D0128622

Reader's
Digest

SAVE $20,000 with A NAIL

OVER 1,900 PRACTICAL TIPS FOR
EVERY HOMEOWNER

Reader's Digest

SAVE $20,000 with A ŃAIL

OVER 1,900 PRACTICAL TIPS FOR
EVERY HOMEOWNER

WITH BRYAN BAEUMLER

Reader's Digest Association (Canada) ULC

Montreal

Project Staff

Consultant **Bryan Baeumler**

Contributing Editors **Deborah Moroz, J.D. Gravenor, Jesse Corbeil**

Manager, Book Editorial **Pamela Johnson**

Cover Designer **Andrée Payette**

Contributing Designer **Ann Devoe**

Production Coordinator **Gillian Sylvain**

Proofreader **Judy Yelon**

Indexer **Cohen Carruth Indexes**

How-to Illustrator ©**Ron Carboni**

Illustrator © **C&T Designs**

Reader's Digest Association (Canada) ULC

Vice President, Book Editorial
Robert Goyette

The Reader's Digest Association, Inc.

President and Chief Executive Officer
Mary Berner

President, Lifestyle Communities
Suzanne Grimes

President, Europe and Global Marketing
Dawn Zier

North America, Chief Marketing Officer
Lisa Karpinski

Text produced for Reader's Digest by GONZALEZ DEFINO editorial & design services (www.gonzalezdefino.com)

Editorial Director **Joseph Gonzalez**

Editor **Patricia Fogarty**

Researcher **Stephanie Johns**

Writers **Jeff Day, Robert V. Huber, Beth Kalet, Aimée Oscamou, Fred Sandsmark, Steven Schwartz**

Library and Archives Canada Cataloguing in Publication

Save $20,000 with a nail: more than 1,900 practical tips for a problem-free home / Canadian consultant: Bryan Baeumler.

Includes index.

ISBN 978-1-55475-055-9

1. Dwellings--Maintenance and repair--Miscellanea. 2. Do-it-yourself work. I. Baeumler, Bryan II. Reader's Digest Association (Canada) III. Title: Save twenty thousand dollars with a nail.
TH4817.3.S28 2008a   643'.7   C2008-903439-2

Address any comments about *Save $20,000 with a Nail* to:
Book Editor, Reader's Digest Association (Canada) ULC
1100 René-Lévesque Blvd. West
Montreal, QC H3B 5H5

To order copies of *Save $20,000 with a Nail*, call 1-800-465-0780

Visit our Web site at **readersdigest.ca**

Printed in China

11 12 13 14 15 / 5 4 3 2 1

NOTE TO READERS The information in this book has been carefully researched, and all efforts have been made to ensure its accuracy and safety. Reader's Digest Association (Canada) ULC and The Reader's Digest Association, Inc., Bryan Baeumler, and gonzalez defino do not assume any responsibility for any injuries suffered or damages or losses incurred as a result of following the instructions in this book. Before taking any action based on information in this book, study the information carefully and make sure that you understand it fully. Observe all warnings. Test any new or unusual repair or cleaning method before applying it broadly, or on a highly visible area or a valuable item. The mention of any brand or product in this book does not imply an endorsement. Price estimates on home-improvement projects and materials are based on averages obtained in a small town; please note that they could vary widely depending on your geographical location and quality of materials used. All prices and product names mentioned are subject to change and should be considered general examples rather than specific recommendations.

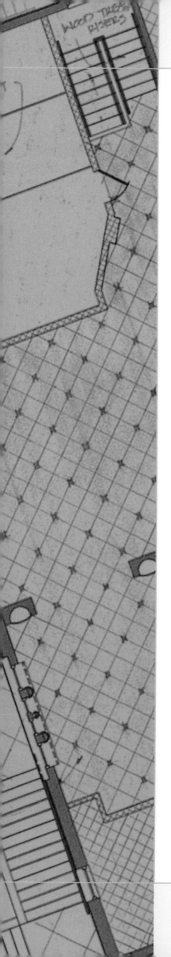

Put Away Your Chequebook

Welcome to *Save $20,000 with a Nail,* your complete guide to preventive home care. Here are simple, inexpensive ways to make sure every part of your home and yard works well for decades to come.

Save $635 with a SPONGE

Ten minutes of cleaning kitchen walls this way, and paint lasts forever.

Save $1,360 with a VACUUM CLEANER

Forget about floors—sweep your walls! Wallpaper will stay like new for decades.

Save $2,700 with TUNA FISH

Believe it or not, an empty tuna can is the perfect tool for healthy lawns.

Save $890 with BLEACH

Air conditioners run smoother and with less energy when you do this.

Save $3,375 with a CHISEL

Doing this common brick-wall repair yourself is both fun and easy.

Save $15,000 with a JAR

That empty spaghetti sauce container can help prevent septic-system breakdowns.

Ready to start saving?

Then grab a few tools—along with some handy household items—
and never again be surprised by an expensive home repair or crisis.

Table of Contents

INTRODUCTION

The Power of a Single Nail

Let's just pretend, for the sake of this story, that a shingle blows off your roof one blustery autumn day. You find it in your yard, and put it in the garage thinking that you really should nail it back into place this weekend.

But, of course, you don't. Something more important comes up, just as it does the following weekend and the weekend after that. And then winter comes.

The shingle, as it turns out, happened to have covered a seam in your roof's plywood that wasn't very well sealed. And then snow starts falling. For a month, there's an ice dam on your roof. Except where the shingle came off, because heat seeping through the gap in the plywood is melting the ice there. And so water starts dripping into your home.

At this point in our story, one or more things could happen: The plywood could get soaked, and in time, start to rot. Or the drip could trickle into a wall, causing mold to grow there. Or the leaking water could soak through your attic's insulation, and the plaster ceiling below it. The water might even seep into a ceiling light fixture, and cause an electrical short or, worse, a fire.

We wish we could say that the tale we're spinning is just a pessimistic, worst-case scenario. But it's not. Meltdowns, if you'll pardon the pun, like this happen *all the time*.

Think about the homes you've lived in. If it wasn't the roof, it was the water heater. Or a backed-up toilet. Or an overloaded wall plug. Who among us homeowners hasn't had to write at least one really big cheque to a repairman for a small problem turned big?

In fact, how many conversations with friends and family quickly turn to horror stories about their homes? Given how common they are, some believe major home troubles are inevitable, even fate. But they're not. And this book is why.

A Health Book for Your Home

Save $20,000 with a Nail has one main goal: to make sure your credit cards and chequebook stay safely in your pocket. No more big, surprising payments for home repairs, we say! Here are smart, easy, practical ways to prevent major home problems from occurring—with an emphasis on *easy*.

Now, we don't mean for you to take this book's title literally. Preventive nails here or there may not always net you windfall-sized savings. But, we hope, the title's message is clear: The tiniest, most seemingly minor attentions that you show your home can have significant, lasting repercussions on its appearance and condition. Think back to the disastrous shingle story for a moment: If that hypothetical homeowner had taken just a few minutes to get up on a ladder and nail in that shingle, all of the damage that we described could have been avoided. Taking a few minutes to replace the shingle, in other words, is kind of like getting paid thousands of dollars for 15 minutes' worth of effort.

We shared that shingle story to illustrate another of this book's main goals: to show you that preventive home care is often about stopping small problems from becoming big. Little problems do happen around a home all the time; this is true for *everyone*, even carpenters and plumbers! So a big part of preventing big-ticket problems is to handle the small ones well. In the pages ahead you'll find easy fix-its, touch-ups, and make-rights to handle most every common house trouble confidently, efficiently, and economically.

We've organized *Save $20,000 with a Nail* very simply. After a few introductory chapters—such as the basic tools you'll need to do the small fixes and preventive measures that fill this book—we gradually work our way through every room, part, and system in your home. Here are preventive-care tips and quick fixes for everything from walls to roofs, toilets to air conditioners, carpets to doorbells. Finally, we show you how to prevent or minimize the impact of several common threats to your home, including natural disasters, bad weather, and pest invasions.

This book is all about giving you the knowledge and confidence you need to maintain and enjoy the biggest investment that most of us will ever make (and by the way, following the valuable tips inside this book will likely increase your home's value!). Never was the phrase "an ounce of prevention is worth a pound of cure" more apt than in describing *Save $20,000 with a Nail*.

Here's to a happy, healthy home— and a little-used chequebook!

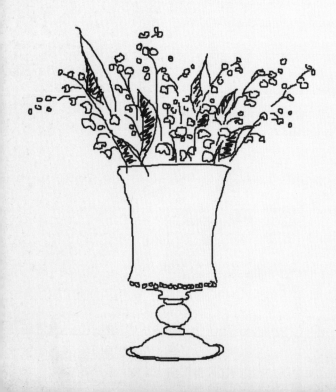

Nailing Down the Right Mindset

The fact that you're consulting this book at all suggests that you understand how important home maintenance is: Maybe your house is in perfect condition, and you want to keep it that way.

Or maybe you already recognize a few things here and there that need to be done around the homestead and just need a little advice about how to do them. Whatever your situation, adopting the right mindset is your first step to achieving a problem-free, well-maintained home.

What do we mean by "the right mindset"? A positive, can-do attitude and the ability to plan ahead—really, that's all you need to keep your house in good working order and avoid thousands of dollars in repair costs. Most homeowners are do-it-yourselfers out of financial necessity and sheer stubbornness: Why should you pay someone else to do what you're perfectly capable of doing? If you have a knack for fixing things, maybe you're a little ahead of the game, yes. But if you're just starting out, relax. If you can read these instructions, you *can* do it—making small repairs really is no more difficult than following a recipe. And stop worrying! You won't hurt yourself if you follow the precautions we provide and use a little common sense. Believe us, there are few things that will make you feel prouder than overcoming your inhibitions, getting your hands dirty, and successfully fixing something you didn't think you had it in you to fix.

We admit there are some home-maintenance projects that are best left to professionals. But that doesn't mean you shouldn't celebrate the small do-it-yourself victories that you achieve. Did you successfully fix that little leak in the upstairs bathroom tub? Give yourself a hearty pat on the back. If you hadn't taken the time to do that, the leak likely would have gotten worse and caused water damage to the bathroom *and* the room below it. Your 10 minutes of effort probably saved you the expense of a plumber's visit, not to mention a new bathroom floor—and the repair of the ceiling below!

This first section of *Save $20,000 with a Nail* contains basic advice on how to get into the groove of doing your own simple home repairs and maintenance. We'll show you how to plan regular maintenance checks and where and when to ask for professional help. You'll also find a description of the basic tools you might need and advice on how to take care of them. You'll be ready to maintain and repair in no time at all!

Preserving Your Home

You know the old saying: "If it ain't broke, don't fix it." Forget that advice! *Do* fix whatever it is, and fix it now. We all know that minor problems can mushroom into major headaches in the blink of an eye; not fixing these problems while they're small will only cost you more money and aggravation in the end. If you want to take some old advice to heart, try this: "An ounce of prevention is worth a pound of cure." You can save a bundle of money in repairs and restoration—and a lot of anguish—if you put an ounce's worth of effort into maintaining your property.

SMART HOMEOWNER

$307,000

The average resale price of a home in Canada in 2007.

The Expense Factor

Owning your own home doesn't come cheaply. In 2007, the average price of a resale home in Canada was $307,000, and that's not the end of your expenditures. Factor in property taxes, mortgage insurance, and homeowners insurance. Then add what the average homeowner spends in a year to maintain (or even improve) his or her property, which can tack on several thousand dollars to your already hefty housing bill. This is why it's so important to prevent problems now, rather than wait until they blossom into full-blown catastrophes later and *then* get around to fixing them.

Can you remember the last time you wrote a repairman a big, fat check for something that you learned you could have fixed yourself? It probably felt like the guy was stealing from you, didn't it? But how were you to know that you could replace the gasket on your dishwasher yourself in 10 minutes? You'll know now! Taking charge of your home's health and putting benign neglect behind you is tremendously satisfying. You'll have a healthier bank account, a more fortified home, and, perhaps most important, you'll remember that *you*—not the plumber or the landscaper—are in control and in charge of your own life and home.

Paying Attention Pays Off

So, your home has many rooms and even more nooks and crannies. How can you stay on top of potential problems? What does a "potential problem" even look like?

You've probably spent thousands of hours in your home, all told, and know your surroundings well enough to be able to find your way around in the dark. But how often do you really "see" your surroundings? The truth is, the best weapons your home has against deterioration are your own senses: It's your eagle eyes, sharp ears, and even your keen sense of smell that will help you recognize the itty-bitty problems early and fix them quickly. Maybe you notice a small hole or chip in your kitchen's plaster wall or detect a musty odor coming from your bathroom. Don't ignore what your senses are telling you. One of the best things you can do for your house is to "visit" it regularly and know it inside out.

We know of one interior designer who tells his clients to walk the perimeter of each room of their houses every so often. Go ahead, try it: Feel the walls. Stand in the far corner of the room and look at the ceilings and floors from points of view that you don't usually have. Stand inside closets and look out into your rooms. Close your eyes, take a deep breath, and smell your living area. You'll get a good feel for what your house's "normal" state is; now you'll notice if something isn't right down the road. We also guarantee you that you'll start noticing things, good and bad, that you didn't notice before. You'll likely develop a new appreciation for your living space and find yourself cleaning, lubricating, painting, and making other such minor adjustments. You're proud of where you live, and you want that to show.

Dedicate the same kind of thoughtfulness that you had "seeing" your home to repairing it. Once you've decided to make some fixes or do some maintenance, plan it out thoroughly. Gather all the tools and materials you need. Proceed slowly and follow instructions carefully.

15 MUST-HAVE ITEMS FOR HOME CARE AND MAINTENANCE

They surely don't count as tools, but the following household items are key to keeping your abode clean and well maintained. Gather them up or purchase them now—many of the tips throughout this book assume that you keep these indispensable items on hand.

- Vacuum cleaner
- Brooms (indoor and outdoor)
- Mops
- Sponges
- Plastic spray bottles
- Scissors
- Pencils
- Wire coat hangers
- Powerful flashlight (and backup batteries)

- Bucket
- Rope
- Clean rags
- Whisk broom
- Steam iron (for such tasks as softening vinyl flooring or reviving a carpet)
- Scrap wood (2-by-4 remnants and shims)

How a Positive Attitude Can Save You Time and Money

When embarking on home maintenance projects, a positive, can-do attitude will save you money, time, frustration—even injury. Bear these points in mind before you begin:

- Be upbeat. Don't let wrinkles in the plan upset you. Negativity leads to defeatism. Keep your sense of humor even when you're mired in a mess.

- Be calm. Having nervous energy and rushing through a job usually lead to mistakes or injuries.

- Be prepared. Read all instructions carefully (in this book, but also on manufacturer's packages where applicable). Follow them to the letter. Collect all tools and gear that you need before you embark on your project.

- Be aware of the details. If you're replacing a shingle, you'll want to note how it fits into place. Take a photo or draw a diagram. When you put in the new piece you want it to fit just right. If you're replacing a faucet, for example, notice the order in which the washers, screws, and other small parts are assembled and disassembled.

- Be creative. If you don't have the tools or materials called for, find substitutes. If you're replacing a brick, for example, and don't have a brick jointer to shape the fresh mortar, use an ice cream stick or a spoon. Sometimes this book suggests such alternatives, but if it doesn't, come up with substitutes of your own. In most cases, the world won't come to an end if you don't have just the right tool.

- Be flexible. Sometimes one problem masks another, and you have to stop in the middle of a job to fix the underlying problem. If you're patching a hole in a wall and discover a leaky pipe, fix the leak first, then return to the original job. You'll save yourself a lot of headaches later!

- Be safe. Most accidents occur when people are tired or in a hurry. Take your time, wear the proper safety equipment, know when to stop and do the job right.

- Be realistic. Many jobs require more time, money and skill than homeowners plan for. Leave yourself a cushion in all three areas and you'll sidestep a lot of frustration.

- Finish what you start. As long as the tools and materials are out, finish up. Otherwise you'll be looking at that unpainted window trim a year from now!

Making Time for Home Maintenance

If you're serious about protecting your home against deterioration and damage, you need to be observant and do regular maintenance checks (with emphasis on the word "regular") around your place. Failing to systematically look for potential problems is only inviting disaster—or at the very least, huge repair bills. As unbelievable as it seems, a small fix here and a thorough cleaning there can keep your house and everything in it running smoothly. Neglect a small problem, though, and it will inevitably grow into a major one.

In the chapters that follow, we'll tell you how to nip all kinds of home maintenance problems in the bud. Some of what you read may be gentle reminders of what you already know but don't necessarily do. Because we tend to brush aside things that don't demand our immediate attention, it's a good idea to come up with some kind of scheduling system that's not daunting but makes sense to you. Maybe you could take one hour out of each weekend to examine one area of the house, and then treat yourself to a nice lunch. Or if you're computer savvy, program a series of pop-up reminders. If you prefer paper and pen, make notes on a regular calendar to do certain jobs on certain days.

Generally, the best time to examine your home's exterior is in warm (but not scorching) weather; the best time to examine indoor systems is when they're not in use. Another good rule of thumb is to do your poking around while certain parts of your home are on your mind, seasonally speaking. Fall is the perfect time to give your home's heating system a once-over: Cold weather is just around the corner and you're already thinking about how high your dreaded heating bill is about to rise. Fall is also when you'll want to inspect your rain gutters and downspouts; you'll have just seen (and hopefully disposed of) the last of the falling leaves.

Even though some chores can be done at any time and some are best done seasonally, there are still other tasks to which you should assign a season or month—even a specific date. You might forget to do them otherwise. The chart on the facing page is a sampling of checks that should be part of your regular home maintenance program. Add these and other jobs to your calendar, adjusting the dates to suit your schedule. Or create your own chart. If you don't want to make extensive notes on your calendar, just write "check maintenance schedule." And then do what your schedule tells you!

SEASONAL MAINTENANCE CHECKLIST

	SPRING	SUMMER	FALL	WINTER
House exterior				
Recaulk joints between siding and other materials	•		•	
Check wood surfaces for deterioration	•		•	
Wash siding and secure loose panels	•			
Putty loose windows and replace cracked glass	•		•	
Clean screens and repair any damage	•			
Replace worn or damaged weather stripping	•			
Caulk around windows and doors if needed	•		•	
Check for carpenter ants and wasps' nests	•		•	
Lubricate door and window locks and hinges		•		
Roof				
Replace damaged shingles		•		•
Inspect flashing at chimney, dormers, valleys, and vents	•			
Replace loose mortar between chimney bricks	•			
Clean gutters, downspouts, and leaf strainers and check for pitch, damage, and leaks at seams	•		•	
Basement, grounds, and yard				
Check wood beams, fences, and posts for decay and insects	•	•		
Check basement for dampness, leaks, or new cracks or movement in old cracks		•		
Repair damage or wear in walks and driveways		•		
Clean debris from storm drains	•	•	•	
Trim trees that may damage house or clog gutters	•		•	
House interior				
Check for and repair cracks in walls		•	•	
Replace cracked floor or wall tiles	•		•	
Check for and repair leaks in plumbing fixtures		•		
Replace loose sealant around tubs, showers, and tile floors		•		
Clean dingy tile grouting	•			
Inspect electric cords, plugs, switches, outlets, and ceiling fixtures for wear or damage		•		•
Inspect refrigerator door gaskets and replace if needed		•		
Change water filter on ice maker or water dispenser	•		•	
Drain sediment from water heater		•		•
Have heating system checked and tuned professionally			•	
Clean out ducts of heating and cooling system	•		•	
Have chimney flue checked and cleaned			•	
Have central cooling system checked professionally	•			
Clean or change air-conditioner and furnace filters	•	•	•	•
Check pressure level in fire extinguishers	•	•	•	•
Check smoke detectors and carbon-monoxide detectors	•	•	•	•
Conduct a family fire drill		•		

Building the Perfect Toolbox

Other than your positive attitude, the most important asset you have in your home maintenance arsenal is your collection of tools and household supplies that can help you get the job done. If you're just starting out, you don't need to have a fully equipped stock of tools and hardware. Every homeowner should have certain essentials on hand; as you take on more complex tasks, you can always add to your toolbox. The gear that we find most useful is described in the following pages. (Tools for specialized tasks like roofing or electricity are covered in the corresponding sections of this book in a recurring feature called "Equipment Spotlight.")

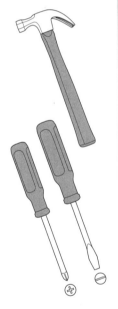

Top to bottom: A claw hammer; a basic, slotted screwdriver; a Phillips screwdriver (with an "X" shape at its tip); and a Robertson screwdriver (with a square tip—not illustrated).

What Every Homeowner Needs

Hammers. Probably the most basic of all tools is the hammer, which is used to drive nails into surfaces to join them. Hammers come in various sizes and weights. Get one that fits your hand comfortably and is the right weight for your strength. The most versatile is probably a good **claw hammer** with a metal head and a hardwood (or sturdy fiberglass) handle. The claw part is used to extract nails.

Screwdrivers. Screwdrivers come in many widths and lengths, with different tip shapes to fit different screws. The three most essential screwdrivers are the **common** or **slotted** screwdriver; the **Phillips** screwdriver, which has a cross-hatch "X" shape at its tip, with corners that are slightly rounded; and the **Robertson** screwdriver or square tip. When choosing a screwdriver, always match the tip to the screw head's type and size; otherwise, you may strip the screw or blunt the driver. The screwdriver tip should fill the slot in the screw head in both thickness and width. A long screwdriver provides more driving power. A short one gives more control and lets you work in tighter spaces.

Nails, screws, and bolts. Every homeowner's toolbox should contain a few basic fasteners. The most widely used are nails, which come in a variety of metals, styles, and sizes for driving into a variety of materials. The **common nail** has a thin, flat head. If you want to drive the nail head below the surface, use a **fini nail**, which has a very small head. Nail sizes are often expressed in pennies, abbreviated "d." Common nails come in lengths ranging from twopenny (2d), which is 1 inch (2.5 cm) long, to sixtypenny (60d), which is 6 inches (15 cm).

Different types of screws are used for joining wood, sheet metal, wallboard, and masonry. Screws also come in various lengths and thicknesses and with many different head types. The most common are **slotted screws**, which just have one straight line that runs across the entire head, **Phillips head screws**, which have an "X" on top, and **Robertson** screws which have a square slot on the head.

A bolt is a flat-ended screw that together with a nut forms a mini-clamp that holds pieces together firmly, yet can be disassembled easily. A **flat washer** is usually placed between the bolt head or nut and the pieces being fastened to spread the pressure and protect the surface.

Drills and drill bits. Home maintenance can involve a fair amount of drilling. You'll need a drill to do even simple tasks around the house, like hanging heavy picture frames. Using a **hand drill** over a period of time is tiring, which is why it's worthwhile to invest in a good **electric drill**. Better yet, you'll be able to use a good **cordless drill**—one that operates at several speeds and in reverse—everywhere, even if you're far from an electrical outlet. Bits for power drills come in many shapes and sizes; they are designed to be drilled into every kind of material, including wood, metal, plastic, and masonry. You'll also be able to use the drill to drive or remove screws. Slotted, Phillips-head, and Robertson screwdriver bits are widely available.

Tape measures and rulers. Measuring a job properly is vitally important if you want to get it right (have you ever tried wallpapering without measuring?). The best multi-purpose measuring tool that everyone should have is a **retractable tape measure**—the flexible, spring-loaded metal rule that's contained in a small square case that you can clip to your belt. If you need to measure odd shapes, such as the circumference of a pipe, it's also a good idea to keep a **cloth tape measure** on hand. Finally (and this one is optional), you may want to purchase a **folding carpenter's rule**, a rigid rule in hinged sections that folds easily and can be extended to give you the length you need.

Level. A **spirit level** will show you when a surface is perfectly horizontal; it's good for easy tasks like hanging pictures (and more difficult carpentry jobs). Simply place it on top of a surface and check its small, liquid-filled vials; when the bubble is at the center of the vial, the surface is level.

Utility knife. Probably the handiest cutting tool is the small utility knife, which comes with a variety of blades to cut wood, vinyl, and other materials. A good straight-handled model will have a button that adjusts the length of the blade or

Above: A cordless drill.

retracts it into the handle for safety. Some models also have storage space in the handle for extra blades.

Basic wood saw. Although different saws are generally needed to make rip cuts (with the grain) and cross cuts in wood, you can make do with a single general-purpose saw with a blade that is 26 inches (66 cm) long and has 9 teeth per inch (2.5 cm). The teeth should have three beveled sides, for razor-sharp cutting, and deep gullets (spaces between the teeth), which make it easier to clear chips away fast.

Metal-cutting saw. For cutting metal you'll need a **hacksaw**, which consists of a sturdy metal frame with a pistol-grip and removable narrow blades. Hacksaw blades are anywhere from 8 inches (20 cm) to 26 inches (66 cm) long and should have 32 teeth per inch (2.5 cm). You can buy an adjustable hacksaw that accepts various sizes of blade. For reaching into tight spots, use a miniature hacksaw.

Gap-filling tools. If you're facing gashes in woodwork, crumbling mortar in the chimney, or gaps between a window frame and your house siding, you'll need to fill the spaces with putty, grout, or caulk. To do so you'll need an assortment of **putty knives** and **trowels** and a **caulking gun**, a device that holds a tube of caulk and dispenses it where it's needed with the squeeze of a trigger.

Sanding tools. At the end of a woodworking job (or after filling small holes or cracks in your wallboard or plaster walls), you'll have to sand the surface smooth before painting or varnishing it. You'll need an assortment of **sandpaper** grades, ranging from coarse to fine. It is also a good idea to use a **sanding block**, a small device that holds the sandpaper to give you a better grip and to maintain a consistently flat sanding surface.

Wrenches. To hold, twist, or turn nuts, bolts, or plumbing pipes, you'll need some wrenches. Your biggest must-have is an **adjustable wrench**, which has an adjustable head to fit various sized nuts and bolts. If you have some plumbing work on the horizon, get a couple of **pipe wrenches** (one for each hand). In time you may want to invest in a set of **open-end wrenches**. The end of each wrench in a set has an opening of a different size; you need to find a wrench with an opening of the right size to fit the nut or bolt you want to turn.

Pliers and clamps. Pliers are good for hands-on holding. Clamps hold things for you and leave your hands free. It's a good idea to stock a supply of **spring clamps** and **C-clamps** (named for their shape) to hold items together while you're working on them or to hold a freshly glued joint together while the adhesive dries. **Slip-joint pliers**, pliers with serrated teeth on the forward parts of the jaws and corrugated teeth farther back on the jaws, are also good to have around. You can easily shift the

Top to bottom: A hacksaw, caulking gun, pipe wrench, adjustable wrench, and slip-joint pliers.

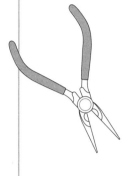

jaws to hold objects of varying sizes, using the set of teeth that fits best. Also get a pair of **needle-nose pliers** for grasping small items or reaching into narrow spaces. If you do your own electrical work, invest in a **multipurpose tool**, electrician's pliers that measure, strip, and clamp wire, and crimp wire connectors.

Indoor and outdoor ladders. You'll need a good **stepladder** to reach high places inside the house. Ladders are graded for loading capacity. Be sure yours will more than hold your weight, plus the weight of the tools and materials you'll be using. Stepladders come in various heights: A 6-foot (2 metre) ladder should be sufficient for indoor projects. For working outside of the house, get an **extension ladder**—a nest of two or three ladders that can be extended or compressed. Many models have pulley mechanisms that make it easier to extend the sections. Ladders are made of wood, aluminum, or fiberglass. Opt for fiberglass. It's lightweight and won't conduct electricity, as aluminum or wet wood will do.

Anchors. If you're driving a screw into plaster, masonry, or wallboard, you'll need to fit an anchor into a predrilled hole to give the screw's threads something to grab hold of. The simplest anchors are **expansion anchors**, plastic or lead sleeves that are closed at one end. To use one, drill a hole in the wall just large enough to accept the anchor and then push or tap the anchor into it. When you drive in a screw, the anchor will expand and grip the edges of the hole. A **molly bolt**, or hollow-wall anchor, is a machine screw in a metal sleeve. When you push it into a predrilled hole in a hollow wall, the sleeve expands or collapses, drawing its shoulders against the inside surface of the wall and permanently holding the sleeve in place. You then remove the screw and use it to mount whatever needs to be mounted.

"Would Be Nice" Gear for the DIY Enthusiast

Pry bars. If you need to remove a nail from a surface and the claw of your hammer won't do the job, use a pry bar, a curved metal tool with two angled blades. One blade is used for pulling nails and the other for prying apart pieces that are nailed together or for pulling off old molding.

Hammering aids. Sometimes it's easier to drive a nail if you make a small starter hole with an **awl**. Position this small, pointed metal tool where you want the nail to go and push it into the wood. If you want to sink the head of the nail beneath the surface, use a **nail set**. This is a small punch with a narrow end that you position over the nail head while you drive it below the surface of the wood with a hammer. A **stud finder** will help you locate the studs behind your wallboard. Inexpensive

Top to bottom: Needle-nose pliers, stud finder, and an awl.

models work magnetically to find the screws or nails that secure the wallboard. Electronic stud finders measure changes in a wall's density.

Electrician's screwdrivers. When doing electrical work, you should use only a screwdriver that is encased in plastic; on an electrician's screwdriver only the tip of the metal blade is not covered with plastic. This plastic coating helps you avoid electric shocks. If you're in an emergency situation and you have to use an ordinary screwdriver to make electrical repairs, wrap overlapping layers of electrician's tape around the entire shaft up to the tip and over any metal parts of the handle. Even then, be sure to turn off the power before you start.

Squares. Used in framing, roofing, and stairway work, a **carpenter's square** is a rigid, steel, L-shaped tool that helps you keep corners squared at exact 90-degree angles; it doubles as a measuring rule and a straightedge. A **combination square** is a steel rule with a sliding head that lets you mark off 90- and 45-degree angles.

Riveters and staplers. To fasten metal to metal or metal to plastic you may need a **pop riveter**, a small tool that applies rivets easily with a squeeze of the handle. To fasten softer materials, get a **heavy-duty stapler**—either a hand-powered model or a power stapler. You'll also need pop rivets and staples to fit these tools.

Wood plane. When working with wood, you'll more than likely need a plane of some sort—for example, to trim a bit from the top of a sticking door. A plane is basically a blade in a holder. A good first purchase is a small **block plane** that smooths and trims wood and makes fine finishing cuts. An adjusting wheel under the palm rest controls the position of the blade. Because of its small size, a block plane can be used in one hand, whereas larger planes require two hands.

Chisels. A chisel is a sharp, usually beveled blade used for cutting or shaving wood or metal. **Wood chisels** are generally fitted with wooden handles and are either driven by hand or struck with a mallet. They are ideal for cutting mortises, or recesses, for hinges or locks. **Cold chisels** are struck by hammers and are used to cut sheet metal or chop off bolts or rivets. A **stonemason's chisel** (also called a straight chisel) is used for cutting concrete block and stone.

Files and rasps. To shape or smooth metal or wood, you may need files or rasps, which are flat, round, or triangular lengths of metal with rows of ridge-like teeth that cut into the material. Files are used on metal and rasps on wood. To save your hands and give you a better grip, get a wooden handle that fits over the end of the file (ask for one at your hardware store). Because files get clogged with the material they remove, get a file card—a small, two-sided tool with a fine brush on one side and a coarser one on the other—to brush away the debris and keep the file cutting properly.

Top to bottom:
A block plane and
cold chisels.

Indispensable Household Supplies

Though some of our advice requires you to pick up your toolbox, many other maintenance tricks can be conquered with household supplies that you use every day. Here's a brief overview of which items under your kitchen sink (and in your junk drawers) can help you keep your home shipshape. Who knew that glue, tape, coat hangers, and TSP could come in so handy?

THE BEST TAPE FOR THE JOB

While tape doesn't usually have as much holding power as liquid or paste adhesives, it can do many things other adhesives can't, such as sealing ductwork or insulating electrical connections. Which type should you use for the job you're working on? Read on.

TAPE	DESCRIPTION	WHAT IT'S USED FOR
Duct tape	Heat- and moisture-resistant tape made of strong, plastic-coated cloth.	For temporary repairs and seals; contrary to its name, do *not* use on ducts.
Metal foil tape	The true duct tape, made from heavy aluminum foil with strong adhesive.	Used to seal seams and joints in air-conditioning or heating ducts.
Masking tape	Lightweight tape made of paper. Various grades or ratings are used for different tasks; longer-rated tapes are less adhesive and will peel off of walls more easily. Painter's tape is often blue or purple.	Holds glued items together while drying; used by painters to cover areas that are not to be painted.
Electrical tape	Flame-retardant, stretchable vinyl tape that comes in a variety of colors.	Insulates electrical switches, outlets, and connections.
Carpet tape	Plastic or cloth tape with adhesive on both sides; waterproof carpet tape is available for outdoor use.	Used to secure carpets and rugs to the floor.
Joint tape	Paper or mesh tape; paper is cheaper and easier to use, but messier.	For covering and strengthening joints in wallboard.

Must-Have Cleansers and Lubricants

Really, one of the easiest ways you can keep your home in good repair is to keep every nook and cranny clean. Dirt is the great destroyer; it clogs moving parts, blocks the free flow of air or water, and corrodes delicate materials.

Household cleaners. Most cleaning jobs are easily done using common cleaning substances, including detergent and water, vinegar, bleach, talcum powder, and household ammonia (though ammonia is found in many commercial cleaning products, including Windex, exercise caution when mixing your own ammonia solutions—never mix it with bleach, and always use it in a well-ventilated area). To scrub away tougher dirt, TSP (trisodium phosphate) or TSP substitute really does the trick. When mixed with water, this white powder, which is available at most hardware stores, cleans away even tough stains and dissolves grease. Caution: Though effective, TSP is not without its dangers. It can be irritating and caustic; its use is banned in some communities because it contains phosphates that can harm the environment.

Compressed air. Sometimes all you need to get something clean is to get dust out of a confined space—for example, from inside your smoke alarm, power drill, computer keyboard, or other electronic equipment. But don't blow it out with your mouth (that will add moisture to the mix, which may make the dirt stick even harder). Instead, use compressed air, which comes in an aerosol can with a nozzle extension. With the press of a button you can blow away dust or other loose, light debris.

Lubricants. If cleanliness is next to godliness, lubrication is right next to cleanliness. A little oil goes a long way in keeping your household running smoothly. For most jobs a lightweight lubricant, such as 3-in-One Oil, is sufficient, but you may need other products. Two of the most popular are silicone spray, available under many brand names, and an anticorrosive penetrating oil in a spray can, such as WD-40. Silicone spray is a water-resistant oil with a silicone base that can lubricate almost anything. It works especially well on porous items, such as plastic parts, and is a good lubricant for locks, hinges, and sliding doors. Because it is water resistant, it can also be used as a rust retardant. Spray penetrating oil is also ideal for lubricating and resisting rust and can double as a cleaning agent. In fact, it is good for any number of home uses, from removing stubborn adhesive labels to exterminating roaches. (The manufacturer of WD-40 claims its product has more than 2,000 uses.)

GLUE, EPOXY, OR CEMENT?

When properly used, a good adhesive makes a bond that may even be stronger than the material itself. Various adhesives are available at hardware stores and home improvement outlets. The chart below will help you decide which adhesive is right for the job at hand.

ADHESIVE	DESCRIPTION	WHAT IT'S GOOD FOR
Carpenter's glue	Thick yellow liquid applied from a squeeze bottle.	Repairing woodwork or furniture
Super Glue, or instant glue (cyanoacrylate) *CAUTION: Don't get any on your skin.*	Liquid adhesive in a tube; also available in gel form.	Liquid version bonds nonporous materials, including metals, vinyl, rubber, and ceramics. The gel is good for wood and other porous materials.
Epoxy	Waterproof adhesive that comes in two tubes of either liquid or putty; mix in equal parts and apply quickly.	Bonding wood, china, glass, and most other materials; especially good for bonding dissimilar materials.
PVC cement *CAUTION: Gives off harmful fumes; use only in a well-ventilated space.*	Paste that is applied with the applicator attached to the container cover; some types require priming with a PVC cleaner.	Joining plastic plumbing pipes and fittings; acts as a solvent that melts plastic and welds the parts together.
Asphalt roof cement (plastic roofing cement)	Mixture of solvent-based bitumen, mineral stabilizers, and other fibers. It is applied with a trowel.	Fastening asphalt shingles and flashing.

Tool Safety

Working with machinery and tools can be dangerous, especially if the equipment is not properly maintained. If your saw is dull or your drill bit is blunted, you have to exert more energy to do the job. When you do this, your tools may wander off course and cause you nasty cuts or other injuries. Do your home maintenance safely by keeping your tools in pristine condition and by keeping a few common-sense safety rules in mind: Ban children and pets from work areas, avoid distractions, don't overexert yourself, and maintain a comfortable pace.

Storage and Maintenance of Hand Tools

Give every tool its own home. When you're not using your tools, keep them in assigned places where they won't be dinged up by other tools. Store cutting tools where their sharp edges won't be damaged (and where they won't damage other tools or fingers). To prevent rust, store tools in a dry place. Spray a rust-inhibiting coating on steel tools or put a few packets of clay or silicone desiccant in the toolbox or cabinet. (Such packets come with most new tools; you can buy them at hardware or home supply stores.) If there are children in your home, keep tools under lock and key.

Store saws and chisels in protective blade covers. This keeps them from being damaged or causing damage to roaming hands. If the tools don't come with blade protectors, make your own: Get a couple of plastic report-cover spines from a stationary store and slide them over the teeth of your saws; cut slits into tennis balls and slip chisel blades inside.

Keep tools dry. Water can rust a blade or warp a wooden handle. If a tool gets wet, wipe it with a soft, dry cloth. If it's sweaty or greasy, clean it with a damp cloth and then wipe it dry with a clean, dry cloth. Avoid oiling hand tools. If oil gets on the handle, your grip might slip, and you could be injured.

Keep saws sharp. There's a saying that it's easier to cut yourself with a dull knife than a sharp one—and it's true of saws as well. Stay safe by cleaning and sharpening the blades on your cutting tools before they get damaged or dull. If they're past repair, replace them. How can you tell if your saw needs attention? Examine its blades under

SAFETY SMARTS FOR DIYers

When you're working on a home project that requires tools or machinery, always wear sturdy shoes with slip-proof soles. Roll up your sleeves and tie back your hair to keep it out of the way as you work. So that you're not juggling a thousand things, carry your hand tools in a tool belt, and keep nails and screws in a canvas nail apron. Above all, use the appropriate safety equipment:

• Wear heavy work gloves when you're doing anything that could smash or scrape your fingers. Use rubber gloves when handling toxic materials. Don't wear gloves when cutting or drilling—the tool could slip out of your hands and injure you.

• Whenever you do grinding, filing, chiseling, or any other work that involves dust or flying chips, wear safety goggles (or even a full face shield) to protect your eyes.

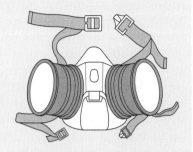

• Wear a dust mask when sanding or doing other work that might stir up particles that could irritate your respiratory system. The most effective masks are marked "CSA-approved" (approved by the Standards Council of Canada). They are generally thicker than cheaper masks and have straps for a tighter seal.

• If you're going to be subjected to harmful vapors or fibers (such as those from insulation), wear a respirator. The best models come with interchangeable, color-coded cartridges to filter out the harmful effects of toxic dust and fumes from specific materials, such as paints and adhesives.

• If you'll be kneeling a lot, wear protective kneepads or kneel on a folded blanket or thick layers of newspaper.

• When you use a loud power tool or otherwise make a lot of noise, protect your ears with foam earplugs or earmuff-style ear protectors.

• Keep a fire extinguisher handy in case a small blaze breaks out.

Before working with flammable or toxic substances—such as paint, kerosene, or contact cement—extinguish any gas pilot lights in the room, open windows, and turn on a fan to ensure proper ventilation. Above all, don't smoke. Many substances give off fumes that could ignite. Also, only buy as much flammable or toxic material as you need (don't buy a gallon of paint thinner if you only need a pint, no matter how great the price might be). Dispose of leftovers as recommended by the manufacturer, or contact an environmental protection agency or your health department for instructions.

a magnifying glass. If the teeth are rounded (not sharp and pointy), take the saw to a pro for resharpening. If a handsaw gets clogged with resin from cutting soft wood, clean it with a bit of oven cleaner, then spray the blade with silicone.

Power Tools

Always follow the manufacturer's instructions for maintaining and operating your power tools. If you've lost the owner's manual, visit the manufacturer's Web site—they usually post old manuals for all of their products. And while you're working:

- Keep power tools unplugged whenever they're not in use. You wouldn't believe how many accidents happen when folks accidentally turn these tools on by brushing against the on/off switch!
- If the tool's air vents become clogged, clean them with compressed air or a vacuum cleaner.
- If your project yields a ton of sawdust or particle filings, use a shop vacuum to suck up the excess. You'll lessen your odds of a fire—these particles are highly flammable.
- If you have cordless tools, use only the battery and charger that came with the unit.
- Never charge batteries for tools in temperatures below 40°F (4°C) or over 105°F (40°C). Batteries rely on chemical reactions that slow down in cold weather and cease altogether at 32°F (0°C). High temperatures release vapors from the battery and diminish its capacity.

Getting Professional Help

If you're like most homeowners, you're probably familiar with the extremes of the do-it-yourself mindset: Some people feel totally inadequate about undertaking any repair or maintenance work, which is absurd. On the other hand, others might feel as though they can tackle *any* job, no matter how complex, which is even crazier. Whatever your level of experience, there will always be certain projects that are best left to the professionals. Almost no one is qualified to work in all fields of home repair and improvement, but even the least skilled homeowner can do a lot of it.

SMART HOMEOWNER

75-100%

Average percentage of the cost of a kitchen remodel that you'll recoup when you sell your home.

Hiring Tradespeople

Work within your comfort zone. As a rule, steer clear of any work that feels dangerous or requires skills that you just don't have. For example, if heights make you dizzy or if you're unsteady on your feet, by all means, stay off the roof.

If you're not licensed, call in someone who is. Don't undertake any job that your local building code says must be done by a licensed professional and requires a permit: If you're caught, you may have to pay significant fines and then have the work redone by pros. Even worse, if your home sustains severe damage, as in a fire, your insurance company won't pay off if you haven't followed codes.

Hunt high and low for top-quality tradespeople. For small jobs, you can hire a lone worker, such as an electrician or plumber. For larger jobs, you may need a contractor, who can coordinate various workers. Ask neighbors for references. Get recommendations from lumberyards, electrical supply stores, and other building-trade establishments.

Take your pick of the contractor crop. Interview at least three contractors and get an itemized estimate from each one. The "best" may not be the cheapest. Opt for quality and durability over a lower-cost, potentially shoddy job, and you'll save money and hassle in the long run. Be sure to compare apples to apples, and read the fine print.

SMART IDEA

Don't pay more than a quarter of the cost of the job as a down payment, and always hold back as much of the payment as you can until the project is completed to your satisfaction. The more the contractor wants up front, the greater likelihood that he has bad intentions.

Spell out your expectations in a contract. Once you've chosen a contractor, work out a written agreement that specifies the work to be done and the materials they'll use. Get the following in writing:

- A description of what the job entails, including who will acquire and pay for any necessary permits (make sure you have copies of all permits)
- Materials to be used, including brand names, colors, stock numbers, weights, and other details
- How long the job will take. Include a monetary penalty if the job is not finished by a certain date (this is generally done only for big jobs)
- The dates and times that workers will be on the premises, along with the names of any subcontractors who have access to your property
- An estimate of the cost (and a maximum price) including an itemization of the work to be done
- Titles and terms of the individual's or contractor's insurance policies, including workers' compensation and liability policies
- A statement of responsibility for any damage caused to your property
- A guarantee of all materials and workmanship
- A declaration that your warranties or guarantees are transferable when the house is sold
- A guarantee of clean-up and removal of debris daily and after the job is completed

Understanding Bids and Estimates

Get everything in writing. Remember the old lawyers' saying, "If it's not on paper, it never happened"? Heed it when hiring professional help. Before embarking on any major renovations or projects, it's a smart idea to get all the details—price, deadlines, materials, and the like—on paper, just to make sure there's no confusion down the road.

Remember that estimates are just that: *estimates.* When you ask for an estimate, a contractor looks at the area to be repaired or renovated, figures what materials will be required and how many hours the job will take, then gives you an estimate of the total. The actual bill may be higher or lower. With a preliminary estimate, make sure the contractor includes:

- The hourly rate. Is the rate the same amount for every person on the job? Does the rate apply to drive time, cleanup time and meeting time?
- Markup on materials. Contractors will often charge the cost of the materials plus a certain percentage; 10 to 15 percent is not unusual.

WHAT TO ASK A PROSPECTIVE CONTRACTOR

QUESTION	WHY IT'S IMPORTANT TO ASK
Are you licensed and bonded to work in this county? Can you provide your license numbers?	You don't want to do business with people who aren't authorized to work in your area (and don't have liability insurance for accidents).
What's your street address?	You should be wary of contractors who only give post office box addresses; it'll be impossible to find them if you have a problem with their work.
How long have you been in business?	Many fly-by-night tradesmen do shoddy work in one town and then vanish after a year or two. Try to find a tradesman who's been in business locally for at least three years.
Can you give me references for clients who have hired you for similar projects?	If the references are few or are not recent, ask why. Check with the Better Business Bureau to see if any complaints have been filed against the contractor.
Will you show me before-and-after photos of similar projects you've done?	You'll want to see what kind of work he does. (Better yet, ask some of his customers if you can come to their homes to see the contractor's handiwork.)
Will you explain what the job will involve and how long it will take? Can you give me a guaranteed end date?	Having him explain the project to you shows that 1) he knows what's involved, and 2) he's willing to communicate with his clients. Though no job goes *exactly* as planned, you should have some assurance that the project won't drag on for months.
Will you provide a written estimate and set a maximum price for the job?	You've heard the horror stories about contractors who bilk their clients for thousands more than they thought the job would cost. Assume that big projects will go 15 to 20 percent over budget; it's a good sign if the contractor is willing to honor the estimate price even if the project takes longer than anticipated.
What is your payment schedule?	Steer clear if the contractor asks for a hefty down payment (he might say it's for materials) before any work begins. This might indicate that he's not established enough to have accounts with local vendors and doesn't have the cash reserves to pay for them out of pocket. For big jobs, negotiate a fee structure in which you pay over three or four installments (the last one being the largest).

The upside to the estimate approach is that the contractor is compensated fairly for time spent on the job. The downside is that expenses can snowball and, if you don't feel the contractor is working efficiently, create conflict. Because they are not binding, estimates are best used for small jobs, and when you've hired people you know and trust.

Know that you can bet on bids. A bid differs from an estimate in that a bid is a binding estimate: The contractor still gives an estimate for the job but the work is done for a set price, regardless of how long the project takes. A bid for a project will often be higher than an estimate, since the contractor has to factor in surprises that he or she may encounter. Nonetheless, most homeowners and contractors feel more comfortable working from a bid, especially on large projects.

SMART PLACES TO PUT YOUR MONEY

As a homeowner, the smartest place to invest your money is in updating the rooms and **spaces you enjoy most** (assuming your house is structurally sound, safe and dry). If you love playing Ping-Pong, finish off that basement!

Some homeowners are more pragmatic about remodeling certain parts of their house, knowing when it comes time to sell, they'll recoup at least part of their investment. Most Realtors will tell you if you're preparing to put your house on the market the best place to invest your time and money is in **inexpensive, cosmetic spruce-ups**. It's hard to beat paint for making a room look new and fresh. New cabinet pulls, carpet, and light fixtures—though more expensive than paint—can also give your home substantial bang for the buck.

Increasing "curb appeal" is another smart tactic. Again, a little paint can go a long way in creating a favorable first impression on prospective buyers. New house numbers, new mulch and foundation plantings, and a new coat of sealer on the driveway also help make your house more attractive at little cost.

For those planning more extensive remodeling projects, a good place to look for information is *Remodeling Magazine*'s annual "Cost Versus Value Report." Although it's American, Canadians can get a good idea of what the **average payback will be if you ever sell your home**. The latest survey shows the projects with the highest paybacks are decks, siding and window replacements and minor kitchen and bathroom remodeling. Some of the projects with the lowest payback include converting a bedroom into an office, installing a back-up power generator, adding a sunroom or another bathroom and reshingling a roof.

These numbers vary according to the value and location of the house and market conditions. But if you're on the fence about whether or not to do a project, these statistics may help you make that decision.

The Inside of Your Home

Things happen to walls, floors, and ceilings that don't happen to other parts of the house. You don't walk on the plumbing, for example, and you'd never dream of driving a picture hanger

through your wiring. But it's all in a day's work for the surfaces of your house.

Eventually this abuse takes its toll: Your floors need refinishing; tiles need replacing; walls need paint or the holes in them need spackle. But there are clever things you can do to slow or minimize wear and tear. These things can be as simple and inexpensive as putting down a throw rug to extend the life of your floor, or vacuuming your walls once a year to prolong the life of your paint, or using hydrogen peroxide to whiten ceiling tiles.

A little maintenance and a few small repairs can go a long way. For instance, a single, cracked ceramic tile can make your kitchen floor look old and outdated. The good news is that replacing it can make the whole floor look brand new. (You can do this yourself. It's only one tile!) Take the money you save to the bank, and whistle a happy tune on the way there. Remember, the better your floor looks, the better your kitchen looks, and the more terrific your home looks overall. The value of a terrific-looking home only goes one way: up!

Wallboard Walls

Wallboard. Drywall. Gypsum board. Plasterboard. Sheetrock. Gyproc. Whatever you call it, it's what the walls in most homes today are made of. It's essentially a layer of chalk-like gypsum pressed between two pieces of tough paper. Screw sheets of it securely to the studs and cover the seams with joint compound, and you've got a wall. And it's a surprisingly sturdy wall that's pretty much maintenance free. Oh, it may get a few nicks and tears, or even worse, be damaged by a leak. But most problems are easily prevented—or repaired.

YOUR COST SAVINGS
$800
The cost to install and tape new sheetrock in a 12-by-12-foot (4 by 4 metres) room.

Care and Maintenance

Keep your eyes open for leaks and other moisture problems. Wallboard and water don't mix. Water will destroy your wallboard in less time than anything else. Any time a wall feels damp, you've got trouble. Also pay attention to brown spots, an almost certain signal of water damage, even if no water is obvious. If you discover signs of moisture, check for a leaky pipe or water that consistently overflows or splashes out of sinks, tubs, or showers or that seeps through poorly grouted or caulked seams in tile work. Look into seepage from the outside, caused by roof problems, leaking eaves, or ice dams that form under snow on the roof and let water work its way indoors.

Install doorstops on every interior door. Wallboard and doorknobs don't mix. Doorknobs are by far the most common cause of holes in wallboard—either because there's no doorstop or because the doorstop has broken. Make sure each door has a solid doorstop. It doesn't matter if it screws into the door, the baseboard, or the floor. Replace puny spring-type doorstops. If you want an inconspicuous doorstop, get one that mounts on top of a door hinge.

Prevent chair dents with chair rail molding. Yet another common cause of wallboard dents and scrapes are chairs and sometimes tables bumping against the wall in a dining room or eating alcove. The answer: chair rail molding. Put it at the correct level, and you'll protect the wall and add style to the room.

Easy Fixes

Replacing popped nails. Wallboard is rarely nailed in place these days; screws work better. But there are still plenty of older walls that have nails in them, and regular as rain, one of these nails will start working its way out of the wall, squeezed by the framing as it dries. If you see a nail popping out, it's simple to fix: Get a small, flat pry bar and pull the nail out. (Be sure to pry against a scrap of wood to avoid damaging the wall.) Then drive a drywall screw in just above or below the pop, dimpling but not breaking the surface paper with the head of the screw. Fill the repair area with spackling, and smooth it with a drywall knife. Let it dry, smooth with sandpaper or, better, a damp sponge. Let dry before touching up.

Quick fixes for scratches and dents. Apply spackling compound using a putty or drywall knife. If the damage is more than 1/4 inch (0.5 cm) deep, do the job in stages. Fill the hole about halfway, let compound dry, and then fill it to the surface. Once the spackling is dry, smooth and level the patch by sanding or wiping with a damp sponge.

Filling cracks. It may seem crazy to make damage worse, but cracks in wallboard are often too puny for the spackling to bond securely in place. The solution? Enlarge

WHICH PATCHING MATERIAL SHOULD YOU USE?

Hardware store shelves overflow with a bewildering mix of similar-looking plaster-type compounds. But they boil down to five basic types. And when it comes to repairing wallboard, only one is really necessary:

YOUR FIRST CHOICE
Spackling compound is designed specifically for making repairs. It won't shrink. Unlike joint compound, it contains strengtheners, so you can fill holes and cracks without the need for mechanical reinforcement like paper wallboard tape or patching screen. Reach for spackling when making almost any wallboard repair, such as filling dents, scratches, cracks, and small holes. It's also fine for small repairs in plaster.

USE ONLY WITH BACKING
Quick-setting joint compound dries harder than regular joint compound but still needs backing, usually fiberglass-mesh tape or a patch. If you're making a repair that calls for tape or patch, you can use quick-setting compound. Because it is harder than regular compound, sanding it smooth before painting won't expose the mesh.

FOR PLASTER WALLS ONLY
Patching plaster is a quick-drying, plaster-based product with added strengthening agents. It simplifies repair of a plaster wall, but it's not meant to be used on wallboard.

STEER CLEAR OF THESE
Joint compound is the plaster-like substance applied over the seams between wallboard panels when a wall goes up. Joint compound needs backing—usually paper wallboard tape or patching screen—or it will crack soon after it dries. It's not for repairs.

Plaster of paris and plaster The first is made of gypsum; the second, of lime. Both are plasters, and both are found near joint compound in hardware stores. Neither is suitable for wallboard repair, and there are better choices for plaster repair.

How to Patch a **Small Hole** *Using a Kit*

The easiest way to patch those doorknob holes and other holes up to 5 inches (13 cm) in diameter is with a repair kit from a local hardware store or home center. A typical kit contains spackling and a stick-on patch of either thin perforated metal or fiberglass mesh. Some kits even supply sandpaper and a putty knife. The kits come in different sizes; get a patch that's the size you need.

1. BRUSH OR CUT AWAY loose paper and crumbling gypsum. Wipe the area with a damp rag to remove any dust or dirt. Let the wall dry.

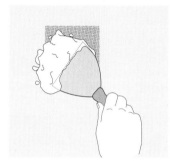

2. TRIM THE PATCH, if necessary. Both metal and mesh patches can be cut with scissors. Remove the backing from the patch, center it over the hole, and stick it on the wall. Press around the edges so that the patch sticks well.

3. APPLY SPACKLING over the patch with a drywall knife, smoothing it out beyond the edges. After the spackling dries, sand and apply a second coat. Finally, apply a third coat to create a smooth wide patch that slopes more gently and is less noticeable.

the crack by cutting along both sides with a utility knife to create a V-shaped groove about 1/4 inch (0.5 cm) wide at the surface. The groove eliminates irregularities and provides enough surface for the compound to adhere to. If the crack is along a seam, remove any loose joint tape and scrape out crumbling compound. Fill the groove with spackling, and smooth it with a drywall knife. Let the repaired area dry, sand or sponge it smooth, and then paint.

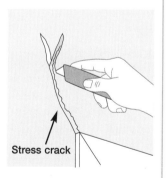

Stress crack

Stopping recurring cracks. You filled that crack and now, two months later, it's back. That's usually because of settling, a common problem in new houses, especially around the corners of windows and doorways. The house eventually settles, but until it does, the trick is to fill those small reappearing cracks with a *paintable* caulk, which is more flexible than spackling. Another trick: Put on a latex glove and wipe

The last stage of any wall repair is to sand the repaired area, and then smooth and paint it. But sanding even a small repair creates copious amounts of fine white dust that's guaranteed to be tracked all over the house. To keep the mess to a minimum, wipe the compound with a damp sponge. It will smooth the surface as well as sandpaper and leave you with much less mess to clean up.

the caulk smooth with your finger. For larger cracks, use flexible ("elastomeric") spackling and apply it with a drywall knife.

Fixing blisters. If a blister forms in the seam tape, the guy who put up the wallboard probably didn't put enough joint compound on the seam. To fix the problem, simply cut out the blistered area with a sharp utility knife; then spackle over the damage. Smooth and touch up the paint.

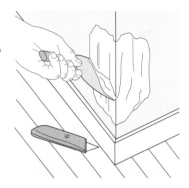

Repairing banged-up corners. Outward-projecting wallboard corners are disasters waiting to happen—just waiting to be bashed by a laundry basket, a kid's toy, a piece of furniture you're moving. Fortunately, the repair is easy. Outside corners are protected by a metal piece, called a corner bead; it wraps around the corner, is nailed to the wallboard, and is then covered with joint compound. If a corner bead is bent, tap it gently back into shape with a hammer and file any sharp edges smooth. Since the existing corner bead will provide backing for any repair you make, this is one case where you can fill gaps with quick-setting joint compound *or* spackling. Fill the damaged area and smooth it with a drywall knife. After the repair dries, sand or sponge smooth; then prime and paint.

DRYWALL KNIVES

If you want to make almost invisible professional-looking wallboard repairs, the secret is to have at least three drywall knives. Plastic ones, which run only a couple of dollars each, are fine for most repairs. When fixing a hole, it's best to cover the patch with up to three coats of compound, each slightly wider than the previous one to create a gently sloping, wide patched area that is not noticeable. The easy way to do this is to put on each coat with a separate drywall knife—each slightly wider than the one before. A good selection would be a 6-inch (15 cm), 8-inch (20 cm), and either a 10- (25 cm) or 12-inch (30 cm) knife.

Plaster Walls

If you have plaster walls, the good news is that a wall made of plaster is more substantial and durable than one made from wallboard. The bad news is that replacing a plaster wall—or having a major repair done with plaster—costs a small fortune today. That's why it's so important to take good care of them. Scratches and dings that damage a wall's surface are easy to fix. But deeper damage—anything that breaks the bond between the plaster and the inner wall—is far more serious. Be good to your plaster walls, and they will last not just your lifetime, but will probably go the distance for your children's and grandchildren's lifetimes, too.

Care and Maintenance

Do a little sleuthing about your plaster cracks. Did you know that the way plaster cracks can often tell you what's causing the problem and how serious it is? Small diagonal cracks above a window or door usually are no big deal and can simply be patched. In a new house, diagonal cracks, often running in opposite directions, are the result of settling. Patch them and forget about them; they'll stop occurring once the house stops settling. If the cracks are large, uneven in width, or recessed, the problem may be structural. Talk to a carpenter or structural engineer and have the underlying problem remedied before you repair the plaster.

Patch small holes as they occur. The weight of loose plaster creates stress on the surrounding plaster. And once the process starts, it continues pulling even more plaster loose. Small holes are easy to fix—don't neglect them and let them become large ones.

Install doorstops. A doorknob that bangs into a wall can damage not only the area it hits, but a lot of the surrounding plaster, too. Make sure that all doors are equipped with sturdy doorstops.

Keep your tools clean. Every now and again, you may find yourself patching small holes or cracks in your plaster walls. It may sound fussy, but make a point of washing and rinsing your tools and pans thoroughly before you mix a second batch of patching plaster. Otherwise, the old leftover patching plaster activates drying compounds in the new plaster, and it can harden before you get it from the sink to the wall.

Be vigilant about your plaster's biggest enemy: water. Leaking pipes, water that spills out of showers, and roof leaks will stain and eventually ruin plaster. Brown spots on your wall can indicate leaks. Fix the leaks first; then repair or repaint the plaster. Before painting over a stain, coat it with a stain killer to prevent show-through.

Easy Fixes

Patching with the right materials. Making surface repairs to plaster is easy if you select the best patching compound for the job:

- Fill small cracks in plaster with spackling compound. Widen a thin crack with the pointed end of a traditional V-shaped beverage opener until it's about 1/8 inch (0.3 cm) wide so the spackling has more plaster to stick to.

SMART IDEA

If you are making a small repair to plaster, use a small rubber kitchen spatula, which is more flexible and easier to use than a putty knife. A spatula is great for applying plaster in areas too narrow for a putty knife.

ANATOMY OF A PLASTER WALL

A plaster wall is built in stages on top of a backing of lath—wooden strips (in older homes), metal mesh, or wallboard-like gypsum—fastened to studs. The first or scratch coat of plaster is pushed through the lath to lock it in place; its front surface is then scratched to help the next coat adhere. The second or brown coat is rich in sand and builds wall thickness. The finish coat is the smooth surface that you see.

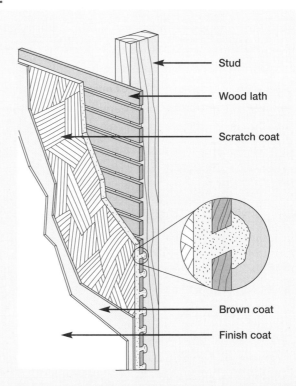

Stud

Wood lath

Scratch coat

Brown coat

Finish coat

- If a crack is persistent—returning after you repair it—put self-sticking fiberglass tape over the crack, and cover the tape with three coats of quick-setting joint compound, which dries harder and covers the fiberglass better than regular joint compound.

- Patch holes with patching plaster—a special mix that is stronger than plaster and seldom requires more than one coat.

Duplicating your wall's texture perfectly. Want a repair to be invisible? Make its surface match the surface of the older surrounding plaster.

- If the wall is textured, duplicate the texture: Depending on the effect you need, try dragging a comb, brush, crumpled newspaper, or sponge on the wet plaster.

- If the wall has a sandy surface, let the patch dry, and prime it. Then apply a top-coat of latex paint mixed with sand.

- If the wall is smooth, just smooth it with a putty or drywall knife, but scrape the knife frequently on a clean piece of wood to keep little pieces of dried plaster from scratching the surface.

How to Repair a Hole in a **Plaster Wall**

1. TAP on the plaster surrounding the hole. A hollow sound indicates plaster has separated from the lath. Pry gently with a putty knife to remove any loose plaster.

2. HOLLOW OUT the area under the edge of the plaster by running a V-shaped beverage opener around the opening. You want the edge to slant inward so that the repair area is wider at the base than at the surface to help anchor the patch.

3. MIX the patching plaster as directed. Dust out the inside of the hole and lightly mist it with water just before you apply the plaster to help it stick.

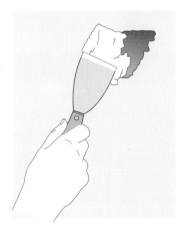

4. APPLY the plaster with a putty or drywall knife. Fill the hole and smooth the patch so it's flush with the wall. If the hole is more than 1/4 inch (0.5 cm) deep, fill the hole halfway; then let the patch dry, and apply a second layer. Once the patch dries, sponge or sand it smooth.

Painted Walls

Most of us don't think twice about the paint on our walls until it starts to look drab and dingy and calls out for a fresh coat. So if you need an incentive to take care of painted surfaces, just stop for a minute and think about all the furniture-moving, scraping, sanding, splatters, drips, and brush-cleaning that go into painting a room. With a minimal amount of care, you can delay that day of reckoning for years. For most walls, all it takes is periodic dusting, prompt spot and stain removal, and occasional patching of scrapes and chips.

Care and Maintenance

Dust your way to clean walls. In most rooms, the easiest way to get rid of the dust, dirt, and cobwebs that shorten the life of your paint is to run a microfiber dust cloth (such as Swiffer) on a long-handled sweeper over your walls every couple of months. You don't need to take down pictures or move furniture. Areas that are covered don't get very dirty—and they don't show anyway. Don't forget the ceiling; despite gravity, some airborne dust collects there. It shouldn't take you more than 10 or 15 minutes to do an entire room. Vacuuming with a soft brush works, too, and so does Grandma's solution: a clean, white cloth wrapped around the head of a broom.

Wash kitchen and bath walls. Remove the residues of cooking and steamy showers by washing the painted areas of kitchen and bathroom walls at least once every year. Do other rooms, too, if they are regularly used by children or a smoker or have a fireplace or wood-burning stove. Start from the bottom. Rub gently with a natural sponge and a soap and water solution (like the ones described in the next hint). Wash and rinse a small area, then move up and do an area that partially overlaps what you've already cleaned. Dry the wall with an old towel. Don't forget to wash woodwork as well.

Make your own wall-washing soap. Homemade soap mixtures do a great job cleaning painted walls. Both of these mixtures are inexpensive, simple to make, and at least as good as commercially available cleaners.

- Mix 1 cup (250 ml) of borax and 2 tablespoons (30 ml) of dishwashing liquid in 1 gallon (4 litres) of warm water. You'll find borax in the cleaning-products aisle at the supermarket.

- Mix 1 cup (250 ml) of ammonia and 1 teaspoon (5 ml) of dishwashing liquid in 1 gallon (4 litres) of water.

Test painted walls before cleaning them. It's safe to wash glossy and semigloss paint, which are commonly used in kitchens and baths and on woodwork. Most modern flat and satin paint are also washable, but always test them in an inconspicuous spot. If paint chalks off on your sponge, don't wash that paint. Never wash with trisodium phosphate (TSP) except when you are about to repaint; it dulls the finish.

Wash high-traffic areas. Even if you don't need to wash an entire room, the areas around switches and thermostats may need an occasional washing. Dust and dirt also tend to accumulate on walls behind TVs or other electronics and above radiators or heating grates. If dusting doesn't get rid of them, wash the area.

Seal in lead paint. Until recently many paints contained harmful lead. The most reliable way to test suspect paint is with a lab test. Mail a chip of paint to the lab for a report (check the Yellow Pages or the Internet for a source). If you have lead paint, seal it off with two coats of high-quality paint. As long as the new paint remains sound, the lead is contained and presents no danger.

SMART IDEA

Apply a light coating of spray starch to walls in high-traffic areas. The starch makes it easier to clean off dirt and grime.

SAVING LEFTOVER PAINT

When you paint a room, save the leftover paint for touch-ups. With care, latex will keep for up to 10 years and alkyd for 15. Odds are, you'll decide to repaint before then.

- If you have less than half a can of paint left, pour the paint into a zip-seal plastic food bag. Squeeze out the extra air as you seal the bag; then put the bag in the original can and seal the can.

- If you have more than half a can, just seal the can. Put a piece of plastic wrap over the can before replacing the lid for an extra-tight seal.

- On the container's lid, write the paint's color, number, and date of purchase, and the room where it was used. On the outside of the can, mark the level of the paint so you can tell how much you have without opening the can.

- Store a can upside down so that any scab that forms will be on the bottom when you turn the can upright. Store paint where it won't freeze or overheat; a basement is better than an unheated garage.

- When you reopen paint, stir vigorously; if it blends well, it's okay to use. If you encounter lumps, strain the paint through a piece of panty hose.

Easy Fixes

Touching up damage. To keep paint looking fresh, touch up damage as it occurs. Sand and touch up a scraped or chipped surface, feathering the paint over the surrounding area. Fill holes first as described for wallboard (page 37) or plaster (page 41). And coat a recalcitrant stain with stain sealer before touching it up. If a leak has caused peeling and bubbling, fix the leak source; then scrape and sand the area and repaint it. Whenever possible, use paint left over from the original job.

Computer-matching your paint color. A leak damages the paint in the corner of the ceiling and a bit of the wall under it. You don't have any of the original paint left over. Must you repaint the entire room? No, just slice through the paint on the wall with a sharp utility knife in an out-of-the-way area and lift off a good-sized chip. Take the chip to a paint store that has computerized paint-matching equipment, which will generate a recipe the store can use to match the color. Computerized color matching is usually free and it may save you from having to repaint the entire room for a few years.

5 KEYS TO A GREAT PAINT JOB

The secret to a successful paint job is choosing materials carefully. Here are some guidelines:

1. Choose the right color. Take paint brochures home and pick the color during daylight in the room you'll be painting. Buy a quart (1 litre) of the color, paint part of the wall, and live with it before making a final decision.

2. Cheap paint is expensive. You're more likely to save money with a top-of-the-line paint. Cheap paint usually requires two coats to cover what's on the wall, thereby doubling your cost. Low-quality latex paint also gets chalky as it ages and needs to be repainted sooner.

3. Get the right paint finish. Paint comes in glossy, semigloss, eggshell, satin, and flat finishes. Use glossy or semigloss on woodwork. In areas likely to get dirty—kitchens and baths—use semigloss or eggshell on walls. The glossier the paint, the more durable and easier it will be to clean. Flat, on the other hand, hides wall defects and touched-up areas better.

4. Match, don't mix. Simplify your life. Use the same color paint on trim and walls even if they're not the same sheen. You'll have to do far less masking, and touch-up is simpler since paint splashed from the walls onto the trim (or vice versa) is virtually invisible.

5. Pick the right applicators. Select a short-nap roller for smooth walls and a longer nap for stucco, concrete, and textured surfaces. Make sure the roller has slightly beveled ends that won't drag paint onto adjoining surfaces. Choose a nylon-wool blend roller for alkyd (oil) paint, but get an all-nylon roller for latex (the water in latex swells natural fibers). Similarly, choose a natural bristle brush for alkyd and synthetic bristles for latex. Look sideways at a brush. A good brush comes to a dull point; a cheap one is cut square. Look at the bristle ends. Split ends (properly called flagged ends) help spread paint for a smoother finish.

How to Prep a **Wall** Before Painting It

A paint job will only be as good as the job you did getting the walls ready for it. Here are four steps to take before you put on the finishing coat.

1. WASH IT. Put on rubber gloves and wash the walls with trisodium phosphate (TSP) or TSP substitute. This strong, non-sudsing cleanser, available at paint retailers, dulls the finish so that paint will adhere better. Rinse with a sponge and water until the water runs clear. Let the wall dry. Wash off any mildew with a 50/50 mixture of water and bleach, and rinse well.

2. FIX IT. Repair holes and cracks in the wallboard (page 37) or the plaster (page 41). Scrape off loose paint and blend in areas with chipped-off paint by sanding the edges of the surrounding paint or by skim-coating the area with spackling. Fill dings and dents in woodwork with wood putty and smaller nail holes with glazing compound; then sand. Finally, lightly sand the surface. Fill gaps between the wall and trim with painter's caulk, and smooth the seams with your latex-gloved finger.

3. MASK IT. Apply masking tape over moldings and trim where they meet the wall; the newer blue tapes are easier to use than traditional masking tape. Protect the floor with a drop cloth.

4. PRIME IT. To keep stains from bleeding through the new paint, seal them with stain sealer, available at paint stores and home centers. Oil-based and shellac-based sealers block stains better than latex ones. Then coat the entire wall with latex primer, which is easier to clean up but just as durable as oil-based primer.

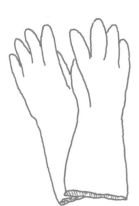

CLEVER WALL STAIN REMOVERS

IF YOUR WALLS HAVE ...	YOU SHOULD ...
Crayon marks	Spray the area with WD-40, then wipe with a soft cloth.
Small spots and smudges	Rub gently with an art gum eraser.
Large spots	Make a paste from baking soda and water. Apply it with a soft cloth and wipe clean with a damp sponge.
Ink and marker stains	Wipe with a rag dampened with alcohol.
Grease marks	Wipe with a rag dampened with mineral spirits.

Wallpaper

We still call it wallpaper, but the correct term is "wall covering" because it's just as likely to be made out of vinyl or some other material as it is paper. (If it is paper, it probably has a protective vinyl coating.) What this means for you is that most wall coverings are very easy to care for. In most rooms, an occasional cleaning is all it takes to keep them looking good. In some cases, you may need to fix the occasional ding, scratch, tear, curling seam, or bubble. All are easy to repair and are a lot easier on you and your wallet than repapering.

Care and Maintenance

Vacuum your wallpaper. The best thing you can do to keep the wall covering in most rooms looking pristine is the simplest: Vacuum it. A soft brush attachment on a vacuum cleaner works best—and is a must if the paper is flocked or has any kind of texture. Start at the top of the wall and work your way down, doing a couple of panels at a time. Be careful of cobwebs. Lift them up with the vacuum; if you try brushing them away, they may streak the wall. Depending on how dusty your house gets, dust every few months. A microfiber cloth on a long-handled sweeper or a clean white cloth wrapped on the end of broom will also work on flat, non-textured wall coverings.

Test unique or textured wallpaper before washing it. Natural coverings—grass, reed, hemp, cork, leather, fabric—and uncoated wallpaper are easily damaged

---

SEAM ADHESIVE AND ROLLERS　　　*equipment spotlight*

Seam adhesive is strong wallpaper glue designed to keep the paper around seams from peeling, and it is also used to repair a seam if it starts to come away from the wall. A seam roller is a nylon, wood, or steel roller about 1 inch wide (2.5 cm), on a short handle. Roll it along seams to press both sides into the adhesive. Don't push too hard; overly compressing the paper and glue will leave a permanent indentation once the glue dries. Don't use a roller if the paper is flocked; it will leave indentations no matter how gentle you are. Use instead a natural-bristle smoothing brush instead.

by water and cannot be washed. To find out if a wall covering is washable, squirt a little dishwashing liquid in water and dab some on the wall in an out-of-the-way spot. If the material darkens or absorbs water—or if the colors run—the covering is not washable. Clean it with wallpaper dough.

Give your kitchen wallpaper an occasional wipe. In rooms where wall coverings are exposed to grease, steam, or active youngsters, dusting is not enough. A light washing every few months is in order. Luckily, the wall coverings used in such areas are usually waterproof sheet vinyl. Give them a quick swipe with a natural sponge dampened in water with a squirt of dishwashing liquid. Make sure that sponge isn't too wet—you don't want water to seep under the seams and loosen the covering. Also, be sure to clean from the bottom up; that way dirty water that you squeeze out of the sponge won't flow down over the dirty areas and leave streaks. Even if the covering is labeled "scrubbable," it best not to scrub hard or to use abrasive cleaners or strong household cleansers. Rinse with a sponge dampened in clean water. Pat dry with a towel. If the paper needs a second washing, let it dry thoroughly first.

SMART IDEA

Don't have a seam roller? In a pinch, use an ordinary rolling pin to press down a seam you have fixed.

WHICH WALL COVERING IS BEST WHERE?

Do you want to get the best new covering for a particular room? Or do you want to know what kind of wall covering you have? Here's a selective guide to wall coverings and the areas for which they are best suited.

FOR ENTRIES AND HALLS
Paper-backed vinyl consists of a solid vinyl surface laminated to a paper backing. It is washable and, since the paper backing gives extra strength to the vinyl, very durable—qualities that make it good for high-traffic hallways and such.

FOR KITCHENS AND BATHS
Sheet vinyl is vinyl through and through with no paper backing.

It's by far the best choice for kitchens and bathrooms because it is resistant both to moisture and to stains and grease and is easy to clean. The absence of a paper backing makes it a bit fragile, however, and it does not hold up well to a lot of wear and tear.

FOR LIVING ROOMS
AND BEDROOMS
Vinyl-coated paper is essentially paper wallpaper that has been coated with vinyl to make it resistant to dirt, grease, and moisture. You can wash it with a damp sponge. It's the most common and best all-round wall covering.

Coated fabric wall covering is cloth coated with vinyl or acrylic.

Because the underlying fabric can absorb moisture, this type of wall covering is best used in low-moisture rooms.

Natural fiber wall coverings are made of grass, jute, cork, hemp, sisal, and other natural materials laminated to a paper backing. They can be very decorative and are good at hiding a wall's imperfections, but they are tricky to hang and to clean.

Foil coverings are made by laminating a thin sheet of aluminum foil or a Mylar-like material onto a paper base. They add drama and reflected light to a room, but are very unforgiving of flaws in a wall. If a wall is less than perfect, apply lining paper first.

Clean delicate coverings with dough. Need to clean a stain off a fabric or reed wall covering? Or off uncoated wallpaper? You can clean a covering that would be damaged by water using a special product called wallpaper dough, sold at paint stores and home centers. Take a handful of dough from the container, roll it into a ball, and then roll the ball across the wall covering to lift the dirt. When the dough gets dirty, knead the dirt into the center of the ball to expose a fresh surface.

SECRET WEAPONS AGAINST WALLPAPER STAINS

IF YOUR PROBLEM IS ...	THE SOLUTION IS ...
Dirt and other stains	Use a slice of soft white bread (instead of commercial wallpaper dough). Trim off the crust and form it into a ball to roll across the wall. When your bread ball won't pick up any more dirt, throw it out, and start with a new slice.
Fingerprints	Rub off gently with an art gum eraser, available at office and art supply stores.
Candle wax	Hold a double layer of paper towels over the spot and press the towels gently with a warm iron.
Grease or other oily stains	Apply a paste made of cornstarch and water. Let it dry; then vacuum it off. If you are worried about using water on the covering, use talcum powder or cornstarch alone.

Easy Fixes

Popping wallpaper bubbles. An air bubble underneath the surface is another common wall covering problem. The solution is simple, but you'll need a glue injector. There are two types of injectors, both of which work well. One looks like a syringe, and the other has an accordion bulb above the needle. You should be able to find them at a wallpaper or home-improvement store. Here's how to get rid of that bubble: Using a sharp utility  knife, cut a small slit in the paper along one side of the bubble. Insert the injector's needle into the slit, and squeeze seam adhesive under the bubble. Press out excess adhesive and wipe it off with a damp sponge. Roll gently with a wallpaper seam roller to flatten the bubble.

Fixing curled seams. Your wall covering's edge has curled up at the seam—no big deal; it's easy to fix. Here's what to do. First, moisten the area with warm water to make the material pliable. Lift the edge carefully and slip seam adhesive under the edge using a strip of index card or a toothpick. (If the paper is solid vinyl, use vinyl-to-vinyl adhesive.) Flatten the seam gently with a wallpaper seam roller and wipe away excess glue.

Regluing peeling borders. Wallpaper borders, which are often used across the top of walls or at chair rail height, are notorious for peeling at the edges. If this happens, just dab white glue on the wall and on the underside of the border with an artist's brush. Roll the edge gently with a wallpaper seam roller.

Painting or repapering over existing wallpaper. If it's untextured, solidly attached to the wall, and only one layer thick, you can paint or repaper directly over old wall covering. To make sure the paper is solidly attached, run your fingers over the wall. If you hear a crackling sound, the paper is loose. Putting paint or wallpaper paste over it will only make it more likely to come off. Check the seams and corners by trying to pry them up. If the paper adheres tightly to the wall, you're in luck. To paper again, just apply the new covering over the old. To paint, first prime the paper with alkyd (oil) paint. (The water in latex paint could dissolve the wallpaper glue.)

SMART IDEA

Painting over a wall covering isn't always a perfect solution—the covering's seams can show through. A good way to disguise them is with a decorative painting technique, such as sponging or rag rolling.

How to Patch a **Wall Covering**

If you had the foresight to save some of the wall covering left over from installation, repairing a damaged section is simple.

1. Cut a piece of the LEFTOVER PAPER so that it's larger than the area you need to patch and large enough to handle easily. Put it over the damaged area, and align the patterns. Tape the new paper in place with easy-release masking tape, and use a straightedge and a *sharp* utility knife to cut through both layers of paper.

2. REMOVE THE TAPE and set aside the top layer, which will become the patch. Peel off the damaged paper. Apply paste (or paste activator if the paper is prepasted) and wait until it gets tacky. Put the patch in place and smooth it with a damp sponge.

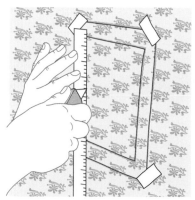

Paneled Walls

Once upon a time all paneling was solid wood—either elaborate frames with inset panels, or simple tongue-and-groove strips nailed next to each other. But today the paneling that lines so many family rooms in converted basements or garages is more likely to be hardboard (Masonite) with a synthetic surface patterned to resemble wood. Sometimes, it's plywood with a wood veneer. Paneling is more durable than paint or wallpaper and relatively maintenance-free. Just keep it clean and do minor repairs as needed, and it will look fine for years. That's why most people install it in the first place: It's the interior equivalent of vinyl siding.

Care and Maintenance

Give your paneling an occasional shine. Paneling that is in good shape rarely needs more than dusting to keep it clean. Wipe both solid-wood and sheet paneling using a soft cloth dampened with furniture polish. Avoid wax or silicone polishes, which may leave streaks on the walls.

Fight stubborn dirt. To get rid of grime, soot, and layers of dust, wipe paneling with a soft cloth dampened with lukewarm water and a squirt of mild dishwashing liquid. Dry immediately with a clean cloth so that the water doesn't damage the finish.

Easy Fixes

Filling scratches with markers. You can cover scratches in both vinyl and wood veneer facings by using either a furniture touch-up marker or wax stick that matches the color of the paneling. Both are available in hardware stores.

Refinishing large scrapes. Larger scrapes in wood veneer paneling call for refinishing. Here's the quick way to do the job: Sand the damaged area with a fine-grit sanding sponge dipped in mineral spirits. Wipe clean with a rag dampened with mineral spirits. Let dry, and apply a matching-color wood stain. Remove excess stain with a dry rag. Let dry, and apply spray lacquer.

Fixing popping paneling nails. Loose nails are not only unsightly, they can snag clothing or even hurt someone. If a nail has come loose, don't just drive it back in. Instead, pull the nail, using pliers or a small flat pry bar with a wood block under it to avoid marring the paneling. Then drive in a new nail about a quarter inch above or below.

Painting paneling. Before you paint paneling, make sure your paneling is really wood—paint won't stick to vinyl or plastic surfaces. Try sanding an out-of-the-way spot—plastic and vinyl will flake. Wood won't. If it is real wood, wash the paneling with a solution of warm water and no-rinse detergent, such as trisodium phosphate (TSP) or TSP substitute. Fill the grooves (if you want), and any holes or dents, with spackling compound, and let dry. Take the shine off the panel surface by sanding lightly with fine-grit (#220) sandpaper. Wear a dust mask and goggles while sanding, and use a window fan to blow airborne dust outside. Clean with a damp rag. Apply a primer designed for paneling. Let it dry, and then apply a finish coat.

Wallpapering over paneling. Another way to hide dark ugly paneling that has a synthetic surface is by wallpapering over it. Wash the paneling and fill the grooves and holes with spackling compound as described above. Then put up wallpaper liner, sold at paint and wallpaper stores, running the liner horizontally across the paneling. Let the liner dry before hanging the wallpaper.

How to Reattach Loose Paneling

Loose or bowed paneling that's coming away from the wall is fairly easy to secure. The paneling adhesive and paneling nails or wood putty you need are available at home centers. If the problem is the result of a leak, be sure to fix it first.

1. Insert a SMALL FLAT PRY BAR under the loose edge and pry the area partly open. Put a wood block under the pry bar to give it more leverage and to protect the paneling's finish. Pull out any old loose nails.

2. Keep the pried area wedged open with a WOOD SCRAP. Apply a generous bead of paneling adhesive to the wall or furring strips behind the paneling. Keep the area wedged open until the adhesive gets tacky, about 10 minutes.

3. Remove the wedge and press the panel in place. Hammer over the area; use a WOOD BLOCK with cardboard under it to avoid marring the paneling. Drive color-matched paneling nails at 5-inch (13 cm) intervals along the glued edge; don't reuse old nail holes. Or use brads; sink them just below the surface with a nail set and fill the holes with color-matched wood putty.

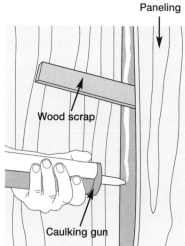

Paneling

Wood scrap

Caulking gun

Molding and Trim

Most of us think that the molding in a room is just a decorative flair—a finishing touch that frames windows and walls. But it does serve a practical function. Chair railings and baseboards protect the wall from collisions with furniture and toys. Toe molding, crown molding, and casings around doors and windows seal and camouflage the gaps where walls meet floors, ceilings, and frames. Over time, molding can lose a good bit of its beauty. It gets dirty, chipped, or otherwise banged up and may even come loose. Letting problems go can mean having to refinish the molding—or replace it.

SMART IDEA

When you're reinstalling molding and need to remove the old nails, a natural inclination is to drive the nails out from the back. But if you do, the nail heads will splinter the front of the trim as they come out. Instead, use this old carpenter's trick: Clamp locking pliers on each nail and pull it out through the *back* of the molding. Put the new nails in different places, predrilling holes for them.

Care and Maintenance

Wash your molding. The best way to keep molding looking its best—and free of the dirt and grime that can eventually ruin its finish—is to simply wipe it every few months with a sponge dampened in a mixture of dishwashing liquid and water. Rinse with a damp sponge and then dry with an old towel to prevent spotting. Most molding has a glossy or semigloss varnish or paint finish, which can withstand a quick wipe down. Trim around entry doors is especially prone to collecting dirt.

Keep molding dry. The key to preserving molding is to keep its finish in good shape. The easiest way to do this is to protect the woodwork against prolonged exposure to moisture. That means closing windows, wiping trim around sinks and showers, and placing pet food bowls far from your trim. The biggest threat of all? Wet mops.

Easy Fixes

Adding storm windows. Yes, storm windows do more than reduce winter heating costs; they can protect your interior woodwork. The moisture that collects on the interior of single-pane windows all winter long can damage the window frame and surrounding trim. On cold days, warm, moist air in the house condenses on the cool glass, water drips down onto the frame and trim, and ultimately the woodwork begins to deteriorate, even rot. The best way to eliminate this condensation is to install storm windows.

Renailing loose trim without damaging it. If you've ever driven a loose nail back into trim, you probably discovered that it doesn't hold very well. When you need to renail molding, there are two tricks to keep in mind.

- The first: Use a new nail, driven in to one side of the existing nail. You can either pull out the old nail with pliers or sink it, depending on what works best.

- The second: To avoid splitting the molding, predrill a hole for the new nail using a nail of the same size as a drill bit. To do this, simply clip the head off a nail with cutting pliers. Put the nail in the drill as if it were a bit and drill the hole. Drive in the new nail; then use a nail set to sink the head slightly below the surface. Fill the new hole and the old one with wood putty that matches the finish.

Using trim screws on warped molding. If your molding is warped slightly or if you just fear a nail might pop again, use a trim screw instead. This narrow, small-headed screw holds better than a nail and doesn't bend while you're driving it. The disadvantage: the head is larger and more obvious. To install a trim screw, first drill a countersink (a depression the same diameter as the screw head and slightly deeper) and then continue drilling a pilot hole with a bit the diameter of the screw shank. After you drive in the screw, conceal the head with wood putty.

Closing gaps in door-frame corners. Don't you hate it when the joint in the upper corner of a door frame opens up, leaving a very visible diagonal gap? It's easy to close using a special clamp called a miter clamp, which you can buy at a home center. First put a bead of carpenter's glue in the opening, and then pull the corners back together with the clamp. Drill a hole at the side and top for a fourpenny (1 1/2-inch or 4 cm) nail that will run through each piece and into the other, pinning the joint together. (To protect the wall from being damaged by your drill and hammer, insert a piece of thin cardboard behind the trim.) Drive nails into the holes, and remove the clamp.

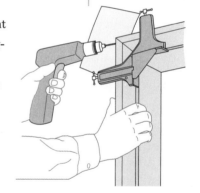

Fixing unsightly baseboard gaps. Gaps often develop between two pieces of baseboard that meet at an outside corner. But if the installer cut the pieces to the right length, you should be able to bring the pieces together using trim screws that go into the wall. To test, try squeezing the ends together with your hand. If you can close the gap, you're in business. (If you can't, just fill the gap with caulk or wood putty.) Predrill and drive a trim screw through one baseboard into the framing at the corner of the wall. Then do the same with the other baseboard.

SMART IDEA

White trim is timeless, goes with every wall color, and is easy to touch up. Paint all your moldings with easy-to-scrub glossy white paint, then use typing correction fluid—like Wite Out—to touch up small dings and dents.

Ceramic Tile Walls

The glazed ceramic tile in our bathrooms and kitchens is just about the most durable, care-free material in our houses. The cement-like grout in the joints between the tiles is what's more likely to give you grief by absorbing dirt or mildew or crumbling. Damage to the tiles themselves is relatively easy to fix, either by touching up or replacing the tile. The biggest challenge to repairing both grout and tile? Matching the color of the original materials.

Care and Maintenance

Wipe down your tiles. Just wiping the tiles regularly with a damp sponge will keep glazed ceramic tiles clean. Do it right after you shower, while the walls are still steamy. If you wash the tiles, use a commercial tub-and-tile cleaner and avoid soapy or oily cleaners. An alternative is to add a capful of rubbing alcohol to a gallon (4 litres) of water and wipe the tiles with that.

Keep the grout clean, too. Routinely wiping your tiles should keep the grout clean by default. But if the grout gets dirty, clean it with commercial grout cleaner. Some spray on; others brush on with a narrow applicator. After applying the cleaner, leave it on for a few minutes; then scrub it off with an old toothbrush.

Bleach grimy grout. For grout that stubbornly resists standard cleaning methods, mix a cup (250 ml) of household bleach in a half-gallon (2 litres) of water. Scrub it

---

GROUTING TOOLS

equipment spotlight

If you are replacing a lot of grout, there are a couple of tools that can speed the process. (For a small job, you can make do with what you have on hand.)

- To remove a lot of old grout, cut it out with a small, hand-held grout saw. Otherwise, just scrape it out with a V-shaped beverage opener.

- To regrout a large area, use a special rubber-bottom grout float. For a smaller area, just press the grout into the seams with your rubber-gloved finger.

on with an old toothbrush, and let it soak for 10 to 20 minutes before rinsing with clean water. Rinse a second time and wipe dry with a clean cloth. If that doesn't do the trick, replace the grout (see page 56).

Easy Fixes

Sealing grout and porous tiles. Once you've got your grout clean, it's easy to keep it that way by sealing it. Make sure the grout is thoroughly dry, and then apply a silicone sealer (available at home centers). Put it just on the grout; grout sealer can stain glazed tiles. Grout manufacturers generally recommend resealing grout joints twice a year. If you have porous tiles, such as slate, stone, or Saltillo, seal the tiles and the grout at the same time by applying a combination tile-and-grout sealer.

Matching your grout's color. Grout comes as colored powder that you mix with water to the consistency of toothpaste. To match the color of new grout with the old, you may need to mix two different colors together. Get a color chart from your tile dealer and match it against the grout on your wall. Make up a few sample batches of grout, varying (and noting) the amount of each color. Let the samples dry at least overnight and choose the closest match.

Finding matching tiles. If you don't have tiles left from the original job, wait until you've removed the tile; then take a large scrap to the tile store and try to match it. A close but not perfect match may be okay under the sink or low in a corner. Otherwise, choose a contrasting accent color and replace a couple of other tiles to make it look like the whole thing was done on purpose. Note that floor tiles are thicker than wall tiles—make sure you get a wall tile.

Replacing cracked tiles. You can't repair a cracked tile; you have to replace it. You'll need a hammer, a cold chisel, a notched plastic trowel, a grout saw, and premixed latex tile adhesive. Wear work gloves and goggles. Start by cutting out the grout around the tile with a grout saw. Then break up and remove the damaged tile and the old adhesive under it with a cold chisel and hammer. Apply adhesive to the back of the new tile with the trowel and press it into place. Let the adhesive dry for at least 72 hours; then apply grout.

Touching up chipped tiles. You can touch up a chipped tile using appliance touch-up paint or the polyester resin made for repairing bathtubs, but it's tricky to find a perfect color match. You may be better off staining the chipped area with a matching-color marker or paint; after it dries, coat the area with clear nail polish.

How to Replace Crumbling Grout

Broken and crumbling grout can let moisture penetrate behind the tiles, loosening the adhesive or even damaging the underlying wall. Replacing grout is actually very simple.

1. Start by REMOVING THE LOOSE OLD GROUT with a grout saw. Vacuum out the debris and wash the area with tile cleaner.

----

2. PACK NEW GROUT into the area with a grout float. Hold the float at an angle to the wall and sweep it diagonally across the tiles. Remove excess grout with the float.

----

3. After 20 to 30 minutes, WIPE THE AREA with a damp sponge. Run the bottom of a toothbrush handle along the joints to pack in the grout. Let the area dry again until a cloudy haze appears. Polish off the haze with a clean rag. Do it right away; if you wait too long, the hazy residue will harden and become difficult to remove. Wait a week, until the grout is thoroughly hardened, and then seal it.

Caulking seams that flex. The seams where wall tile meets the bathtub, or where two walls meet, are particularly vulnerable to water infiltration and damage. These seams also need to be allowed to flex since the bathtub moves as it empties and fills. The solution is to apply color-matched caulk in the seams instead of grout. Fill the tub before caulking the seams so they don't stretch later.

Ceiling Tile

With no moving parts and a surface well above most of our reach, ceiling tiles have only two natural enemies—gravity and airborne dirt. Ceiling tiles are either suspended from a metal grid or attached directly to the ceiling, and there are simple fixes for those that come loose or are damaged. When it comes to cleaning, what matters most is what the tiles are made of: Most new tiles have a vinyl coating that you can spray-wash. Older tiles and new ones designed for maximum sound absorption aren't coated and require a special dry-sponge cleaner.

YOUR COST SAVINGS
$375
What you would pay to have old, acoustical tiles removed and replaced with new ones in a 12-by-18-foot (4 by 6 metres) room.

Care and Maintenance

Vacuum your ceiling yearly. Manufacturers brag that ceiling tiles are virtually maintenance-free, but that doesn't mean you shouldn't clean them. Vacuum your tiles with a soft brush attachment at least once a year; more often if they are in the kitchen. If you put off vacuuming until the tiles begin to look dirty, you're waiting too long.

Give your tiles the cotton-ball test. If your tiles are so dirty they need more than vacuuming, find out first if they have a protective plastic coating. Dampen a cotton ball and dab it on the ceiling. If the water beads up and drips off, you have coated tiles that you can clean using a wet solution. If the water soaks in, the tiles are absorbent and need a moisture-free cleaning method.

Spray your tiles clean. Hydrogen peroxide is mild bleach that will clean and brighten washable ceiling tiles. Buy ordinary 3 percent hydrogen peroxide solution at the drug store. Mix an ounce with a quart of water in a spray bottle, and spray it on the ceiling. That's all you have to do. It's that simple. You don't have to rub or rinse—the peroxide will do its job, and all you need to do is let the tiles air-dry.

"Dry clean" non-sprayable tiles. Since uncoated tiles can't be sprayed with a wet solution, you need to use a special dry-cleaning sponge, such as Wonder Sponge. It's made of natural rubber treated with a specially formulated cleaner. Just wipe the dry sponge across ceiling tiles using smooth, even strokes.

take care

Cleaner that you spray on the ceiling can end up in your eyes or running down your hands and arms. That's why it's a good idea to wear safety goggles and rubber gloves. Fold the glove ends into cuffs so that drips will collect in the cuffs not on your arms. Also make sure that you have a sturdy ladder—be careful up there!

Call in a pro for the really tough cleaning jobs. If a ceiling is too big or too dirty to wash by yourself and you have room in your budget, hire a ceiling tile cleaning company. They have special equipment and cleaners that can make fast work of cleaning a ceiling. Rates charged by professional cleaners are generally between 30 cents and 45 cents per square foot. That's about $50 for a 10-by-12-foot (3 by 4 metres) room.

Easy Fixes

Resetting suspended tiles. Suspended ceiling tiles fit loosely in a grid and are held there by gravity. Any number of things—even the breeze created by closing a door—can jostle them. If they slide around enough, they'll fall out and often break on impact. If you can see the edge of a tile, it's slipping out of place. Get out the ladder, lift the tile gently, and slide it back where it belongs.

Troubleshooting attached tiles. If an attached tile—one that's glued directly to the ceiling—falls on the floor, the cause is usually water leaking from above that's caused the glue holding the tile to give way. Fix the leak, whether it's in the plumbing or the roof, before you replace the tile.

How to Replace an Attached Ceiling Tile

Instead of being suspended from a metal grid, attached ceiling tiles are either glued directly to the ceiling or stapled to narrow wood furring strips on the ceiling. They're usually 1 foot square (0.1 metre square) and have flanged edges.

1. With a utility knife, cut a line close to each edge of the damaged tile to CREATE A SQUARE that you can pry out with a putty knife. Scrape away debris and any adhesive you've exposed.

- -

2. CUT OFF THE FLANGES from the replacement tile to fit it in the space you've cleared. If the tile was glued to the ceiling, put four golf-ball-sized dabs of ceiling tile adhesive on the back about 2 inches (5 cm) from the edges, and then press the new tile into place. If the old tile was stapled to furring strips, apply carpenter's glue to the strips and to the parts of the new tile that touch the strips. The glue will hold the tile in place as you drive twopenny (1-inch or 2.5 cm) nails at each corner to hold the tile to the furring strips. Sink the nails just below the surface with a nail set.

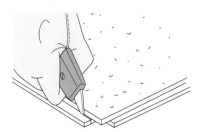

- -

Wood Flooring

For sheer natural beauty and warmth, there's nothing like a hardwood floor. It is also surprisingly durable. With just a little regular care, a floor can go decades without needing to be sanded and refinished or even needing a new coat of varnish. The kinds of problems to be on the lookout for are ones that affect the surface finish—scratches and scrapes, water damage, and a variety of stains. These problems are easy to prevent and simple to fix when you catch them early.

YOUR COST SAVINGS

$425

What you would pay a floor refinisher to sand and refinish a hardwood floor in a 12-by-18-foot (4 by 6 metres) room.

Care and Maintenance

Vacuum your floor every week. You probably do this already, but it always bears repeating. The reason: underfoot, the fine grit in dust is just like sandpaper and will slowly but surely wear through your wood floor's finish. So a good vacuuming protects the finish as well as keeps up its appearance. Use an attachment with a brush or a felt surface that runs along the floor. Attachments with rotating brushes or a beater bar can scratch the finish. Disengage the beater bar on an upright. If you don't feel like hauling out the vacuum, a dust mop or one of the newer microfiber sweepers (such as Swiffer) will work just as well.

Use an extra-long "walk-off" doormat. Doormats, inside and out, earn their keep and then some. While vacuuming and spot-cleaning are great, keeping the dirt out in the first place is even better. Get a 4- to 6-foot-long (1 to 2 metres long) "walk-off" mat for the front door. The longer the mat leading up to the door, the more people will rub dirt and moisture off their shoes as they walk in, even if they don't stop to wipe them.

Protect high-traffic zones with area rugs. Walking across an area several times a day eventually wears down a wood floor's finish. Nice-looking throw rugs are the easiest way to reduce the wear. But make sure they don't have a backing. Vinyl or rubber backing traps humidity, which can ruin your floor's finish and stain or damage the wood.

Watch the hairspray. And the furniture polish. Both of them can cloud your floor's finish. Wipe them up immediately with a damp cloth. For a more thorough cleanup, spray with non-ammonia window cleaner.

Keep out the rain. Water can not only ruin the finish on a hardwood floor but can penetrate deep into the wood and stain it. Close windows when you're expecting rain. Put trays under potted plants and, of course, immediately wipe up any water you see.

Remove residue with no-wax wood floor cleaner. Keep it in the hall closet or another convenient location so that you can get to it quickly to clean up small problems before they become big ones. Wipe up spills and dirt immediately; then use the cleaner to remove the residue. Dirt can damage the finish or get ground in. Liquids can damage the finish or stain the floor.

Know the rules about using waxes and restorers. You can rejuvenate a wax finish with more wax. But never use wax on a surface finish such as shellac, varnish, or polyurethane. It not only makes the floor far too slippery, it also interferes with subsequent finishes. If the finish is polyurethane, use a polish made for polyurethane. If it's another type of surface finish, get a general-purpose floor restorer, test the restorer on an inconspicuous area to make sure it won't peel off.

How to Recoat a Polyurethane Finish

Sanding and refinishing a floor is a job for a pro. But anyone who's at all handy can bring a dull polyurethane finish back to life with a new coat of polyurethane varnish. You can't put down new polyurethane if you've used wax on the floor. If there's wax on your floor, remove it with commercial wax remover. You'll need to rent a buffer and a 150-grit sanding screen to roughen the old finish.

1. To make sure the new coat will stick, TAPE OFF A COUPLE OF 6-INCH (15 CM) SQUARES in an out-of-the-way area. Sand them with 100-grit paper and wipe clean. Brush on some polyurethane; wait 24 hours. If coating hasn't developed an orange-peel texture and it doesn't flake when scratched with a coin, it's safe to recoat the floor.

----

2. SAND THE ENTIRE FLOOR using the buffer. Clean up the dust *thoroughly:* vacuum and wipe down the floor with an alcohol-dampened rag.

----

3. APPLY THE FINISH using a long-handled applicator and a disposable paint tray. Plan your exit, so that you can paint your way out of the room.

Easy Fixes

Fixing color variation. If a scratch is lighter in color than the floor, it means the scratch has penetrated the finish and stain under it and exposed raw wood. It's easy to mask such deep scratches with a furniture marker. Get a marker that matches the color of your floor, and dab it on to replace the stain. Let it dry, and apply a coat of the finish used on your floor. Apply additional coats if needed to make the new finish flush with the old. On a small scratch, you can use clear nail polish as described below.

Touching up floor scratches. You can touch up a small surface scratch on a varnished floor with clear nail polish. Thin the polish by about half with lacquer thinner, and brush it over the scratch with the nail polish brush. Let it dry thoroughly. Sand it gently flush with the surrounding finish using 220-grit paper backed with a block of wood. Keep sanding with progressively finer grits until the sheen matches the surrounding floor. Hardware stores usually stock papers no finer than 400 grit, but you can get finer grits at an auto supply store. The finer the grit you sand with, the shinier your floor will be.

Making patched holes blend in. Patch small, deep holes with wood putty using a shade darker than your floor color. The patch will never be invisible, but if it's slightly darker than the surrounding wood, it will look like a tiny knot instead of badly matched putty.

Replacing floor boards. If you have boards that are too damaged to touch up, call a good carpenter or floor installer to replace them. The job typically involves cutting down the center of the damaged board and chiseling or prying it out. Usually the lower lip on the new board's grooved edge is cut off so that the board can just drop into place.

take care

A lot of cleaners that *seem* innocent enough may be disastrous if you use them on your wood floor. First, you must determine what kind of finish is on your floor. For polyurethane finishes, never use ammonia-based cleaners, detergents, bleach, polishes, oil soap, abrasive cleansers like Comet and Ajax, or vinegar or other acidic products. Some, like ammonia, can etch the finish. Others, like wax used on a varnished or shellacked floor, get in the way of products meant to clean or rejuvenate the finish.

HOW IS MY FLOOR FINISHED?

When you get right down to it, most wood floor finishes look pretty much alike. Ever wonder what the finish on your floor is? It's easy to figure out, and proper maintenance depends on knowing whether the finish is shellac, varnish, polyurethane varnish, or simple wax. Here's how to figure out what's underfoot:

Wax turns white a few minutes after you drip some water on it.

Varnish flakes when scratched.

Shellac flakes when scratched and dissolves in alcohol.

Polyurethane won't flake, whiten, or dissolve.

10 QUICK REMEDIES FOR YOUR FLOOR'S BIGGEST ENEMIES

Here are a few secret weapons that'll help you remove pesky messes and stains from your wood floor:

CHEWING GUM

Any finish: Cool gum with an ice-filled plastic bag until it is brittle enough to crumble; then remove with a plastic scraper.

CRAYON OR CANDLE WAX

Wax or penetrating stain finish: Put a brown paper bag over the crayon or wax, and heat with an iron until the bag absorbs the stain.

Shellac, varnish, or polyurethane finish: Use a cleaner designed for hardwood floor finishes.

DARK SPOTS AND INK STAINS

Wax or penetrating stain finish: Treat like water stains. If they remain, soak with bleach or vinegar for an hour. Wipe with a damp cloth, then wipe dry. Sand lightly with fine sandpaper. Stain to match original color. Apply wax with a cloth.

Shellac, varnish, or polyurethane finish: Use a cleaner designed for hardwood floor finishes.

DRIED MILK OR FOOD STAINS

Wax or penetrating stain finish: Rub gently with a damp cloth. Rub dry; then apply wax.

Shellac, varnish, or polyurethane finish: Use a cleaner designed for hardwood floor finishes.

GREASE AND OIL STAINS

Wax or penetrating stain finish: Saturate a cotton cloth with hydrogen peroxide and place it over the stain. Saturate a second cotton cloth with ammonia and put it on top of the first. Repeat if necessary. Let dry; then buff with a cloth.

Shellac, varnish, or polyurethane finish: Use a cleaner designed for hardwood floor finishes.

HEEL SCUFFS

Wax or penetrating stain finish: Apply a small amount of wax with fine steel wool; rub in and buff with a cloth.

Shellac, varnish, or polyurethane finish: Use a cleaner designed for hardwood floor finishes.

MOLD OR MILDEW

Wax or penetrating stain finish: Apply a cleaner designed for wood.

Shellac, varnish, or polyurethane finish: Use a cleaner designed for hardwood floor finishes. Sand and refinish areas where the mold or mildew is beneath the surface.

SCRATCHES

Wax or penetrating stain finish: Apply wax.

Polyurethane finish: Fix with a touch-up kit made for urethane finishes and sold at flooring stores.

Shellac or varnish finish: Fix with a hardwood floor finish restorer.

WATER STAINS OR WHITE SPOTS

Wax or penetrating stain finish: Rub with 000 steel wool dipped in wax. If the stain or spot remains, sand with fine sandpaper. Follow up with 00 steel wool dipped in mineral spirits. When mineral spirits evaporate, stain to match original color. Apply wax and buff.

Shellac, varnish, or polyurethane finish: Use a cleaner designed for hardwood floor finishes.

WAX BUILDUP

Wax or penetrating stain finish: Remove the old wax with a stripper made for wax. (Do not use furniture stripper.) Remove residue with a cloth and fine steel wool. Let dry, then wax and machine buff.

Shellac, varnish, or polyurethane finish: Don't wax these finishes. It can make the floor dangerously slippery and interfere with subsequent finishes. If you have used it, take it off with a commercial wax remover.

Floor Structure

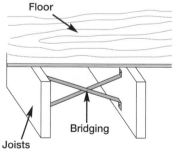

We tromp on our floors all day long, day after day, and they carry not only our weight but also the weight of all of our furniture and possessions. It should really come as no surprise that after a few years a floor begins to squeak and flex when you walk across it. Both of these structural problems—squeakiness and bounciness—are easy to fix.

YOUR COST SAVINGS

$250

What you would pay a carpenter for tracking down and fixing a large number of floor squeaks.

Easy Fixes

Quieting noisy floors. There's nothing quite like a squeaking floor to drive you bonkers. Floors squeak when the floorboards rub together or against nails. If the squeak is minor, you can often fix it by simply putting talcum powder between the boards to act as a lubricant. Sprinkle the powder over the crack between the offending boards, cover with a towel, and rub in the powder with your foot.

Shimming large, squeaky gaps. If the gap above a joist is particularly wide, try putting a shim into it to silent the squeak. You can get a package of ready-made shims at a home center. Put construction adhesive on both sides of the shim. Then put a block of wood against the end of the shim, and hammer the wood block to drive in the shim. Clean up any stray adhesive with paint thinner.

Pouring wax between the cracks. If the floor has a wax finish, try pouring liquid floor wax between the floorboards. Don't try this on a varnish finish.

Screwing the subfloor to the floor. Sometimes a squeak or a bouncing floor results from a gap between the floorboards and subfloor. If you suspect this, drive screws from below through the subfloor and into the floor. Drill pilot holes and have someone stand on the floor above as you drive the screws in. Use screws no more than 1 1/4 inches (3 cm) long so that you don't poke through your finished floor. Slip a washer over the screws before you drive them to keep the screws from going in too far.

Floor

Bridging

Joists

Using a glue gun to stop squeaks. If you can get underneath the floor—from the basement or a crawl space—try silencing a squeak with your hot-melt glue gun. Have someone walk across the floor so you can pinpoint the squeaky spot. Look especially for gaps between the subfloor and the joists supporting it. Then apply hot-melt glue along each side of the joists.

Caulking gaps. Instead of hot glue, you can inject polyurethane caulk into the gaps between the joists and the subfloor. Push the caulk into the gaps with a plastic spoon.

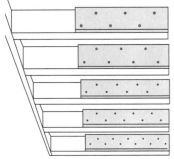

Bracing joists. Another way to reinforce joists is by nailing strips of 3/4-inch (2 cm) plywood to them. Put the strips on one side of the joists or both, depending on how bouncy the floor is. Have your lumberyard cut strips of plywood to the same width as the joists. Apply construction adhesive to one side and the top edge of a strip, put it against a joist, and nail it in place with two rows of nails, staggering them so that no nail is directly above another.

Firming up a bouncy floor. Floors flex because there isn't enough support beneath them. Add support by putting diagonal bridging between the joists. Metal bridging, sold at home centers, is easy to install under floors with accessible joists. Just drive a nail through each end of each crosspiece to attach the bridging to the joists. Leave a space between pieces of bridging so they don't rub together and make noise.

How to Fix Squeaks *from Above*

What if you can't get to the underside of the floor? Don't despair. You can get rid of squeaks from above by screwing the floor to a joist. And you can do it without the repair being very obvious.

1. Find the joist with a STUD FINDER. Remember joists often line up with the studs in the walls and run at right angles to the direction of your flooring. (As a last resort, drill a small hole in the floor and probe for the joist with a piece of coat-hanger wire.)

----

2. Screw the floor to the joist with a TRIM-HEAD SCREW, which has a small head that is not too noticeable. Drill a hole for the screw that goes diagonally through the floor and into the joist—get a combination drill bit designed to drill a recess for the screw head. Stand directly above the joist to weight down the floor as you drive the screw in.

----

3. Fill the space above the screw head with WOOD PUTTY, and touch up.

Vinyl Flooring

No-wax vinyl flooring is one of the greatest innovations in flooring ever. It's coated with a polyurethane finish that gives it a long-lasting shine and makes care a breeze. You can choose no-wax tiles or sheet vinyl. It's easier to replace a single tile than to repair damaged sheet vinyl, but seepage is less of a problem with sheet vinyl because it's a continuous piece. If you're not sure whether you have no-wax vinyl or flooring that requires waxing, here are some hints: If your floor was installed in the last 20 years, it is almost certainly no-wax. Embossed tiles are also generally no-wax. Old 9-inch-square (23 cm square) tiles likely need waxing. If you're still not certain, ask the sales staff at a flooring store.

YOUR COST SAVINGS

$1,500

What you would pay to have a new vinyl tile floor installed in a 12-by-18-foot (4 by 6 metres) room.

Care and Maintenance

Keep out dirt and chemicals with a doormat. A doormat helps keep out your vinyl floor's two greatest enemies: dirt and chemicals. Tracked-in dirt means extra broom time. Grit acts like sandpaper, removing the finish from your floor. And even though you can't see them, chemicals from asphalt can stick first to your shoes and then to the floor, causing it to yellow.

Keep your floors clean. The key to keeping any floor in good shape is to keep it clean, and sheet vinyl is no exception. Get the dirt off before it gets ground in, and your vinyl will last longer. Sweep frequently. It's a good idea to get in the habit of quickly running a soft broom across the kitchen floor every evening after you put the dishes in the dishwasher.

Shampoo away hair spray. If you have hairspray buildup on your vinyl floor, just shampoo it away. It works on your hair, doesn't it? Mix a squirt of shampoo with a gallon (4 litres) of warm water. Mop, then rinse with a damp mop.

Learn low-impact cleaning techniques. Resist the temptation to blast away dirt with heavy-duty cleaners. Instead, clean your vinyl floor using the mildest possible method. Sweep or vacuum it every evening, and wipe up spills right away. To clean dirt that the broom or vacuum can't get, use a mop dampened with warm—not hot—water. If all else fails, use soap, but make sure the soap is designed for your flooring.

Use the right cleanser. If your no-wax vinyl needs cleaning, wash it with a cleaner made specifically for no-wax floors, following the directions on the container. If you have older vinyl that requires waxing, clean it with warm water and detergent. Dampen a mop or sponge with the mixture, and rub the floor just enough to loosen the dirt. Try not to rub off the wax because you'll just have to reapply it. Rinse with clean, cool water—no matter what the soap label says about not needing rinsing—otherwise you'll leave a residue on the floor.

Don't drench your vinyl. Water from an overly wet mop will work its way into the cracks, seams, and edges. Once there, it can destroy the glue bond that holds down the vinyl, causing it to come loose or corners to curl.

Rinse well to remove all soap. Soap may get your floor clean, but soap scum leaves a film that actually collects dirt. Until your floor needs a serious cleaning, stick to damp mopping with just water. When you do need to wash the floor, use two mops—one for washing and a second one just for rinsing.

Preserve the sheen. "No wax" really means "Don't wax." No-wax vinyl has a clear polyurethane coating that makes it shine. Wax won't adhere well to the coating and will leave behind a mess that you'll have to strip off. (Don't use mop-and-wax products, either.) If your no-wax floor loses its shine, restore it with a polish or sealant made for no-wax flooring. Make sure the floor is thoroughly clean and apply one or two thin layers as directed. It should keep your floor shining for at least a year with only routine damp mopping. If you have an older floor that requires waxing, wax when it loses its sheen, but use only the amount called for on the container label.

Outfit your furniture and large appliances with protective "feet." The weight of heavy items (such as tables and refrigerators) that occupy permanent places in your kitchen can dent vinyl flooring. Prevent these dents by fitting your furniture with floor protectors, which you can find at hardware stores and home-improvement centers.

Forgo rolling casters. These, too, can damage the surface of your tile. Instead, consider fitting chairs with felt tips, which won't harm your vinyl.

Before big moves, put appliances and other heavy items on a plywood path. More often than not, when we replace or move appliances, we drag or push them across the floor rather than lift them—but dragging them will only scratch and scuff

SMART IDEA

Tile adhesive sticks to *everything* and is virtually impossible to get off your tools. Make short work of the job by wrapping your tools in plastic wrap and putting them in a freezer overnight. (Unwrap the tools before you start the next job.) You'll be delighted at how easy it is to chip off the frozen adhesive.

your vinyl flooring. To keep your vinyl in tiptop condition, lay a piece of plywood sheeting along the route that you are going to take out of the room, and push or "walk" the appliances out along the plywood path.

Easy Fixes

Fixing a blister. Has your vinyl flooring developed a blister? Fix it before it starts to wear unevenly. Just slit the blister and about 1/2 inch (1 cm) of the vinyl on either side of it with a utility knife. Then cover the spot with aluminum foil and warm it with an iron. Pull up each edge of the slit and slip vinyl adhesive under it with a putty knife. Press the blister flat, and wipe up any seepage with a sponge dampened with water or the recommended solvent. Cover the area with a board weighted with a heavy object for 24 hours.

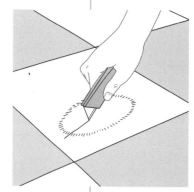

Protecting exposed edges. Vinyl edges that end at a doorway or at the transition to another room need to be protected. If they're not, poorly glued edges might curl, or a heel could catch and chip the vinyl or trip you. A screw-down metal threshold strip is simple to install and will protect the vinyl and give your feet a smooth transition.

How to Replace a **Vinyl Tile**

When replacing a tile, ask an employee at your local tile store for the proper adhesive for your type of tile. Also get the right disposable notched applicator; the adhesive manufacturer will recommend a specific notch size to control the amount of glue that goes on the floor.

1. To make the old tile pliable and easy to remove, cover it with ALUMINUM FOIL and warm it with an iron on moderate heat. Run the iron back and forth to heat the whole tile. When the tile is pliable, cut into its center with a putty knife and pry outward to remove it. This will help you avoid damaging surrounding tiles.

2. Scrape the OLD ADHESIVE from the floor with a scraper or putty knife. Test to make sure the new tile will fit the opening. If it won't, trim it to size with a utility knife and straight edge.

3. Warm the REPLACEMENT TILE with your iron until it's flexible. Apply the adhesive to the floor with a notched applicator and set the tile in place. Clean up any excess with a sponge dampened with water or the recommended solvent. Cover the tile with a board, and weight it with a heavy object overnight.

What can you do
to remove those
black heel marks
on your clean
floor? Smear a
drop of baby oil
over the mark,
wait a few min-
utes, and then
wipe it off with
a rag.

Adhering loose tiles. If you have a loose or curled tile, put adhesive under the edges with a trowel. Drive a small finishing nail into each corner and one along each seam. Fill the nail dimples with matching-colored caulk.

Don't have a match for a tile you need to replace? Steal one from a closet or from under an appliance. Tiles with a printed pattern all have a factory-applied pressure-sensitive glue on the back and can be easily removed. (Old solid or swirled color tiles are held down with stronger mastic glue and are virtually impossible to remove.) Heat the tile with a hair dryer, and gently slip a putty knife under it. Keep warming the tile until you can lift it up entirely. Use it to replace the damaged tile as described in the sidebar on page 67. Replace the tile that's now missing with a new tile—because it will be hidden, it doesn't need to match.

How to Patch Damaged Sheet Vinyl

There it is for all to see: a big gash in your vinyl flooring. Don't worry. If you have a matching piece of vinyl, you can make a repair that's nearly invisible.

1. Put a MATCHING PIECE OF VINYL that's larger than the damaged spot over the area. Align the patterns and tape it firmly in place. Cut through both pieces at the same time with a sharp utility knife guided by a straightedge. Set the upper piece aside for use as a patch.

----

2. Heat the damaged area with a HAIR DRYER, and pry it up with a putty knife, being careful not to mar the surrounding area. Scrape up the old adhesive. Test-fit the patch and sand or trim the edges if necessary.

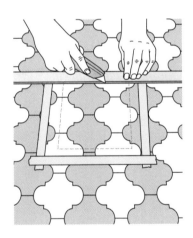

3. Apply multipurpose TILE ADHESIVE to the floor, clean up any excess, and let the floor dry. Put the patch in place, weigh it down with a board, and let it sit overnight.

----

4. To fuse the seams and make them unnoticeable, treat them with SEAM SEALER, available at flooring stores. Make sure you buy sealer that has a gloss that matches the one on your floor—high gloss or low gloss, for example.

Going vinyl "shopping" in hidden places. If you can't find a matching piece of sheet vinyl to replace a damaged area in a visible location, borrow a piece from an inconspicuous place—like under the refrigerator. You can cover the new "hidden" bare spot with an inexpensive vinyl tile of any kind.

Out, out, black spot. Does your vinyl floor have a small black spot that won't wash away? Look closely. Chances are the color in the vinyl has worn away, exposing the dark inner material. The cause of this wear is a chunk of dirt, a small stone, or a nail head underneath the vinyl that has raised the spot just enough that foot traffic has worn through the top. With large damaged areas, the only cure is to replace the tile or patch the sheet vinyl. Repair kits are available for smaller areas. The process involves mixing special paints (supplied in the kit) to match the floor color, painting the damaged area, and drying it with a hair dryer. Next pour the filler powder and bonding agent over the damaged area, level it, then let it harden for 15 minutes. Finish by brushing the clear acrylic finish over the repair. Kits are available at home centers and hardware stores.

Ceramic Tile Floors

If we can go by all the surviving examples in Roman ruins, a ceramic tile floor is virtually indestructible. Of course, a chipped or cracked tile is almost inevitable in an active household or a settling house, but either is a problem that you can easily fix yourself. Actually, the problems that concern homeowners most are far more mundane: stained grout and tile surfaces dulled by soapy buildup. They are even easier to fix. If you choose the right cleaners and clean about once a week, your floor will practically take care of itself.

Care and Maintenance

Sweep or vacuum, then mop. Depending on how much you use the room and how much dust and grit the floor collects, the only regular cleaning a ceramic floor needs is an occasional sweeping or vacuuming. If you vacuum, avoid using a beater bar (the rotating brush). Once a week, after sweeping or vacuuming, damp-mop using an alkaline floor cleaner such as Spic and Span or Mr. Clean.

Stay away from oily or waxy cleaners. No matter what your mother, uncle, or the advertising council tells you, do not clean your ceramic tile floors with oil- or wax-based cleaners, such as Murphy's Oil Soap or Pine Sol. These cleaning products will leave a greasy or waxy film on the grout, which will just collect more dirt.

Bleach grimy grout. When dirt builds up on grout, it's time to bring out a scrub brush and a little elbow grease. First, try cleaning the grout with a scrub brush and an alkaline cleaner. If that doesn't work, mix a cup of bleach with a half-gallon of water. Make sure the area is well ventilated—open the doors and windows and turn on any exhaust fans—and put on a pair of rubber gloves. Scrub the dirty areas with a nylon scrub brush, and let the solution soak for 10 to 20 minutes. Rinse twice with clean water, and wipe the area dry with a clean cloth.

Apply a sealer. You'll be glad you did. Grout sealer keeps water and dirt from penetrating and staining grout, saving you a lot of work and possibly damage to the underlying structure. If the tile

take care

Much as we love vinegar for cleaning, it's not good to use on grout. Vinegar and other acids, like muriatic acid, are often recommended for cleaning dirty grout. And they do work. The problem is they work because they dissolve the grout. Stick to alkaline cleaners or bleach to clean grout.

is glazed, you don't need to seal it, and you should be careful not to get the sealer on the tile surface. If the tile isn't glazed, use a combination grout-tile sealer to seal the tile at the same time as you seal the grout.

Easy Fixes

How can I tell if my tile is sealed? With some matte-finished ceramic floor tiles, it's hard to tell if they are glazed or not. To find out, just sprinkle a few drops of water on a tile. If the surface darkens after a few minutes, the tile needs to be sealed.

Caulking perfect seams. What looks like a grout line between the floor and tub is actually a gap filled with caulk to keep water from seeping into the subfloor. If the caulk starts to look ragged, pry it out with a screwdriver and apply a caulk recommended for bathroom use. To get an ultra-neat seam, run strips of masking tape on either side of the seam and use an ice cube to smooth the caulk. The ice cube's slippery surface glides quickly over the caulk. Then carefully remove the masking tape.

Touching up chipped corners. If there's a chip in the corner or along the edge of a tile, touch it up using matching appliance touch-up paint. If the chipped area is deep, fill it with epoxy and let it dry before painting. If you can't match the color, color the damaged area with paint or a marker and then cover it with clear nail polish.

SMART IDEA

Canned goods falling out of the cupboard are almost guaranteed to chip tile. Put a rug in front of your cupboard to help prevent damage.

How to Replace a Broken Tile

It's relatively easy to replace the tile and leave the area looking like new. If you don't have a replacement tile left over from the original installation, take a chip of the damaged tile and its dimensions to a tile store and get the closest replacement you can find.

1. Remove the grout around the damaged tile with a GROUT SAW.

2. Wearing work gloves and safety glasses, hit the tile with a HAMMER and cold chisel to break it. Chisel out the tile along the crack lines. Then chisel the old adhesive out of the opening.

3. Apply mortar to the back of a new tile using a NOTCHED TROWEL. Press the tile firmly into place and let it dry overnight. Mix grout as directed, apply it, and wipe off the excess with a damp sponge. When a haze forms on the tiles a few minutes later, buff it off immediately with a clean rag. Seal the grout after a couple of weeks—the wait varies; follow the directions on the sealer.

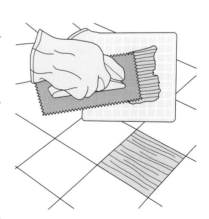

Carpeting

Most of us install carpeting because we like the way it looks and feels. But carpeting also has some valuable practical functions: It insulates against the cold. It absorbs sound. And it cushions the floor. On top of that, modern carpeting is highly durable, stain-resistant, and easy to care for. But carpeting's ability to last for decades is often undermined by the detrimental effects of spills, pet and baby mishaps, dust, grime, sunlight, and, of course, being constantly underfoot. With a little attention and some precautions, you won't have to replace it prematurely.

Care and Maintenance

Change the room's traffic flow. To distribute the wear on your carpet and extend its life, move your furniture every few months in a way that changes the way people walk through the room. If you have a moveable rug, just rotate its position in the room.

Use protective runners or rugs. An easy way to prevent excess wear and dirt on your carpet is to put runners or throw rugs in high-traffic areas, especially in entries and hallways. The runners can be strips of similar or contrasting carpeting hemmed along the edges. It's much, much cheaper to replace a runner or rug than an entire carpet.

Block those UV rays. To prevent your carpet from fading, keep direct sunlight off it. Close drapes or blinds on the sunny sides of the house during peak daylight hours.

Take your shoes off, but leave your socks on. If you can get everyone in your family to do it, taking off your shoes when you enter the house is a great, simple way to reduce both wear on your carpet and tracked-in grime. But leave your socks on so that oil from your bare feet doesn't rub off; it will attract dirt and shorten the life of your carpet.

Lift—don't drag—furniture. Don't drag furniture when you rearrange a carpeted room. Pulling furniture over carpet causes unnecessary wear, but more important, it can snag a loop of yarn, rip a carpet seam, or bunch and wrinkle the carpet. Moreover, if the carpet is nylon, as most are, the friction caused by dragging can actually melt the fibers. Always pick up furniture to move it.

Vacuum your carpet every week. We may not always feel up to it, but frequent vacuuming—weekly or more often, depending on traffic—is the best way to keep your carpet in good shape. Here's how to get the most out of your vacuuming efforts:

- Go back and forth. Set your vacuum cleaner for the pile level of the carpet unless your vacuum automatically adjusts. When you vacuum, use slow, even strokes, and go back and forth several times, flipping the nap by going alternately against and with the grain. Finish with strokes that all go in the same direction.

take care

Avoid carpet-cleaning methods that use shampoos, dry powders, and powerful rotating brushes. Whether done by you or a pro, none are as effective as a professional steam cleaning and may cause harm from the force of the brushes or by leaving behind residual detergent or solvent.

WHAT KIND OF CARPET SHOULD I BUY?

There are two types of carpet pile—loop and cut. Loop pile is formed by yarn stitched in loops. Cut pile is made by cutting the loops. Cut pile is plusher, but not as durable as loop pile, so you may want to protect cut pile with runners in high-traffic areas. Some carpets have a combination of cut and loop pile, and many have pile of both types that is curled or twisted and heat-set for more durability. Another key to long carpet life is the material used to make the carpet. Here, according to the Carpet and Rug Institute, are the main types and their characteristics:

- Nylon is used in more than two-thirds of carpets in North America. It's no wonder, since nylon is wear-resistant and resilient, and it withstands the weight and movement of furniture while providing brilliant color. Nylon resists soils and stains and can stand up to heavy traffic. Solution-dyed nylon is colorfast because color is added in the fiber production.

- Olefin (polypropylene) is the stuff indoor-outdoor carpeting is made of because it resists wear and permanent stains and is easy to clean. The color is added when the fibers are made, so it is colorfast. Its only shortcoming is that the fibers crush easily.

- Polyester has a luxurious, soft feel when used in thick, cut-pile textures. It has excellent color clarity and retention. It's easily cleaned and resistant to water-soluble stains.

- Acrylic offers the appearance and feel of wool at a lower cost. It has a low static level and is resistant to moisture and mildew. It's commonly used in velvet and level-loop carpets and often in bath and scatter rugs. It's not as strong as nylon.

- Wool is very durable and luxuriously soft and thick. It's available in many colors, but it's much more expensive than synthetic carpeting.

- Blends of the materials above are also common. Wool-nylon combines the great look and comfort of wool with the durability of nylon. Other good combinations include acrylic-olefin and nylon-olefin.

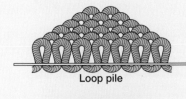
Loop pile

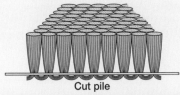
Cut pile

- Use attachments. Vacuum under furniture as best you can with extension attachments. About twice a year, move the furniture and vacuum the area under it thoroughly.

- Get rid of fluff and hair. New carpeting produces a lot of extra fluff. Don't worry. It's normal. If your vacuum cleaner won't suck up cat hairs, threads, or other fine items, use a lint roller or a piece of doubled-over tape to pick them up.

- Change the bag. Keep in mind that as the bag fills up, the suction power reduces. Changing your bag when it is about half full will keep the suction going strong.

Hire a pro to do the steam cleaning. Periodic steam cleaning—say, every 6 to 18 months, depending on room use—is the best way to really renew your carpet. Even with regular vacuuming, dirt eventually works its way deep into the pile where the vacuum can't reach it. It's best to hire a professional carpet-cleaning company. The pros will use very hot water throughout the cleaning process as well as a powerful vacuum, which will suck up all the water that the cleaner puts down. The cost is generally less than $100 a room.

Or steam clean on your own. If you opt to do steam-cleaning yourself, rent the most powerful steam cleaner you can find, follow the instructions closely, and change the water frequently to keep it hot and clean. Also rent a strong wet-dry shop vacuum and use it to suck up water that the steam cleaner leaves behind. Open windows and let the carpet dry thoroughly—typically overnight—before walking on it or replacing furniture. Trapped moisture can rot fibers and encourage the growth of mold and mildew.

SMART IDEA

Do you see deep impressions in the carpet after you move the furniture? Bring the crushed fibers back to their original shape with a steam iron. Just set the iron on steam and hold it about 1/4 inch (0.5 cm) above the carpet. Use a screwdriver to help fluff out the fibers.

How to Patch Carpeting

Patching a damaged area of carpeting is easy. The only special materials you need are double-faced carpet tape, which is sticky on both sides, and carpet seam cements—both available at home centers and carpet outlets.

1. Cut out the damaged carpet area with a sharp UTILITY KNIFE held against a straightedge. Then, using the cutout piece as a guide, cut a patch from a spare piece of carpet or from carpet in an inconspicuous place like a closet. Make sure the pattern matches.

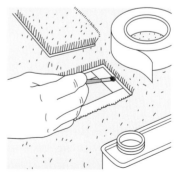

2. Slide DOUBLE-FACED CARPET TAPE partway under the edges of the hole in the carpet. Then apply carpet seam cement to the carpet edges of the hole and the patch. Press the patch in place and weight it down until the glue sets.

Easy Fixes

Repairing cigarette burns. These days, no one smokes anymore, right? Well, somehow cigarette burns still happen. To fix a surface burn, just snip off the charred tips of the tufts with sharp scissors. If the carpet is plush, it helps to feather out the area by lightly tapering the nap in a circle a little wider than the damaged area. For a deep burn, see "Cookie cutter" patching.

Repairing torn carpets. A tear in a carpet nearly always occurs along a seam where two carpet sections are glued or sewn together—often because somebody dragged furniture over it. To fix a ripped seam, thread some heavy fishing line through a large, curved upholstery needle. Stitch the tear together, pushing the needle through about 1/2 inch (1 cm) from the edges of the tear and spacing the stitches about 3/4 inch (2 cm) apart. Your stitches will be less visible if you make the top of the stitches square to the tear and the underside diagonal. If the seam was previously glued together, you may find it tough to work the needle through the old glue tape. Use needle-nose pliers to help push the needle.

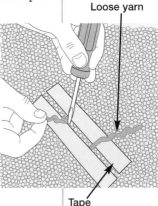

Loose yarn

Tape

Replacing loose or missing yarn. Furniture moving is often the culprit when a carpet develops loose or missing yarn. To repair loose or missing yarn, all you need are a small screwdriver and some carpet seam adhesive.

- If the yarn is still attached to the carpet, just glue it back in place. First protect the area around the run with masking tape; then squeeze a heavy bead of adhesive into the run. Use the screwdriver to press each scab (where the original adhesive clings to the yarn) down into the carpet backing until each new loop is at the right height.

- If the yarn is missing, count the number of carpet loops it will take to fill the run. Then pull a piece of yarn from the edge of a scrap (or hidden) piece of carpet and count the curls in the loose yarn; cut it to provide the right amount of yarn to fill the run.

"Cookie cutter" patching. A carpet "cookie cutter" kit is great for replacing a small bit of carpet that's badly stained or deeply burned. The spot-patch kit comes with a circular tool with a center pivot and blades attached to the outside. You just rotate the tool to cut out a 3-inch (8 cm) circle containing the damaged area; then do the same to cut a patch from a piece of spare carpet or carpet in a hidden area such as inside a closet. Then put down the double-stick tape that comes with the kit and plug in the patch. Make sure the patterns match when you cut out the patch. If the patch looks a lot less worn than the rest of the carpet,

Carpeting **75**

roughen it by rubbing it on concrete. If you need to replace a larger area, see "How to Patch Carpeting," on page 74.

Replacing carpet tiles. Since these tiles are usually held in place by self-adhesive or double-stick carpet tape, you can usually lift the tile by slipping a putty knife under an edge. Then you just insert a new one using the same type of tape to attach it. Rather than using a bright new tile that will stick out like a sore thumb, exchange the tile with one from a hidden or less noticeable area. To remove a stubborn stain on a carpet tile, try taking it up and washing it under cold water; let it dry completely before replacing it.

REMOVING STAINS FROM CARPETING

TYPE OF STAIN	HOW TO GET IT OUT
Animal urine	Immediately blot excess with paper towels. Soak with club soda. Blot again. Scrub with diluted carpet shampoo.
Blood	If fresh, blot with cold water (not hot). If dried, cover with equal parts cold water and meat tenderizer. Let set for 30 minutes. Sponge off with cold water.
Chewing gum	Freeze with a plastic bag full of ice cubes, then scrape off with a butter knife and blot with trichloroethylene (dry-cleaning fluid, available at drug and hardware stores).
Coffee, beer, and milk	Blot excess with paper towels. Scrub with diluted carpet shampoo. Cover with paper towels weighted down for two to three hours.
Fruit juices and soft drinks	Blot excess; sponge with a solution of a teaspoon of powdered laundry detergent and a teaspoon of white vinegar dissolved in a quart of warm water.
Grease, oil, lipstick, and butter	Blot excess with paper towels. Sponge with dry-cleaning fluid, working from edges to center.
Shoe polish, ink, and dried paint	Dab with paint remover. If that fails, use dry-cleaning fluid.
Wax	Scrape off as much as possible, then place a brown paper bag over the area and run a warm—not hot—iron over it. The bag will act as a blotter and absorb the wax.

Stairs and Banisters

The staircase is often the grand centerpiece of a home—as well it should be—because it's the most complicated piece of carpentry in the home. Keeping stairs looking good requires little more than regular dusting, cleaning, and vacuuming. Here are a few tricks that'll make stair cleaning a breeze, along with easy carpentry secrets and balustrade repair tips that can save you the cost of an expensive replacement down the road.

YOUR COST SAVINGS

$625

What you would pay to have a single flight of stairs recarpeted.

Care and Maintenance

Vacuum from the bottom up. If your stairs are carpeted, the carpeting is dirtiest just before you vacuum it. And you're just grinding in the dirt when you stand on an uncleaned step as you vacuum your way down the stairs. Instead, vacuum from the bottom of the stairs up, so you're always standing on a clean piece of carpet. Don't forget to vacuum the risers occasionally, too, to remove the dust that the carpeting traps there.

Buy extra extenders for your vacuum. Is your back aching from hauling that awkward vacuum up and down the stairs? If you have a canister model, consider buying a couple more extension tubes, which can extend your reach several feet, enabling you to clean the steps from just one or two spots. If you have an upright with a hose, you can also add a couple of extension tubes.

Turbo-charge your vacuum. An air-powered beater brush, called a turbo tool, attaches to the end of the vacuum hose and brushes across carpeting on stairs the same way an upright vacuum brushes across a carpet on the floor. Use a turbo tool to loosen and suck up lint, hair, and dirt you would otherwise miss.

Keep your banisters clean. Dust painted banisters with a soft, damp cloth. If the banister is especially dirty, add a couple of drops of dishwashing liquid to warm water. When using soap, wring out the rag, and wash small sections at a time, rinsing them immediately with a second damp cloth. Dry thoroughly with a separate cloth. If your banister has a natural varnish finish, dust it with a soft cloth dampened with a little furniture polish.

The main parts of a staircase are the treads and risers. Treads are what you walk on; the rounded front edge is called the nosing. Risers are the vertical boards between treads. The treads and risers are supported by stringers—boards with sawtooth notches for steps or with slots that the treads slide into. Some stairways have both types of stringers. The balustrade, comprising a row of balusters topped by a rail, is often the most elaborate and pretty part of a staircase. Balusters are the vertical pieces that support the banister, or handrail. The newel post is the large post that the railing is nailed to, at the bottom and top of the stairs.

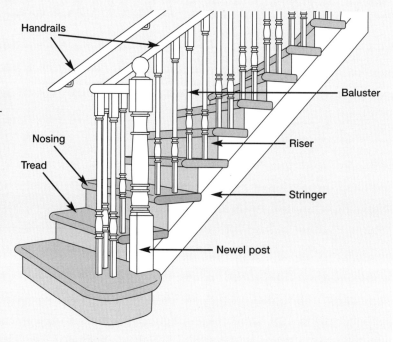

Powder a squeak. If you have a squeaky stair that needs silencing, sprinkle talcum powder into the seam at the back between the tread and the riser. You'll need to apply it again when the powder works its way out of the joint. Powdered graphite—just scrape a pencil lead—also works.

Easy Fixes

Identifying the source of a squeak. Stairs squeak when you step on one piece of wood and it rubs against another. Isolate the problem by walking up and down the stairs to see which step is squeaking. Try to tell if the squeak is coming from the back, the front, or the side of the step. Better yet, if you can get underneath the stairway, have someone walk on the steps so you can pinpoint and mark the squeaky spots from below.

Caulking stubborn squeaks. One easy, long-lasting way to quiet a squeak is to apply a thin bead of caulk under the step nosing, so that it cushions the joint where the tread meets the riser. After applying the caulk, run a plastic spoon along it to shape it, remove the excess, and push some caulk into the squeaky joint. Clean up any stray caulk as directed on the tube before it dries. If you can get to the steps from the underside, caulk the seams of the squeaky step from there, too.

Reinforcing steps. Another simple way to eliminate a squeak is to add some reinforcement on the stairs' underside. Screw one leg of an L-bracket to the riser, leaving a small gap between the other leg and the tread. Run a bead of glue between the tread and riser, and then screw the bracket to the tread, pulling it down slightly in the process. Make sure the screws are at least 1/4 inch (0.5 cm) shorter than the tread's thickness so that the screw tip doesn't come out the other side.

4 Ways to Fix a Wobbly Newel Post

Over the years, newel posts—the large posts at the top and bottom of a stair's railing—get a lot of stress and strain and can start to wobble. How you fix it depends on how its base is attached.

1. In newer homes, most newel posts are secured to the stair's framework with lag screws. The lag screws are hidden by wooden plugs that are difficult to get out. Drive in EXTRA LAG SCREWS instead. Drill a pilot hole for each screw along with a deep countersink hole for the head. Fill the hole with a wood plug (sold at home centers) or wood putty.

2. If the newel post goes through the floor and is attached to a joist that you can access in the basement, try driving a few EXTRA NAILS through the post and into the joist. If this doesn't work, nail pieces of wood to the joist, as braces that press solidly against the post on each side.

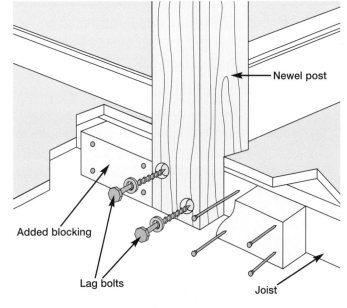

Newel post

Added blocking

Lag bolts

Joist

3. If the wobbly post is attached to the floor by a metal plate, the screws have come loose in their holes. Back out the old screws, and drive in NEW, LARGER-DIAMETER SCREWS.

4. In an older home, some newel posts are anchored by a threaded rod that runs the entire length of the post. To tighten the post, just TIGHTEN THE ROD from below.

Shimming squeaks. Use shims to fill small gaps between treads, risers, and stringers so that loose boards can't rub against each other and squeak. Dab a little construction glue on a shim and drive it into a joint gap with a hammer. (Buy ready-made shims at a home center.) It's best to do this on the underside of the stairs. If this isn't possible and you want to shim a gap between riser and tread from above, make the repair less noticeable by using a utility knife to trim the shim flush with the riser as shown.

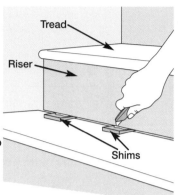

Reinforcing steps with wood blocks. Instead of brackets, you can also secure wood blocks beneath the stairs at the seam where tread meets riser. Drill pilot holes for the screws in each block. Apply glue to adjacent faces of the block. Put the glued surfaces against the tread and riser and then screw the block to each surface.

Fixing a loose baluster. If the top of a baluster that is nailed in place comes loose, it may be because the baluster is too short. If so, pull the nails from the top of the baluster, coat a shim with a bit of glue, and slip it between the baluster and the banister. Drill a pilot hole and drive a screw up at an angle through the baluster and into the banister. Trim the shim flush with a utility knife.

Repairing a broken baluster. A broken or splintered baluster can often be glued back together without removing it. Brush the broken surfaces with glue. Draw rectangular pieces together with clamps, wipe off any excess glue, and leave the clamps on overnight. Clamp round pieces by wrapping rope around the break and tying it. If the damage is minor, you can use masking tape instead of rope.

Removing damaged balusters. If a baluster is too damaged to fix, take it out and find a replacement. Some balusters are held in place by a molding that runs along the side of the stairs. To remove one of these balusters, pry off the molding and pull out the baluster. If the baluster is nailed in place, drive the nails all the way through the baluster and into the tread or railing with a hammer and nail set, and then ease the banister out. If there's no visible way to remove a baluster, there's no visible way to put it back in either. Consult a carpenter.

PART 3

The Outside of Your Home

Maintaining the exterior of your house isn't just about keeping your curb appeal (and property values) high—doing so also has a lot to do with the amount of comfort, security,

and safety you experience when you're indoors. From roof to foundation and windows to siding, the building "envelope" is a complex array of surfaces and materials that require year-round vigilance. Not keeping your eyes open for the well-being of your home's exterior can result in both headaches and hefty repair bills.

Structural elements and finicky finishes are big-ticket items when they have to be overhauled or replaced (have you priced a new roof lately?), but it's possible to prevent or at least put off such expenses by working steady maintenance and incidental fixes into your home-care calendar. In this part, we'll tell you when to schedule exterior checkups, what gear gets the job done, and how to care for and rehabilitate your home's siding, doors, windows, and roof. You'll also learn how to patch a foundation crack, keep water out of your basement, lengthen the life of your deck or porch, and securely seal your home against the elements.

Exterior maintenance can be labor-intensive, especially when it places you up on the roof or down in the basement. Don't hesitate to call in the pros as needed. But there's an awful lot you can do on your own to preserve the health and beauty of your home's outer shell—and save a bundle in the process.

Wood Siding

Your house's siding is its skin. Like your skin, siding provides a protective shield that keeps out external intruders. To do its job, siding must be watertight, airtight, and able to withstand repeated bouts of driving rain, searing heat, icy cold, and even abundant sunshine. Despite all the stress that siding is exposed to, even traditional wood siding doesn't need a lot of upkeep. With a just little care and foresight—and maybe an occasional paint job—you can prolong wood siding's life indefinitely. Remember, the appearance (and curb appeal) of your home will only be as sharp, clean, and attractive as its siding.

YOUR COST SAVINGS

$3,780

Cost to replace the deteriorated clapboard siding on one side (40 by 20 feet or 12 by 6 metres) of a house.

Care and Maintenance

Poke and prod your siding. Once a year, pick a day when the weather is fine and take a stroll around the perimeter of your house. Carrying a screwdriver or an awl, seek out loose caulking or rotted wood. If you find a bad spot, prod it, like a dentist probing for cavities, to determine the depth of the damage. Scrape away the bad material and replace it as described in this chapter.

Give your house a bath. Every spring or summer, wash down your wood siding. For a light cleaning, you don't need to use soap. Just wet the siding using a garden hose, and scrub off surface dirt with a long-handled brush. Be sure to scrub under the edges of slats or shingles, where dirt tends to cling.

For tough dirt, use soap. If your house is *really* dirty, or if you live in an area where mildew is a problem, scrub the siding with special deck and siding cleaner. Or just mix together 1 quart (1 litre) of chlorine bleach and 1/3 cup (80 ml) of household detergent in 3 quarts (3 litres) of warm water (don't use ammonia). This solution will remove heavy dirt and prevent mildew. Rinse with a garden hose. Every few years (or before painting your home), clean your siding with a power washer.

Watch out for standing water. If water tends to collect on the ground near your house, the moisture may ultimately damage your home. Add more soil (nonporous clay works well), sloping the ground so that it drains the water away from the house, or install a drain system. It may cost a bit, but it could save you a lot more in repairs.

After a rainstorm, look for and fix broken or clogged gutters, downspouts, or drains that are spilling water on your siding.

Trim back foundation plantings. Nice shrubbery is an easy and inexpensive way to boost your home's curb appeal; the key is keeping the greenery from crowding your siding. If the sun can't reach your wood siding, moisture will build up, peeling the paint and rotting the wood. Plant new shrubs and bushes at least 18 inches (46 cm) from the siding, and trim back plants that touch the house. Another good reason to leave some space between plants and siding is that the closer plants are to your siding, the better access insects have to your home.

Easy Fixes

Gluing splits back together. If you spot a split in your clapboard, fix it before it gets worse. Gently lever the split open with a putty knife. If the split is large enough, slip a small wooden wedge under the bottom edge of the damaged board to keep the inside of the split exposed. Apply waterproof glue along the exposed edge of the split, then remove the wedge, push the siding back into place, and wipe away excess glue with a damp cloth. Drive several small finishing nails at an angle under the repaired section and bend them up to hold the bond tightly together. Remove the nails when the glue dries and plug the nail holes with caulk or exterior wood putty.

Using auto-body putty to fill rot. To repair rotted wood, dig away the rot with a knife or chisel, then mix up a batch of auto-body filler (available from home centers

WHAT'S INSIDE AN EXTERIOR WALL?

Siding is what you see on the outer surface of an exterior wall. A typical exterior wall consists of a wood frame made from studs and covered with either plywood or board sheathing. The sheathing is usually covered by a waterproofing layer of thick building paper or breathable plastic house wrap. Wood siding—generally horizontal rows of overlapping boards (clapboard or lap siding) or panels (shingles or shakes)—is nailed to the sheathing or underlying studs.

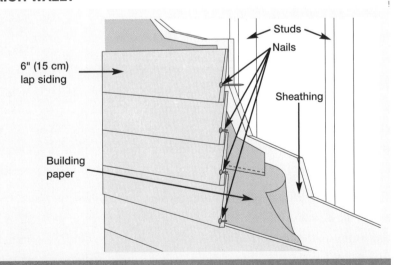

6" (15 cm) lap siding

Studs

Nails

Sheathing

Building paper

or auto supply stores) and fill the hole with it, smoothing or shaping the patch with a putty knife. Sand it to match the surrounding wood. Prime and paint the area.

Banishing board bulges. Has a board in your siding developed a bulge? Just screw it down. Drive a long wood screw through the siding and the sheathing beneath it, then into a stud. (To find a stud, look for a pattern of nail heads or seams between boards.) To avoid splitting the board, drill a pilot hole for the screw. Then drill a second, larger, shallow hole at the surface (called a countersink) for the head of the screw to sink into. Drive the screw in as far as it will go. Cover the screw head with exterior-grade wood putty and sand it smooth. Prime and paint the area.

Making good use of roof cement. If you accidentally cut the building paper or housing wrap behind the siding while replacing a section of siding or making another repair, just seal the damage with asphalt roofing cement.

How to Replace a Damaged Shingle

Some houses are faced with cedar or redwood shakes or shingles. The main difference between the two is shingles are smooth-cut on both sides, and shakes are left rough on one side. Generally, neither is painted, but sometimes they are treated with semitransparent or even solid-color stains. Replace a damaged shingle (or shake) as follows:

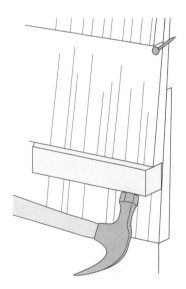

1. Use a HAMMER and a wood chisel to split the damaged shingle in several places, being careful not to damage the underlying shingles. Then pull out all the pieces.

---

2. Slip the blade of a MINI-HACKSAW under the overlapping shingle and cut off the nails that held the damaged shingle. (Pull out any exposed nail heads using a claw hammer.)

---

3. Measure and SAW a replacement shingle's width to fit, allowing a 1/8-inch (3 mm) gap between the new shingle and the shingles on each side.

---

4. Slide the NEW SHINGLE under the overlapping shingles to about 1/2 inch (1 cm) below its final position. At 1/2 inch (1 cm) in from each side edge, drive in 3d (1 1/4-inch or 3 cm) rust-resistant shingle nails at a slightly upward angle. Tap the shingle into place with a hammer and a block of scrap wood. The nails will straighten and be hidden under the overlapping shingles.

Clapboard, also called lap siding, bevel siding, or weatherboard, comes in a variety of widths and styles. The boards are nailed in overlapping rows to the sheathing behind. If you need to replace a badly damaged section of board, remove the damaged section and take it to a lumberyard to find the closest match. All clapboards are installed and replaced in the same way.

1. Use a COMBINATION SQUARE to mark cut lines on the section of clapboard you're replacing.

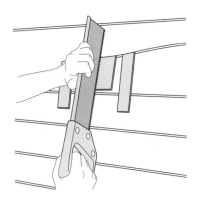

2. Gently lift the BOTTOM EDGE of the damaged board using a pry bar resting on a wood scrap. Drive shims under the raised edge to separate the damaged board from the board below it. Using a wood scrap to protect the board below, cut along the cut lines with a backsaw.

3. Gently lift the BOTTOM EDGE of the board overlapping the damaged one, and wedge shims under it. Use a keyhole saw with the teeth pointed outward to complete the cuts at the top of the damaged board.

4. With the SHIMS still in place, slip the blade of a mini-hacksaw under the damaged board, feel for the nails, and cut through them. (If a nail head is exposed, just pull the nail.) Remove the damaged board.

5. Cut the REPLACEMENT BOARD to size, and treat its sawed edges with wood preservative. Then tap the board into place with a hammer and a piece of scrap wood. Pre-drill nail holes and secure the board with galvanized siding nails. The nails should go through the lower part of the replacement board and into the sheathing 1/4 inch (0.5 cm) above the top of the clapboard below it. (Never nail through the underlying course of siding because this will impede the ability of the wood to expand and contract and may result in cracks that allow moisture to seep in.)

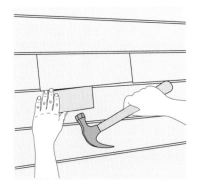

6. CAULK OR PUTTY over the nail holes and the seams. Then sand, prime, and paint the new board to match.

Painting Your House

As a tough outer membrane that stands up against the ravages of weather, paint plays a key role in protecting your house. As such, you want to keep it in as good condition as possible. How often you have to repaint depends on your climate, the quality of the paint used, and other factors, but once every five or six years is typical. But if you clean and touch up your siding regularly, you can put off repainting much longer. Weather conditions and how well you prep the surface can make a big difference in the quality of the job and how long it will last.

YOUR COST SAVINGS

$6,100

Cost to have a 2,400-square-foot (225 square meters) house with wood siding and badly weathered paint prepped, primed, and repainted.

House Painting Tips

Paint the bottom edge first. When painting clapboard siding, use a brush or pad to paint the bottom edges first, then paint the face of the siding with broad horizontal strokes. When spray-painting, spray up, painting the bottoms of the boards first, and then spray head on.

Only paint in a Goldilocks season. Paint in the spring or autumn, when the air temperature is neither too hot nor too cold. Not only will you be more comfortable, but the paint will stay wet longer, giving you more time to brush it out. Obviously,

5 TIPS FOR PERFECT PREPPING

Here's how to get your siding ready for a great-looking, long-lasting paint job:

1. **Fix caulk.** Scrape out and replace any crumbling caulk in joints between siding and trim.

2. **Hide nail heads.** Sink any visible nails with a nail set. Coat the nail heads with primer, fill the holes with exterior putty, and sand flat.

3. **Remove loose paint.** Scrape off all loose, cracked, alligatored, and peeling paint. Soften stubborn spots with a heat gun (but never use a propane torch!). If paint won't come off, it has probably bonded to the wood; you can safely paint over it.

4. **Sand smooth.** Sand down the edges around all scraped areas so that the difference between areas with and without old paint won't show through the new coat. Start with extra-coarse sandpaper, then switch to medium.

5. **Prime raw areas.** Prime all scraped wood, caulk, or putty.

To scrape off loose exterior paint, you'll find that a long-handled scraper or a hook scraper with replaceable blades works fine in most cases. If you need extra reach, try using a garden hoe with a sharpened edge. A V-shaped bottle opener is a great tool for scraping out loose caulk.

don't paint on a rainy day or just before rain is expected; the paint could be washed away before it adheres.

Test for lead paint. If your house was built before 1960, it may contain lead paint. Lead-based dust and paint chips can cause health problems, especially in young children. Before scraping or sanding, test for lead using a lead test kit. If lead paint is present, special precautions need to be taken when scraping or sanding. Visit http://www.cmhc-schl.gc.ca for further information.

Do the Band-Aid test. Before any big repainting job, test the bond of the new paint in an inconspicuous area. Apply a little paint to a small, clean spot. Two days later, stick a Band-Aid over it, then yank it off. If paint comes off with the tape, the surface needs more cleaning or a good primer. If paint doesn't come off, the surface can be painted.

Prevent paint blisters by chasing the sun. The sun beating down on a fresh coat of paint can cause blistering. So don't paint areas that are about to be hit by bright sunlight. Instead, chase the sun through the day. For instance, in the early morning paint the north side of the house. Paint the east side in the late morning, and in the mid-afternoon shift to the south side. Finally, paint the west side in the late afternoon (when the sun is weakening) or wait until the next morning.

WHAT'S WRONG WITH MY PAINT JOB?

It looks like alligator skin!
Possible causes: Outer coat was applied over a poorly prepared surface, an undercoat that was not dry, too many undercoats, or an incompatible paint, such as latex over oil.
Solution: Strip to raw wood; prime and paint.

It's blistering and bubbling!
Possible cause: Prick one of the blisters. If it shows paint inside, temperature was too warm while painting.
Solution: Sand clean and repaint.
Possible cause: If a pricked blister reveals bare wood, moisture has seeped in from somewhere.

Solution: Check for faulty caulking, leaky gutters, or ice dams; fix before repainting.

It's shedding a chalky powder!
Possible cause: Exterior paints are formulated to gradually release powdery chalk that washes off dirt when it rains.
Solution: There's nothing for you to do; it's not a problem. Because new paint doesn't really adhere to a chalky surface, power wash the siding before repainting.

It's cracking and scaling!
Possible causes: Moisture or pollution. When paint becomes old, it often loses its elasticity, allowing moisture to seep in and lift off the paint.

Solution: Fix the moisture problem; then strip and repaint.

It's flaking and peeling!
Possible cause: When your surface is dirty or has too many layers of old paint, new paint generally has a hard time sticking to it.
Solution: Strip and repaint.

It's mildewed!
Possible cause: Moisture and a warm, dirty surface, as well as inadequate venting or improper caulking.
Solution: Scrape off mildew and scrub with one part chlorine bleach and three parts water. When dry, coat with mildew-resistant primer and repaint.

Vinyl and Aluminum Siding

Vinyl and aluminum siding are not totally maintenance free, but they're close to it! An annual washing is almost all the care this kind of siding needs for the first decade or two. But eventually it suffers from wear and tear and the detrimental effects of weather and dirt. Aluminum siding does dent, and its factory finish may discolor or flake off. Over time, vinyl siding will fade. Vinyl may also sag in hot weather or become brittle in cold weather; it can crack if it's hit by something hard. With a few simple repairs, however, you can keep aluminum or vinyl siding attractive and weathertight for a very, very long time.

YOUR COST SAVINGS

$2,530

Cost to remove deteriorated vinyl siding on one side of a house (40 by 20 feet or 12 by 6 metres), replace building wrap, and install new siding.

Care and Maintenance

Wash your siding every spring. Over time both aluminum and vinyl siding collect dirt and become chalky, leaving a whitish residue that can break down into dark permanent spots if it's not removed. Use a mop or long-handled brush to scrub off the chalk, along with any dirt, grease, or mildew. For a cleaning agent use either trisodium phosphate (TSP) or mix 1/4 cup (60 ml) of bleach-free powdered laundry detergent with 2 gallons (8 litres) of warm water. Wash the wall from the bottom up. Rinse with a garden hose, moving from the top down. If your siding is really dirty, use a power washer, but always spray downward to avoid forcing water under the siding panels.

Got a loose panel? Metal and vinyl siding panels interlock along their top and bottom edges. If you notice a loose panel when you are cleaning, it's easy to fix. Just hook its bottom edge with the hooked end of a zip tool (see below) and press against the panel above it with your other hand until the two panels snap together.

SMART IDEA

Working alone replacing a panel of aluminum or vinyl siding? Use a strip of duct tape to hold one end in place while you install the other end.

ZIP TOOL   equipment spotlight

A zip tool is a small, handheld tool that helps you "unlock" pieces of vinyl siding from adja-cent strips. It has a small, curved blade with an easily gripped han-dle. Zip tools can be purchased at home improvement stores for $5 to $10.

Easy Fixes

Repairing minor dings. You can repair scratches or small cracks without removing the panel of siding from the wall. To fix a small scratch in aluminum siding, simply sand it, apply metal primer, and brush on a dab of matching acrylic latex paint. To repair a shallow crack in vinyl siding, use a toothpick to gently pry up one side of the crack, apply a bit of PVC cement from a vinyl-siding repair kit, then press the crack closed.

Fixing large cracks in vinyl. For a larger crack in vinyl siding, put a patch on the back of the panel using a vinyl-siding repair kit. Remove the damaged panel and turn it over. Prepare the back of the panel with PVC cleaner, apply some PVC cement, and press on the patch, finished side down. Replace the panel. (For directions on removing and installing a panel, see "How to Replace Damaged Vinyl Siding," next page.)

Pulling out dents. It's not unusual for aluminum siding to get dented, but removing a dent is easy. Just drill a 1/8-inch (3 mm) hole in the deepest part of the dent, install a sheet-metal screw with a flat washer, and use pliers to pull the screw toward you, bringing the dent out with it. Remove the screw, fill the screw hole and any remaining depression with auto-body filler, and sand it smooth. Apply metal primer and two coats of matching spray paint.

CAN I PAINT VINYL OR ALUMINUM SIDING?

One of the great things about vinyl and aluminum siding is that they don't need to be painted. Aluminum siding comes with a factory finish, and vinyl siding is manufactured with color infused throughout. But years after you install it, when either of these types of siding begins to show its age, you may want to freshen it by painting it. But be warned: Once you start painting, you'll have to keep doing it every five or six years, just as you would with wood siding. Before painting, clean the siding thoroughly so the paint will adhere well.

PAINTING ALUMINUM SIDING

Scrape off any loose paint. Then spot-prime the bare metal with two thin coats of a latex metal primer. When it's dry, smooth with fine sandpaper. Apply two *thin* coats of latex paint; a thick coat might crack as the aluminum expands and contracts.

PAINTING VINYL SIDING

Just apply two coats of latex house paint. You don't need to prime unless the surface is pitted or porous. If that's the case, use latex primer. Don't use alkyd paint, which is less flexible and may crack or peel. Also, never paint vinyl siding a darker color than the original. The darker color will absorb more heat, which can cause the siding to buckle.

Matching new siding to old. When you replace an old section of vinyl siding, don't use a brand new panel that will stand out like a sore thumb. Instead, steal a matching weathered panel from a less noticeable or hidden part of the house, and replace that panel with the shiny new panel.

How to Replace Damaged Vinyl Siding

Replacing a badly damaged panel of vinyl (or aluminum) siding is easy. When you buy the replacement panel at a home center, pick up a packet of the recommended nails and a zip tool, which lets you easily unlock the siding panels. Work on a warm day; vinyl may crack in cold weather.

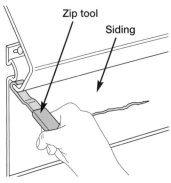

Zip tool
Siding

1. Unhook the DAMAGED PANEL from the one above. Hook the curved end of a zip tool under the bottom edge of the top panel and pull down on it as you slide the tool along the seam.

----

2. Prop up the TOP PANEL with shims, and use a pry bar on a wood block to pull out the nails holding the damaged panel. Remove the panel.

----

3. Set the REPLACEMENT PANEL in place. Lock the bottom edge over the top of the panel below it and overlap adjacent panels the same way as the old panel did. If an end goes into trim at a corner or a window, leave a 1/4-inch (0.5 cm) space at that end to let the panel expand. Using aluminum siding nails, nail the top edge of the new panel in place through each nail slot. Don't drive the nails flush; leave a 1/8-inch (3 mm) space under the nail head for siding expansion. Also, don't drive the nails into old nail holes; move a bit to one side.

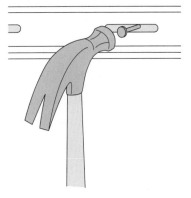

4. Lock the TOP PANEL to the replacement panel by pressing against it or by using the zip tool to pull down while you push in.

Brick Veneer

A brick house is the ultimate symbol of sturdy construction. The Big Bad Wolf can huff and puff, but he'll never blow it down. But that was once upon a time, when brick houses had solid walls that were two or three bricks thick. In most of today's brick houses, a single layer of bricks is used as a veneer, or facing, over a wood frame. But even brick veneer houses are strong. Not only is the underlying weight-bearing wood frame sturdy, but the bricks provide an almost mainte-nance-free exterior. Blows to the surface, moisture, mold, and plain old dirt may cause problems—moisture may even cause a wall to set-tle. With a little care, however, you can avoid serious damage.

Care and Maintenance

Inspect your exterior. Once or twice a year, walk around your house on a nice bright day and examine the bricks in the exterior walls. Make note of any crumbling mortar joints, cracked bricks, mildew, and other stains. You don't have to rush to fix the problems, but the sooner you do, the better.

Keep your eyes peeled for moisture problems. After a heavy rainfall, check the house's downspout and gutters to make sure no water is collecting on the ground near the outer walls. Clear away any clogs, and make any needed repairs to gutters and downspouts. If standing water is a problem, add soil to regrade the ground near the house so that it slopes away from the building.

Clean weep holes with pipe cleaners. A couple of times each year inspect the weep holes in your brick veneer to make sure they're not blocked. Trapped moisture can rot windows, doors, and sheathing, leading to thousands of dollars in repairs. Clean them out with a pipe cleaner.

Hose bricks before cleaning them. Before applying a cleaning compound to your bricks—if you need to remove a stain, for example—wet them thoroughly with a garden hose. It will help the compound penetrate better.

take care

When applying any strong cleaning agent to your bricks, wear protective goggles and gloves and cover nearby plants and grass with plastic. Don't use a metal brush; it may scratch the bricks and leave behind metal particles that will rust. Don't use muriatic acid; it may stain or bleach bricks or corrode aluminum window frames. Before applying a clean-er to century-old bricks or bricks with a light or unusual color or an unusual fin-ish, test the cleaner in a hidden spot.

WHAT'S INSIDE A BRICK VENEER WALL?

Brick veneer consists of a single thickness, or wythe, of bricks that rests on the house's foundation. Behind the bricks is a wood frame of studs covered with plywood sheathing and a thick layer of building paper or house wrap. The bricks are anchored to the wood structure with small metal ties. A 1-inch (2.5 cm) space between the inner wall and the bricks lets moisture trickle down inside the wall. Near the bottom of the wall, metal flashing prevents the water from seeping into the foundation, directing it instead out through small drains called "weep" holes. Flashing and weep holes are also used above and below windows and doors.

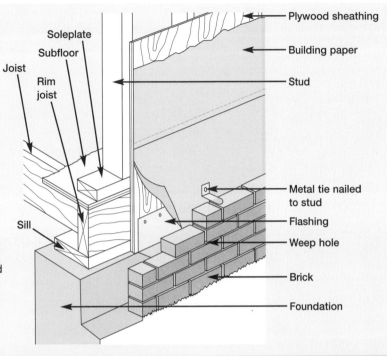

Mix your own mortar. You can buy premixed mortar for repointing or replacing brick, but you'll get a smoother joint if you mix your own. Just combine three parts builder's sand and one part type N masonry cement (this is the type recommended for exterior, above-grade walls). Mix in enough water so that the mortar forms a stiff paste that retains its shape when rolled into a ball. Let the mortar stand for about an hour to become firm enough to stay in place. You'll then have about 30 minutes to use it. If it gets stiff, throw it out and mix a fresh batch.

Easy Fixes

Matching new mortar joints to old. To shape a new mortar joint to match the old ones, you don't need a mason's jointer tool. To form the common concave shape, smooth the joint with an ice-cream stick, a piece of metal tube, or an old spoon. For other shapes, carve a scrap of wood to the shape.

"Aging" new joints. To "age" new joints so they match old ones in color, pat the mortar, while it's still a little damp, with a wet tea bag. It's easier than adding commercial colorant to the mortar mix.

Replacing a broken brick. This is not as hard as you think it might be! Wearing safety goggles, chisel out the old mortar from around the brick with a hammer and a cold chisel, being careful not to chip the surrounding bricks. Then use the chisel to break apart and remove the damaged brick a piece at a time. Clean and dampen the opening and the new brick, then spread mortar along the bottom of the cavity and along the top and sides of the new brick. Support the brick on a trowel or a wood scrap and slide it into place. Add more mortar as needed to fill the joints, then shape them to match the other joints.

Hiding a mismatched replacement brick. If you replace a brick in a wall and the replacement doesn't match the surrounding bricks, try staining it the same color as the existing ones.

How to Repoint Crumbly Brick Joints

If the mortar in the joints between bricks is cracking and crumbling, you need to repoint it—that is, replace old loose mortar with fresh mortar. Whether you do it yourself or hire a handyman or mason, repointing is simple:

1. Use a COLD CHISEL to chip away loose mortar to a depth of from 1/2 to 1 inch (1 to 2.5 cm)—until you reach solid mortar. Wear safety goggles. Brush out any debris, and rinse the surface with a garden hose.

----

2. Put some MORTAR on the back of a trowel or a board, and push it into the openings with a tuck pointer tool. Or just roll the mortar into a "sausage" and press it in. Let it dry until you can press it gently with your thumb and leave a print.

----

3. Smooth and SHAPE THE JOINT to match the surrounding ones; use a brick jointer tool or improvise using an ice-cream stick, piece of metal tube, or old spoon. After the mortar has set, brush away any excess.

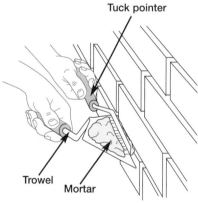

Tuck pointer

Trowel   Mortar

Repointing bricks

Painting brick siding. Although you *can* paint brick, it's not a good idea. Painting brick changes it from a relatively maintenance-free exterior into one that will need repainting every five to seven years. Also, if you or another owner later wants to remove the paint from the brick, the job will be expensive (and the results iffy). That said, if you're dead-set on painting your brick siding, power wash it first and use proper masonry primer and paint. Apply the paint with an airless paint sprayer, then roll it out with a thick-napped roller.

GET THIS STUFF OFF MY BRICKS!

IF THE PROBLEM IS ...	TRY THIS ...
Dingy spots	Apply spray-on oven cleaner; let sit 15 minutes, then scrub with a stiff brush. Repeat, then rinse with water.
Dirt	Hose off while scrubbing with a stiff brush. For a tough job, rent a power washer.
Efflorescence (chalky buildup)	Mix masonry detergent with water according to package directions, and apply it with a stiff brush. Rinse.
Graffiti	Apply commercial spray-paint remover, following label directions.
Mold or mildew	Prepare a 50-50 mixture of bleach and water and pour into a plastic spray bottle. Spray on mixture; wait one hour, then flush area well with water. Alternatively, scrub the area with full-strength white vinegar and a stiff nylon brush.
Paint	Blot wet paint with paper towels; then wipe with a rag soaked with paint thinner for alkyd paint (if the paint is latex, use water). If the paint has dried, scrape it off; then remove residue with commercial paint remover.
Rust	Dissolve 1 pound (0.5 kilogram) of oxalic acid crystals in 1 gallon (4 litres) of water. Brush on; wait three hours, then scrub and rinse.
Soot or smoke	Scrub with scouring powder; rinse well. For stubborn spots, make a paste of talc and liquid chlorine bleach, apply, and let dry before brushing off.
Tar or asphalt	Scrub with scouring powder. Make paste of talc and kerosene, apply, and let dry. Brush off, then scrub again and rinse.
Water stains (as from lawn sprinklers)	Scrub with an acid-based commercial brick cleaner and a stiff brush.

Stucco

Stucco is a remarkably durable and attractive siding. It doesn't need to be painted and, with care, it can last 75 to 100 years. Made of cement, sand, lime, and water, stucco is applied like plaster over metal or wood lath or directly over concrete or masonry. Although problems are rare, look out for cracks or flakes. Be particularly concerned if you find long cracks—they may indicate that the supporting wall is settling, and you may need to get help to prevent severe structural damage.

Care and Maintenance

Check for cracks. Once a year, examine your stucco walls for cracks. You can ignore hairline cracks, but seal larger ones (see sidebar on opposite page).

Duct tape test to spot a dangerous crack. If you find a long crack, attach a length of duct tape across it with epoxy. Watch the tape over the next two months. If it splits or twists, the wall behind the stucco is shifting and the foundation may be settling, which could cause significant damage to the entire house. Have an expert evaluate the problem.

Beware of crustiness. Do you have a white crumbly or flaky crust forming on your stucco? It's efflorescence. Salts inside the material are being leached out by moisture coming from inside. Get professional help from a mason or stucco specialist.

Bleach away ugly mildew. Gray or black stains on stucco are most likely mildew. To get rid of them, just clean the area using a solution of one part household chlorine bleach and three parts water. Wear rubber gloves and protect any nearby plants or grass with plastic sheeting.

Easy Fixes

Using tape for neat crack repairs. If you find a crack that is no more than 1/8 inch (3 mm) wide, fill it with acrylic latex caulk. Clean out the crack using a stiff brush. To keep the caulk from smearing, cover the crack with a strip of wide masking tape and slice the tape with a utility knife to remove the area that needs filling. Put a tube of caulk into a caulking gun and fill the crack. Smooth the surface with a trowel or putty knife. Before the caulk hardens, remove the tape. Fill larger cracks with pre-mixed stucco repair compound.

Whitewashing stucco. Stucco remains fresh looking for decades, but over time it can become dingy and stained with age. Freshen it the old-fashioned way with whitewash. Make white-wash by mixing white Portland cement with water to the consistency of pancake batter. Wet the stucco with a hose and apply the mixture with a masonry brush or a whisk broom.

Color-washing stucco. If you want to give your home a new look, you can color the whitewash with masonry dye. But if you do, plan to do the entire wall in one session using the same batch of dyed whitewash because it will be almost impossible to match the shade using a new batch.

How to Patch Damaged Stucco

If you need to patch a large area in a stucco wall, call a mason or stucco specialist. But if the damaged area is no more than a couple of square feet, you can easily patch it, using premixed stucco repair compound.

1. Wearing SAFETY GOGGLES, clean out the old damaged stucco with a wire brush. Using a hammer and cold chisel, undercut the edges of the opening to make it wider inside at the base than on the surface. Brush out any loose material, then wet the area with a sponge.

2. Use a TROWEL to pack stucco into the opening, overfilling it slightly. Let the stucco dry for 15 minutes or as directed. Then smooth the stucco and scrape off any excess.

3. Further SMOOTH THE SURFACE with the trowel, feathering (smoothing out) the edges to blend with the surrounding surface. Then use a whisk broom or trowel to give the patch a matching texture. Cure the stucco by wetting it with a fine spray from a garden hose once each morning and evening for the next three days.

Painting stucco. For a longer lasting finish, paint faded and cracked stucco. Fill cracks with a paintable exterior caulk; if they are wide or deep, use premixed stucco repair compound. Clean the surface thoroughly; if you use a power washer, hold it three feet away from the surface to avoid crumbling the stucco. Apply two coats of high-quality acrylic latex. Apply the paint with a thick-napped roller, and use a masonry brush to get into crevices. Work the first coat into the stucco by rolling or brushing in several directions.

Painting cracked stucco. If the stucco on your house tends to crack, use elastomeric paint, a paint that has a special coating that makes it thicker, tougher, and more pliable.

Keeping out moisture. Preventing moisture from sneaking behind stucco is the most important step you can take to prolong the life of your stucco. Replace damaged or missing flashings around chimneys, vents, and other roof openings. Check windows and doors—especially along the tops—to make certain they're properly flashed to keep water out. Repair any surface cracks or damaged areas immediately.

Double-Hung Windows

A double-hung window consists of a top and a bottom sash with windowpanes that slide up and down in channels on the sides of the window frame. While contemporary models incorporate such conveniences as tilt-in sashes and removable dividers (technically called "muntins") for easy cleaning, even vintage double-hung windows are easy to keep in tip-top shape with just a little bit of care. The maintenance is worth the effort, as anyone who's ever replaced windows knows—the windows themselves are expensive enough, but the installation costs can be *twice* the cost of the window!

YOUR COST SAVINGS
$425
Cost to replace a 2-foot-10-inch-by-4-foot (0.8 by 1 metre) double-hung window with a new double-glazed wood window with screen.

Care and Maintenance

For smoother sliding on the sash, use candle wax. If your window is sliding up and down with difficulty, clean the channels that the sashes ride in and rub them with a candle stub or a bar of soap. For longer-lasting results, lubricate them with silicone spray, which is available at hardware stores.

Clean windows regularly, frames to glass. No one likes to "do windows," but it's an essential task if you want to prolong the life of your windows. Do a thorough cleaning every few months, with the timing adjusted for local weather and grime conditions. Start by vacuuming the frames and sills, then clean their surfaces with a soft cloth and the appropriate cleaning agent—oil-based wood cleaner for clear-finished natural wood frames; mild dishwashing liquid and water for painted wood and other materials. Finally, clean the panes.

Overlap the glass with paint. When painting windows, keep in mind function as well as appearance. To extend window life and seal out moisture, allow paint to overlap onto glass panes by 1/16 of an inch (2 mm).

Don't let paint cause a window to stick. To prevent stuck sashes, open both sashes partway before you begin painting, give the sash channels one thin, carefully applied coat of paint, and after the paint has dried to the touch, slide sashes up and down a few times.

SMART IDEA

Erase a shallow scratch in a windowpane with toothpaste. Use a traditional paste of the "extra-whitening" variety, which contains the most abrasive (avoid gels). Use a soft cloth to apply a bit of the toothpaste to the scratch, rub vigorously for a few minutes, and wipe the glass clean.

Easy Fixes

Reaching the exterior of windows to clean them. If cleaning the outside of your windows is difficult, tightly shut the windows and spray them with a garden hose. (Do it very gently—just misting the windows. Too much pressure could force water into the house or crack a pane.) Attaching a long-handled car wash brush to your hose is also helpful.

Gluing cracks in glass. A small crack in a windowpane can morph into a big problem if left unattended. As soon as you see a crack, fill it with cyanoacrylate—better known as Super Glue. Squirt the glue directly from the container into the crack. Capillary action will suck it right in. Any excess will dry to a clear, invisible finish.

Replacing crumbly window putty. In addition to preventing drafts from sneaking in around pane edges, glazing compound, also known as window putty, keeps water from soaking into the wood sashes and rotting them. Replace cracked or brittle compound by carefully chipping it out with a chisel or a five-in-one painter's tool and spreading on a new coat.

Repairing rotted windowsills. Rotted windowsills are easy to rebuild, using liquid consolidant and puttylike epoxy filler, both sold at hardware stores. Chisel away the rotted wood and scrape paint from other soft areas. Drill several 1/4-inch (0.5 cm) holes in the damaged areas, and soak them with liquid consolidant. Before the consolidant hardens, apply the epoxy filler, gradually building up the sill to its original level. Smooth with a putty knife dipped in lacquer thinner to prevent it from sticking. Smooth with 100-grit sandpaper; prime and paint.

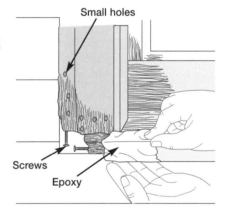

Small holes

Screws

Epoxy

Giving the filler a grip. If you have to reconstruct a corner of a rotted sill with epoxy filler, put in a couple of screws first so that the filler will have something to hold onto.

Making your windows more secure. Double-hung windows are susceptible to break-ins, even when they're locked. With the window closed tightly, drill a hole through the top of the lower sash going into the bottom of the upper sash. Then insert a nail in the hole. Do this on both sides of the window. If you are worried about someone smashing the glass and pulling out the nails, clip the nails flush with the wood and keep a magnet handy to pull them out.

Adding locks for extra security. Though there are a number of types of supplementary locks for double-hung windows, these two are particularly useful:

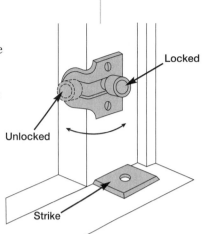

- Ventilating locks let you lock a window in a slightly open position. It attaches to the upper sash, slightly above the center where the two sashes meet, with its strike plate attached to the top of the lower sash. Install one lock on each side of the sash.

- Key turnbuckles replace your window's existing clamshell latch with a key-lock mechanism. For ease of operation, particularly in emergencies, arrange for all locks to be operated with the same key; keep spares within reach but hidden from prying eyes.

How to Replace a Broken Window Pane

Replacing a broken single-thickness pane is a straightforward repair. Measure the opening and buy a piece of glass cut 1/8 inch (3 mm) smaller in width and length. You'll also need work gloves, a chisel, a heat gun or hair dryer, pliers, boiled linseed oil, a putty knife, glazing compound (also called window putty), and metal glazing points with extending "ears."

1. Wearing gloves, carefully REMOVE THE BROKEN GLASS. Then use a chisel to chip out all the old compound around the opening, being careful not to damage the wood. Use a hair dryer or heat gun to soften stubborn chunks. As you work, pull out the original metal glazing points with pliers.

2. Coat the EXPOSED WOOD in the opening with linseed oil and let it soak in well. Then line the opening with a thin bead of compound, and press the new piece of glass into place.

3. Use a PUTTY KNIFE to push new glazing points into place against the glass every 4 inches around the perimeter. Don't use the old holes.

4. Apply more COMPOUND over the glazing points and around the exposed edges of the glass, occasionally dipping the putty knife in linseed oil to keep it from sticking to the compound. Let the compound cure for about a week before repainting.

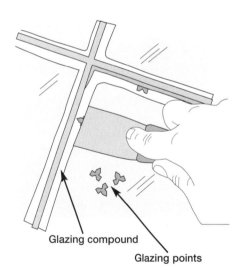

Glazing compound

Glazing points

Classic double-hung windows rely on counterweights for opening, closing, and staying put. A cord or chain attached to the sash runs up to a pulley and down to a weight in a cavity inside the window frame. Over time the cords can fray and break. If this happens, quit propping the sash open with a stick, and replace the cord with a flat-link brass or steel sash chain.

1. Working on the side with the BROKEN CORD, unscrew or pry out the inner stop—the vertical molding strip that holds the sash in place. Also remove and save any metal weather stripping.

----

2. Swing the SASH out from the frame, and remove the end of the broken sash cord from the channel in the side of the sash. Disconnect the sash cord from the other side of the sash, and if it's intact, tie its end to a pencil to keep it from slipping over the pulley. Set the sash aside.

----

3. Unscrew or pry open the COUNTERWEIGHT POCKET DOOR on the side with the broken cord. Pull out the weight and remove the cord. Use cutting pliers to cut a chain 1 foot (30 cm) longer than the broken cord.

----

4. To install the CHAIN, slip a nail through a link in one end to keep it from running over the pulley. Then feed the other end over the pulley into the weight chamber and pull it out through the access hole. Loop the chain end through the eye of the weight, securing it with wire or manufacturer-provided clips. Slip the weight back inside the chamber.

----

5. Put the SASH back on the sill and refasten the intact cord. Pull the new chain down until the weight hits the pulley; then lower it about 2 inches (5 cm). Remove the nail from the free end of the chain, and secure it to the sash with 3/4-inch (2 cm) No. 6 wood screws through two of its links.

----

6. Holding the SASH in its track, slide it all the way up until the sash weight is visible in the access hole—it should be about 2 inches (5 cm) above the bottom of the window frame. Adjust the chain length as needed at its connection to the weight, then replace the weight door, weather stripping, and stop.

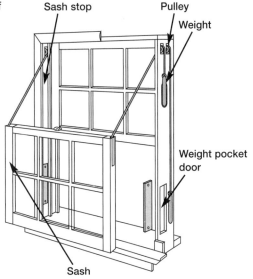

Sash stop

Pulley

Weight

Weight pocket door

Sash

Sliding Windows

Sliding (sometimes called "gliding") windows are essentially double-hung windows turned on their sides. They're often the most affordable windows, but they do have disadvantages: The bottom tracks on which the windows glide are notorious dirt catchers, the aluminum frames spot easily, and the seal isn't terrifically strong. With good care and a few security measures, you can easily keep yours rolling in the right direction.

YOUR COST SAVINGS

$375

Cost to replace a 5-foot-by-3-foot (1.5 by 1 metre) sliding window with a new vinyl thermopane unit.

Care and Maintenance

Keep the bottom track clean and lubed. The bottom track of a sliding window tends to be a natural landing point for the kind of grime that can gunk up the window's mechanisms. Cleaning it is easy: Simply vacuum the tracks whenever you are cleaning the room and occasionally scrub them with a mild dishwashing solution. To banish hardened dirt, use detergent and an abrasive sponge or fine steel wool. After wiping them dry, lubricate both the lower and upper tracks with silicone spray.

Protect aluminum frames with auto wax. Window frames face constant exposure to the elements, and oxidation can leave older, uncoated aluminum frames looking dull and blotchy. To return their sparkling, sleek finish, first clean them with detergent and fine steel wool or a mildly abrasive cleanser. Dry them completely, and then apply a light coat of automotive paste wax to seal out future oxidation.

Easy Fixes

Removing a sliding window sash. You may need to remove sliding window sashes to clean them better. Just slide the sash to the center of the frame. Grab the sash on both sides and push it up into the top track, then swing the bottom edge out toward you.

What to do if you can't get the sash out. If the window doesn't budge after you push it into the upper track, try tightening the screws in the upper track. This will effectively push the track up and away from the sash and expand the opening.

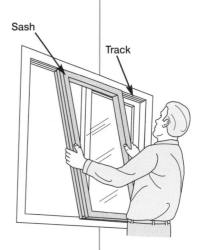

Sash

Track

Removing a stationary sash. If you need to remove the fixed sash in a sliding window, unscrew the brackets that secure it to the frame at the top and bottom corners. Then unscrew the bumper in the lower track in the center that keeps it from moving. Slide the sash to the center, lift it up, and tilt it outward. Sometimes, the outside edges of this sash are sealed with caulk and paint, which may have to be cut and scraped away before you can remove the sash.

Burglarproofing sliding windows. Much like their double-hung siblings, sliding windows can be an easy mark for intruders. To keep sashes from sliding at the wrong moment or being lifted out completely, try this approach: Drive a screw or two going vertically into the top of the upper track of the window frame (upper picture). This will prevent the sash from being lifted up and removed.

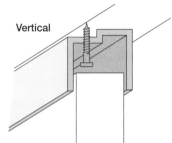

Vertical

Stopping the slide. You can limit how far a sliding window sash slides by putting in a screw that goes horizontally through both sides of the upper track to block the sash's movements (lower picture). Caution: Don't do this on any window that also serves as an emergency exit. Instead, use a track stop.

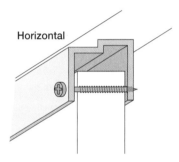

Horizontal

Affixing supplemental locks. Don't want your windows to slide unless you say so? Here are a few auxiliary locks that will keep them in place:

- Track stops prevent sliding by fitting directly over the track and locking in place with either a bolt-and-handle combo or a heavy-duty tab-head screw.
- Keyed track stops are track stops that use a lock and key rather than a bolt and handle. If you choose this style, keep things simple and safe for emergencies by making sure that all track stops in a room share the same key, and stow that key within reach but out of sight.

HOW A SLIDING WINDOW WORKS

A sliding window has two sashes that slide side to side; sometimes one is stationary. Tracks along the top and bottom of the window frame guide the sashes. Usually a groove in the bottom of each sash fits over a ridge in the bottom channel. There may be additional glides or rollers on the sash that ride on the ridge. A latch handle at the point where sash frames overlap locks the sashes together when the window is closed.

Casement Windows

Casement windows operate like doors, swinging open, rather than up and down or side to side. Constant use can wear down a casement window's opening mechanisms, but you can prevent this—and make sure that your casement windows have a long life—by lubricating the mechanisms as soon as you notice that the cranks are growing stiff. As is true of any windows, replacing these windows is expensive, but newer models will at least save you a bundle on energy costs.

YOUR COST SAVINGS

$425

Cost to replace a 3-foot-by-5-foot (1 by 1.5 metre) casement window with a new thermopane unit.

Care and Maintenance

Clean your casements, inside and out. On most casement windows you have to remove the screen to reach the glass. But once you do, it's simple to clean the inside of the glass—and then the outside because the sash swings out on hinge arms giving you access to the pane exterior. When cleaning, be sure to wipe the gasket around the perimeter with a mild soap solution.

Lubricate the mechanism. If a casement window's crank is not moving as easily as it once did, the opening mechanism probably needs attention. Loosen the setscrew at the base of the crank handle and remove the handle; then pop off the operator cover. Give a shot of silicone spray to any visible gears and all pivot points, including those on the guide arm. If you don't see any gears, it means the gears have been permanently encased and lubricated; just spray the pivot points. Reassemble the operator components, and your casement window will come back swinging.

Keep the windows shut when it rains. Be sure to close casement windows during inclement weather to keep the operator block and crank handle away from harmful, corrosive moisture.

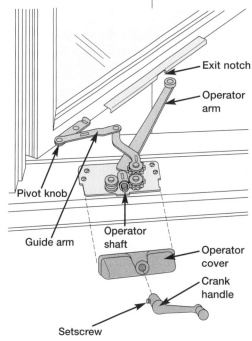

Exit notch
Operator arm
Pivot knob
Guide arm
Operator shaft
Operator cover
Crank handle
Setscrew

4 SECRETS TO SHOPPING FOR REPLACEMENT WINDOWS

Even after years of tender loving care, there may come a day when your windows need to be replaced. Today's "smart" windows not only match the good looks of your originals but can help pay for themselves by keeping heating and cooling dollars in your pocket. Here are the major points to consider:

1. Match the original window, then go one better. Replace existing windows with new units of the same configuration (double-hung with double-hung, casement with casement), and look into features that make them easier to clean (such as tilt-in sashes) and more securely locking.

2. Choose a frame that's a good balance of care and cost. Contemporary manufacturers offer a range of framing materials, including wood, vinyl- or aluminum-clad, and all-vinyl. Wood looks great but is high maintenance. All-vinyl is very energy efficient, low mainte-nance, and lowest in cost but can crack or warp from extreme cold or hot weather. Vinyl- or aluminum-clad windows are covered with vinyl or aluminum on the exposed out-side surfaces with wood on the inside. They are low main-tenance with great energy efficiency and longevity but are expensive.

3. Choose an energy-saving glass. Double-glazed win-dows will give you maximum energy savings. Nontoxic, odorless, colorless gases such as krypton and argon are set between double panes for extra insulation, and coatings on "low-E" glass reflect infrared light to keep heat out-side during summer and inside during cooler weather.

4. Know your U-factor. Look for the Canadian Energy Rating (ER) System sticker, which rates the window's energy performance. The U-factor, for instance, indicates how well the window keeps heat from escaping. Other ratings tell you how effectively it blocks the sun's heat, how much light it lets through, and the rate at which it lets air seep in.

How to Replace a Worn-Out Operator

With all the use they get on some windows, casement operators are bound to wear out. Replacement is relatively simple.

1. Loosen the handle's SETSCREW and remove the handle. Then gently pull off the cover. If the cover won't come off, go to the next step.

----

2. Pry up the STOP that hides the operator's arms. Partially open the window and press down on the operator arm so that its end slips out of the exit notch in the sash track.

----

3. Slide the GUIDE ARM off the pivot knobs. Remove screws holding operator and replace the operator.

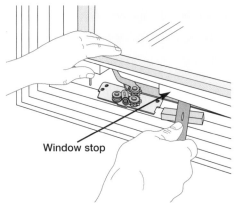

Window stop

Easy Fixes

Using carbon paper to figure out where a window sticks. Weather conditions, overzealous applications of insulation, and the natural settling of a house can all lead to swelling and sticking in wooden casement windows. Pinpoint problem spots by slipping a piece of carbon paper between the sash and the frame in different places around the window's perimeter, opening and closing the window as you go; binding points will be revealed with carbon marks on the sash side. Level the high spots on the sash by sanding them down or by using a hand plane to remove a few shavings. Touch up the bare wood.

Remedying crank problems. If your crank is loose or just not turning smoothly, try tightening the setscrew near the handle's base. If that doesn't do the trick, loosen the setscrew, pull the handle off, and check the teeth inside it. If they are rounded, replace the handle. Finding an exact handle match can be a problem, but you can get a generic replacement kit that offers enough shaft adapters to accommodate a range of casement mechanisms.

Keeping blinds from getting caught in the hardware. Window blinds tend to catch on (and are sometimes damaged by) the standard long crank handle on casement window operators. Replace the handle with a more blind-friendly T-handle.

HOW A CASEMENT WINDOW WORKS

The third basic window type has side-mounted sashes that are opened from the inside by an operator block and its crank handle. Guide and operator arms connect from the operator mechanism to the underside of the sash to control its movement and positioning. Casement windows also offer secure sealing thanks to a one-piece, sash-surrounding gasket and locking system. Screening is located on the windows' interior.

Hinged Doors

In most homes, you'll find two types of hinged doors: solid exterior doors and hollow-core interior doors. No matter where they are or what kind you have, hinged doors can fall prey to changes in temperature and humidity, the rigors of frequent use, and the breakdown of their mechanical components. In fact, few other moving parts of a house see as much use—and sometimes abuse—as its doors. Replacement doors can be had inexpensively, but this is one case in which you really do get what you pay for: Is a few extra bucks worth your family's security?

Care and Maintenance

Wash your exterior doors. Facing the elements and daily household traffic, the outside surfaces of entry doors can pick up dust and grime that not only dulls their appearance but also corrodes their hardware and finish. That's why you need to clean your door every few months. First, do a thorough dry wipe-down to remove surface dust. Follow with an application of a water-based cleaning compound. For stained wooden doors, use a wood oil soap, such as Murphy's. For painted finishes, use a homemade mix of a cup (250 ml) of ammonia and a good squirt of mild dish-washing liquid in a gallon (4 litres) of warm water. Using a natural sponge, scrub the door in small circular motions from the bottom up; rinse the sponge often and make a new batch of cleanser if needed to avoid re-dirtying the door.

Polish the hardware. Once the door is dry, give its trimmings some attention. Protect surfaces around the doorknob, knocker, kick plate, and other hardware with plastic wrap secured with masking tape; then polish the hardware with a metal cleaner. Clean glass or ceramic doorknobs with a soft cloth dampened with rubbing alcohol.

Tighten a loose doorknob. Do you have a doorknob that's a little wobbly? Simply loosen the setscrews holding the knobs in place on either side of the door and center the spindle on which they turn so that it extends equally on both sides of the door. Then reposition the knobs and adjust the setscrews for a snug but not binding fit.

Lubricate locks with graphite. Never use an oil-based lubricant on locks; it can attract dust and grime. Instead, give locks an occasional blast of powdered graphite, a dry lubricant that comes in a squeeze bottle for easy application. It's sold at hardware stores. Powdered graphite can also be applied to latches and hinges.

Silence hinges with a little oil. Keep hardworking hinges from squeaking with a touch of light machine oil such as 3-in-One. To apply, pry up the hinge pin slightly by tapping a screwdriver with a hammer and aim a few drops of oil onto the shaft just above the hinge's upper barrel. With a towel at the ready to catch any drips, swing the door back and forth a few times to distribute the oil over the hinge mechanism.

Keep your exterior doors weathertight. Sealing your exterior doors is an important step toward home energy savings. Whether your door is a newer model with built-in weather stripping or an old favorite in need of retrofitting, do a checkup each year before cold, damp weather arrives and add these if your door needs them. For more on each option, see the "Weather Stripping" chapter.

• Weather-strip the frame's top and sides. Several weather-stripping materials are available, and they often come in convenient kits.

SMART IDEA

If you don't have any powdered graphite on hand, just scrape off some pencil lead with a knife. To get the resulting powder in the lock, rub the powder on a key and insert it in the lock a couple of times.

ANATOMY OF AN ENTRY DOOR

The typical entry door connects to its surrounding frame via three hinges on one side and knob-controlled latches and locks on the other.

Solid-wood paneled doors are made up of vertical stiles and horizontal rails with panels in between; there are expansion gaps between all of these elements so they can expand and contract with changes in humidity.

Solid-core flush doors usually have a particleboard or wood-block core sandwiched between two plywood surfaces.

Hollow-core doors are lighter-weight versions for interior rooms that have a cardboard-lattice core.

Steel- and fiberglass-clad doors often mimic the look of wood

paneled doors and are common in new construction. They have a core of rigid insulation that provides superior energy

conservation. They are also more durable and maintenance-free than wood doors.

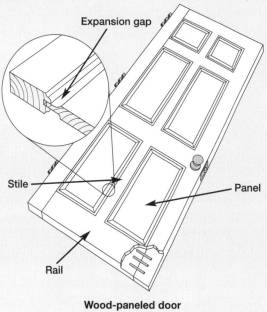

Wood-paneled door

- Install a sweep on the door's bottom edge. A sweep has a metal flange with a rubber strip that acts as a seal against the threshold.
- Or install threshold weather stripping. Close the gap under your door with the less-obtrusive configuration of a rubber gasket installed in an oak or metal threshold. Make your selection based on aesthetics and what will work best for your door, as well as some comparison shopping.

How to Get a **Binding Door** *Moving Smoothly*

Changes in humidity and natural shifting of your house may leave you with a swollen, sticking door, but you can often fix it using this trial-and-error approach.

1. Try tightening all HINGE SCREWS. Fix any that are stripped as described in "Fixing loose hinges" on the next page.

2. If that doesn't solve the problem, hold a block of wood against the NON-HINGED side of the door and give it a whack with a hammer to see if that widens the opening enough to stop the binding.

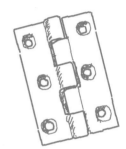

3. If the door STILL BINDS, close it and examine it closely to find the sticking points along its edges. Use a pencil to mark them.

4. SAND DOWN the problem areas, using first coarse, then fine, sandpaper. If you need to remove more than 1/8 inch (3 mm) of wood, you may use a small block plane.

5. Once you unstick the door, PRIME AND PAINT exposed wood to prevent moisture from seeping in. Use thin coats of paint.

Easy Fixes

Silencing rattling doors. If your door rattles, the problem is that the door doesn't fit snuggly against the doorstop, the strip of wood on the frame that the door hits when it closes. Here is one easy adjustment you can make: Remove the strike plate—the catch on the frame that the latch bolt goes into—and use pliers to slightly bend out its tongue-like flange so that it will hold the door more tightly against the doorstop.

Quieting rattling doors, part two. If adjusting the strike plate doesn't stop the rattling, try moving the doorstop so that it fits more tightly against the door. To do this, use a sharp utility knife to free the stop from surrounding paint along both of its sides;

then use a hammer with a wood block to tap the stop about 1/8 inch (3 mm) so it is closer to the door. Close the door to test the fit (it should hit the stop and the latch at the same time), then use a few finish nails to secure the stop in its new position.

Curing a self-closing door. If a door swings shut and you don't want it to, its frame is likely out of plumb due to faulty installation or the natural settling of your house. An easy way to correct the problem is to increase resistance at the hinges by removing the hinge pins and hitting them with a hammer to bend them slightly so that they fit more snugly into their hinge holes.

Fixing a hard-to-close door. Do you have to give a door an extra shove to get it to close all the way? Likely, the door is either warped or has bound hinges (meaning they're completely closed before the door is). Rule out warping (which is best fixed by replacing the door) by closing the door and checking to make sure it's hitting all the stops along the top and sides. If it is, then adjust the hinges by cutting strips of thin cardboard that are the same length as the hinges and half their width. Unscrew the hinges from the jamb one at a time (put a supporting wedge under the door), and place a strip in each hinge mortise against the barrel side of the hinge. Experiment with the thickness and numbers of strips needed to unbind the door.

Quelling wood swelling and sticking. Wooden doors can be magnets for moisture, which causes them to swell and stick. Keep moisture at bay by making sure that both the top and bottom edges of a door are painted or varnished to properly seal the end grain. Give paint strength and staying power with an undercoat of primer.

Filing door latches. If a door won't latch properly because the strike plate is higher than the bolt, a little filing could do the trick. First observe how the latch bolt hits the strike plate on the frame when the door closes. Look for wear marks left by the bolt. Carefully file the opening in the strike plate to enlarge the hole a bit at a time until the bolt fits in. You can also use your file to slightly round the edges of the bolt itself.

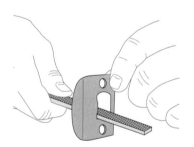

Fixing loose hinges. If some of a hinge's screw holes have become stripped—the screws just spin when you turn them—you have two choices:

- Replace the screws with ones that are the same size, but about an inch (2.5 cm) longer so that they will penetrate into solid wood in the framing.
- Remove the screws, and plug the holes with wood toothpicks that have been dipped in carpenter's glue. When the glue has dried, shave away the protruding

SMART IDEA

You can paint the hard-to-reach bottom edge of a door without removing it by using a carpet scrap as your brush. Cut the scrap to a width that can be held comfortably in both hands, slather its pile side with paint, and slide it under the open door, pulling the carpet scrap back and forth for a smooth and easy coating.

toothpick ends with a utility knife. Then drill new pilot holes, and drive the screws back into place through the hinge plate.

Replacing strike plates. If a door won't latch because the old plate and jamb are worn or damaged, buy a slightly larger strike plate from a well-stocked hardware store and install in place of the old one. You'll have to slightly chisel the mortise—the slot on the jamb the plate fit into—to enlarge it.

Raising the strike plate. If a door won't latch because the bolt doesn't reach all the way to the strike plate, make the strike plate protrude more by putting one or more layers of thin cardboard behind the strike plate. Remove the strike plate and use it as template to mark cut lines on the cardboard.

Installing a kick plate. If you've got a wooden door that sees a lot of traffic and a bit of roughhousing, consider installing a kick plate. Lending surface protection and a touch of style, these easy additions are made to span the bottom rail and the lower portions of the adjoining stiles. Apply them to interior or exterior doors, on one side or both. Finishes ranging from traditional brass to black steel are available to complement any design scheme.

Patching a hollow-core door. There's no need to replace a hollow-core door with a hole in it if you've got a little aluminum foil and powdered wood filler on hand. Carefully remove the splintered wood surrounding the hole, and then pack the hole with a wad of foil. Prepare the wood filler and apply it with a putty knife to fill the space between and over the foil, smoothing the repaired area. After it dries, give the surface a good sanding, and you're set to prime and paint either the patched area or the whole door.

PENETRATING OIL SPRAY: A LOCK'S BEST FRIEND

GET A STUBBORN LOCK TURNING

If it's difficult to turn your door lock, first try an application of penetrating oil spray, such as WD-40, to clean and lubricate the mechanism. Have a cloth in hand to catch any resulting runoff. (If this doesn't turn things around, the problem may be a poorly cut key; have a new one made from a functional original.)

REMOVE A TRAPPED KEY

It's not uncommon for older locks to trap keys as a result of dried-out, misaligned pins. Get your key out by giving the lock a dose of WD-40 or other penetrating oil spray and then rotating and jiggling the key. The key should come right out, but if it doesn't, pinch the key as your other fingertips touch the lock for leverage, and slowly work out the key.

OPEN A FROZEN LOCK

If a lock responds to wintry weather by giving you the freeze-out, loosen it by spraying a little of the lubricant into its mechanism (avoid oil-based lubricants—they'll only make matters worse). Another way to thaw things out is by carefully preheating your key with a match before inserting it in the lock.

5 WAYS TO MAKE YOUR FRONT DOOR MORE SECURE

No matter how solid your door, it's ultimately only as strong as its heavy metal. Here are a few hardware upgrades to consider if you want to beef up your home's security.

1. Add a heavy-duty dead bolt. A dead bolt is a low-cost, high-value addition to your security system. Varieties include double-cylinder dead bolts, which are keyed on both sides, and single-cylinder dead bolts, keyed on one side. Whichever type you choose, make sure it has a grade 1 security rating, and follow the next suggestion below to connect it securely and solidly to the frame.

2. Add a strike box. A strike box toughens up your entry and deters intruders by replacing existing strike plates with a structure that includes a metal pocket, oversized plates, and a solid connection into the wall stud behind the doorjamb with 3-inch (8 cm) screws. To accommodate this addition, you'll need to enlarge both the hole in the jamb and the cover plate recess.

3. Add a reinforcer plate. Three-sided metal reinforcement plates add an extra layer of security by encasing a door around its handset or dead bolt. To select the correct size for your door, measure its thickness, the handset or dead bolt hole diameter, and the distance between its edge and the center of the handset or dead bolt (known as the setback). A reinforcement plate will typically extend the door's edge a bit, so you may need to deepen the hinge mortises on the other side of the door to prevent catching and sticking.

4. Rekey the lock. If you're not the first to live in your present abode, rekeying the entry locks is yet another way to enhance its security. Rekeying kits matching most lock brands can be found at hardware stores and

home-improvement centers and work on both entrance and dead-bolt locks. They also allow up to six locks to be rekeyed for the same key.

5. Install a wide-angle peephole. You'll be able to do a larger-scale screening of unexpected visitors with a wide-angle peephole viewer. This easy-to-install safety accessory is designed to fit any door up to 2 inches (5 cm) thick.

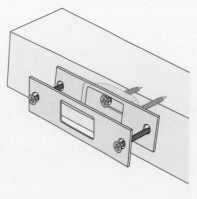

Sliding Doors

Sliding patio doors are popular for several reasons. They not only have a convenient, space-saving design, but their expansive glasswork lets in ample sunshine and provides a largely unobstructed view of the landscape. They can also be more energy-efficient than you might expect—especially the contemporary models that feature specially coated glass and well-insulated frames. The only tasks you're left to worry about are maintaining the mechanisms that keep your door gliding along and ensuring that it's always secured against intruders.

Care and Maintenance

Wipe metal frames with window cleaner. Many patio door frames are made of aluminum because it's affordable, rust resistant, and easy to maintain. They are also usually finished with a tough protective coating, so all that's needed to maintain their good looks is an occasional wipe-down. So if you've got a bottle of window cleaner in hand to clean the door's glass, go ahead and use it on the frame as well. A shot of all-purpose household cleaner in water is also fine for cleaning them.

Treat the track with alcohol. Dust and grime just love to settle in a patio door's bottom track. Every time you vacuum nearby flooring, give the track a once-over. Then every few weeks, clean the track with a soft cloth wetted with denatured alcohol.

Lube the track with wax. After you finish cleaning your patio door's bottom track, run a bar of paraffin wax along the track in long, even strokes to further smooth its way.

Easy Fixes

Getting your door back on track. The heavy use that patio doors get in high-traffic areas can lead to occasional sticks and skips. It's smartest to do the preemptive tune-up described on this spread, but if your door already has problems when you slide it, don't panic. Survey the gaps along its top and bottom edges. Then grab your screwdriver and find the roller adjustment screws, located along the edge of the door's bottom rail. Remove the button-size covers and turn the screws counterclockwise to lower the door in its track, or clockwise to raise it. Then, check the gaps again to confirm that they're uniform; if they aren't, grab your screwdriver again and adjust as needed.

"Locking" your door with screws and a stick. Patio doors may be heavy, but clever crooks know how to exploit their weak points. So, as with sliding windows, keep your door and your stuff from being lifted by driving a couple of screws into the top track, allowing their heads to protrude; this way, the door can't be removed from its track unless the screws are removed first. Supplement this setup by placing a cut-to-fit dowel in the lower track to prevent the door from being jimmied open.

How to Tune Up Your Patio Door

Keep your patio door rolling along with occasional attention to its wheels. You'll have to remove the door to get at the rollers, and since patio doors tend to be heavy, have an assistant on hand to help with removing the door and moving it to a place where you can work on it.

1. To REMOVE THE DOOR, retract its rollers by turning the adjustment screw completely counterclockwise (see illustration); then lift the door up and out of the bottom track. Some sliding doors have a retaining strip, or head stop, screwed to the top inside edge of the frame. You may have to remove the stop to get the door out. If that's the case, have your helper hold the door to keep it from falling into the room. Then place the door on your work surface.

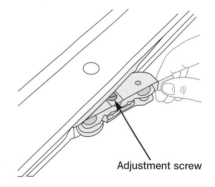

Adjustment screw

2. Carefully REMOVE THE ROLLERS from their pockets along the bottom edge of the door and inspect the assemblies. Damaged rollers can be easily replaced at a well-stocked hardware store or home center; take the old ones along to get a matching replacement. If the rollers are simply grimy, remove any loose dirt and wipe them clean with a soft cloth and denatured alcohol. Finish with a shot of silicone spray, and replace the rollers in their pockets, making sure the assemblies are in a completely retracted position (you may have to tap them in gently with a hammer).

3. Use the same CLEANING AND LUBING routine (denatured alcohol followed by silicone spray) with the head stop (if any) and head track.

4. Reattach or replace any WEATHER STRIPPING that's missing, damaged, or lost its elasticity. Wipe the bottom track clean as described on the facing page.

5. REINSTALL THE DOOR and, if necessary, reattach the head stop. Slide the door just short of its closed position, and turn the adjustment screws clockwise to release the rollers and bring the door into a position parallel with the jamb.

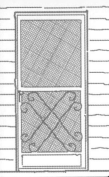

Storm Windows, Doors, and Screens

Screens and storm windows strengthen your home's exterior seal, filtering out insects and airborne irritants and blocking the effects of weather. Storm windows in particular add an extra layer of insulation that increases energy efficiency, lowers your heating bills, and diminishes noise pollution and sun damage. Storms and screens are relatively low maintenance and long lasting. It's easy to extend their lives by including them in your upkeep routines.

Care and Maintenance

Clean your screens. Insect screens are magnets for surface gunk. But it's easy to clean them if you first hose them off and then use the right cleaning solution. If you take down screens for winter, clean them before putting them away for the season. Otherwise, clean them in the spring.

- Take them down. Remove the screens from doors and windows, and lay them on the driveway or other flat, protected outdoor surface, preferably with a drop cloth or tarp underneath.
- Make your own cleaning solution. In a bucket, mix up a cleaning solution of 3 quarts (3 litres) warm water, 1 quart (1 litre) ammonia, 2 tablespoons (30 ml) borax, and 2 good squirts of dishwashing liquid.
- Hose, spray, and wait. Wearing rubber gloves, fill a spray bottle with the solution, and after rinsing screens thoroughly with a garden hose, treat both sides with the cleaner. Wait five minutes for the cleaning solution to loosen grime, and follow up by gently scrubbing with a soft-bristle brush. Rinse again.
- Dry them standing up. Prop the screens vertically and let them air-dry.

Wrap screens for the winter. Prepare your screens for the off-season by wrapping them for storage after cleaning them. Plastic sheeting, ink-free newsprint, and brown wrapping paper are all great options.

Check the closer mechanism. Once a year, wipe a screen or storm door's closer—the mechanism that pulls it shut gently—with a lightly oiled cloth. Snug up any loose screws in the closer bracket by replacing them with wider ones.

Avoid "sweaty storm window" syndrome. Along the bottom edge of a storm window's frame, you'll find small vents called weep holes. They allow trapped moisture to escape, and they need to be kept clear to do their job efficiently. Clean weep holes before the onset of winter using a pipe cleaner or toothpick. If you don't, the trapped moisture will damage the window.

Easy Fixes

To patch or replace a screen? The location and extent of the damage are the key factors when deciding whether to patch a screen or replace it. If the area is small and well away from the frame's edges, a patch or even a dab of nail polish will suffice, but a larger rip, especially near an edge, calls for replacement. In either case, tend to the tear immediately to prevent bigger problems.

Sealing holes with nail polish. Mend a small hole in screening with an application of clear nail polish. Prepare the area by straightening the torn strand ends, then dab on the polish and spread with the bottle-cap brush. Before the polish is completely dry, use a toothpick or pin to pierce clogged openings in the surrounding area. You can also do the same trick with epoxy glue; apply it with a cotton swab.

Patching metal screens. Repair an aluminum screen with a patch of the same material. Neatly trim the damaged area and cut a patch 2 inches (5 cm) larger all around than the hole. Remove a few strands from all four sides of the patch and bend the exposed ends 90 degrees. Then carefully push the ends through the screen around the hole and press the ends flat against the other side to secure them.

Patching fiberglass screens. Cut a patch of scrap fiberglass screening a half inch larger all around than the hole. Apply a thin bead of epoxy around the patch and glue it over the hole, aligning the pattern. Smooth and blot off excess glue before it dries.

Lifting sagging screen doors. Taking the droop out of a wooden screen door is simple with a door brace and turnbuckle kit from your local hardware stores. Install the brace diagonally across the door, with one end at the top, hinge-side corner and the other at the bottom, latch-side corner. Tighten the turnbuckle until the sag is gone.

SMART IDEA

When removing storm windows or screens for cleaning or storage, prevent mismatches by writing a number on each window frame in a hidden spot, and then mark the frame of the corresponding storm or screen with the same number. Store fasteners in individual self-sealing sandwich bags and write the same number on the bag.

On a metal frame screen, the screening is usually held in place by a spline—a long, thin piece of vinyl that fits into a groove around the frame's inside edge. Always buy new spline; take a piece of the old spline to the store to get the right size. Also pick up an inexpensive tool called a spline roller, which you need to force the spline into the groove.

1. Place the SCREEN on a flat work surface, and use a small screw driver to pry out the old spline. Remove the damaged screening.

- -

2. Cut NEW SCREENING about an inch wider than the opening on all sides. Place it over the frame, making sure it's straight. Clamp one long side in place with clip-on clamps.

- -

3. Starting at a CORNER on the side opposite the clamps, pull the screening taut by hand and gradually force the new spline into the groove with a spline roller.

- -

4. Continue around the PERIMETER. As you approach each corner, clip metal screening at a 45-degree angle to the frame to prevent bunching. (It's okay to let fiberglass bunch up.) Use a screwdriver to press the spline down at corners.

- -

5. TRIM AWAY excess screening around the edges of the groove using a sharp utility knife held at an angle.

- -

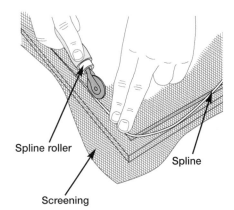

Spline roller

Spline

Screening

Garage Doors

Your garage door is your home's biggest moving part, with a hardworking but sensitive behind-the-scenes network of springs, rollers, hinges, and tracks. And because it can pose a hazard to your safety—say, if it accidentally closes on you or is rigged open by a home intruder—it's best to stay on top of its upkeep. While electronic door openers are more convenient, they add a few more to-dos to the maintenance list. Keeping everything in good working order isn't hard, though. You'll be glad you did when you find out how much your neighbors are paying to have these doors and opening systems replaced!

YOUR COST SAVINGS

$1,000

What you would pay to install a single, sectional garage door and opener.

Care and Maintenance

Lubricate all its moving parts. It's essential: you must oil all moving parts every year. Apply lightweight oil such as 3-in-One to roller and hinge pivots; apply spray-on white lithium grease to the opener's chain- or screw-drive, and a cleaner-lubricant such as WD-40 to the springs. Go easy, though—too much oil will collect dirt. Clean tracks by wiping them with a cloth dampened with oil. Follow your owner's manual if its instructions differ.

Test your door's auto-reverse with a 2-by-4. Test your garage-door opener's auto-reverse safety feature every month. Raise the door. Place a 2-by-4 flat on the ground in the door's path, and hit the remote again. The door should instantly reverse as it touches the 2-by-4; if it doesn't, increase its close limit, following the guidelines in your owner's manual.

Test the door balance. Pull the release cord or lever to disconnect the opener. You should now be able to lower the door halfway and have it hold its position, with only a slight movement above or below the halfway point. If the door rides back up or falls, have a pro adjust the spring tension.

Wash and wax your door. Extend your garage door's life by protecting its surfaces from dirt and corrosion. Dust the door both inside and outside, then wipe it down with a mild household

take care

A garage door's weight is counterbalanced by either a torsion spring mounted on the header above the door or a pair of side-mounted extension springs above the roller tracks. These tightly coiled springs can injure you if they snap or come loose. If they need adjustment or replacement, call a garage door installer. Always have both springs in a pair replaced. Also call a pro if the lift cables, attached to the bottom bracket, are frayed and need to be replaced.

detergent in water. Spray lightly with a hose to rinse. If the door is metal with an enamel finish, apply car wax on the exterior to seal out damaging grime and moisture.

Keep water away. Water splashing on the bottom of your garage door will eventually cause problems—rust on a metal door or peeling paint and rot on a wooden one. Make sure that your gutters keep water away from the door and that the surrounding landscape doesn't drain water onto the drive in front of the door. Clear away snow before it melts and refreezes, sticking the door to the driveway.

Seal out moisture with caulk and paint. On a multi-panel wood garage door, protect the vulnerable bottom section from moisture by caulking the seam where the bottom horizontal rail meets the panels. Seal the door's bottom and side edges and all seams around panels with paint.

Keep weather stripping clean and flexible. Every couple of months, wipe the weather stripping around the edges of the garage door frame and along the bottom of the door with vinyl cleaner. Then spray with silicone lubricant to keep it pliable. This also helps keep the bottom seal from sticking to the snow.

Send the kids to the ball field. Why do kids seem to think that garage doors are the perfect backstops for batting practice? Tell them to hoof it to the park—balls can dent a metal door and cause any garage door's parts to loosen or become misaligned. (And even though everybody does it, it's not a smart idea to put a basketball hoop over the door either.)

Easy Fixes

Quieting the rattling. Loose, rattling components are usually the culprits behind noisy garage doors. Do a systematic check to find the source of the noise. In particular, check and tighten the bolts on loose hinges and roller mounts. Also keep moving parts well lubricated. Chain drives tend to be the biggest noisemakers.

Is the problem the tracks or the opener? If your garage door's operation becomes sluggish, pull the release cord or lever to disconnect the opener. If the door opens fine manually, the electric opener is the problem; check your owner's manual or call for help. If the door is still hard to open manually, the problem is rollers binding in the tracks. Lubricate the rollers and look for damaged rollers or tracks that are out of alignment.

Repairing broken rollers. To replace a bent or broken roller, just unbolt and remove its hinged bracket; take the roller with you to a home center or garage door dealer to get a matching replacement. Do not, however, remove the bottom roller bracket to which the door's lift cables are attached; if it's broken, call a pro.

Realigning tracks. Measure between the tracks on either side at several locations to figure out where they are not parallel. With a roll-up door, check the radius sections of the track extra carefully. If a track is off, it's easy to shift it a smidgen because its mounting bolts are in elongated slots. Just loosen the mounting bolt in the area that needs adjustment and use a hammer and a small block of wood to nudge the track. Then retighten the bolt.

Stopping rusting and flaking. Sand the areas down to bare metal using emery cloth. Apply metal primer, then two coats of spray paint matching the original finish.

Touching up peeling paint. Sand the affected areas until smooth. Then apply a mildew-resistant primer and two finish coats of paint. (This also works on black smudges that indicate mold.)

Repairing a cracked seal. If the seal along your door's bottom edge is cracked or broken, replace it with a matching one to maintain robust weather resistance and reliable door security. Most seals come with instructions and are simple to install; just make sure any wide flanges face inward, especially if you live in a cold climate; a protruding flange can freeze to the driveway.

Asphalt Shingles

You can expect an asphalt shingle roof—the kind that most homes have—to last for 20 years or more. This figure can vary, depending on the quality of roofing material and its exposure to severe weather. How long your roof lasts also depends on watchful care—being able to spot and repair or replace damaged shingles as soon as possible. Yes, it's that important to be vigilant about your shingles: Not only is replacing a roof one of the most expensive home-improvement projects that you can undertake, but unattended damage to your home's uppermost surface means that interior wall stains, floor damage, and costly moisture remediation are soon to follow.

Care and Maintenance

Inspect your roof with binoculars. You don't have to climb up on your roof to check it out. Every spring and fall, go outdoors on a sunny day and examine your roof from ground level, using binoculars. Shingles with bare areas indicate that the granules on the surface are wearing away; look for loose granules in gutters or below downspouts. Watch these shingles closely for signs of future damage. Fix any curled or cracked shingles. Also check for other roof problems such as crumbling chimney mortar and deteriorating flashing.

Trace that leak's twisted path. Once or twice a year or anytime you see evidence of a leak (such as a stain on a ceiling or peeling paint), inspect the underside of your

WHEN IS IT OKAY TO PUT NEW SHINGLES OVER OLD ONES?

Even with the best care, you'll eventually have to reshingle your entire roof. Should you add the new shingles over the existing ones? This can usually be done once, if your local building code permits, and you'll get a good-as-new roof and not have to pay for someone to tear off and dispose of the old shingles. If you live in a heavy-snow area, however, you may not want to do this; the weight of snow over two sets of shingles may prove too much for the framing. Get expert advice from a local roofing professional.

roof inside the attic. Using a flashlight, check for watermarks left by a leak on rafters and insulation. A leak rarely travels in a straight line. Even better, trace the leak when it's active during a downpour. When you pinpoint the source, mark the spot and measure the distances from there to the roof's peak and to an outside wall or chimney. Use your measurements to locate the problem's rooftop source.

Disguise a blemish with caulk. To fix a small gouge in a shingle, clean the area thoroughly and apply a bead of silicone caulk. Then use this trick to disguise the repair: Rub together the top surfaces of two scraps of shingle above the blemished area. Granules will come loose and embed themselves in the fresh caulk, disguising the fix.

Easy Fixes

Repairing damaged shingles. To avoid worse problems down the line, repair a damaged shingle as soon as you can.

- If a shingle is partially lifted or curling, just glue it down with a dab of roofing cement under the corner.
- If a shingle is torn, apply roofing cement under both sides of the tear and then press down firmly. Drive roofing nails around the edges of the tear and cover the nail heads with roofing cement.

How to Replace a Damaged Shingle

A shingle with mild damage—a tear, small hole, or turned-up corner—can be fixed as described above, under Easy Fixes. But if the damage is more severe, it's best to replace it.

1. Gently lift the SHINGLES overlapping the damaged one and remove the nails from the damaged shingle with a pry bar. Being careful not to crack the good shingles, pull out the bad shingle. Slip a new shingle underneath the raised edges of the shingles above.

2. Use a HAMMER and the pry bar to nail down the new shingle. Angle the pry bar under the overlapping shingle, with the far end of the pry bar over the nail; with the hammer, drive the nail by striking the near end of the pry bar. This keeps you from bending the overlapping shingles too far up and cracking them.

3. Dab roofing CEMENT under all the affected shingles. Press them down firmly.

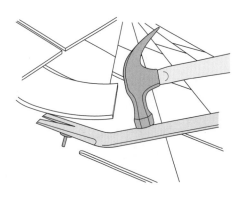

- Seal a hole smaller than a nickel or a crack less than 1/2 inch (1 cm) long with roofing cement. Fill an enlarged nail hole the same way, but first, drive the nail down below the shingle, using a nail set.

Using metal patches. Instead of replacing a heavily damaged shingle, especially on an old roof or in an inconspicuous area, use a metal patch. Cut it from sheet aluminum and coat one side with roofing cement. Slip it, cement side down, under the damaged shingle. Then dab roofing cement on top of the patch and embed the shingle in it. This quick patch doesn't require nails.

Patching ridge shingles. If a shingle along the peak, or top ridge, of the roof is damaged, repair it with an asphalt shingle patch. Cut the patch to overlap the damaged area by 3 inches (8 cm) on all sides and gently bend it to fit. Cement the patch into place and secure its corners with roofing nails, but before you finish driving in the nails, dab the area around them with roofing cement. Afterward, cover the nail heads with cement as well to prevent leaks.

Ladder Safety

Whether you climb up on the roof yourself or hire a handyman to take care of repairs on your roof or eaves, you want make sure you have the right kind of ladder for the job, and that it is in tip-top shape and set up safely. Wear soft-soled shoes with a bit of grip and comfortable clothing that is not too snug or too baggy. Sweep a roof clean of any debris that you might slip on—and beware of slippery moss and algae. If your roof is steep (with a pitch of over 30 degrees) or is two or more stories off the ground, hire a pro. He'll use a safety harness and other protective gear.

YOUR COST SAVINGS
$87
According to the Canadian Institute for Health Information, the average cost to the Canadian taxpayer for an emegency-room visit.

A Safe Ladder

Buy a sturdy model. Make sure your ladder can handle your weight and the weight of the tools and materials you'll be carrying. Ladders are rated for load capacity. Always buy a ladder rated Type I (heavy duty) or Type II (medium duty); they're sturdier and safer than Type III (light duty).

Does it wobble? If you haven't used your ladder in a while, inspect it for loose rungs, cracks, dents, and rot or rust. If a wood ladder feels shaky, tighten the nuts on the reinforcing rods. On an extension ladder, make sure that the safety feet pivot freely, that the sliding sections move easily and lock solidly into place, and that the pull rope is not frayed. Check a stepladder for loose hinges.

Ladder Set-Up

Check your ladder's angle. To make sure you've got your ladder at the correct 75-degree angle, stand straight with your toes at the foot of the ladder. From that position, you should be able to stretch out your arms and rest your hands on the rungs at your shoulder height.

Keep your ladder from sinking. You need to give your ladder firm footing when the ground is rain-soaked or muddy. Set the ladder's feet on a wide board or a solid piece of plywood staked into the ground. To keep the ladder's feet from shifting, nail cleats to the board at the base and at the sides.

SMART IDEA

If you plan to use a ladder to access your roof, make sure that the weather forecast for that day is favorable. Work on a dry, mild, wind-less day after the dew evaporates. Severe heat and cold, wet and icy surfaces, and gusty winds are all hazardous.

SMART IDEA

Never store a ladder outside or in an unlocked garage. A burglar may use it to reach an unlocked window that would otherwise be out of reach. If you have to leave a ladder out, chain it securely to a tree or a fence post.

Put boots on a ladder's feet. On more solid ground, you can create a foothold for a ladder that doesn't have rubber feet by slipping the ladder's feet into an old pair of rubber boots. This will give the ladder added traction and keep it from sliding while you're climbing. You can also tie a ladder's feet to stakes in the ground.

Put socks on the ladder's tips. Before leaning the top end of a ladder against your siding, slip a couple of old heavy socks over each top end and tie them in place with string. You can also tie old rags around the ends or put old work gloves over them. Or you can buy rubber covers that fit over the ends.

Extend your ladder 3 feet. When you are using a ladder to climb onto the roof, make sure to extend it so that the top is at least 3 feet (1 metre) above the edge of the roof. This gives you something to hold onto when you are stepping onto or off the roof. Always start from a rung below the roof edge and step *up* onto the roof.

Is a window in the way? If a job calls for you to rest the top of your ladder on a window, buy a U-shaped stabilizer bar that attaches to the top of the ladder to span windows.

Don't let an opening door topple your ladder. When putting a ladder in front of a door, lock and brace the door so that no one can unknowingly fling it open, toppling the ladder (and you). Warn other people in your household where and when you'll be working from such heights.

Avoid being shocked by power lines. When you are setting up or moving a ladder and when working on it, be careful to stay away from power lines. A metal or wet wood ladder is especially hazardous.

On the Ladder

Remember the "three points of contact" rule. Use both hands to steady yourself as you climb. When working, keep your weight centered between the side rails. Overreaching may end in disaster. You'll be okay if you remember this rule: Always maintain three points of contact with the ladder—either two hands and a foot or two feet and a hand.

Use a pull-up bucket or tool belt. Don't carry your tools and materials in your hands while climbing a ladder. Instead put them in a bucket with a long rope and haul them up once you're safely on the roof or at your working height on the ladder. Or carry them in a tool belt secured around your waist, with the weight evenly distributed to keep them from throwing you off balance.

Wood Shingles and Shakes

A wood shingle or shake roof not only has a welcoming natural look but surprisingly lasts years longer than an asphalt-tile one. Wood is an organic material, however, and it is subject to mold, mildew, and fungus—all of which are precipitated by moisture and can eventually cause the wood to rot. Whether you do it yourself or hire a handyman, the way to extend the life of a wood roof is by keeping it clean and by fixing small defects before they become major problems. Debris standing on the roof traps moisture and promotes destructive growths. A lifted edge or crack in a shingle can grow into a serious leak. And like a deck, a wood roof should be coated with preservative every few years.

YOUR COST SAVINGS

$9,785

What you would pay a contractor to strip the roof off a 2,400-square-foot (223 square metres) home and reroof with cedar shingles.

Care and Maintenance

Sweep off moisture-trapping debris. Wood-eating fungus thrives in moist places. So make sure the rain runs off your wood roof into the gutters and downspouts. Occasionally sweep the shingles clean. You may be able to do it from a ladder with a long-handled broom. Pine needles, leaves, and debris can hold in moisture after a rain and act as a perfect nest for fungus.

Use bleach and detergent to kill mildew. If your wood roof develops mildew, fungus, moss, or algae, get rid of it before it spreads. First, sweep the roof clean and prepare as much solution as you need, adding a cup of laundry detergent and a cup (250 ml) of chlorine bleach for each gallon (4 litres) of water. Cover any foundation

DO YOU HAVE SHINGLES OR SHAKES?

Both shingles and shakes are made of western red cedar, white cedar, or (less often) spruce. Shakes are hand-split and then sawn in half, giving them a rough surface on one side and a smooth surface on the other.

Shingles are machine-sawn on both sides, resulting in thin, tapered panels that are smooth on both sides. Both shingles and shakes are usually installed in single, overlapping courses. On some roofs, however, double

courses overlap one another to add depth. If you remove a shingle or shake from your roof, the pattern used will be obvious. Follow it in replacing any panels.

plants with plastic sheeting and wear rubber gloves. Start at the top of the roof and work down. Pour the solution over the shingles or spray the solution using a hand-pump garden sprayer, and then carefully sweep or brush away the growths or stains. Watch your footing, though, because the wet wood will be slippery. Once the roof is thoroughly clean, rinse with a garden hose.

Extend the life of your roof. Extend the life of your wood roof for years with a wood preservative. First, clean the roof thoroughly and rid it of any mildew or other growths, as described above; then apply a commercial wood preservative according to directions. Repeat this treatment every five years or whenever the wood starts to look dry or brittle.

Keep moss away with zinc strips. If you live in a humid climate and your roof is subject to moss and algae growth, install zinc strips at the top ridge. (They are available

How to Replace a Wood Shingle

Replacing a badly split or warped shingle (or shake) is much easier than you may think.

1. Use a WOOD CHISEL and a hammer to split the damaged shingle into pieces so you can slide it out. If the overlapping shingles are holding the damaged one tightly, gently drive wooden wedges under them to ease the pressure.

2. Use a HACKSAW BLADE with tape wrapped around it as a handle. Slip the blade under the overhanging shingles and cut off the nails that had been holding the damaged shingle. Cut a new shake 1/4 inch (0.5 cm) narrower in width than the space it goes in. This will let the shingle expand as the weather changes.

3. Slide the NEW SHINGLE under the overlapping shingles; nudge it into place by tapping it with a hammer and a block of wood. If the shingle won't go in, check for nails you may have missed. Don't force the shingle; you'll split it.

4. In the GAP between the shingles in the overlapping course, drill pilot holes and drive in two galvanized roofing nails. Use a nail set to drive the nails flush. Then cover the nail heads by sliding a small square of metal flashing under the overlapping shingles. Push screwdriver blades under the overlapping shingles to raise them a bit, if needed.

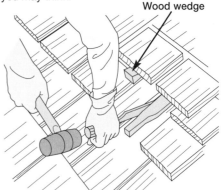

Wood wedge

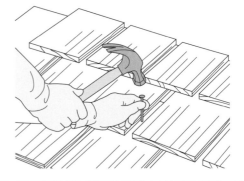

at roofing supply stores.) When rain hits the strips, they release zinc ions, which travel down the roof and inhibit the growth of moss and algae.

Easy Fixes

Straightening a curled shingle. If a shingle curls, just nail it down. Depending on how much moisture your roof is exposed to, this fast fix will take care of the problem for a few months or a year or more. But eventually the wood will swell and crack, so plan to replace the piece (see previous page).

Repairing a leaking shingle. If a wood shingle or shake cracks and is causing a leak, fix it temporarily with a piece of sheet metal. Cut a piece of sheet aluminum and slip it under the cracked shingle. Use a hammer and a block of wood to drive the sheet in, if necessary.

Aging new shingles. A new shingle on an old roof can stand out like a sore thumb, but it's simple to make a new shingle look like the other weathered shingles. Before installing the shingle, dip it in a solution of a half-pound (227 gm) of baking soda in a quart (1 litre) of water and set it aside. It will "age" to a nice gray in a couple of hours. Coat it with wood preservative before installing it.

Flashing

Flashing is the unsung hero when it comes to protecting your home from nature's watery intrusions. These sheet-metal shields line the valleys between roof sections and fit around vent pipes, skylights, and chimneys to prevent water from seeping in. If your flashing shows signs of corrosion, gets bent, or isn't covered properly by shingles, leaks are sure to follow—along with a whopping bill for water damage repair. Luckily, most flashing repairs are simple for homeowners to fix themselves.

Care and Maintenance

Get a good gander at your flashing. When you check your roof with binoculars, make sure to take a good look at all the flashing, too. Be on the lookout for corrosion, twigs and leaves clogging valleys, flashing coming loose from the chimney or pipes, and lifted shingles that are not covering flashing adequately.

Easy Fixes

Plugging small holes. First scrub the damaged spot with a wire brush to clean and roughen the metal surface. Then fill the hole with gutter sealant and smooth the patch with a putty knife. Wetting the knife with paint thinner (mineral spirits) will help you put a smooth finish on the patch.

HOW DOES FLASHING WORK?

Flashing can be made of copper, galvanized steel, or most commonly, aluminum. It doesn't create a waterproof seal but rather it overlaps or is overlapped by the roofing, diverting rainfall so that it runs harmlessly off the roof. Every joint is vulnerable, especially if it joins materials that shrink or expand at different rates, like vent pipes and shingles. Joints may also pull apart as the house settles. Chimney flashing is especially complex. To let the chimney move independently from the house, it has two-part flashing: a base flashing on the roof overlapped by a second flashing on the chimney.

Patching corroded areas. Scrub away the corrosion with a wire brush; then clean the surface thoroughly with soap and water and rinse. Cut a piece of fiberglass mesh large enough to cover the rusted area and extend beyond it at least an inch on all sides. Apply a coat of plastic roof cement to the flashing area and press the fiberglass over it, then top with a second coat of the sealant.

Sealing leaky valley joints. Valley joints—those troughs where two roof sections meet—are especially vulnerable to leaks. Usually the problem is not the flashing itself, but rather that the edges of the overlapping shingles have curled up slightly, letting water seep in. It easy to fix this problem using a cartridge of plastic roof cement in a caulking gun. Starting at the lower end of the flashing, one by one, lift the edge of each shingle that overlaps the flashing, and apply a heavy bead of roof cement to the edge of the flashing and to the top of the shingle below. Then gently press the shingle into the cement.

Capping vent pipes. If small animals and debris keep falling into your plumbing vent pipes, cover the top with hardware cloth and glue it into place with plastic roof cement.

take care

Whenever you or your contractor is on the roof, avoid stepping or kneeling on flashing or exerting any pressure to the area within 12 inches (30 cm) of it. The weight may damage the joints beneath the roofing.

How to Replace Vent Pipe Flashing

Get a telescoping two-piece flashing unit, which has a base that goes on the roof and a separate sleeve that fits snugly over the pipe.

1. Carefully LIFT THE EDGES of the shingles that overlap the vent flashing with a pry bar. Use a putty knife to scrape away any old adhesive from the undersides of the shingles. Pull out the nails holding the old flashing and remove it, being careful not to damage the surrounding shingles.

- -

2. Fit the new BASE FLASHING over the vent pipe and slide the sleeve over the pipe. Lift the shingles above and on both sides of the vent pipe and slide the new flashing underneath, rotating it as you do to ease the installation.

- -

3. Nail the FLASHING to the roof at the top and sides, making sure that the surrounding shingles will cover the nails. Seal the nail heads with roof cement. Press the surrounding shingles over the new flashing. The bottom edge of the flashing should be over the shingles below it so that it will shed water, not trap it.

- -

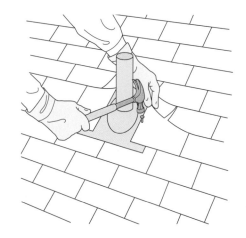

Flat Roofs

A flat roof provides less surface area to fix and care for than a sloped roof. But a flat roof—which may be gently pitched—doesn't shed rain as quickly, which is why it's essential to keep it watertight. Traditionally, flat roofs were covered with alternating layers of builder's felt and hot tar, topped with a layer of gravel. Today, the more common covering is asphalt-roll roofing, so named because it comes in rolls like carpeting. Other common flat roof coverings are usually metal—aluminum, copper, or galvanized steel—or a rubber membrane called EPDM. Most problems with metal roofs result from electrolysis, a chemical reaction that occurs when dissimilar metals touch. Fasteners, vents, and gutters should always be made of the same metal as the roof.

Care and Maintenance

Check for surface damage. Every few months, inspect your flat roof. Depending on the architectural style of your home, you may be able to inspect your flat roof by looking out a second-story window. In other cases, you'd have to access your roof by climbing a ladder. Look for holes, tears, blisters, and loose seams on an asphalt-roll roof or for rust and pitting on a metal roof. Make repairs or add patches to prevent leaks. Also check the edges of the flashing to make sure water can't seep under it.

Slather on sunblock. To protect an asphalt-roll roof against damage from the sun's ultraviolet rays, paint it with reflective asphalt aluminum paint. The paint will also lubricate the roofing and reseal the surface against water.

Give your old roof a topcoat. After a while, many asphalt roofs become a patchwork of repairs. If this is true of yours, revive the surface by simply brushing on asphalt roof coating. If the roof has any slope at all, start at the highest part and work your way down.

Renew tar and gravel over a leak. If your old-fashioned felt-and-tar roof springs a leak, scrape the area clean of gravel and apply fresh roof tar. Be sure to replace the gravel before the tar hardens. If you can't pinpoint the source of a leak, cover the entire suspected area with tar.

Easy Fixes

Lancing blisters. If you find a blister on your asphalt roll roofing, the culprit is usually trapped moisture. Slit the blister down the middle with a utility knife to release the moisture. Let the blister dry, then fill its cavity by squeezing in roofing cement from a caulking gun. Drive a row of roofing nails on each side of the split, then apply more roofing cement to the slit and the nail heads. Cut a patch of similar roofing material a couple of inches longer and wider than the damaged area. Nail the patch over the repaired area and seal the patch's edges and the nail heads with roofing cement.

Patching an aluminum roof. It's easy to fix a leak in an aluminum roof with fiberglass mesh. Cut two pieces of mesh, each large enough to generously cover the damaged area. Clean the area with a wire brush and coat it with roofing cement using a flexible putty knife. Apply one fiberglass piece over the fresh cement and cover it with more cement. Then position the second piece over the cement, and cover that piece with the final coat of cement.

Coating a pitted metal roof. Got a garage or shed with an old metal roof that has seen better days and has developed deep pitting or pinholes? You can buy another year or two of life for it with a coat of asphalt-base liquid sealant. Apply it with a stiff push broom, starting at the higher end of the roof.

SMART IDEA

When it does come time to re-roof a flat roof, consider using a reflective roof product—especially if you live in a warm climate such as the Okanagan Valley. Products like these can reduce roof surface temperatures by as much as 100°F (38°C), in turn lowering your cooling bills by up to 50 percent.

How to Patch Asphalt-Roll Roofing

1. With a UTILITY KNIFE, cut out a rectangular area surrounding the damage. Using the cutout piece as a pattern, cut a patch from new roll roofing.

2. Brush the CUTOUT AREA clean; then apply roofing cement. Use a putty knife to work the cement under all the cut edges and completely coat the opening.

3. Slip the PATCH into place. If the top of the patch is not flush with the rest of the roof, add a second patch in the same way. Secure the edges of the patch with a series of roofing nails.

4. Cut a COVER from roll roofing that is about 2 inches (5 cm) larger all around than the patch. Apply roofing cement to the top of the patch and its surrounding area. Center the new cover over the patch and press it firmly into place. Make sure all edges are sealed.

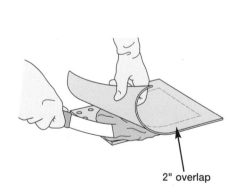

2" overlap

Gutters and Downspouts

We all hate to clean rain gutters. Is there a more thankless home-maintenance job? You can't even stand in front of your house afterward and take pride in how nice and clean they look. But whether you do the job yourself or get your yard man to do it, take comfort in knowing that your gutters and downspouts are clean and in good repair, because they are a crucial first line of defense in protecting your house from damage. By diverting runoff away from the house, they prevent it from seeping through foundation walls and literally undermining your home.

Care and Maintenance

Clean gutters around Easter and Thanksgiving. There are two times each year when you need to clean your gutters—in spring, to remove debris that has collected over the winter, and late autumn, after the last of the leaves have fallen. Clumps of wet leaves can cause wooden gutters to rot and metal ones to corrode. And their weight can cause a vinyl gutter to sag or pull loose.

Tidy your gutters. Cleaning gutters is fairly easy but you need to be organized and work systematically. Here's how to go about it:

- Use a pull-up bucket. Attach one end of a long rope and an S-hook to the handle of an empty bucket (you can make the hook by bending a wire coat hanger), and put work gloves, a trowel, and a whisk broom into the bucket. Starting near the down-spout, climb a sturdy ladder to the gutter and pull up the bucket with the rope and hook it over a rung of the ladder.

- Work from low end to high. Put on work gloves. Sweep all debris toward the higher end of the gutter. Scoop up the debris with the trowel and dump it into the bucket. Clean only as far as you can reach comfortably, then move the ladder and do the next section—until you finish at the high end of the gutter.

- Use a hose to pinpoint problems. Once the debris is all out, use a garden hose to flush the gutter from the high end. It also lets you check for leaks and other damage. If you see standing pools of water, the gutter is sagging and needs realignment. If the water won't go down at all, the downspout is clogged.

Clear a clogged downspout. The fast way to clear a clog in a downspout is with a garden hose. And surprisingly it's best to do it from the bottom up. Wrap rags around the nozzle of a hose and wedge it into the bottom of the downspout. (You may have to remove a section to gain access.) Turn on the water full force. If that doesn't blast the debris out, use a plumber's snake, working from the bottom up.

Easy Fixes

Conquering leaking gutters. Most gutter leaks occur at the joints where two sections meet. To stop a leak, apply silicone sealant from a squeezable tube along the joint's inside seams. Smooth the sealer's edges so that they won't collect debris. If the leak recurs, disassemble the sections and put a bead of caulk between parts at each seam.

Tightening sagging gutters. Straighten a gutter by tightening the fastener that holds it to your house. The most common fastener is a spike driven through both the gutter and a ferrule (a sleeve inside the gutter that acts as a spacer) and into the end of a rafter. To pull up a sagging section of gutter, strike the spike head up and in with a hammer to drive it deeper into the rafter. If the gutter is fastened with metal brackets, use pliers to bend the strap that bridges the gutter, and the gutter will perk up accordingly.

Patching metal gutters. If a gutter section is rusty and leaky, replace it. But if there's just one bad spot, the few minutes it takes to patch it is time well spent. Just scrape the area clean of rust with a stiff wire brush and wipe with paint thinner. Cut a fiberglass patch large enough to overlap the damaged area by 2 inches (5 cm) on all sides. Using a putty knife, cover the area with plastic roof cement. Smooth the patch into the cement using a dry, wadded cloth. Cover the patch with another coat of roof cement, feathering the edges and avoiding ridges that could impede water flow.

Diverting water from your house. If your downspout doesn't empty into an underground drain, attach a few feet of extra downspout to an elbow at the bottom of the downspout to carry the runoff away from the foundation.

SHOULD YOU USE GUTTER SCREEN GUARDS?

Using wire mesh screens to keep leaves out of gutters may seem a great idea. But leaves sometimes cling to the screens and divert water over the gutters. The screens can also be tricky to remove when you want to clean the gutters. A more practical solution is to put a bulb-shaped leaf strainer in the top of each downspout—just be sure to check them every couple of months to make sure they have not become clogged.

Roof Ice and Snow

Ice dams are the bane of homeowners in snowy climates; they're the principle cause of leaks and other roof problems. Ice dams form when heat from the attic melts snow on the upper reaches of the roof. The water runs down under the unmelted snow on the lower roof and refreezes at the roof's edge, which is colder because it's not directly over the attic. Insulated by a blanket of snow, the ice then prevents subsequent melt-off from draining into the gutters. The result? The water backs up under the shingles and works its way into your house, causing costly damage not just to your roof, but also to your home's interior.

Care and Maintenance

Cool down your attic. Because ice dams form as a result of heat rising from the attic, the best way to prevent them is to lower the temperature in your attic. A three-pronged attack will correct this problem and save your paint job and wallboard inside.

- Seal everything. Don't let any air travel up through the walls to the attic. Light fixture boxes, electrical outlets or switches, and openings for pipes or ducts can all serve as routes for warm air to move up. Use caulk, expanding foam insulation, or other sealants to close any openings. Also go into the attic, pull away the insulation, and apply a sealant to the top edges of the drywall or plaster. You'll cut down on ice dams and your heating costs.

- Increase your attic insulation. Check the insulation on the floor of your attic. If it already fills up the space between the joists, add another layer of insulation, running at right angles to the joists. You should have at least a foot of insulation with a heat retention value above R-32. If you have a finished heated attic, add a layer of rigid foam insulation panels to the existing ceiling and cover it with wallboard to create a second ceiling,

- Ventilate the attic. Once your attic floor is better insulated, it is a good idea to increase the ventilation in the attic to move out any trapped warm air. The simplest way to do this is to have roof vents installed near the ridge. This is a simple, relatively inexpensive job that can be done by a roofing contractor; get bids from a couple of them. You may also want to add vents under the eaves.

take care

You may be tempted to use salt (or a similar deicing chemical) to melt ice on your roof. After all, it works great on walks and driveways. Don't do it: The salt can damage not only the shingles but also the wood, gutters, and foundation plantings.

Rake off fresh snow. The no-brainer way to avoid ice dams is to keep your roof as snow-free as possible. If there's no snow, there can't be any ice dams. Use a snow rake with an extension handle to manually remove fresh snow from your roof after every major snowfall. Just be careful not to hit any overhead power lines or send snow cascading down on someone's head. (If your home has more than one story, the extension-handled rake will probably not be long enough to reach the top floor— you may have to call for professional help.)

Easy Fixes

Identifying an ice dam. If you spot a damp ceiling or wall area or any other symptom of a leak in snowy weather, suspect an ice dam. Go outside and take a good look at your roof. If the snow has holes or thin areas, or icicles are hanging from the eaves, thicker layers of ice may have already formed.

Installing an electric deicing cable. Overrun with ice dams? You can install deicing cable, which is designed to heat up and keep snow from collecting along the lower part of the roof by melting it. Buy the exact length you need, because it can't be cut. Following the manufacturer's instructions, mount the control box to the soffit (the underside of the eaves). Snake the cable around all parts of the roof overhang and a bit above and into the downspout. *Caution:* Carefully follow the manufacturer's instructions. Incorrect installation can lead to electrical shock or fire.

Creating drainage channels. One simple way to deal with an ice dam on your roof is to use an ice pick or a hatchet and hammer to chip vertical grooves in the ice every 3 feet (1 metre) or so to let the water drain off the roof. But be very careful not to cut or break the shingles underneath, since they will be brittle from the cold. To play it safer, hire a contractor to steam the ice away. And watch out for falling icicles!

ELIMINATING ICE DAMS ONCE AND FOR ALL

Next time you get your roof reshingled, add a weatherproofing membrane directly to the sheathing along the eaves before adding the shingles. The membrane bonds to the boards and seals itself around nail holes to form a watertight surface. The membrane, which comes in 3-foot (1 metre) widths, should extend at least 2 feet (0.5 metre) above the point where the outside wall of the house meets the roof. If your house has wide eaves, install two rows. Also install membrane around dormers and in valleys.

Chimneys

Keeping your chimney clean is a matter of life or death. Over time, residual gases and resins from wood condense on the inside of the flue, mix with soot and tar, and form a dark coating called creosote. If it is not removed, it can grow into a thick layer and block the flue or dissolve mortar joints, allowing smoke to leak through the sides of the flue. Worse, it can catch fire and spread through cracks in the flue into your house. If you use the fireplace regularly, have the chimney cleaned once a year by a chimney sweep. While he's there, you may want to have the chimney sweep do some of the chimney checkups described below, especially the ones that require inspecting the top of the chimney.

Care and Maintenance

Only burn well-seasoned firewood. If you have a fireplace, you should only use wood that has been seasoned for at least a year. Because green, unseasoned wood contains up to 50 percent water, it burns poorly and produces a lot of smoke, which leads to creosote on the chimney's walls. Avoid softwood, too, which burns fast and gives off more smoke than heat. Keep your firewood dry. When you store it outside, keep it off the ground and uncovered during nice weather; pull a tarp over it when it rains or snows.

Look for obstructions. The best time to check a chimney is in the spring, right after you've finished using it for the season. From the roof or a ladder, check the top of the chimney first; look for anything that might block it, such as a bird's nest. Then use a powerful flashlight to look down the flue for obstructions. If you find any you can't reach, call a chimney sweep.

Be on the lookout for creosote buildup. With the flashlight still shining down the flue, check how much creosote buildup the chimney has. Also check the flue from the fireplace. If the creosote is more than 1/8 inch (3 mm) thick in any part of the flue, have the chimney cleaned.

Cap your flue. If your flue doesn't have a cap, get one attached. It will keep out foreign objects, small animals, and water. If your chimney has two flues—usually one for the fireplace and a smaller one to vent a gas furnace—put a cap on each.

SMART IDEA

Concrete caulk is especially sticky and hard to spread. The solution is to use an ice cube to smooth it out and spread it into the joint.

Inspect the chimney flashing. Make sure the flashing around the chimney is securely in place and intact. If it's loose or corroded, it won't keep out water, and you'll have plenty of problems to complain about. Chimney flashing is complicated to install; have it replaced by pros.

Check the chimney's crown. The crown is the concrete slab on the top of the chimney that surrounds the flue and acts as a roof to protect the brickwork beneath. If it is seriously cracked, have it replaced by a professional. If it is only slightly cracked, fill the crack with fresh concrete mortar. Also, if the joint between the crown and the flue has deteriorated, recaulk it.

Do a nighttime inspection. At night with most of the lights in your home turned off, have someone shine a bright work light up the flue from the fireplace while you check all the exposed areas of the chimney throughout the house and attic. If you see any light leaking through, repoint the bricks and have the flue relined by a professional.

Trim back encroaching trees. Make sure no trees hang over the top of the chimney. They can be ignited by escaping sparks or create a canopy causing your fireplace to smoke. Trim the trees back so that they're at least 10 feet (3 metres) from the chimney.

Check for a damaged cap from inside. A missing or damaged chimney cap can result in moisture inside the chimney. An easy way to check a cap without climbing onto the roof is to place a single sheet of newspaper at the base of the flue the next time it rains. If the paper becomes fairly wet, the cap probably needs repair or replacement.

Easy Fixes

Filling joints at the chimney crown. If you find a gap in the joint between the flue and the chimney crown, put a tube of caulk rated for use on concrete into your caulking gun and apply a thick bead of caulk around the entire circumference of the flue where it meets the crown. Push the caulk down into the gap to fill it, then round it off and smooth it.

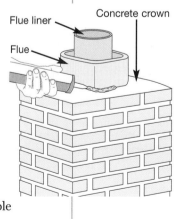

Flue liner

Concrete crown

Flue

Sealing brickwork. As hardy as it is, brick is subject to wear. Years of rain will eventually roughen its surface, which will cause the brick to begin absorbing water. In winter, water in the bricks may freeze and expand, crumbling the material. Putting a halt to this process is easy: Just spray the chimney with Siloxane, or other clear, water-repellent masonry sealer available in home-improvement centers. Follow the directions on the label.

Foundations

House foundations rarely cause homeowners any trouble, but when they do, it can be serious—and seriously expensive. (Repair can be a multi-thousand-dollar endeavor!) If cracks in your foundation walls are wider at the top than at the bottom, there may be a problem with the footings beneath the foundation; consult a structural engineer. The more likely cause, however, is water that seeps into your home. It's vitally important to keep water directed away from the foundation, or you're sure to have trouble. This page contains plenty of suggestions for how to keep your foundation dry; you'll find even more in the "Basements" section.

SMART IDEA

When you are caulking cracks and gaps between the foundation and siding, use a mirror to see under the edge of the siding so that you don't have to hunch over. You may have to prop the mirror on a block of wood to position it at the best angle.

Care and Maintenance

Caulk gaps in foundation joints. Check the joints between the foundation of your house and your patios and porches. If you find a gap, brush the area clean. Then use a caulk gun with a tube of urethane or silicone-modified acrylic caulk rated for concrete to fill the gap. Smooth it to blend with the surrounding surfaces. Caulk gaps between the foundation and siding the same way. Also caulk cracks in the foundation itself if they are no more than 1/8 inch (3 mm) wide (see "How to Patch a Foundation Crack," opposite, if they are wider). For more information, see the "Caulking" section.

Easy Fixes

Installing a vapor barrier. It's easy to overlook what's going on in a crawl space, but if you do, you may pay for it in the long run. Trapped moisture can damage your

---

HEADLAMPS   equipment spotlight

Slithering around in a tight crawl space is much easier if you get a light with an elastic band that straps around your head and keeps your hands free. You can get them at camping and mountaineering supply stores. They're great for any job that requires a flashlight.

house's wooden understructure. If your house rests on perimeter foundation walls with a dirt-floor crawl space beneath, keep the crawl space dry with a vapor barrier of 6-mil polyethylene film. It's easy to install:

- Dig a 2-inch-deep (5 cm) ditch around the interior perimeter of the crawl space.
- Lay sheets of polyethylene film over the ground, overlapping them at least 2 feet (0.5 metre) and extending their outer edges into the ditch.
- Return the excavated soil to the ditch to anchor the plastic. If you can't dig a trench, weight down the plastic with gravel or bricks.

Preventing crawl-space mold. To keep mold from growing under the house, mix a half cup (125 ml) of chlorine bleach with 3 cups (750 ml) of water in a spray bottle. Spray the plastic vapor barrier and then wipe it off. Wear rubber gloves, goggles, and a mask while working with the bleach mixture.

How to Patch a Foundation Crack

Patch a crack in your foundation that's more than 1/8 inch (3 mm) wide. If it extends below ground level, dig a small trench to reach it, saving the dirt to refill the trench.

1. Wearing a DUST MASK, goggles, and work gloves, scrape off any dirt around the crack; then clean the area with a stiff-bristle brush and mists of water from a spray bottle. Let the wall dry. Don't hose; it'll take too long to dry.

2. Chip away any CRUMBLING MATERIAL with a cold chisel and hammer. Then chisel the crack to undercut the edges, making the crack wider inside than on the outer surface. This will lock in the patching material when it hardens.

3. Prepare a small batch of CONCRETE PATCHING COMPOUND, mixing in enough water to make it pliable but not runny. Use a pointed trowel to force the mixture into the crack, slightly overfilling it; then smooth the surface with the trowel to blend the compound with the surrounding surface.

4. After the repair has hardened, SEAL THE SURFACE with masonry waterproof coating. Let dry; then paint to match surrounding surface.

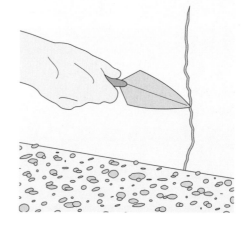

Stopping foundation leaks. To keep water from leaking through a stone foundation onto the dirt floor of a crawl space, seal the joints between the stones both outside and in. Wear work gloves and goggles.

- On the outside, rake out crumbling mortar using a hammer and chisel and clean with a stiff brush. Dampen the joints and fill the voids with a packaged mortar mix, as you would when repointing a brick veneer wall (see "Brick Veneer" section).
- Inside the crawl space, repeat the process. Then seal the interior surface with masonry waterproof coating. If you don't mind losing the look of the natural stone, you can also waterproof the exterior and paint over the waterproof coating.

Checking cracks between foundation sections. If the foundations of your house and an adjoining garage or add-on were poured separately and a crack appears between the two sections, test the joint for stability. Paint a line across the crack and make a note of the date and the crack's width at the painted line. Remeasure the crack occasionally over the next six months. If it gets wider, the foundation walls may be moving apart; call in a structural engineer. If the crack does not widen, fill it with urethane caulk. Don't use mortar or patching compound, which are not flexible and will crack as concrete sections expand and contract.

Basements

If you have an unfinished basement, the most important thing you need to do for it is to keep it dry. Most problems in the basement result from dampness, which can be caused by condensation of humid air, slow seepage of outside moisture through the walls, or outright leaks through cracks or holes. You can usually reduce condensation with increased ventilation and contain seepage by waterproofing the walls. (Doing so significantly lessens the probability that your basement will develop mold.) Cracks and holes in the walls or floor can lead to real damage and should be fixed as soon as possible. If you fill a crack and it reopens, you may have a major structural problem; consult a structural engineer.

YOUR COST SAVINGS

$3,250

Amount it would cost to have an interior drainage pipe and sump pump installed in a 30-by-40-foot (9 by 12 metres) basement.

Care and Maintenance

Scrub especially dirty basements with a cleaning solution. If a concrete or concrete-block surface is especially dirty, add detergent and a quarter cup of ammonia to a bucket of warm water and brush the solution over the surface with a stiff nylon brush. (Never use a metallic brush; metallic fibers can get trapped in the concrete and rust.) For really stubborn dirt, get extra kick by adding trisodium phosphate to the wash water. TSP is available at hardware stores. Rinse with a hose and let dry. Use a shop vacuum to remove excess water.

Freshen a smelly basement with bleach. Mildew that takes up residence in a basement gives off an unpleasant, musty odor. Open windows to let in air, use fans to improve air circulation, and install a dehumidifier to remove moisture. To get rid of the fungal growth that's the source of the smell, mix up a brew of 1 to 2 ounces (30 to 60 ml) of household bleach per quart (litre) of water in a spray bottle. Spray the walls and floors with the solution and scrub them with a nylon-bristled brush.

Treat the floor with bleaching powder. An easier solution for the floor in a smelly basement is to sprinkle it with chlorinated lime (bleaching powder; sold in the supermarket's laundry section). Let it sit there, soaking up the bad odor and microorganisms that cause it, for a day, then sweep or vacuum it up. Dispose of the sweepings outdoors. If the odor persists, seal the concrete with concrete sealer.

A THREE-PRONGED APPROACH TO PREVENTING BASEMENT MOISTURE

CUT DOWN ON CONDENSATION

Increase ventilation in the basement by closing windows in hot, humid weather and opening them in cool, dry weather. Use a fan to keep the air moving.

Install a dehumidifier to dry the air. Even a small roll-around model will remove gallons (litres) of water. Attach a plastic tube so that the water it collects goes directly into the basement drain.

Insulate sweating pipes with self-sticking, foam insulating tape or pre-slit foam sleeves. Fix any leaky plumbing connections.

Vent clothes dryers to the outside. Make sure bathroom and laundry room moisture is vented to the outside; install an exhaust fan if there's none.

REDUCE SEEPAGE FROM OUTSIDE

Repair gutters and downspouts and make sure roof runoff is not accumulating next to the foundation. Use splash blocks and downspout extensions to carry water away from the house.

Waterproof basement walls with a crystalline waterproofing material (CWM).

Thin out foundation foliage and organic mulch that keep the ground next to the house from drying out after a rain.

If you have a sump pump, make sure it is functioning.

PREVENT LEAKS

Caulk leaky joints between walls and doors or windows and around floor drains—and make sure the drains are not blocked.

Don't pile snow against outside walls or let it accumulate there or in basement window wells. If you get a lot of snow, install window-well covers—clear plastic bubbles that let in light but not rain or snow.

Check for cracks or holes in basement walls and repair them before they get worse.

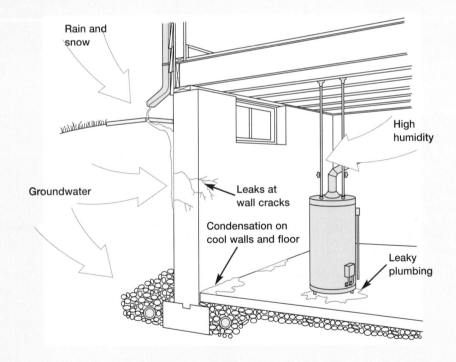

Rain and snow

High humidity

Groundwater

Leaks at wall cracks

Condensation on cool walls and floor

Leaky plumbing

Easy Fixes

Ditching the efflorescence. The white powder that sometimes accumulates on the concrete walls or floor of a basement is efflorescence, soluble salts that remain when water seeps through concrete and evaporates. Clean it off with a rigid, nylon-bristled brush or a wet rag or mop. If it returns, you may need to waterproof your basement walls.

Removing rust stains. Do away with a rust spot by sprinkling it with dry cement and rubbing with a small piece of flagstone (the kind used to pave patios). The combination of dry cement and stone acts like pumice and should remove the stain.

Giving your basement floor a makeover. Tired of your dull gray concrete basement floor? Give it a new look with a waterproof stain. The stain and other supplies you need are all sold at home centers. The process is simple:

- Scrub the floor with trisodium phosphate (TSP) or a similar strong alkaline cleaner-degreaser and rinse with a hose.

- While the floor is still wet, sprinkle it with muriatic or phosphoric acid and scrub with a stiff-bristled nylon brush for a minute or so. This roughens the surface so that it will accept the stain better. After 20 minutes, hose the floor three times to rinse away all the acid and stop the etching action.

- When the floor is dry, use a short-nap paint roller on a long handle to apply the stain in 3-by-3-foot (1 by 1 metre) sections. Let the stain dry for 24 hours before walking on it.

SMART IDEA

Before painting a concrete floor, you can apply a coat of white vinegar instead of muriatic or phosphoric acid. It will clean the floor and lightly "etch" or roughen the surface, so the paint adheres better. Vinegar works well for preparing metal before painting, too.

WHEN YOU HAVE TO CALL A CONTRACTOR

If your basement still gets wet after you have taken all the measures suggested here, you're going to have to bite the bullet and pay a contractor to fix the problem. Here are two possible professional solutions to your moisture problems:

Redo your exterior drainage. Your yard should slope away from the house at a rate of 6 inches (15 cm) for every 10 feet (3 metres). To ensure that the slope sheds water rather than absorbing it, have a

layer of clay added beneath the topsoil. If water runs downhill onto your house, have a swale dug around the house, about 6 feet (2 metres) away. A swale is a shallow drainage ditch with gently sloping sides that is filled with crushed stones and then covered with topsoil and grass. It catches the water before it can reach the house.

Beef up your interior drainage. If you have a high water table, have perforated drainpipes installed

under the basement floor, along with a sump pump that can operate on both normal house power and a battery. Water will collect in the pipes and be discharged to the outside by the pump. If you already have an old sump pump in your basement, supplement it with a battery-operated model so that you can pump water out even after a storm cuts off your electricity. Add a cover to the sump pump and an alarm to alert you to flooding.

Using aluminum foil to find sources of moisture. Before you can deal with basement dampness, you'll need to know what's causing it. Determine the cause with this simple test: Dry an area on the wall or floor with a hair dryer. Fasten a square of aluminum foil over the area, sealing all four edges with duct tape. After two days, peel off the foil. If the wall behind the foil is dry, the problem is condensation from humid inside air. If the wall is wet, moisture is seeping—or possibly, leaking—in from outside.

Waterproofing basement walls. If water is seeping through your basement walls, coat them with a crystalline waterproofing material (CWM). Unlike other water-resistant products, which simply coat the surface, this powdered blend of cement and sand with a chemical catalyst penetrates into the concrete, so it won't peel off over time. Follow package directions for application instructions.

How to Patch Concrete Basement Walls

Patch cracks and small holes in a concrete wall with hydraulic cement—a remarkable compound, sold at hardware stores, that hardens even under water. Because it expands when it dries, hydraulic cement bonds firmly with the surrounding concrete.

1. Wearing GLOVES AND SAFETY GOGGLES, enlarge the crack (or hole) with a chisel and hammer, angling the chisel to make the opening larger inside than out so the cement will be locked in. (Don't cut deeper than 3/4 inch (2 cm) into a concrete-block wall or you may break through to the hollow core.)

----

2. Clean the opening with a STIFF BRUSH, then vacuum out any remaining debris. Moisten the opening slightly with a wet sponge. Mix a batch of hydraulic cement with cold water to the consistency of soft modeling clay. It starts to set very quickly so mix only as much as you can use in three minutes.

----

3. FILL THE CRACK with the cement, using a trowel, to within 1/2 inch (1 cm) of the surface. Wait 10 minutes; then fill the crack with more cement, holding it in by pressing the trowel against it until it hardens. Trowel the surface smooth.

----

4. TO FILL A HOLE, form the prepared cement into a cone about 4 inches (10 cm) long. The base of the cone should be about 1 inch (2.5 cm) wider than the hole. Push the cone into the hole and hold it there until the cement hardens. Trowel the surface smooth.

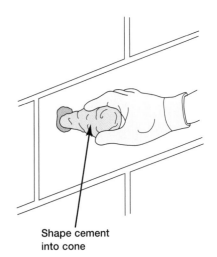

Shape cement into cone

Concrete Steps

The good news is that concrete steps need little maintenance or special care. Edges or corners may chip or crumble, but not for many years—unless you drop a refrigerator on them as you're moving it into the house. Even chipped edges and corners can be fixed without too much trouble (unlike that fridge). On the other hand, steps do get dirty, thanks to our daily traipsing in and out, so you'll need to keep them clean, as much to protect your interior floors as the steps themselves.

YOUR COST SAVINGS

$870

What you would pay to replace a three-tier flight of concrete porch steps.

Care and Maintenance

Keep steps clean. Keep concrete steps well swept, and hose them down to get rid of muddy footprints and other abrasive material that will wear down the steps' surface and can be tracked into the house to do worse harm.

Seal and waterproof your steps. To keep steps from getting stained, scrub them with detergent and water and rinse well with a hose. When they dry, apply a masonry waterproof coating, which will make future cleaning jobs far easier. Don't worry; the coating won't make the steps slick.

Easy Fixes

Caulking narrow cracks. Seal narrow cracks in concrete steps before winter comes; water that gets inside and freezes will expand and make the crack worse. Brush away any loose concrete and dirt. Then fill the crack with an exterior urethane or silicone-modified acrylic caulk rated for use on concrete. The caulk comes in tubes that fit in a regular caulk gun. Smooth it to blend with the surrounding surface.

Installing upside-down bolts. Railings attached to concrete steps often work loose because their bolts rust or water gets into the bolt holes, freezes, and expands, pushing out the bolts. If you have a loose railing, fix it, but also improve the original installation: Anchor new bolts upside down to make the railing sturdier. Here's how to go about it:

SMART IDEA

If your steps' surface becomes grease-stained, sprinkle some dry cement over the stain and let it sit for an hour to absorb the mess. Then sweep it up with a broom and dustpan. If you don't have dry cement, try plain sand or cat litter.

- Detach the railing from the wall by removing the screws or wall brackets. Then use a pry bar to lever up the floor-mount bracket and pull the old bolts out of the concrete.
- Use an electric drill fitted with progressively larger masonry bits to widen the bolt holes until they will accept the heads of new bolts.
- Brush the insides of the bolt holes with masonry bonding agent, then slip the new bolts into the holes upside down. Mix and pour special-purpose anchoring cement around the bolts, and let it set for at least an hour.
- Once the anchoring cement is firm, apply a masonry waterproof coating around the bolts. Then reposition the railing and secure it with nuts and lock washers.

How to Fix Chipped Concrete Steps

To fix a chipped corner or edge on concrete steps, you need to make a temporary wooden form to hold the wet concrete patch in place while it dries. A corner requires two boards nailed together at right angles, while an edge requires only a single board. Use boards that are as wide as the step is deep and brace them with bricks or heavy blocks to keep them in place. Use a concrete patching compound, mixing it with enough water to make it thin for pouring but not runny.

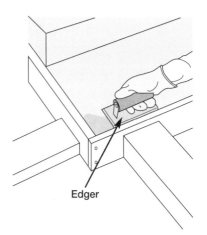

Edger

1. Wearing WORK GLOVES AND GOGGLES, clean loose concrete away from the damaged area with a cold chisel and hammer. If you're fixing a corner, use a masonry bit to drill 1 1/2-inch-deep (4 cm) pilot holes for two or three concrete screws. Drive in the screws, letting 1 inch (2.5 cm) protrude. Vacuum or brush the area clean, then coat the surface with a brush-on masonry-bonding agent.

- -

2. Create a TEMPORARY FORM and brace it with bricks or blocks. Fill the area with wet patching compound, pack it firmly with a trowel, and round the edges with an edging tool (a trowel with one rounded edge, as shown). When the new concrete is firm enough to hold its shape, remove the form boards and smooth the surface of the concrete with a trowel.

- -

3. Fix a CHIPPED EDGE as you would a corner, but instead of adding screws, use the chisel to flatten the area, forming a horizontal ledge for the patch to rest on. Slant the ledge slightly down toward the back. Clean the area, brush on bonding agent, brace a board against the area, fill with patching compound, and shape and smooth it.

- -

Insulation and Venting

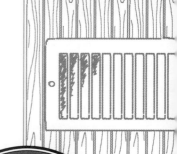

Though you probably never think about such things, how comfortable you are inside your home largely depends on the effectiveness of your home's insulation and ventilation. A properly insulated attic can make a substantial impact on your energy use—in fact, it can reduce your home heating and cooling expenses by as much as 30 percent. Start by learning the recommended R-values for your area, and add additional layers of insulation, if needed. Periodically check for air leaks and uninvited four-legged guests, and ensure that vents are free of any obstructions. Don't forget to seal the small gaps around pipes and wiring. Always wear protective gear when handling insulation materials.

YOUR COST SAVINGS

20%

Amount you can reduce your heating and cooling costs by simply sealing leaks and upgrading your insulation.

Care and Maintenance

Are your walls insulated? Current building codes require homes to have insulated exterior walls, but this wasn't required of houses that were built before 1965. Here's how to tell if your walls are insulated: Remove a switch plate or outlet cover on an exterior wall (be sure to shut off the power first), and with a flashlight, look for insulation around the electrical boxes. You can also use a hole saw to cut a small hole inside a closet and inspect from there. If the walls are not insulated, you may want to explore having blown-in insulation installed, especially if you live in an area with cold temperatures.

If yours is lacking, add more attic installation. A poorly insulated attic can cost you plenty in terms of heat loss and high utility bills. On a cool, comfortable day, grab a ruler and head up to your attic to measure the depth of the insulation; if it's less than 7 inches (18 cm), add at least one more layer. You can lay rolled blankets or batts (precut lengths) of unfaced fiberglass insulation on top of existing fiberglass or loose-fill insulation. (This second layer of insulation needs to be unfaced to avoid trapping moisture between the two layers. Place a plywood platform across the joists to support your weight.) Working from the eaves toward the center of the attic, lay the new batts over the tops of the joists at right angles to the existing insulation. Be careful not to block ventilation, especially at the eaves.

Seal small gaps. It may be hard to believe, but those small spaces around the plumbing vent pipes and electrical cables in your attic can result in significant heat loss during the winter months. Fiberglass batts or loose-fill insulation alone won't block such air leaks. If insulation is already in place, carefully remove it, and pack strips of fiberglass batts into the gaps as backing. Then fill in the spaces with expansion foam sealant and replace the insulation. Holes around the openings for electrical junction boxes also create air leaks. Plug them by placing a bead of silicone caulk around the box. Make sure the caulk has cured (this typically takes 24 hours) before putting the insulation back in place.

Check for rodents and other critters. The same loose-fill insulation material that keeps your home comfortable can make a cozy winter residence for mice, squirrels, and even raccoons. Check your attic insulation for any unwanted guests in early winter. If you see droppings, disturbed fill, or any signs of chewing, contact a pest-control specialist. Make sure any service you hire will remove the animals and eliminate their point of entry.

Vent the attic well. All homes have some form of attic ventilation, if only the screened gable vents that are found in most houses built before 1980. Doing a periodic check to make sure that there's good airflow in your attic will ensure that the space is cool and dry all year round. Make sure all vents are open and free of obstructions, and that insulation is not blocking soffit vents or impeding the flow of air into the attic.

Attend to icicles and ice dams on your roof right away. In addition to causing significant damage to your roof, ice dams can produce leaks that back up into your house to rot rafters, stain interior walls, and ruin your insulation. A well-insulated and vented attic is the best insurance against this type of damage. If your attic isn't cold in winter, it needs additional layers of insulation. For details on how to preventing ice dams, see the "Roof Ice and Snow" section.

THE BARRIER RULE

Vapor barriers keep moisture out of your home and should almost always be installed between the drywall and insulation, facing your living quarters. The paper or foil facing on fiberglass batts and blankets and on rigid board insulation serves as a vapor barrier; loose-fill insulation requires a layer of plastic or polyethylene.

Do not stack faced insulation; moisture can collect between the layers, reducing the effectiveness of the insulation and may cause water damage inside your home.

WHICH TYPE OF INSULATION SHOULD I USE?

The answer depends on where you live, when your home was built, and a variety of other factors. This chart will help you make the right decision for your home and your family.

TYPE	R-VALUE/INCH	PROS	CONS
Fiberglass	R-3.0–R-3.8	Easy to install	Can irritate skin and lungs
		Comes in standard stud and joist widths	Air gaps may form during installation
		Can be trimmed to size	
		Available with or without vapor barrier backing	
		Low cost	
Loose fill (cellulose, rock wool)	R-2.2–R-4.0	Can be poured or blown into walls	Can be messy to use
		Excellent coverage over trusses and in irregular spaces	Variable quality
		Low cost	Materials can shift or settle
			May require mechanical blower
Expanded foam	R-3.8–R-4.3	Lowest-cost foam insulation	Not for underground use
			Needs to be covered by drywall or fireproof material
Extruded foam	R-5.2	Provides excellent thermal and moisture resistance	Expensive
		High compressive strength	Needs to be covered by drywall or fireproof material
		Good for underground use	
Sprayed urethane foam	R-6.0–R-7.3	Provides a dense, seamless thermal and moisture barrier	Very expensive
		Covers irregularly shaped surfaces	Must be professionally installed
		Enhances structure strength	Needs to be covered by drywall or fireproof material

Easy Fixes

Filling your attic's cavities. You may think your attic is well insulated, but large, empty voids can lurk in joist spaces and in the areas above stairwells, soffits, and dropped ceilings. To fill these energy-sucking vacancies, cut a large square piece from an unfaced fiberglass batt, fold it in half, and place it in a plastic garbage bag. (Be sure you're wearing protective gear and clothing.) Punch several holes in the bag on the attic side, and insert it into the open cavity.

Cutting insulation to fit. Fiberglass and rigid insulation often need to be cut to fit properly into an allotted space. Cut rolled fiberglass or fiberglass batts by placing the insulation, faced side up, on a piece of plywood. Position a 2-by-4 or a straightedge across the cut line, and press it down with your knee. Use a sharp utility knife to cut through the fiberglass. To slice through thick rigid foam insulation, place it on a solid, raised surface, such as a table or workbench, and use a power saw with a fine-tooth blade or an electric carving knife to make the cut. Thin foam insulation can simply be scored with a utility knife then snapped.

Sealing off the crawl space. Moisture rising from the bare ground under a crawl space can damage floor joists and floor insulation. The solution? Lay a 6-mil polyethylene film vapor barrier directly over the soil.

Insulating rim joists. The rim joist area—where floor joists connect to a band of wood around the perimeter of your house—is an area that's often overlooked when insulating. Cut blocks of rigid foam insulation and friction fit them into the spaces between the joists where they meet the rim joist.

How to Install a **Soffit Vent**

Installing exterior soffit vents can reduce moisture in your attic in the winter and keep it cool in summer. The vents are easy to install, although you'll probably need to put in more than one. (The precise number you'll need will depend on the size of your attic; estimate one soffit vent for every 100 square feet (9 square metres) of attic space.) Note, too, that soffit vents draw air *into* the attic. To achieve proper ventilation, your roof should also have sufficient roof vents, which let air flow *out* of the attic. Here's what to do:

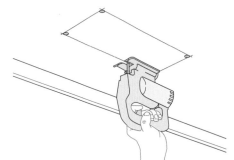

1. Place the VENT ON THE SOFFIT and trace its area with a pencil. Measure 1 inch (2.5 cm) in on all sides, and fill in that outline (erase the initial tracing). Drill holes on all four corners.

---

2. Using a SABER SAW, cut along the outline to make the opening for the vent.

---

3. Install the VENT OVER THE OPENING, and screw it into place with stainless-steel, self-tapping screws. (Be sure to angle the louvers so that air flows into the attic.)

Insulating floors. To insulate a floor above an unheated basement or crawl space, push fiberglass batts, with the vapor barrier facing up, into the spaces between the overhead floor joists. Secure the batts by stapling wire mesh (chicken wire) to the lower edges of the joists, or by pressing lengths of heavy wire—cut slightly longer than the width of the cavity— between the joists every 18 inches (0.5 metre) or so. Bow the wires up slightly. Although the wires should hold the batts firmly in place, make sure they are not compressing them.

Weather Stripping

It's important to have weather stripping on windows and doors; the material keeps out the winter cold and the summer heat. Insulation around doors tends to receive the most stress, which is why it's important to inspect it annually and make necessary repairs or modifications. When shopping for weather stripping, bear in mind that price is usually a good indication of durability and effectiveness—go ahead and spring for the good stuff. You'll replace it less frequently.

Care and Maintenance

Test for air leaks. Before you can seal an air leak, you need to find out where it is. On a windy day, light a stick of incense and move it slowly alongside windows, doors, attic hatches, and other fixtures where outside air might enter. When the incense smoke moves horizontally, you've found a leak that may require weather stripping, caulking, or sealing. You can also detect drafts by feel. Dampen the back of your hand and move it along the perimeter of exterior doors and windows; you'll feel coolness when air is coming through.

Inspect exterior doors annually. In addition to the wear and tear of ordinary use, the weather stripping around exterior doors will shift as your house shifts and settles. Check the weather stripping around these doors once a year to see if it needs to be adjusted or replaced.

Replace threshold gaskets. When it's time to replace a worn threshold gasket, take the old one with you to the hardware store to ensure a good match. A gasket has two splines (narrow, projecting strips) that fit into grooves in the threshold; these may tear off and stay in place as you remove the old gasket. If so, use a narrow screwdriver to pry the splines out, and make sure no pieces remain in the grooves. To install a new gasket,

SMART IDEA

Here's a rule of thumb for determining whether air is leaking around an inside window or its storm window: If moisture forms on the windowpane, cold air is leaking past the storm sash. If condensation appears on the storm window, warm air is leaking around the inside window.

press its splines into the grooves using your fingers, then push down with a wood block to complete the job.

Prepare surfaces for weather stripping. When applying self-adhesive weather stripping to windows, start with a clean, dry surface. Any residual moisture, dirt, or oil will prevent the adhesive from adhering to the frame and forming a tight seal. If the area is dusty or grimy, use a small amount of rubbing alcohol on a cloth or paper towel to clean it off. Use a hair dryer on its highest setting to thoroughly dry the surface and remove trapped moisture. Before installing weather stripping on a door, check that none of the hardware is loose and that the door latches tightly.

WHAT KIND OF WEATHER STRIPPING SHOULD I USE?

When selecting weather stripping, be sure to compare cost to durability. Felt is very inexpensive, for example, but it is also one of the least durable and least effective types of weather stripping.

TYPE AND DESCRIPTION	USE	PROS	CONS
Interlocking metal Two metal strips that interlock when affixed to the frame and joint edges.	Use on high-traffic doors and windows.	Reliable and permanent; inconspicuous.	Expensive; difficult to apply joint edges (strips must be perfectly aligned to form seal); should be professionally installed.
V-Strip Flexible vinyl or metal (bronze, aluminum, copper, or stainless steel) strip with adhesive backing.	Use on low-traffic doors and windows.	Durable; seals well on even surfaces	Needs to be installed on flat, smooth surfaces; can increase resistance in opening or closing.
Vinyl or rubber tubing Flexible tubing with slots along the back; stapled or nailed in place.	Use on windows and doors.	Easy to install; fits irregular surfaces; creates a tight seal.	Tubing susceptible to damage; can become stiff and less effective if painted.
Foam strip Reinforced with wood or metal backing. Applied with adhesive backing or nails.	Use on little-used doors and windows.	Effective; easy to install.	Unattractive; wears easily; needs to be replaced after 1–2 years.
Felt Sold in rolls, either plain or backed with a flexible metal strip; stapled or tacked in place.	Use on doors and windows.	Inexpensive; easy to install.	Least effective; should not be exposed to moisture; very visible; needs to be replaced after 1–2 years.

Easy Fixes

Stopping window leaks. An easy way to seal gaps around a leaky double-hung window is to install a flexible vinyl or rubber tubular gasket on the bottom of the window sash. When left unpainted, gaskets can stay pliable even in freezing temperatures. Although they provide an airtight seal, they are also pretty hard to hide. V-strips, made of aluminum, bronze, stainless steel, or vinyl, are less conspicuous alternatives. They can be installed in both the side and bottom sash channels, and are especially effective on older wooden casement windows. Double-hung windows may require V-strips on the side channels and a gasket on the bottom.

Coating cold windows with insulating film. If you live in an area with bitterly cold winters or steaming-hot summers, you may want to coat your window glass with clear or tinted insulating window film. The film won't obscure the view, and it can significantly reduce your heating and cooling bills. Look for film labeled "low-e" for "low emissivity," which means that it has been coated to suppress radiative heat flow.

Stopping weather stripping from sticking. Gradual shifting in weather stripping can cause doors to stick or become difficult to close. To get it swinging smoothly again, loosen the weather stripping on the doorjamb enough to be able to slide a credit card between the insulation and the door when it is closed. Then check that the insulation is making contact with the door to form an airtight seal.

How To Install Vinyl Tubing on a Door

Before you start, make sure the doorjamb is clean and the door hardware is tight.

1. Measure the HEAD AND HINGE sides of the doorjamb at the inside stop, and cut tubing to fit. Start nailing the strip to the jamb on the hinge side with the tubular part flush against the stop.

----

2. NAIL THE STRIP to the stop along the top and latch sides. Let the tubular part extend slightly over the edge so that it barely touches the door when it's closed.

----

3. INSTALL A SWEEP—cut to fit with a hacksaw, if needed—on the inside door bottom. Position the sweep so that it touches the threshold with the door closed. Mark screw holes with an awl and screw it into place.

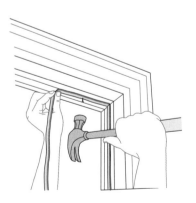

Caulking

Caulk is one of the most versatile products around. It's relatively inexpensive, and the amount of money it saves you in energy costs and leak repairs more than makes up for the money that you lay out for it. Caulk can be used with virtually any building material found inside and outside the home—everything from drywall, glass, plastic, wood, and tile to asphalt, concrete, metal, stone, and brick. Although it performs just one essential task—sealing gaps—it does the job extremely well.

YOUR COST SAVINGS

$125

Amount you can save annually by recaulking an older home.

Care and Maintenance

Check the caulk. Early spring and fall are the best times to examine your home's exterior caulking. Do a walk-around inspection at least once a year to make certain that all joints are watertight and ready for harsh weather. Test caulk by poking it with a screwdriver. It should have some give; if it cracks or tears, replace it.

Before you apply caulk, prep the area. Clean the surface. Wipe off any dust or dirt, and remove oils or deposits with mineral spirits or a manufacturer-recommended solvent. Most important, remove any existing caulking with a putty knife, razor blade, or screwdriver, or with liquid caulk remover. For exterior doors or windows, scrape off old paint, clean the area with a mild soap solution, and let dry.

Cut the caulk nozzle carefully. The success of any caulking job depends on applying the right amount of caulk. One of the most common mistakes that DIYers make is cutting the nozzle too far down, creating a large opening that dispenses too much caulk. For best results, the hole should be about half as wide as the crack or seam you'll be caulking. Cutting the tube at a 45-degree angle also facilitates a neater job, although some pros claim that a V-notch cut in the tip makes it easier to caulk corners.

Tool the bead. A bead of caulk is what you get once you squeeze caulk out of its gun onto a seam. To do its job, the bead needs to be tooled, or compressed, to fit into the seam. Tooling the bead to an "hourglass" shape ensures better adhesion and flexibility. (You want the caulk to be thick where it adheres to both sides of the joint but thinner in the middle.) With practice, you can use the cut end of the spout itself to tool the caulk as it's applied. A wet finger is the traditional tooling choice, but be

SMART IDEA

Be sure to test old silicone caulk before using it. Squeeze a little onto a nonporous surface; if it doesn't cure (harden) within 24 hours, you'll need to use a fresh tube.

Most exterior caulking compounds should not be used outdoors when the thermometer dips below 45°F (7°C). In addition to taking longer to cure, some compounds, especially those containing silicone, become thicker and more difficult to work with. If you need to caulk in the cold, store the tube in a warm location (or in warm water if the tubes are plastic) until the time you use it. Keep it warm by sliding a piece of pipe insulation over both the tube and the caulk gun before you start working. You can also use caulking cord for temporary emergency repairs around windows and doors in temperatures below 45°F (7°C).

sure to wear latex gloves if you're using silicone, polyurethane, butyl rubber, or any other caulk that may cause skin irritation. You can also tool with an ice cube (this is especially good because it will never stick to caulk), a Popsicle stick, or a plastic spoon.

Keep caulk in line with masking tape. If you're new to caulking, or if you need a straight, neat caulk line, try working with a border of masking tape or carpenter tape. Place a strip of tape on each side of the seam before you start caulking. Make sure the tape is straight and spaced evenly to the width of the tooled bead. Apply about 3 feet (1 metre) of caulk at a time, and tool the bead when done. Then slowly remove the tape.

Stop up the caulk. What can you do with a half-full caulk tube? Either look for something else to caulk, or reseal it and save it for next time. The trick to reusing caulk is to keep the remaining adhesive from hardening. Plug the nozzle with a rustproof, 2-inch (5 cm) machine screw or nail. Wrapping the tube with plastic wrap can also help keep the caulk from hardening.

Don't caulk everything! Lap siding needs to "breathe" and have a way for any trapped moisture to escape. Don't caulk the horizontal joints of lap siding. Also, most storm windows have small weep holes along the bottom edge to allow moisture to escape; don't caulk these either.

Easy Fixes

Caulking big gaps. Don't waste caulk trying to seal a gap that's wider than 1/4 inch (0.5 cm), or deeper than 1/2 inch (1 cm). Chances are it won't hold up, and you'll soon be buying more caulk to do it over the right way. The way to approach a deep crack is to press a backer rod (available in different sizes at most hardware stores) into the gap before you caulk. The rod lets you tool the bead more effectively, and provides an additional support surface that lessens stress on the caulk.

Reaching difficult areas. Every so often you'll need to caulk an area that's hard to get to. Use a piece of duct tape to affix a piece of plastic tubing or a plastic drinking straw to the end of the tube nozzle. You'll still need to guide the caulk into the seam, but the added inches (centimetres) can make the job much easier.

Prime, caulk, paint. If you've stripped your siding down to bare wood (or have new siding) the correct order is to prime the bare wood first, caulk the seams, then paint.

10 MUST-CAULK SPOTS

Caulk seals the seams of a house's shell, preventing water, cold and hot air, and pests from getting in. Want to keep your house well sealed and watertight? Caulk here:

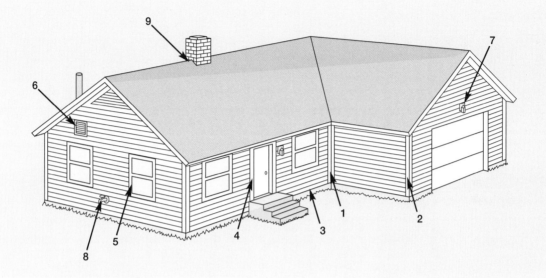

1. Along seams at inside corner moldings

2. Along seams at outside corner moldings

3. Along joints where siding meets the foundation

4. Along joints between door frame and siding

5. Along joints between window frames and siding

6. Around vents from dryer, bathrooms, and kitchen

7. Around through-wall holes made for outdoor electrical outlets or lights

8. Around through-wall plumbing pipes and utility lines

9. Along joints between flashing and the chimney and around the chimney flue where it meets the crown

10. Along the joints between the foundation and a patio or porch (not shown)

WHICH CAULK SHOULD I USE?

These four caulking compounds can be used for most interior and exterior tasks. Whenever possible, buy a premium product for the best durability, and choose a caulk that suits your specific needs. Be sure to read the manufacturer's directions for a description of the compound, its proper usage and curing time, and any required solvents.

CAULKING COMPOUND	USE	DURABILITY	STRENGTHS	WEAKNESSES
Acrylic latex and acrylic latex with silicone	Primarily interior. Use around doors, windows, molding, fixtures, glass, tile, and smooth, nonporous materials.	5–25 years	Good flexibility; water cleanup; low shrinkage; low odor; inexpensive; available in various colors.	Low moisture resistance (non-silicone); may not adhere to metals and nonporous materials; acrylic latex with silicone may not be paintable.
Silicone	Interior/exterior. Use around metal flashing, primed wood, glass, tile, and smooth, non-porous materials.	12–30+ years	Excellent moisture resistance, flexibility, and resiliency; low shrinkage; resists mold, mildew, and UV rays.	Can't be painted; messy; strong fumes; solvent cleanup; not for use on vinyl or masonry; expensive.
Butyl rubber	Exterior. Use around concrete, brick, foundations, gutters, aluminum siding, and metal flashing.	3–10 years	Excellent flexibility; paintable; water resistant; holds up well to extreme temperatures.	Low durability; toxic; strong fumes; cures slowly; solvent tooling and cleanup; not for use on masonry; may be difficult to find.
Polyurethane/Urethane	Exterior. Use around concrete, brick, stone, wood, metal, plastic, fiberglass. (Some urethane caulks can be used indoors.)	20–30+ years	Excellent flexibility and strength; water, temperature, and stress resistant; paintable; adheres to painted surfaces.	Long curing time; messy; flammable; toxic; strong fumes; solvent cleanup; expensive.

Porches

An attractive, well-maintained porch serves many purposes: It welcomes the outside world to your home, serves as a gathering place for guests, provides the perfect perch for taking in the passing scene, and offers a naturally cool living space in summertime. A porch's roof provides protection against the elements, so maintenance is somewhat easier in this space than for a fully exposed deck. Keep your porch clean and structurally sound, and it will reward you with many years of easy living.

YOUR COST SAVINGS

$2,300

How much it would cost to have floor joists and top boards replaced on an 8-by-20-foot (2.5 by 6 metres) porch.

Care and Maintenance

Do a seasonal inspection. Prepare for the wear and tear of rough winter weather with an annual fall inspection of your porch's structural elements. Before the new season rolls in, repair damaged steps, leaking roof, loose boards or rails, split or rotting wood, missing nails or screws, and loose or missing anchors where the porch attaches to the house.

Prevent rot and banish pests. Proper maintenance of a porch starts at the top—of your house, that is. Roof edges and clean gutters should allow rainwater to drain well away from your porch's footings; otherwise, accumulating moisture will be an open invitation for the rot and pests that can cause structural damage. Also make sure that mulch and soil don't come into direct contact with wooden porch posts (another place for moisture and its resulting problems to develop). Every year, prevent dampness from soaking into the porch floor by sealing any raw floorboard ends with a water-repellent wood preservative and topcoat of porch paint.

Break out the broom regularly. Fallen leaves and pine needles aren't just an eyesore on your porch—if you let them accumulate, they can shorten the life of the structure. Such debris captures moisture, which in turn attracts rot, mildew, and such pests as the dreaded termite. Sweep your porch once a week (and more often if needed), making sure to get the bristles between the floorboards and into other collection points, such as the bottoms of porch posts. A putty knife works well if you need a little extra help clearing out debris that has gathered in narrow crannies.

SMART IDEA

When painting
your porch ceil-
ings, think blue.
Light, bright blues
ranging from
turquoise to peri-
winkle have long
been favorite hues
for porch ceilings,
which is no sur-
prise when you
consider the
expansive, sky-like
feel such shades
lend to an
enclosed space,
the natural calm
they impart, and
the way they help
to reflect and
extend natural light
as the sun sets.
Many folks have
also found that a
blue porch ceiling
helps to banish
bugs.

Plan ground-level plantings carefully. Perennial plantings can add color as well as an attractive screen around the base of your porch, but you need to be cautious about where you plant them. As they grow and fill out, shrubs and other plants can reduce proper air circulation if they're too close to the porch, and the water they need to thrive can end up drifting toward foundations and footings. Before you begin planting, know what the full-grown dimensions of your plants will be, and position them at least half of that full-grown width away from your porch's base. Use mulch to keep moisture near plant roots and away from your porch's structural elements.

Hang plants correctly. Baskets of plants are a welcoming sight on any porch, but if the water you give them ends up draining directly onto your porch's railings and floorboards, they can do more harm than good. Be sure to position hanging plants so that water drains over and away from railings and floorboard edges.

Line it with lattice. A great way to conceal a porch's framing and whatever might lie under it—without restricting essential airflow—is to install a perimeter lattice enclosure, or skirt, between the porch's floor and just above the ground (to protect the skirt's edge from moisture). Ready-made lattice is sold by the sheet at most home-improvement centers, in finished and unfinished wood varieties or made from synthetic materials.

Use the right paint for your porch's various surfaces. The right finishes will enhance the beauty and longevity of your porch, but you'll need different types of finishes for different parts of the porch. Posts and railings look best painted with exterior gloss or semigloss paint, both of which are durable and easy to clean. For the floor, use specially formulated porch floor paint made to stand up to a steady flow of foot traffic.

Easy Fixes

Stopping slips. Keep your family and guests safe with smart surface applications to help them maintain their footing. Self-adhesive, nonskid strips in 1- or 2-inch (2.5 or 5 cm) widths can be applied in double bands to step treads (be sure to thoroughly sand and clean surfaces before laying the strips). For all-over traction that's especially helpful in wet weather, apply a porch paint that includes a nonskid additive, or mix a little sand into standard porch floor paint before applying it.

Steadying wobbly rails and posts Porch railings get their strength and solidity from vertical structural supports—newel posts at the ends and evenly spaced porch posts at intervals in the handrail. If a newel or porch post is unstable, your railing will be, too, creating a serious safety hazard. Tighten any loose vertical supports by driving a 4- or 5-inch-long (10 to 13 cm), 5/16-inch (0.5 cm) lag screw (with washer) through the post's base into the porch floor's framing. First, drill a 1-inch (2.5 cm) diameter, 1-inch (2.5 cm) deep countersink (a depression to accommodate the head of the screw) at an angle into the base of the post. Continue by drilling a pilot hole using a 7/32-inch (0.5 cm) bit. Drive in the screw, making sure the post is level before tightening the screw all the way. Finish the repair by covering the screw head with a plug cut from a 1-inch (2.5 cm) diameter wooden dowel.

SCREENING YOUR PORCH

When screened porches came into vogue, there wasn't much choice in materials or installation techniques. That's not so today. Screening itself is available in either fiberglass or aluminum varieties and in a range of colors. Fiberglass is often the better bet as it's easier to work with, can be stretched out more tightly than aluminum, and is more cost-efficient; select it in a dark shade such as black, which is less reflective and provides clearer visibility than lighter screen tones. As for installation, there are now much better options than the traditional method of tacking the screening directly to post and railing surfaces with a narrow wood strip for cover. Look for new screening systems that provide handy tracks and a spline to hold the screening in place, topped with attractive snap-on trim.

Decks

Decks are valuable outdoor living spaces, not only for the day-to-day enjoyment they allow as an extension of your home's square footage, but also for the great return on investment they can provide if you sell your home. But to sustain its value a deck needs to be well maintained. Regular cleaning, periodic refinishing, and the timely repair of potential structural problems are the three keys to prolonging the life of your deck and keeping it looking its best.

Care and Maintenance

Give it a clean sweep. Just as with porches, you need to sweep decks regularly to get rid of leaves, twigs, and other debris that can stain wood surfaces and trap moisture, resulting in mildew and rot. Use a heavy-duty broom to sweep your deck clean, making sure the bristles get into the gaps between floorboards to clear out any trapped leaves and needles. If even after a good once-over with a heavy-duty broom you still see gunk lodged between floorboards, use a putty knife to clean out the gaps.

Keep your deck dry. Standing water is another invitation for rot, so make sure any roof runoff is directed away from your deck. Clean, strategically placed gutters are the best means of keeping rainwater from forming puddles on a deck. Another option is to install rain diverters on the roof to direct water runoff away from the deck.

Keep screws and bolts tight. As the wood in a new deck dries, connections that were bolted or nailed together can loosen and become unsafe. Periodically, check below the deck and tighten every nut and bolt you see. Hammer in any nails that are about to pop (see "Fixing popped nails" tip). While you're at it, look for discoloration, mold, or other signs of rotting wood, both below the deck and on its surface. Poke a screwdriver into wood surfaces that look suspect; if the tip penetrates the wood easily and tears its fibers apart, replace that piece.

take care

Pressure-treated wood is basically plywood or lumber that has been treated with potentially toxic chemicals that protect wood from termites and decay-causing fungi. When handling pressure-treated lumber, wear eye protection and a CSA accredited dust mask. Wash up well before eating, and launder your work clothes separately. Finally, don't use pressure-treated wood for any structural elements that could come into contact with drinking water or food.

Let air circulate. Good air circulation underneath a deck is essential to preventing moisture buildup that can cause rot and attract termites. Clean out below your deck periodically to keep leaves, needles, and other moisture-trapping debris from building up. If you want to conceal the area below a deck, use a lattice enclosure, or skirt, which hides untended ground or stored items while allowing air to flow freely. Make sure the skirt sits at least an inch (2.5 cm) above the ground so that its bottom edge doesn't get moist.

Exercise caution when caring for composite deck material. Composite deck materials such as Trex may have maintenance requirements that differ from those listed here. For example, it is not advisable to pressure wash composite surfaces, and certain cleaning supplies may fade the composite material. Ask your contractor or home-improvement store how to care for your composite deck.

Easy Fixes

Bleaching stains. Remove mildew and stains with a relatively gentle but effective oxygen bleach wash. Mix 1 to 3 ounces (30 to 90 ml) of sodium percarbonate per gallon (4 litres) of water (don't substitute chlorine bleach, which can break down the lignin that binds wood together and harm nearby plants). Apply the solution to stained areas with a mop or brush, let it sit for 15 to 20 minutes, then use a hose to rinse off the solution. Some commercial deck cleaners also contain bleach and are specially formulated to remove tough stains, mildew, and unsightly tree sap. Whether you use a commercial or homemade bleach-based cleaner, you'll have to reapply wood sealer after washing since bleach removes it along with dirt and stains.

take care

A power washer may seem like the perfect tool for deck cleaning, but in inexperienced hands it can do more harm than good. Too much water pressure or the wrong spray angle can end up disturbing wood fibers and raising the grain, making for a fuzzy surface that doesn't wear or weather well. In most cases, a standard garden hose with an adjustable nozzle (in conjunction with a deck-cleaning solution) is a much better tool for the job.

DECK FURNISHINGS DOS AND DON'TS

- Don't place mats or outdoor rugs on deck surfaces because they'll collect rot-inducing debris and moisture. If you must have a mat or a rug on your deck, remove it regularly to clean and air the underlying surface, and don't replace it until the surface is completely dry. Pick up a mat or rug that's gotten rain-soaked and dry it out thoroughly before replacing it.

- Do elevate planters on rolling plant stands instead of placing them directly on your deck.

Placing a saucer underneath a planter isn't enough, because the saucer can leave stains.

- Do move furniture pieces often to clean underneath them, especially if they have closed-weave or otherwise solid constructions.

Fixing popped nails. Over time, nails used in the construction of your deck can pop out, creating safety hazards and possibly leaving rust stains. If the nail head is just barely above the surface of the wood, hammer it back in. If the nail has worked itself loose, pull it out as soon as you notice it, and instead of driving a replacement nail, use a 3-inch (8 cm), stainless-steel decking screw. It will bite more deeply and securely into the wood; it's also rust resistant and won't stain wood decking.

How To Clean and Seal Your Deck

Depending on your family's traffic patterns and the local climate, your deck will be due for a good washing once or twice a year. This may also be your opportunity to reseal the deck, a job that needs to be done every two to three years. To see if your deck needs resealing, splash a glass of water on the deck boards. If the water beads up, the surface is still water-repellent; if it soaks in, it's time to reseal. Gear up for this job with rubber boots, eye protection, and rubber gloves, and select an overcast day to tackle it. Warm, sunny weather will cause your deck-cleaning solution to dry before it has a chance to de-gunk the surface.

1. REMOVE FURNISHINGS and planters from the deck, and trim or tie back any branches that are touching its surface. Also moisten and cover any nearby foliage that might come in contact with the cleaning solution.

2. Mix a ready-made DECK-CLEANING SOLUTION following manufacturer's directions; unless your deck is badly stained, use a bleach-free formulation. In general, use a stiff-bristled brush to scrub all parts of the deck (railings, steps, and floorboards) with the solution. For best results, start at the top of the railings and work your way down to the floorboards. To make washing floorboards easier on your back and knees, use a long-handled floor brush.

3. Allow the CLEANING SOLUTION to sit on the wood surface for about 15 minutes, then rinse away all residue with a garden hose. Also rinse nearby plants that have been splashed with cleaning solution. Let the deck dry completely (usually three to four days) before replacing furnishings and planters.

4. If you also need to RESEAL YOUR DECK, sweep it thoroughly once it's dry, and apply a clear or staining wood sealer. Use a roller attached to a pole for the deck boards and a natural-bristle brush for the railings and anyplace else the roller can't reach; or use a pump-style garden sprayer. Treat the entire surface of the wood (top, sides, and bottom), and pay extra attention to the ends of the deck boards, as they're the easiest entry points for damaging moisture.

Garages and Carports

Garages and carports provide your prized wheels protection against the elements. A garage can also do double and triple duty as a workshop and covered storage area. Carports, especially those made of steel, aluminum, or vinyl, are relatively maintenance free. The most maintenance-intensive part of a garage is its door and door opener. These can not only be costly to repair or replace, they can put your family, your home, and its contents in jeopardy if your garage is attached to your home and someone gains access through your garage door.

Care and Maintenance

Give your garage floor a new look. The right finish will give your concrete garage floor an easy-to-clean surface and a polished look. Paint options include acrylic latex and epoxy formulated especially for garage floors. Concrete sealers and stains are easier to apply but require more frequent cleaning and reapplication. Whichever finish you choose, make sure the floor is clean first. Wash the floor with trisodium phosphate (TSP) or a similar cleanser and rinse it with a hose, starting at the back of the garage and working your way forward. You may also need to roughen the surface with a commercial etching solution that will allow the coating to adhere better. Once the floor is ready for the new finish, make sure the area is well ventilated, then apply the paint, stain, or sealer following the manufacturer's directions. Allow the floor to dry for at least 24 hours before walking on it. Allow as much as a week before parking a car on it.

Mark off your parking spot. Avoid damage to your car and the garage wall by marking off the parking zone within your garage. Use colored electrical tape or spray paint to designate the drive-in stopping point, or suspend a tennis ball from the ceiling so that it hangs at the spot where you need to stop.

take care

A well-sealed garage can make a great work area or protected storage space, but it can also be a trap for carbon monoxide gas generated by cars and other machinery such as lawn mowers. Never run any such items in a detached garage unless the door is open for ventilation. Never run this kind of machinery in an attached garage even if the door is open, because carbon monoxide can seep through the garage walls into the house.

Easy Fixes

Keeping oil stains from setting. Oil dribbles are pretty much a given in a well-trafficked garage or carport, but they don't even have to hit the floor if you're careful. Place a garage floor mat or a pan lined with cardboard under cars and leaking machinery to intercept drips, and if you miss a few, don't let them sit and soak in. There are all sorts of products available for removing oil spills from a garage or carport floor, but none works better than ordinary clay-based cat litter. If the stains are fresh, cover them with cat litter, wait about an hour, and sweep it up. For old stains, pour paint thinner on the stain, cover with cat litter, wait 12 hours, and then sweep clean.

Stripping out the elements. Want to keep cold air, vermin, and debris out of your garage? Close the gaps around your garage door with weather stripping. You can create a good seal between the bottom of the garage door and the floor by tacking 3/4-inch (2 cm) foam pipe insulation to the bottom of the door, with the slit side of the insulation facing down. To keep the insulation out of sight when the door is closed, set it back about 1/2 inch (1 cm) from the door's front edge. (See "Garage Doors" section.)

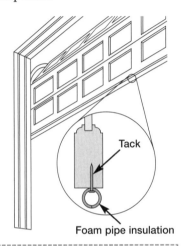

Tack

Foam pipe insulation

---

7 TIPS FOR AN ORGANIZED GARAGE

With just little time and planning, you can transform your garage from a cluttered mess to an organized, convenient oasis. Here are some easy ways to overhaul your garage quickly:

1. Sort the contents of your garage into "keep," "sell/give away," and "toss" piles. If you're hesitating about a certain item, remember the two-year rule: if you haven't used or worn something in two years, it's time to let it go.

2. Group the "keep" pile by season (or by use) so that these items can be stored together when you put them back inside the garage.

3. Install cabinets or roll in freestanding, open shelving units, if you don't have them already, for effective, off-the-ground storage. Bins and boxes in an array of sizes and shapes can be added for extra convenience.

4. Suspend overhead bins or an over-the-car-hood rack from ceiling joists. If you've got a high ceiling in your garage you can turn the overhead space into a storage bonanza.

5. Wall racks can be installed for easy access to athletic equipment, yard-work gear, and tools.

6. Station recycling bins near the entrance to your home for easy sorting and disposal.

7. Create a workbench with pegboard paneling above it for displaying tools and, alongside it, cabinets or shelves for storing other tool gear.

Your Home's Systems

Like your body, your home has so many interdependent parts—washers, dryers, sinks, furnaces, drains, refrigerators, doorbells, lights—that thinking about them and how

one's performance can affect another can make your head swim. The inner workings of your home will make a lot more sense when you start thinking about them not as discrete parts, but as a series of systems.

As a child, it was probably easier for you to understand how the heart worked after you understood its relation to your body's veins, arteries, and capillaries. Similarly, you'll get a much better handle on how your electrical outlets work if you first understand the ins and outs of your circuit breakers and interior wiring. Home-care professionals, too, think in terms of systems: You don't hire one person to fix the tub and another to fix the sink, do you? The same guy who fixes your furnace is the one you'd call to fix your air conditioner, because they're both part of your heating and cooling system. If you think of your plumbing system as basically a water supply and a bunch of drains, fixing the sink is little different than fixing the tub.

One key to keeping house systems running smoothly is regular maintenance, which often involves little more than cleaning. Clean the coils on the refrigerator and it will run more efficiently. Clean the striker on the doorbell and that faint chime will return to its loud peal. It's as simple as that. In this part, we'll show you how to handle basic house-systems maintenance and repair jobs. We'll also warn you about more dangerous projects (especially those involving electricity and heating and cooling equipment) that you should leave to professionals.

Electrical Smarts

We've all plugged "just one more" appliance into an already overloaded extension cord or dangled a hair dryer just a little too close to running bathwater. But mishandling electrical wiring can mean injury for you, not to mention potentially extensive (and expensive!) repairs that you'll have to pay a professional to do. Using common sense is the best tool you have to keep your wiring in tip-top shape: The job is more than half done if you inspect visible wires, cords, appliances, and lamps regularly, and keep kids, pets, and water away from outlets and appliances at all times.

YOUR COST SAVINGS
$55
What you'd typically pay per hour for the services of a licensed electrician.

Care and Maintenance

Check cords and plugs for signs of damage. Examine electrical cords attached to appliances and lamps for cracked or worn insulation, exposed bare wire, and black spots (the latter are caused by sparks). Inspect the plugs, too, and make sure that there are no bent or corroded prongs or missing insulation disks. If you spot any of these problems, have the cord and/or plug replaced—or replace the appliance altogether.

4 ELECTRICAL MISTAKES TO AVOID

Preventing trouble with your home's electrical system doesn't take much effort—it probably has more to do with the stuff that you *shouldn't* do than it is about things that you really *need* to do. For example:

1. Don't splice damaged cords. Splices can fall apart and cause fires. Chuck the appliance with the spliced cord and buy a new one, or have it repaired by a professional.

2. Don't overload your outlets. Multiple extension cords and "octopus" plugs that turn a single outlet into multiple outlets can overheat and cause a fire. Instead, plug some appliances into other outlets. If you live in an older home with an inadequate number of outlets, consider hiring an electrician to add more.

3. Don't use outlets that screw into light sockets. They're easily overpowered, causing overheating, melted wires, and possibly a fire.

4. Don't get too used to those ugly extension cords. Extension cords are supposed to be temporary, not permanent, parts of your décor. And it's not just that they're tacky to look at—these cords can cause dangerous circuit overloads. And who among us hasn't taken a spill after tripping over an extension cord?

Pull the *plug*, not the cord, from the outlet. If you tug on the cord you're bound to loosen some connections inside, which will cause a short in your system.

Keep cords away from heat sources. Because they're so ugly to look at, electrical cords tend to get tucked along baseboard heaters or snaked around the toaster. Bad idea. A toaster can melt through a cord; a warm-water baseboard heater won't melt a cord, but the heat can cause the insulation to crack.

Keep outlets covered. Make sure that the covers for floor outlets are screwed in tightly. If you have small children or pets in the home, it's a good idea to plug outlets you're not using with childproof covers.

Don't put your life in the hands of a $3 outlet adapter. You know those adapters that allow you to use a three-prong grounding plug in a two-prong outlet? They basically rely on the cover plate's screw to serve as a substitute ground connection. And believe us, the screw is rarely adequate as a grounding device. If the adapter's grounding wire is not properly attached to the screw, it can cause a fire—or lethally shock you. If your home only has two-prong outlets, consider upgrading them to ground fault circuit interrupters (GFCIs).

PLAYING WITH WIRES = PLAYING WITH FIRE

Electricity is a powerful and potentially lethal force; as such, you should approach it cautiously. Professional electricians follow these guidelines when they're working with wires, plugs, and all that other hot stuff. You'd do well to follow their example.

ALWAYS …

- Wear safety glasses when working around electricity.
- Unplug a lamp or appliance before attempting to repair it.
- Turn off power to a circuit at the service panel before working on it.
- Use a voltage tester to make sure a wire isn't live. Do this *before* you touch the wire!

- Use plastic-handled tools for electrical work. Even better, do as electricians do and use plastic-handled tools with rubber jackets.
- If you're in doubt about the safety of any electrical repair or test, call in an electrician.

NEVER …

- Stand on a wet or damp floor when working with electricity. Put as much insulation as possible between you and the source of a shock. Wear rubber-soled shoes, and stand on a rubber mat.
- Touch metal plumbing or gas pipes or fixtures when working on electrical wiring or appliances. Touching these pipes and fixtures connects you to ground and will allow any shocks that you might receive to course through your body.
- Use two hands to open a service panel, pull out a fuse, or test an outlet or switch. If you use two hands and come in contact with electricity, a shock can run up one hand, through your heart, and out the other hand. If it can be done with one hand, just use one hand.
- Use aluminum or wet wooden ladders if you're working near overhead power lines or testing a live circuit.

Wiring, Fuses, and Circuit Breakers

The heart of your home's electrical system is called the "main service panel," but you know it by a more common name: It's a fuse box if your electrical system dates back, say, pre-1960's. If your electrical system is newer, it's probably a circuit breaker. Your service panel's purpose is to distribute electricity through-out the house via branch circuits; it also prevents individual circuits from drawing too much power—if that happens, your wires could overheat (and increase your risk of fire). Each circuit is protected at the service panel by an "overcurrent protection device"—either a fuse or a circuit breaker. Aside from resetting a tripped breaker or replacing a blown fuse, there's not much maintaining to do to fuse boxes and circuit breakers. Repairs and upgrades are jobs for licensed electricians.

YOUR COST SAVINGS

$14,500

Average insurance claim in Ontario due to faulty wiring.

Care and Maintenance

Get a gander at the service panel. Look for signs of moisture and rust in the service panel; if you see any, call an electrician. Once a year, trip and reset circuit breakers to prevent corrosion from set-ting in. A corroded breaker may not trip when it needs to.

Turn power off before doing any electrical work. At the main service panel, trip the circuit breaker or remove the fuse that controls that circuit that you're working on. Use a voltage tester to make sure the switch or outlet you want to work on isn't live. To turn off power to the entire house, trip the main breaker in the circuit-breaker panel; if you have a fuse box, remove the main pull-out block or turn the lever switch to "off."

If you're not sure which circuit to turn off, listen to the radio. Plug a radio into the outlet you want to work on and turn it up loud enough that you can hear it from the service panel. Switch off breakers or unscrew fuses until the radio goes off.

Replace blown plug fuses. Make sure that you're standing on a dry surface. Using one hand only, open the service panel, turn off the main power switch, grasp the blown

take care

The CSA's Canadian Electrical (CE) Code sets minimum safety standards for wiring. Even if your home's electrical system was up to code when it was installed, it's a good idea to keep on top of new code requirements (check local building codes, too, as they are often more stringent than the CE), and consider upgrades that could make your house safer. Before altering or adding to your electrical system or undertaking anything but minor repairs, call your electrical or building inspector for up-to-date code information and any necessary permits.

fuse by its glass rim, and turn it counterclockwise. Replace the fuse with one of the same amperage rating, *never* with one of a higher rating. (A fuse whose amp rating exceeds its circuit's capacity could overheat wires and cause a fire.)

Invest in a time delay, not more amps. Heavy power tools and large appliances, such as air conditioners and clothes dryers, usually need more power to start up than they do to remain up and running. Though circuit breakers can withstand these momentary start-up surges, standard fuses often can't. Installing a higher-amp fuse is definitely *not* the answer. Replace the standard fuse with a time-delay fuse of the same amperage. Time-delayed fuses are designed to handle power spikes without blowing.

Keep a flashlight near the service panel. This is a good idea in case you have to replace a fuse or reset a breaker in the dark. Attach Velcro to the wall and to the flashlight to hold it in place.

HOW DOES ELECTRICITY WORK?

The answer to this question can either be simple or really, really complicated. Here's the short answer: Electricity must flow in a closed loop, or circuit, from a power source to a load, such as a lightbulb, and back to the source. If something interrupts the circuit (like an open switch or a tripped circuit breaker), current flow stops.

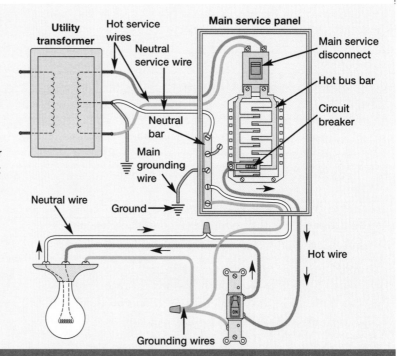

Easy Fixes

Unlocking electrical mysteries with fuses. Unlike a tripped circuit breaker, a blown fuse gives you a visual clue as to what caused the circuit to fail. Take a look at the fuse's glass window. If the metal strip inside is broken but the window is

AMPS, VOLTS, AND WATTS: WHAT DO THEY ALL MEAN?

The rate at which electric current flows through a conductor such as copper wire is measured in amperes (amps). The pressure that causes current to flow through a conductor is measured in volts. Electricity's power, or ability to do work, is measured in watts. What do they all have to do with each other? The basic formula tying the three together is simple: watts (power) = amps (current) x volts (pressure). For example, 1/2 amp of current at 120 volts will power a 60-watt lightbulb.

In Canada, current is delivered to homes and offices at 120 volts (for lighting and small appliances) and 240 volts (for electric ranges and other heavy-duty appliances). Modern three-wire services are rated at 100 to 400 amps, with branch circuits typically rated at 15 or 20 amps.

clear, the circuit is overloaded. If the window is discolored, you probably have a short circuit.

Upgrading your electrical service. If you don't know how many amps your electrical system delivers, check the service disconnect—the amps rating is usually stamped on there. A three-wire (120/240-volt) electrical service with a 60-amp fuse box, once the residential standard, is barely adequate for smaller homes with just one 240-volt appliance. The more modern electronic conveniences you have in your home, the more amps you'll need: If you have a 60-amp, three-wire service, consider upgrading to a three-wire service with a 100-amp or larger breaker panel. If you just have 30-amp, two-wire service, you should definitely upgrade.

WHAT'S CAUSING MY CIRCUIT PROBLEM?

Circuit failure is usually due to one of two problems: Circuits can be overloaded, which is what happens when too many appliances are running on the same circuit. Or they can be short circuited, which is when a worn hot wire touches a worn neutral (or another hot) wire, or the ground wire, or any metal that's grounded, creating a shortcut for a large current surge. Here's how to identify the problem.

Your circuit is probably overloaded if you've just plugged a high-wattage appliance into an outlet and everything just stops working. If you're overloaded, try moving smaller portable appliances to another circuit that's not being used as much. Switch off or unplug the high-watt load, then reset it. Not doing these things will cause the breaker to trip again almost immediately.

If you reset the breaker or replace the fuse and your circuit still isn't working, you probably have a short. Do a little sleuthing to figure out what's causing the short: First unplug all lamps and appliances on the circuit. Then check the plugs and cords for damage: If a fixture, switch, or outlet is discolored or has a faint burned smell, it's likely the culprit. Replace the damaged cord, switch, or outlet if needed.

Before you plug anything back in, reset the breaker or replace the fuse. If the circuit still doesn't work, you'll need to call an electrician because the problem is likely interior wiring. Now, start plugging a few things in again. If the circuit fails only when you turn on a specific lamp or appliance, you've found your short.

Wiring, Fuses, and Circuit Breakers   **175**

Making sure your home has enough juice. If you suspect that your home's electrical system can't accommodate your appliances, electronic equipment, and other modern "toys," consider these general circuit guidelines. Your electrical system should have:

- One 15-amp general-purpose circuit for every 600 square feet (56 square metres) of floor space
- No more than a total of 10 lights and outlets per 15-amp circuit
- Two 20-amp circuits for kitchen receptacles
- One 20-amp circuit each for bathroom and laundry receptacles

How to Map Electrical Circuits

You're standing in front of the breaker box or fuse box, and you want to turn off the circuit that controls the kitchen window air conditioner. How do you know which circuit that is? A map of your home's electrical system, like the ones that you sometimes see taped to the inside of your breaker's cover, is a great help in figuring out which switch or fuse controls which circuit. Tracing circuits isn't difficult. Here's what to do:

1. SKETCH A PLAN of each floor of your house, labeling all rooms and areas.

----

2. On the floor plan, MARK THE LOCATION of every switch, receptacle, and fixture, using the symbols shown in the illustration key.

----

3. At the SERVICE PANEL, shut off the first circuit by tripping its breaker or removing its fuse, and mark a "1" next to it.

----

4. WALK THROUGH THE HOUSE turning on lights and plugging in a radio at each receptacle. If a light or the radio doesn't go on, that switch or receptacle is part of the first circuit. Mark a "1" on your floor plan next to all the switches and receptacles on the dead circuit.

----

5. REPEAT THE PROCESS for all the other circuits, using a different number for each.

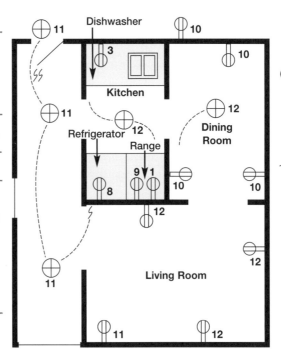

Receptacle
Light fixture
Switch
2 switches
10 Circuit number
Switch to light circuit

Wall Switches and Receptacles

There may be miles of wiring behind your walls, but none of it would mean much to you if it weren't for switches and receptacles (what we often call "outlets"). Receptacles give you access to power; switches let you control it. While usually long-lived and problem-free, receptacles and switches can sometimes fail. Both switches and receptacles can also be incorrectly wired, dangerous, and yet fully functional, until something else goes wrong. Fortunately, switches and receptacles are easy to check and replace, as long you follow the safety precautions outlined in this part of the book.

YOUR COST SAVINGS

$3,000

What it would cost you to replace basic home theater and computer systems that are not protected by a surge protector and are damaged by lightning.

Care and Maintenance

Test your GFCI outlets every month. A ground fault circuit interrupter (GFCI) is designed to sense leaks of electrical current that could cause deadly shock (especially if you're in a moist environment, like a bathroom) and instantly shut off power to everything plugged into it or that comes after it on its circuit. GFCIs that aren't working, of course, won't help you. Testing is quick and easy. First, press the GFCI's "Reset" button to make sure the unit is on. Then plug in a radio and turn it on. While the radio is playing, press the GFCI's "Test" button; the radio should go off. Press "Reset" again; the radio should go back on. If the GFCI fails this test, have it checked by an electrician and replaced if necessary.

Power down before you do any repairs. This is a key step to keep from injuring yourself. Before working on a switch or receptacle, always turn off the power to its circuit at the service panel, and then use a voltage tester to make sure power really is off. Keep kids and pets away from an open electrical box, and never leave the box unattended.

Ditch the heavy metal. Metal switch and outlet faceplates may be pretty, but plastic is the safer bet. A metal plate that comes in contact with a loose hot wire can deliver a nasty shock if you touch it.

take care

If an appliance makes a crackling noise, smells hot, or sparks when you turn it on, don't risk a shock or a burn by unplugging it or touching the outlet. First turn off power to the circuit at the breaker panel or fuse box. Then, with dry hands, cover the plug with a dry towel and pull it out.

Know what the slots mean. The number and shape of the slots in a receptacle tell you a lot about it:

- Two-slot receptacles, found in older houses, lack a grounding terminal that would enable them to be connected to a circuit's grounding wire. Although it's not required, it's a good idea to replace two-slot receptacles with safer, grounding-type, three-slot receptacles, but only if the new receptacle can be properly grounded.

- Three-slot duplex receptacles rated 15 amps/120 volts are the standard household receptacle today. Each of the receptacle's two outlets has two vertical slots—with the neutral slot longer than the hot slot—and a U-shaped grounding slot that should be (but isn't always) connected to a circuit grounding wire.

- T-slot receptacles are used for appliance circuits. They have one T-shaped slot, one vertical slot, and a U-shaped grounding slot and are rated 20 amps/120 volts.

- Certain large appliances require 240- or 120/240-volt receptacles rated 30 amps or more. A large-appliance receptacle's amp and voltage ratings determine its slot configuration, which matches the plug configuration specific to that appliance.

Figure out what kind of wiring you have. Homes built in the 1960s and 1970s may have aluminum wiring, which can be unsafe if it's not properly installed and connected. The trouble with aluminum wiring is that it expands and contracts at different rates than copper. If it's improperly connected to a copper wire or a terminal that's not designed for it, the connection can degrade or loosen and possibly cause a fire.

With a little sleuthing, you can find out what kind of wiring you have: Exposed cables in the basement or attic will tell you all you need to know. Aluminum wire sheathing will be marked "AL" or "ALUMINUM" (copper wire sheathing is marked

---

GFCIS AND AFCIS

equipment spotlight

A ground fault circuit interrupter (GFCI) is a terrific invention: It protects you against shock by instantly shutting down a circuit when it senses a misdirected flow of current to ground, known as a ground fault. A ground fault may not trip a standard breaker, but it can give you a bad shock—a potentially lethal one if you're standing, say, on a wet bathroom floor using a hair dryer with loose or worn wiring. GFCIs are available as breakers, receptacles, and plug-in adapters. Because the rooms are prone to moisture, receptacles in kitchens, bathrooms, workshops, laundry rooms, and garages (plus any that you have outdoors) should be GFCI protected.

An arc-fault circuit interrupter (AFCI) is a relatively recent development. It protects your home against fire by shutting a circuit down when it senses an arc fault, or an unintentional electrical discharge that sparks the circuit. AFCIs are required for bedroom branch circuits; statistics show that a high percentage of home electrical fires occur in bedrooms.

"CU"). If your wiring is aluminum, replacement switches and receptacles must be marked CO/ALR or AL-CU. (You'll also be able to recognize the bare wire by color: aluminum is gray, and copper is orange.) Special connectors are required to join aluminum to copper wires. To be on the safe side, have an experienced electrician do any work on an aluminum wiring system.

Easy Fixes

Keeping the plug plugged in. A receptacle that won't hold a plug snugly in its slots is defective or worn from heavy use. It is a potential fire hazard and must be replaced with one of the same ampere and voltage ratings.

Replacing outlets. Outlets don't often conk out, but they can crack or be shorted out by a faulty appliance. The good news is that it takes just a few minutes (and a few dollars) to replace them. Replacing a faulty receptacle or outlet is not unlike replacing a switch. Turn off power to the receptacle, and use a voltage tester to make sure the receptacle is dead. Remove the cover plate and mounting screws. Pull the

---

MAKING CONNECTIONS

Making correct and secure wire connections is essential to trouble-free electrical installations or repairs—but not everyone knows how to pigtail, hook, or splice. Here's a quick rundown of the most basic wire-connecting skills you'll need:

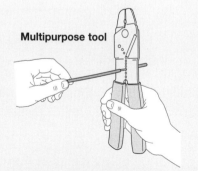

Multipurpose tool

- Strip. Joining wires usually requires removing about 3/4 inch (2 cm) of insulation from their ends with a wire stripper or a multipurpose tool. To strip wire with a multipurpose tool, insert the wire in the correct size notch, then close and rotate the tool until the insulation is cut through and you can slide it off.

- Splice. Use a screw-on wire connector (wire nut) to join wire to wire. Hold the stripped ends of solid wires together and twist the wire nut on clockwise. Twist the bare ends of stranded wires together, then screw on the connector.

- Hook. To connect wire to a screw terminal, use needle-nose pliers to bend the stripped end of the wire into a loop. Wrap the loop clockwise around the screw, and tighten the screw.

- Pigtail. Pigtails are used so that a failure in an outlet won't interrupt the whole circuit. When joining two wires to a switch or receptacle terminal, use a wire connector to join the two wires to a short length of wire called a pigtail; connect the pigtail to the screw terminal. Never connect more than one wire to a single terminal. (This isn't a hard rule to remember—most terminals are designed to hold only one wire.)

This is one of the simpler electrical do-it-yourself jobs you can undertake, but it doesn't mean that you should be any less careful. Assume any wire is hot until you've proven other-wise. Bear in mind, too, that switches are wired to a circuit's hot side only, never to the neutral side (unlike receptacles, which are wired to both the hot and neutral sides of a circuit). The following directions are for a single-pole switch, which controls a receptacle or fixture from one location. Three- and four-way switches (which control receptacles and fixtures from two and three locations, respectively) are wired in a similar fashion, but there are more terminals and wires to keep track of and connect.

1. TURN OFF POWER to the switch, remove the cover plate, and loosen the switch's mounting screws. Gently pull the switch out of the box and use a voltage tester to make sure the circuit is dead.

----

2. Loosen the switch's SCREW TERMI-NALS and disconnect the wires—depending on the circuit, they both may be black, or one may be black and the other white with black tape around it (a white wire, usually neutral, is recoded black to indicate that it's functioning as a hot wire).

----

3. CONNECT THE NEW SWITCH by hooking the hot wires' bare leads clock-wise around its terminal screws. Tighten the screws.

----

4. The new switch will have a GREEN GROUNDING SCREW, which the old one may not have had. In that case, run a pigtail from the green screw to the ground-ing wires in the box (see the "Making Connections" box).

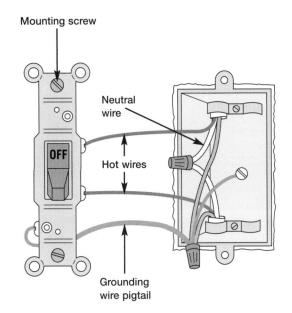

Mounting screw

Neutral wire

Hot wires

Grounding wire pigtail

5. PUSH THE WIRES AND SWITCH BACK INTO THE BOX. Screw the switch to the box, reinstall the cover plate, and restore power.

----

receptacle out of its box and disconnect the wires. Check to see whether its break-off tab has been removed (this allows the receptacle's two outlets to be wired to different circuits). If the tab is gone, bend the same tab on the new receptacle back and forth with needle-nose pliers until the tab breaks off. Connect the wires to the new receptacle in the same configuration they were to the old: black wires to brass screws, white wires to silver screws, grounding pigtail to green screw. Remount the receptacle and restore power. (Installing or replacing a GFCI receptacle is a little trickier. You'll probably want to call a licensed electrician.)

Replacing like switches or outlets with like. When you need to replace a defective switch or receptacle, remember that the new device must have the same amperage and voltage ratings as the old one. You'll find this information and much more on a switch's metal mounting yoke or on a receptacle's case. Don't forget to look for the "CSA" mark on any electrical device you buy.

Getting your system grounded. Building codes now require all switches and receptacles in new installations to be grounded. If you have an older electrical system with two-slot receptacles or if a circuit tester reveals that your three-slot receptacles are not grounded, consider having an electrician assess your system. If it turns out that your system does include grounding wires (or other means of grounding, such as metal conduit), you're in luck. You can replace two-slot receptacles with three-slot ones or rewire existing three-slot receptacles so that they're properly grounded. If your system lacks a means of grounding, you have two options: You can replace standard receptacles with ground-fault circuit interrupters to provide protection against shock, or you can have new cable that includes a grounding wire run throughout your house. The latter is a major undertaking.

SURGE PROTECTOR

equipment spotlight

Surges in the power line—sudden spikes in voltage usually caused by lightning—can damage computers and other electronic equipment. A surge protector keeps the spike from getting through to and damaging any devices connected to it. Plug-in surge protectors require three-slot grounded receptacles; whole-house protectors are also available.

ARE YOU *SURE* THE POWER'S OFF?

Always prove that there's no power in a circuit before you attempt to do any work on it. An easy way to check a circuit is with an inexpensive device called a noncontact voltage tester: It's the size of a magic marker and lights up (or makes a noise) when it comes in contact with a hot wire. The device is battery powered, so make sure it has fresh batteries before you test anything. (You'll know it's working when you hold the device next to a lightbulb or near an outlet that you know is live and the tester flickers or beeps.) A noncontact tester is not reliable when testing wires coated in metal sheathing.

Here's how to do two basic voltage tests:

Testing for power at a switch: Shut off the switch's circuit by removing its fuse or turning off its breaker at the service panel. Leaving switches in the "on" position, remove the switch's cover plate and loosen the screws fastening the switch to the electrical box. Without touching wires or switch terminals, touch the probe's nose first to one switch wire terminal, then the other.

Testing for power at a receptacle: Shut off power to the receptacle's circuit at the service panel (sometimes there's more than one circuit to an outlet, so make sure you shut them all off). If the outlet is connected to a wall switch, make sure that the wall switch is on. Insert the nose of the tester into or against one of the plug's slots (test the "neutral" or bigger one, which should give you a proper reading no matter what—even if the outlet was wired incorrectly). Check all of the plugs in the outlet; sometimes the top and bottom plugs are wired separately. If you don't hear consistent chirps or see consistent beeps on the reader, the power is probably off.

But let's just double-check. A faulty receptacle can give you a faulty reading. Remove the receptacle's cover plate and loosen its mounting screws. Pull the receptacle gently out of the box without touching the wires or terminals. Touch the tester to the bare ends of each pair of hot (black) and neutral (white) wires; then insert the nose deeper into the box to test other wires in the box that are not connected to the receptacle. If you find any hot wires, turn them off at the service panel and retest. If the tester doesn't light in any of these positions, the circuit is dead.

Ceiling Light Fixtures

Because ceiling fixtures tend to last a long time—after all, when was the last time you nudged into one accidentally and broke it?—they are generally replaced for decorative reasons, not because they fail. Caring for your high-hanging light fixtures is simple, as is replacing one if you want a change. Here's how to keep fixtures gleaming and install replacements when the time comes.

YOUR COST SAVINGS

$285

What you would pay an electrician to install a new ceiling light fixture.

Care and Maintenance

Give your crystal the white-glove treatment. When a crystal chandelier gets really dirty, your only option is to remove the crystals and wash them by hand—what a job! Regular maintenance, however, will help you avoid such an arduous task. A couple of times a year, set up a stepladder and apply the two-glove cleaning method. Put on a pair of white cotton gloves, available at most home centers, and dampen one of them with glass cleaner. Rub each crystal with the damp glove and wipe it immediately with the dry one. Wipe the chandelier frame with a dry cloth.

Install "rough service" bulbs. Installing long-life bulbs in hard-to-reach fixtures means you'll climb up to replace bulbs less often. Vibration near doorways, however, causes even long-life bulbs to burn out early. When a bulb near a constantly slamming door burns out, replace it with one labeled for "rough service" (they're available at most electrical supply stores).

SMART IDEA

Keep light fixtures, shades, and bulbs clean by including them in your regular vacuuming routine.

HOW MUCH LIGHT DO YOU NEED?

How bright (or how dim) you want your home to be is a matter of personal preference. But here are some rules of thumb to follow if you like a cheery, well-lit home. For fluorescent light requirements, divide the wattages below by a third. Watts indicated are for square metre of floor.

ROOM	WATTAGE
Living rooms, dens, and bedrooms	11 to 22 watts of incandescent lights per square metre
Kitchens, laundry rooms, and workshops	32 to 54 watts per square metre
Bathrooms	66 watts per square metre and 30 to 40 watts per running 30 centimetres of vanity top

Stick with the right wattage. If a label on your light fixture says not to use bulbs beyond a certain wattage, heed the warning. Larger bulbs generate more heat in the socket than the fixture is designed to handle. Excess heat trapped in a fixture can shorten the life of a bulb, and over the long run, it can cause the wire's insulation to give out and the socket to fail.

How to Replace a Ceiling Light Fixture

The hardware used to mount fixtures to the ceiling box varies depending on their size and design. Lighter one- or two-bulb fixtures are screwed directly to mounting tabs in the ceiling box or to a mounting strap attached to the box. Center-mounted fixtures are fastened to a threaded nipple with a nut. Follow the fixture's installation instructions carefully. (Never hang a ceiling fan from a standard ceiling box that's set up for a light fixture. Ceiling fans require special boxes that are secured to the ceiling framework.) In general, here's what involved:

1. TURN OFF POWER to the fixture at the service panel. Remove the fixture's globe and the screws or nuts that hold it in place. With the wiring exposed, use a non-contact voltage tester to make sure the power is off. Disconnect the wires; remove the old fixture and its mounting strap.

2. Attach the new fixture's MOUNTING STRAP to the ceiling box with the screws provided.

3. HAVE A HELPER HOLD THE NEW FIXTURE while you connect its wires to the circuit wires with wire connectors: hot (black) to hot and neutral (white) to neutral. (If the new fixture has a lamp-style cord rather then black and white wires, the cord's neutral wire will have ribbed sheathing or be identified with writing.) Run a pigtail from the green grounding screw on the mounting strap to the green or bare circuit, ceiling box, and fixture grounding wires. If the fixture lacks a grounding wire, run a pigtail from the mounting strap's grounding screw to the other grounding wires in the box.

4. TUCK THE WIRES INTO THE BOX. Fasten the new fixture to the mounting strap with screws or to the threaded nipple with a nut. Install the lightbulb(s) and globe, if any.

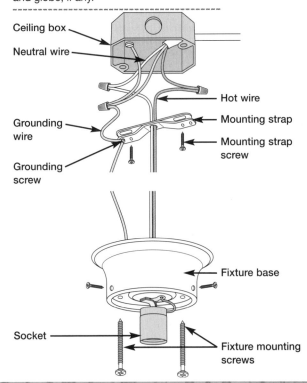

Ceiling box

Neutral wire

Hot wire

Grounding wire

Mounting strap

Grounding screw

Mounting strap screw

Fixture base

Socket

Fixture mounting screws

Fluorescent Light Fixtures

Kitchens, baths, workshops, and offices have long relied on the brightness, low heat emission, and reduced energy consumption of fluorescent lighting. For the most part, these fixtures are trouble-free. When something goes wrong, the culprit is often the ballast, the transformer that boosts household current to get a fluorescent tube's internal gases and phosphor lining glowing and then reduces voltage to the level required to keep the tube lit.

YOUR COST SAVINGS

$35

Amount you'll save per bulb over five years by switching from incandescent to compact fluorescent bulbs.

Care and Maintenance

Leave the lights on. Turning off lights doesn't always conserve energy; turning a fluorescent light on and off frequently wastes power and shortens bulb life. If you're going to be out of a room for less than half an hour, leave fluorescent fixtures on. (The same applies to compact fluorescent bulbs.)

Replace light tubes with ease. Need to replace a fluorescent light tube? How you do it depends on what type it is. Rapid-start tubes have two pins at each end. To remove a double-pin (rapid-start) tube, give it a quarter turn so that the pins line up with the slots in the sockets, then gently pull the tube out. The other type of fluorescent tubes, instant-start tubes, have one pin at each end. One of the sockets that holds a single-pin tube is spring-loaded. Press the tube toward the spring-loaded socket and gently pull the opposite end out.

take care

Fluorescent tubes contain trace amounts of toxic mercury. When a fluorescent bulb fails, recycle it. Check with your county or city for nearby recycling centers.

COMPACT FLUORESCENT LIGHTS

equipment spotlight

It's not just about saving money anymore. There's no doubt that compact fluorescent lights (CFLs) save electricity, last longer, and pay for themselves quickly. But these days, compact fluorescents are about the future: Just one CFL in every house would eliminate the amount of greenhouse gases that 800,000 cars emit over the course of a year. CFLs screw into a regular light socket, use 75 percent less energy than incandescent bulbs, and last 10 times as long. Even better, CFLs are getting cheaper, and they now come in a variety of sizes and wattage equivalents, as well as in three-way and dimmable versions.

SMART IDEA

When buying a replacement ballast, check out fixture prices, too. It may be cheaper and more efficient to replace the entire fixture, especially if it's an older, starter-type model.

Easy Fixes

Choosing color-true bulbs. The rap against fluorescent light used to be that it was too cool and too harsh and didn't render colors well. That's no longer the case. Today you can get more natural lighting with fluorescents by choosing tubes according to their color temperature, measured in degrees Kelvin (K). Light from high-temperature bulbs (4000K and above) contains a high proportion of blue, which is harsh and cool. Light from lower-temperature bulbs contains more red, which is warmer and softer. A 3500K tube provides the most accurate rendition of colors. Light from a 2700K bulb most closely resembles that given off by a regular incandescent bulb.

Using low-temperature bulbs. Fluorescent tubes start up slowly when the temperature is below 50°F (10°C). If you have fluorescents in the garage or in a workshop that gets cold, install a bulb rated for low temperatures. If the problem persists, replace the ballast with a low-temperature one.

TROUBLESHOOTING FLUORESCENT LIGHTS

Fluorescent bulbs last longer than other bulbs, but they have a few quirks that may fool you into thinking they've gone bad when they're just fine: A cold room, a faulty ballast, or even a bulb that's slightly askew can make you think the bulb is bad when it really isn't. Before discarding the bulb, check the following chart.

PROBLEM	POSSIBLE CAUSE	SOLUTION
Light blinks on and off	Tube is wearing out	Shut off power; rotate tube to clean terminals. Make sure tube is properly seated in its sockets. If problem persists, replace tube.
Tube is hard to start	Defective starter in older fixture; faulty ballast in rapid- or instant-start fixture	Replace starter or ballast The starter is a small metal cylinder found next to the socket in older fixtures. To replace it, turn off power to fixture, push down on the cylinder, and turn it counter-clockwise. Reverse the procedure to install a new one of same rating.
Light flickers or appears to swirl through tube	New tube or cold temperature	Leave new tube lit for several hours to stabilize. Install low-temperature ballast in cold areas.
Fixture hums or vibrates	Loose parts or loose mounting screws; ballast short-circuiting	Tighten all connections. If hum continues, replace ballast.
Tube ends are blackened	Tube is wearing out	Replace tube.

Doorbells

It's easy to take for granted the bell, buzzer, or chimes that announce visitors to your home—that is, until something goes wrong with them. Traditional signaling systems consist of one or more push buttons, a sounding device, and a transformer that steps down household current to the lower voltage that most systems require. Except for keeping the sounding device clean, doorbell systems pretty much take care of themselves. Following are guidelines for figuring out what might be causing a problem and what to do.

YOUR COST SAVINGS

$195

What you would pay an electrician to install a new door chimes unit.

Care and Maintenance

Use alcohol to keep your doorbell clean. If you can't hear your doorbell ding when visitors announce themselves, it may be because your doorbell or chimes are dirty. Dirt, oil, or grime can slow down or stop the motion of a mechanical chime's plungers or a bell's clapper and gong. To restore the sound, remove the sounding device's cover and clean the plungers or clapper contacts with a cotton swab or toothbrush dipped in alcohol. Electronic doorbells can't be cleaned—you'll need to buy a new one if it stops sounding.

Bend the clapper back into shape. A doorbell's sound may be muted because the clapper isn't striking the gong quite right. This usually happens because the clapper arm is bent. Use pliers to gently bend the arm back into shape. If the sound from your mechanical door chimes is getting softer, check the rubber grommets (pads) attached to the unit's tone bars (see illustration). If they are worn or hard and brittle, buy replacements at a hardware or electrical supply store.

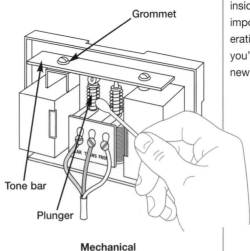

Grommet

Tone bar

Plunger

Mechanical chimes

SMART IDEA

Do you need to install a new doorbell? Consider going wireless. Wireless door chimes can be installed in minutes without snaking wires inside walls—an important consideration unless you're dealing with new construction.

Easy Fixes

Getting the doorbell to ring. If your doorbell doesn't make any sound at all and there's no power outage, suspect the push button; constant use and exposure to weather and dirt can cause it to fail. To inspect the button, remove the screws securing its cover plate, if there are any. If the plate or button isn't fastened with screws,

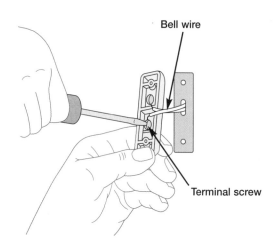

use a screwdriver or a flat knife to gently pry it up. Tighten wire connections, and check contacts and terminals for corrosion, removing any with fine sandpaper. If there's still no sound, disconnect the button wires and touch their ends together. If the bell rings, the button is defective and needs to be replaced. Connect the existing wires to the new button's terminal screws and remount the button.

Tightening and splicing wires. Loose connections and broken wires are common causes of signaling system problems. Check and tighten wire connections behind the push button, inside the sounding device, and at the transformer (with the power off). Check visible doorbell wiring for breaks and frayed insulation. Wrap frayed wires with electrician's tape. Splice breaks by stripping both wire ends and joining them with a wire connector.

take care

Doorbell and chime systems operate on low-voltage current, so it's generally safe to work on everything but the transformer without turning off power at the service panel. (Even so, shutting off power is never a bad idea.) Because the transformer is wired to a 120-volt house circuit, you *must* turn off power to it before working on it.

REPLACING A DOORBELL

Replacing the sounding device, whether it's because it's faulty or you just want to upgrade it, is simple. Make sure the new unit's voltage rating matches the transformer's. In a nutshell, here's what to do: With the power off, remove the existing unit's cover and disconnect the wires from their screw terminals, noting which wire went where. Detach the old unit from the wall. Run the wires through the back of the new unit, and mount it on the wall. Connect the wires to the correct terminals on the new unit, and restore power.

Outdoor Electrical Fixtures

Having electricity outside can make a world of difference. It gives you power to run tools, motion detectors, and security lights, even a pump for a decorative pond—all without having to deal with awkward and possibly dangerous extension cords. While wiring techniques are the same indoors and out, outdoor receptacles, switches, and fixtures need to be protected from the elements and rated for use in wet conditions. The following pages will show you how to stay illuminated *and* safe while working with outdoor electrical fixtures.

Care and Maintenance

Clean the bulb sockets annually. Once a year, turn off power to outdoor light fixtures at the service panel, remove their lightbulbs, and use a ball of very fine steel wool (grade 0000) to clean corrosion from inside the sockets. This will help keep the bulbs from jamming in the sockets and make removing them easier.

Don't break from the code. The combination of moisture and electricity can be lethal. That's why the Canadian Electrical Code requires that all outdoor receptacles have ground-fault circuit interrupter (GFCI) protection. Check your outdoor receptacles, and if any are not of the GFCI type (or are not protected by a GFCI breaker at the service panel), have them replaced with GFCI receptacles. Also, be sure to test your GFCI receptacles every month.

Go solar. Using solar-powered rather than low-voltage outdoor lighting prevents two things: First, this is the surest way to avoid spending a whole afternoon fiddling around with wiring. Some second-generation, solar-powered landscape lights give off as much light as their low-voltage cousins and are easier to install. Put them in the ground, aim them, and they'll turn on automatically when it gets dark. It won't take you more than 20 minutes to poke six or eight solar lights into the yard. Installing these lights in the land around your driveway will light a bright path to your front door and prevent you and your guests from tripping or falling in the dark.

Weatherproof your electrical boxes. Receptacles and switches that are exposed to the elements must be housed in weatherproof electrical boxes. In addition, the

Canadian Electrical Code now requires that exterior electrical boxes housing GFCIs be waterproof while in use. That means having a cover that's deep enough to close completely even when something is plugged into the receptacle. (The cords come out through a notch in the bottom edge of the cover.) If you have an insufficiently protected GFCI, install an "in-use" watertight cover. Some covers can be retrofitted to existing boxes.

Check seals and seams. Caulk seams between outdoor electrical boxes and the house to seal out moisture and cold. In addition, periodically inspect outdoor receptacles to make sure their cover hinges and gaskets are in good shape. If either has deteriorated, replace the cover so that you can keep moisture and debris out of the receptacles.

How to Install Low-voltage Lights

There's certainly no shortage of inexpensive low-voltage outdoor lighting kits, but you're probably better off paying more for a better-quality system; you'll get more out of it in terms of long life and dependability. Whichever you choose, the elements will essentially be the same: fixtures, low-voltage cable, and a transformer that steps down 120-volt household current to 12 volts. The installation procedure will be pretty much the same. Here's what you need to do:

1. SPEND TIME PLANNING your outdoor lighting scheme: number of fixtures, what types (path, pond, cone, spotlights, floodlights, etc.), and where you want them.

2. MOUNT THE TRANSFORMER near an outdoor GFCI receptacle fitted with an "in-use" cover. Follow the mounting and wiring instructions that came with your unit.

3. LAY THE LIGHT FIXTURES ON THE GROUND at their intended locations. Starting at the transformer, run the cable along the ground from light to light.

4. CONNECT THE CABLE to the fixtures. Connection methods vary depending on the design of the fixture. Most kit fixtures come with press-on connector fittings that "bite" through the cable insulation and into the wire to make the electrical contact. For other fixtures, the connection is made by joining fixture and cable wires with weatherproof wire connectors. Either way, follow the kit or fixture manufacturer's instructions.

5. DIG A HOLE about 8 inches (20 cm) deep for the fixture's ground stake (driving the stake into the ground without digging first could damage the light). Insert the stake into the hole and pack it with dirt. Bury the cable in a shallow trench.

6. CONNECT THE CABLE wires to the terminal screws on the transformer. Plug the transformer into the adjacent GFCI receptacle and turn it on to test the installation.

5 QUESTIONS TO ASK BEFORE YOU BEGIN AN OUTDOOR LIGHTING PROJECT

Embarking on an outdoor wiring project? It pays to plan ahead. Here are a few questions to ask yourself before you start digging and wiring:

1. What do the local codes say? You (or your contractor, if you've hired this work out) need to be absolutely sure that your plans mesh with those allowed by local building and electrical codes. Consult your town's building inspector, too, about any special restrictions or requirements in your area. Obtain all necessary permits.

2. How and where do I plan on running power from the inside of my house to the outside? There are several options: You can tap into an existing general-purpose lighting circuit, as long as it's not already operating near capacity. A convenient way to do this is to have a cable run through an exterior wall from an existing interior receptacle to a new outdoor GFCI receptacle. Or if you're planning extensive outdoor wiring, consider having a new circuit run from the service panel (if there's room) to new outdoor receptacles and fixtures. Finally, the simplest alternative is a low-voltage outdoor lighting system. It's flexible, safe, and relatively inexpensive, and since it doesn't involve extensive rewiring or deep digging, it's easy to install.

Options 1 and 2 are best left to a licensed electrical contractor. For more on low-voltage lighting, see below.

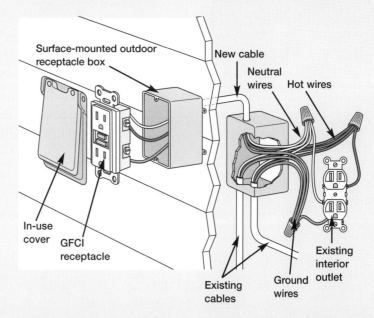

Surface-mounted outdoor receptacle box

New cable

Neutral wires   Hot wires

In-use cover   GFCI receptacle

Existing cables

Ground wires

Existing interior outlet

3. Where'd I put that circuit? It's easy to forget where an outdoor electrical cable is buried, until it's rediscovered by a spade or a tiller. Map out an efficient route for the new outdoor circuit, and keep a record of it. Waterproof UF (underground feeder) cable can be buried directly in the ground in a trench that's at least 24 inches (61 cm) deep. The trench can be shallower if the wiring runs through plastic (PVC) conduit (18 inches or 46 cm deep) or rigid metal conduit (6 inches or 15 cm deep). Low-voltage wiring can

be laid on the ground and covered with mulch, but it's best to get it out of the way by burying it in a shallow trench.

4. Am I going to hit a utility line? Before having a trench dug for underground wiring, check with your local utilities to make sure you won't hit a utility line. Look up your "Call before you dig" number for information on all buried utility lines in a given area and to get your underground utilities marked.

5. Are the neighbors going to hate me? When planning outdoor lighting, take into account glare and its possible effects on your neighbors and passersby.

Buy the right lightbulbs for outdoor fixtures. Use weatherproof bulbs in your outdoor light fixtures—they resist shattering in severe weather better than regular bulbs. And if you're tired of climbing up a ladder to change a hard-to-reach outdoor floodlight bulb, replace it the next time with a long-life outdoor bulb. Energy-saving (and long-life) compact fluorescent bulbs can be used outdoors, as long as the fixture is sheltered from the elements by your porch, for example, or by an enclosed light fixture.

Easy Fixes

Removing a broken bulb with a potato. Outdoor lightbulbs sometimes burst in their sockets because of exposure to moisture or sudden swings in temperature. Before you try to remove what remains of the lightbulb, turn off power to the fixture at the service panel. Use a tester to make certain that the power is off. Since there's not much of the bulb left to grab, getting it out of the socket is tough, but a potato can rescue you! Cut off the end of the tuber, and press it into the bulb's base. Turn the potato to unscrew the bulb. Once the bulb is out, clean the socket with very fine steel wool (grade 0000). If that doesn't work reach up into the bulb's metal base with needle-nose pliers, and open them until the tips are pushing against the inside of the base. Turn the pliers to remove the bulb.

Keeping bugs away from outdoor lights. Porch and door lights that are left on for hours at night attract a lot of insects, and they often wind up indoors. Here are a couple of ways to keep them at bay:

- Turn off outdoor lights when you don't need them. Better yet, consider installing motion sensors, which turn lights on when movement is detected and turn them off after a few minutes—before insects have a chance to gather. Outdoor light fixtures with built-in motion sensors are available at home centers and electrical supply stores.
- Use yellow-coated, all-weather bulbs in outdoor fixtures. The yellow pigment makes light less visible, and therefore less alluring, to flying bugs.

Sinks and Their Fixtures

Sinks are the workhorses of your kitchen and bathrooms; they see a lot of action, so keeping them clean should be high on your list of home maintenance chores. They're also very easy to take for granted—that is, until something (a clog, leak, or malfunctioning stopper, for example) goes wrong. Heed our advice and your sinks will stay in tip-top shape for many years to come.

YOUR COST SAVINGS

$460

What you would pay a plumber to install a new stainless-steel, double-bowl kitchen sink and faucet set.

Care and Maintenance

Scrub that dirty sink. You'd think that with all the soap and water that flow through sinks that they'd be perpetually clean—but that's not so. Soap deposits, food stains, rust, and water spots will all build up if you don't stay on top of them. How often you should scrub a sink depends on how much use it gets: Scrub a bathroom sink after about 30 uses. A good recipe for a clean sink is a squirt of dishwashing liquid added to a bowl of warm water. Dip a sponge in the mixture, and scrub gently. If you want to give the sink a more thorough scrub, try an all-purpose cleaning spray or a nonabrasive cleaner.

Make your porcelain sparkle. Here's a trick that will bring back the gleam to a white porcelain enamel sink. Line the sink with paper towels and soak them with bleach. Let the towels sit for 30 minutes, then discard them, and rinse the sink with running water. Don't use bleach on colored porcelain, however, as it may cause the color to fade. Use a mild liquid detergent, vinegar, or baking soda instead.

Protect sinks from scratches and stains. Replacing a kitchen sink makes no small impact on your wallet. Once you've got a shiny new one in place, there are many easy things you can do to keep it in like-new condition:

- Install a perforated plastic mat in the bottom of your sink. This will protect the sink's surface from scratches and mars and will protect your dishes, too.
- Don't let fruit, vinegar, salad dressing, or other acidic foods linger on the surface of a porcelain enamel sink. Long-term exposure to acids can cause staining and could etch the surface.
- Don't use scouring powders to clean your sink. Instead, use the warm water and dish detergent formula we describe above.

SMART IDEA

Before breaking
out the plunger,
use a funnel to
pour 1/2 cup
(125 ml) of borax
down a clogged
drain, followed by
2 cups (500 ml) of
boiling water.
Flush with hot
water after
15 minutes.

Use baking soda to clean solid surfacing such as Corian. Sinks made of non-porous, acrylic-based solid surfacing are relatively stain-resistant and easy to clean. But they do need to be kept up. For routine cleaning, use soapy water or a solid-surface cleaner specially formulated for solid surfacing. Rub out stains with baking soda and water mixed to a toothpaste-like consistency. Apply the paste with a nonabrasive white scrubbing pad, and rinse thoroughly.

De-stain surfaces with lemon juice. We've got a sure remedy for stained sinks: Erase those spots with a paste made of one-half cup (125 ml) of powdered borax and the juice of one-half lemon. Dab a sponge in the mixture, rub, and rinse with running water—it'll work like a charm whether your sink is made of porcelain enamel, stainless steel, or any other material.

Use vinegar on your lime. The white spots that you have so much trouble cleaning off the faucets are lime deposits from mineral-rich hard water. They're very easy to remove with a secret ingredient that's already in your pantry: vinegar. Soak a paper towel in vinegar, and wrap the towel around the spotted area. Wait 10 minutes and then buff with a dry paper towel. This works well on all fixtures except brass or colored fixtures; using vinegar on these surfaces may discolor them.

Rid rust with WD-40. Wipe WD-40 (lighter fluid works, too) on the spot with a cloth and then rinse thoroughly. For rust stains on porcelain enamel sinks, pour salt on half of a lemon and rub it on the stain.

Keep your drain free of clogs. Mix up 1 cup (250 ml) of baking soda with 1 cup (250 ml) of salt and 1/4 cup (60 ml) cream of tartar in an airtight container. Every few weeks, pour 1/2 cup (125 ml) of the mixture down each drain, followed by a quart (litre) of boiling water. Do your best to keep debris out of your sink drains in the first place. Following these few steps should keep you clog-free!

Easy Fixes

Unclogging an aerator. If water runs out of your faucet slowly or without much pressure, the aerator may be clogged. Unscrew it from the faucet and take it apart, if possible, keeping careful track of which part goes where (you might want to take a photo of what it looks like before you take it apart). Soak the parts overnight in

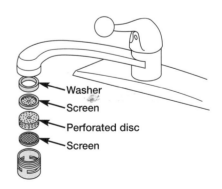

Washer
Screen
Perforated disc
Screen

white vinegar, then scrub with a toothbrush. Flush out debris from the faucet, reassemble the aerator, and put it back on the faucet. If the problem persists, replace the aerator.

Fixing an aerator with a sandwich bag and a rubber band. Sometimes the aerator sticks and won't come off the faucet spout. If that happens, there's still a way to

5 WAYS TO CLEAR A CLOGGED DRAIN

Any number of things can clog a sink drain or cause it to drain slowly. Similarly, there are a number of ways to unclog a sink, but some are easier than others. Start with the easiest solution at the top of this list, and work your way down until water flows freely.

1. If the clog is in a bathroom sink, you're probably dealing with a pop-up stopper (see "How to Adjust a Pop-up Sink Stopper" on the following spread). To clear the drain, try **pulling out the pop-up stopper,** removing any accumulated debris, and washing the stopper with soapy water and a toothbrush. Replace the stopper and turn on the water. This typically resolves the problem.

2. If the sink is still clogged, try **using a plunger.** In bathroom sinks, the overflow opening lets air into the drainpipe as you're plunging, preventing the plunger from getting any suction. The solution is to stuff the opening with a wet cloth before you start plunging. Position the plunger cup so that it completely covers the drain hole, then fill the sink with enough water to cover the cup. Make the first plunge a slow one to allow air to escape from the cup, plunge

vigorously up and down about 15 or 20 times, then remove the plunger abruptly. Repeat several times as needed.

3. If you're this far down in the list and still haven't resolved the problem, you've got a serious clog. It's time for a little direct action. **Bend a hook in a coathanger wire** and feed it down the drain. Fish for the clog, and if you catch it, pull it out slowly. Run some water down the drain, and then give it a good plunging to remove any buildup left in the pipes.

4. Still no luck? If the curved pipe underneath the sink (called a P-trap) has a clean-out plug, you can also approach the clog from there. Put a bucket under the trap,

unscrew the plug with an adjustable wrench, and let the water drain out. **Probe inside the P-trap** for the clog with the hooked wire. If the trap doesn't have a plug, remove the entire trap by loosening the coupling nuts above and below it with a pipe wrench.

5. If you still can't locate the clog, it's probably located farther down the line, out of your reach—perhaps even in the main drainpipe. It's time to **call a plumber.**

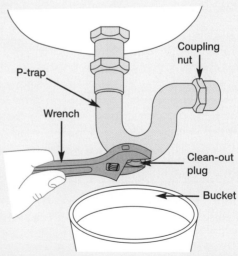

Chemical drain cleaners will not only eat through a clog, they'll eat through anything, including your pipes (albeit rather slowly). Try to avoid them whenever possible. If you must use a chemical drain cleaner, wear rubber gloves, long sleeves, and safety glasses. Never use a plunger on a drain into which you have just added a chemical cleaner. Water that splashes out of the drain as you work will be loaded with caustic chemicals.

dissolve the mineral deposits that may be clogging it. Pour white vinegar into a plastic sandwich bag and use a rubber band or duct tape to secure the bag around the spout, making sure that the aerator is fully immersed in the vinegar. Let it soak overnight. Note: This may discolor brass and other fixtures.

Saving a faucet sprayer. Like a faucet aerator, the nozzle of a kitchen faucet's sprayer attachment can become clogged with mineral deposits. Before you take action on the sprayer's inner workings, check under the sink to make sure the hose is not twisted or kinked. If it's worn or permanently kinked, have it replaced.

If that doesn't work, chances are your sprayer is clogged. To unclog it, turn off the faucet and use a rubber band to hold the sprayer handle in the open position. Soak the sprayer head in a cup of warm white vinegar for 30 minutes, then run the sprayer at full blast to clean out any debris. Repeat if needed. If the sprayer is still sluggish, take the sprayer head apart and clean the nozzle's parts with a toothbrush. Open any clogged holes with a straight pin. Reassemble the sprayer head, making sure to replace parts in the proper sequence.

Repairing faucets. The first step to all faucet repairs is to turn off both water-supply shutoff valves under the sink (if there are none, turn off the main water-supply valve; see the "Plumbing Emergencies" section) and open the faucet handle(s) to drain the faucet. Next, remove the faucet handle, which is almost always held in place by a screw or setscrew. Sometimes, the screw is exposed at the top of the handle; in other cases, you'll need to pry off a decorative cap to access the screw.

How to Repair a Leaky Cartridge Faucet

1. TURN OFF THE WATER SUPPLY and remove the faucet's handle.

2. UNSCREW THE RETAINER PIVOT NUT with a pair of pliers. (In some models, there may be a plastic retainer ring that you'll need to remove.)

3. LIFT OFF the spout sleeve and spray diverter, if any, and check the O-rings on

the faucet body. If they're worn, pitted, or otherwise damaged, replace them.

4. Pry out the cartridge's RETAINER CLIP with a small screwdriver. Use pliers to pull out the old cartridge and replace it with a new one, following manufacturer's directions.

5. REASSEMBLE the faucet.

Plugging leaks in the P-trap. If water is leaking from a sink's drainpipe, it's probably coming from the P-trap—more specifically, from the coupling nuts that hold it in place. Tighten a leaking coupling nut with two pipe wrenches, or with a pipe wrench and groove-joint pliers. Wrap the jaws of both tools with duct tape to keep them from marring chrome pipe surfaces. Grip the lower pipe with one tool and tighten the nut with the other. If the leak persists, call a plumber.

Replacing a compression faucet washer. With the handle removed, use an adjustable wrench to remove the packing nut. Pull up the stem assembly, unscrew the brass screw holding the washer in place, and replace the washer with a duplicate. If the leak persists, the valve seat may have to be replaced. Call a plumber.

SMART IDEA

When repairing a sink, be sure to keep track of those tiny parts. Put a saucer over the drain to keep parts from falling down it. To make reassembly easier, line up parts in the order in which you removed them.

How to Adjust a Pop-up Sink Stopper

A pop-up stopper needs to be readjusted when it doesn't seat properly and either fails to hold water in the sink or doesn't lift high enough to let water drain out freely. Here's how the stopper works: It is moved up and down by a three-part linkage consisting of the lift rod at the back of the faucet, the clevis (a metal strip with holes in it), and the pivot rod, which supports the stopper or is actually connected to it.

Some of these steps involve working on the underside of the sink, which can be awkward. Make sure you clear out the area before you start, and keep all your tools (including a flashlight) within easy reach.

1. If a POP-UP STOPPER won't seal tightly, first check for debris that might be preventing it from dropping far enough into the drain opening to keep water from escaping. Some pop-ups lift straight out, others are twisted out, while still others require pulling out the pivot rod to which they're attached. To take out the rod, use an adjustable wrench to loosen the retaining nut securing the rod to the drain body, then pull out the rod to free the stopper.

2. WASH THE STOPPER (at a different sink) and check the rubber seal at the bottom of the stopper head. If it's dry or cracked, replace it.

3. REVERSE THE REMOVAL PROCEDURE in step 1 to reinstall the stopper. If the seal still isn't good, use pliers or your fingers to loosen the setscrew holding the lift rod and the clevis together. Pull the lift rod up, push the stopper down, and retighten the setscrew (enlist a helper, if necessary).

4. IF THE PROBLEM PERSISTS (or conversely, if the stopper doesn't lift high enough to let water drain out freely), try moving the pivot rod to a different hole in the clevis. To do this, squeeze the spring clip on the clevis while sliding the rod out of it. Move the clip and the rod to the next hole up.

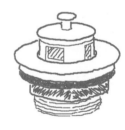

WHAT KIND OF FAUCET DO YOU HAVE?

The most common and exasperating of sink problems is a leaking faucet. Faucet repairs are relatively simple, but because they often involve a lot of little parts that you need to keep track of and reassemble in the exact order in which you found them, you might want to ask a plumber to take over. Before attempting any repair, you need to know what type of faucet you're dealing with. Here's an overview of the four main types:

Compression faucets have separate handles for hot and cold water. Inside each handle is a brass stem assembly with a rubber washer screwed to its bottom end. When you turn a handle to the off position, the washer is compressed against an opening (seat), shutting off the water flow.

A worn washer is a common cause of leaks.

Cartridge faucets can be double- or single-handled. Leaks (and repairs) usually involve just one part: the cartridge that moves up and down inside the handle(s) to control water flow.

Ball and ceramic disc faucets are single-handled. Like cartridge faucets, these faucets are washerless, although they do contain O-rings and other types of seals that can wear out. Repairing these more complex faucets can be tricky and is best left to a plumber.

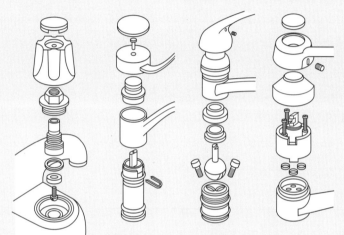

Left to right: compression faucet, cartridge faucet, ball faucet, and ceramic disc faucet

Tubs, Showers, and Their Fixtures

Like other bathroom plumbing, tub and shower fixtures are built to last—and it's a good thing, too, considering the amount of use and abuse they're subjected to over the years. Maintaining tubs and showers takes nothing more than a little regular diligence, but not attending to these small leaks and drips promptly can mean major problems for you down the road: If water from your shower seeps behind your tiles and mold and mildew flourish, your wall will probably need to be taken down to rectify the problem. Even worse, leaks from a second-floor bathroom can mean disaster (and big repair bills) for the room underneath the bathroom.

YOUR COST SAVINGS

$525

What you would pay a plumber to replace a stained, rusty bathtub with a new porcelain enamel on steel tub.

Care and Maintenance

Buy the right caulk. For durability and moisture-resistance, use a silicone-based bathroom caulk containing a mildewcide or fungicide. If you need to match a specific color, get a high-quality acrylic latex bathroom caulk, which comes in a wide range of colors. For more on caulk types and caulking techniques, see the "Caulking" section.

Wipe your tub and go. There's really no big secret to keeping your tub looking good: Just wipe it down with water and a cloth or sponge after every use. This helps prevent water spotting and soap scum buildup. When simple rinsing isn't enough, use a cleaner that's right for the tub's material, and rinse well after each application.

- For porcelain enamel, make a paste of borax and water, and scrub it on with a soft scrubber sponge.
- For fiberglass, spray on a household cleaner or a tub-and-tile cleaner, and wipe with a nonabrasive sponge.
- For stainless-steel fixtures, rub gently with baking soda on a damp sponge.

Use orange to banish rust. Orange oil–based wood cleaners remove rust and clean wood. Rub in the cleaner with a circular motion on the stain, and rinse with water. Alternatively, try scrubbing the rust stain with a mixture of lemon juice and salt.

SMART IDEA

When applying caulk between the tub and the wall, fill the tub with water. The water's weight will open the gap between wall and tub as wide as possible, preventing the caulk from cracking in the future.

Reduce the danger of slipping and injury by putting peel-and-stick antiskid tape on the floor of your tub.

Get your tub as shiny as a new penny. Blue-green stains on a bathtub are caused by water with high copper content. To remove these stains, mix 1 tablespoon (15 ml) of cream of tartar with 1 tablespoon (15 ml) of baking soda, and add enough lemon juice to make a paste. Rub the paste into the stain with a soft cloth. Leave it on for 30 minutes, rinse, and repeat if necessary.

Make your shower tiles gleam. Using dishwasher detergent (liquid or powder) is a great a way to keep tiled shower walls and floors sparkling. Mix 1/4 cup (60 ml) of detergent with warm water in a small trigger spray bottle, and shake to dissolve the detergent. Spray the solution liberally on shower walls and doors, let it sit for several hours, and then scrub with a sponge. (Use a sponge mop on the floor and to reach high spots.)

Keep shower doors crystal clear with vinegar. Done with soap scum? Put white vinegar in a trigger spray bottle, and spray it on the shower door. Rinse the door well with water, and dry it with a soft cloth. If your doors have lots of mineral buildup, spray the door with vinegar and let it sit for a few minutes. Combine equal amounts of baking soda and salt, rub the mixture over the door with a damp sponge, and then rinse well.

"Paint" your shower door runners clean. To keep shower door runners from sprouting mildew, run the head of a small, dry sponge paintbrush along the bottom runner channels after each shower.

Switch spouts. To redirect the water to the showerhead in many tubs, you pull up the plunger on top of the spout. If only some (or none) of the water is being diverted to the showerhead, the simplest solution may be to replace the entire spout. While some require loosening a setscrew beneath the spout, most simply screw on and off.

FIXING TUB FAUCETS

Tub faucets are available in the same types—compression, cartridge, ball, and disc—and with the same operating parts as sink faucets. They can also drip and leak as sink faucets do. Repairing tub faucets is done in much the same way as for the sink; for example, replacing a worn washer in a compression faucet or the cartridge in a cartridge faucet (see "What Kind of Faucet Do You Have?" in the "Sinks" chapter). The trick with tubs is that accessing the faucet's working parts can be tricky, as it may involve breaking into the surrounding tile and wall from the back side. Further complicating matters are combination tub-shower arrangements in which a diverter valve directs water to either the showerhead or the tub spout. Unless you've really honed your plumbing skills, you should probably call a plumber to deal with tub faucet leaks.

Easy Fixes

Avoiding a blast of cold (or hot) water. The change in temperature is caused by a change in pressure; this usually happens when an appliance (like your dishwasher or clothes washer) is running. Hot water that was being directed to your shower is now flowing to the appliance, leaving you naked and shivering. (When you're showering and someone flushes the toilet, cold water is diverted from the shower to the toilet, leaving you with a potentially dangerous hot blast.) The solution is a pressure-balancing, or anti-scald, valve, which maintains water temperature no matter what else is going on in the system. You can either have a pressure-balancing valve installed on the hot- and cold-water lines that feed the shower faucet or have a plumber replace the faucet with a pressure-balancing model.

SMART IDEA

To create a tighter seal between plunger and drain and increase suction over the clog, coat the rim of the plunger cup with a thick layer of petroleum jelly.

How to Replace a Showerhead

Installing a new showerhead is not much harder than screwing in a lightbulb, and it can do a lot to upgrade your bathroom. If you've got an old water-saving showerhead (or one that doesn't save water at all), you can replace it with a new water-saver that delivers a full stream of water. Other easy-to-install options include a pulsating showerhead or a hand-held unit. Head to a plumbing supply store or home center to see what's available.

1. To remove the OLD SHOWERHEAD, turn its collar counterclockwise with pliers or an adjustable wrench. If the collar doesn't budge and the shower arm starts to twist as you turn the wrench, wrap the arm with a protective cloth or with duct or utility tape and hold it in place with a pipe wrench while you unscrew the showerhead.

2. Wrap the SHOWER ARM THREADS with three to five clockwise turns of Teflon pipe-thread tape to prevent leaks. If a washer is supplied with the new showerhead, install it following the manufacturer's directions. Screw on the new showerhead or handheld shower attachment, and tighten with the adjustable wrench.

3. If you're installing a HANDHELD SHOWER ATTACHMENT, screw the hose onto the attachment and the shower-head onto the hose, using all required washers or gaskets.

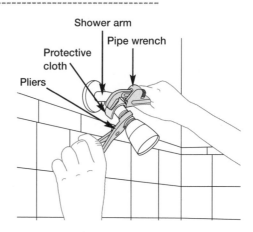

Shower arm
Pipe wrench
Protective cloth
Pliers

Filling in bathtub chips. A chip or nick in a porcelain enamel surface need not be permanent. Home-improvement stores stock many types of repair kits, ranging from simple touch-up paints to two-part epoxy compounds. The latter come in a variety of colors and are usually your best bet. The package directions will explain how to apply the material, but here's what's usually involved: Scrub the chipped area with soapy water, let it dry, then use a small piece of medium-grit sandpaper to remove any rust and give the epoxy a rougher surface to cling to. Mix the epoxy components together as directed, and brush the compound onto the damaged area, but not beyond—don't try to blend the new with the old. If the chip is deep, apply a second coat eight hours later. Wait at least 24 hours before allowing the repair to get wet. Wait a week before scrubbing it.

Caulking the tub. The difference between water that stays in the tub and water that seeps through to the walls is a good caulking job. Caulk seals the cracks between the tub and adjoining walls and floors. There are three places you want to make sure are well caulked: between the tub and the wall, between the tub and the floor, and between the wall and the plumbing fixtures. Some inside wall corners are caulked, too. Before applying new caulk, use a putty knife or a razor blade to remove old caulk.

Unclogging drains. More often than not, when a tub drain gets clogged or is slow to drain, the culprit is a buildup of hair and soap scum on the tub's pop-up stopper. This is a problem that can be quickly solved. Just pull out the stopper and the rocker arm attached to it, remove the accumulated gunk, and wash the stopper mechanism with soapy water and a toothbrush.

Plunging drains. If cleaning the pop-up stopper doesn't unclog your bathtub, try using a plunger. Position the plunger cup so that it completely covers the drain hole, then fill the tub with enough water to cover the cup. Hold a wet towel over the tub's overflow plate to seal it, and plunge vigorously to dislodge the clog (see "5 Ways to Clear a Clogged Drain" in the "Sinks" chapter).

Going down under. If, from the basement or crawlspace, you have access to the P-trap connected to the bathtub drain, you can attack the clog from there. Loosen the two large nuts that hold the lower U-shaped section in place. Then, with an assistant holding a bucket to catch any water or gunk, remove the section. Clear out the U-shaped piece and any other parts of the drain you can now reach. See the sidebar "5 Ways to Clear a Clogged Drain" in the "Sinks" chapter for more details. If the clog persists, call a plumber.

Unclogging strainer-style drains. Hair and soap scum lurking underneath a shower drain's strainer cover are the likely suspects when a shower gets clogged or drains too slowly. Usually, a quick cleaning or a bit of plunging is all it takes to get your tub or shower back in shape.

- First, check the strainer cover itself: If gunk is visible in its openings, try cleaning them out manually. Run the water and see if that did the trick.
- If water still isn't draining properly, remove the strainer cover. Some types snap into place and can be lifted out with a screwdriver; others are held in place by screws. With the cover off, shine a flashlight into the drain and see if you can spot the clog. If you can, try fishing it out with a hooked length of coat-hanger wire, taking care not to push the clog farther down the drain.
- Still no luck? It's time to pull out the plunger. If that doesn't work, call a plumber.

Unclogging your showerhead. A buildup of lime and mineral scale in a shower-head can reduce the shower stream to a trickle. To restore the flow, pour white vinegar into a plastic sandwich bag and pull it up over the showerhead, making sure that the entire head is immersed in the vinegar. Secure the bag to the shower arm with duct tape and leave it on overnight. (Note: Vinegar can discolor some brass and other finishes.)

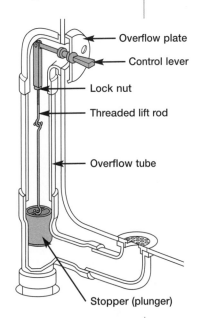

Adjusting a plunger-type stopper. In some tubs, both the stopper (in this case, a plunger) and the lift assembly are inside the overflow tube. The control lever on the overflow plate raises and lowers the plunger by way of a threaded lift rod. To service and adjust the lift assembly, unscrew the overflow plate and pull out the assembly. Loosen the adjusting lock-nut on the lift rod, and raise the rod for better drainage or lower it for a better seal.

Toilets

Toilet maintenance is certainly not high on anyone's list of favorite household chores, but it must be done regularly to keep the fixture sanitary and in good working order. Clogs are the most common toilet ailment, but the vast majority of them are easily taken care of with a plunger. A toilet is a major consumer of water, and if it has worn or leaky parts, the water it wastes can cost you a mint. Worse yet, the damage to your home that is caused by a toilet overflowing with waste can be both financially and emotionally distressing. Fortunately, the parts of a toilet's flush and refill mechanisms that tend to fail are also easy to adjust or replace.

Care and Maintenance

Clean your toilet from top to bottom. You've got to do it, so you might as well do it efficiently. When cleaning a toilet, start at the top and work your way down in this order: tank, seat, inside of the bowl, and base. Use a spray-on bathroom cleaner, preferably one with ammonia. Spray the cleaner on the exterior surfaces and wipe it off with an absorbent dry cloth; change rags as they become soaked. To clean inside the bowl, spray cleaner under the rim and on surfaces above the waterline. Use a rounded bowl brush to scrub first under the rim, then the bowl itself, and finally the drain opening.

Use a pumice stone to get rid of toilet bowl rings. Pumice stones are sold at drugstores and bath supply shops; their main purpose is to rub calluses off feet. (Pumice scouring sticks are also available at hardware stores and home centers.) Keeping the pumice wet, rub it on the ring until it's gone. Pumice won't scratch white vitreous china, which is what most toilets are made of, but it will scratch enamel, fiberglass, and other materials.

Flush only toilet paper. We're not sure how it comes to pass that people put things like petroleum-based products (like oil or paint thinner), pesticides, photo chemicals, and gum down the toilet but boy, can they clog up your toilet and mess up a septic tank (see the "Septic Systems" section) in a second. The same is true of items such as paper towels, facial tissue, bandages, diapers, and personal sanitary products. Toilet paper—and only toilet paper—is all that you should flush. Use the wastebasket next to the toilet for other items.

Peek inside the tank. Every now and again, it's a good idea to take off the tank lid and check up on what's going on inside. Doing so will help keep your toilet from clogging, overflowing, or experiencing other troubles. Here's what you should look for:

- The water level should be half an inch (1 cm) below the rim of the overflow tube. If it's too high, water can spill down the tube and into the bowl between flushes. If it's too low, the toilet may flush sluggishly. Either way, the water level needs to be adjusted.

HOW A TOILET WORKS

Most home toilets are of the gravity-flush type shown here. The main parts are the base, comprising the bowl and the hollow rim and siphon-jet chambers surrounding it, and a water-storage tank, containing a ball cock (fill-valve assembly, including a ball float and arm) and a flush (outlet) valve. When you flush the toilet, the trip lever and lift chain (or wire) pull the rubber flapper (or tank ball) out of the flush-valve seat, releasing water from the tank into the bowl through the rim and siphon-jet holes. The rush of water into the bowl creates the siphon effect that carries waste out of the bowl and down the waste pipe. As the tank empties, two things happen: the flapper drops back into the valve seat, plugging the outlet, and the float ball drops, lowering the float arm and opening the ball cock fill valve. The open fill valve sends water from the supply pipe into

the tank through the tank refill tube and into the bowl through the bowl refill tube that runs down the overflow tube. As the tank refills, the float rises until it reaches the point at which the fill valve closes, shutting off the water flow.

Instead of a float ball, some ball-cock assemblies have a float cup that slides up and down the ball cock's shank as the water level rises and falls; floatless ball cocks control water level with a pressure-sensing device.

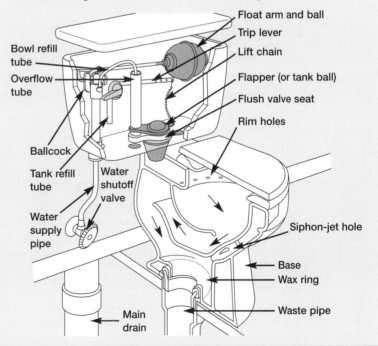

- Next, check the flush valve. To keep water from running into the bowl between flushes, the flapper or tank ball must fit tightly in the valve seat, and the seat should be smooth and free of mineral deposits, which can keep the flapper or tank ball from seating properly. To adjust the flapper or tank ball and clean the valve seat, see "Easy Fixes," below.
- If the flapper or tank ball is worn, cracked, or no longer pliable, replace it.
- If the float ball is cracked or waterlogged, replace the entire ball cock assembly (including the float ball) with a float-cup or floatless ball cock.

Easy Fixes

Stopping a leak. If you see water puddling on the floor under the toilet tank and the tank isn't sweating, try tightening the water-supply line connections on the underside of the tank and the bolts connecting the tank to the base. If there's leakage on the floor around the base, tighten the nuts on the flange bolts on either side of the base. (To avoid cracking the toilet, tighten the flange-bolt nuts alternately, a little at a time on each side.) If tightening the connections doesn't work, call a plumber.

Fixing flushing problems. If a toilet won't flush, make sure that its water shutoff valve, usually located under the tank, is open. Then look inside the tank. Chances are that the lift chain is disconnected from the trip lever. (Lift wires are less likely to come loose.) Just slip the hook at the end of the chain into one of the holes in the trip lever. The chain should hang straight down with about 1/2-inch (1 cm) slack. Adjust the chain length, as needed, by moving the hook to another hole.

Tightening the handle. A toilet's failure to flush can also be caused by a loose or disconnected handle. Remove the tank lid, and hold the handle with one hand. Reach inside the tank with the other hand and tighten the handle locknut with a wrench.

Adjusting the water level. To raise the water level in a toilet with an older ball cock/float ball assembly, bend the float arm up slightly from the center; to lower the water level, bend the arm down slightly. Newer models have a screw at the top of the ball cock that allows you to adjust the float level. In a float-cup ball cock, pinch the clip on the side of the cup and slide the cup up to raise the water level and down to lower it. Turn a floatless ball cock's adjustment screw to raise or lower the water level.

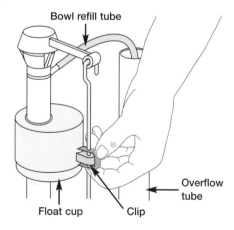

Bowl refill tube

Overflow tube

Float cup

Clip

Adjusting a tank ball or flapper. If the tank ball isn't fitting tightly in the valve seat, turn off the toilet's shutoff valve and flush to empty the tank. Loosen the setscrew on the tank ball's guide arm, and reposition the ball so that it drops straight into the valve seat. If a flapper doesn't seat properly, adjust the length of its lift chain. If necessary, use needle-nose pliers to remove a link from the chain. Replace a chain that's too short.

Cleaning the valve seat. If a brass valve seat is caked with mineral deposits, empty the tank as described above, and use fine steel wool to scour it; use a plastic scouring pad on a plastic valve seat.

Fixing slow flushes. Clogged rim holes (the holes underneath the rim of the bowl) can slow flushing; bacteria in clogged holes can also cause a foul odor to be released with each flush. Check for clogged rim holes with a mirror, and clean them out with a curved length of coat-hanger wire (use the mirror to help you see what you're doing). Afterward, pour several cups of household bleach down the overflow tube. The flow of bleach through the rim holes into the bowl will kill any bacteria lurking in them. If the odor persists, call a plumber; an obstruction in your roof vent may be backing up sewer gases.

How to Clear a Toilet Clog

The day will come when you'll have to know how to do this, so you may as well learn now! Below are a few ways to clear clogs. Start with the first one, which is the easiest, and proceed from there as needed. If you suspect a clog, whatever you do, don't flush the toilet. Doing so will just create an overflow problem.

1. PLUNGER. Bail out excess water from the toilet but leave enough in to cover the plunger cup. If possible, use a plunger with a funnel-shaped cup. Put the plunger over the drain opening so it seals it completely. Plunge vigorously 10 or 12 times, then yank the plunger out with force. Repeat if needed.

----

2. HANGER. If you can see the clog, bend a hook in a coat-hanger wire and try to fish out the clog with it.

----

3. THE BIG GUNS. If neither the plunger nor the hanger worked, it's time for a closet (toilet) auger. This is a crank-handled version of a plumber's snake designed to get a cable with a hooked spring tip past a toilet's trap and into the drain to grab or break up a clog. You might want to leave this job to a plumber.

Water Supply and Drainage Pipes

Plumbing is a simple mechanical system, complicated by a maze of different-sized pipes and connections. The pipes that bring water into your home and the pipes that take it away are prone to three (sometimes four) problems: leaks, clogs, and noise (and in cold climates, freezing). The first two can cause water to go where it shouldn't go, and while some plumbing noises are normal, others are a sign of a problem somewhere in the system. There's plenty you can do to keep your plumbing in good shape: be vigilant, correct small problems (like minor leaks and sluggish drains) before they become big headaches, and develop good waste-disposal habits. When a pipe problem occurs, how accessible the troubled pipe is often spells the difference between an easy repair that you can do yourself and one you should leave to the pros.

Care and Maintenance

Be kind to your drains. What's the most common cause of drain clogs? *You*— rather, the stuff that you throw down sinks and toilets that you should be tossing in the trash can. Grease is a major culprit. It solidifies and collects along the sides of a pipe, attracting food debris and eventually clogging the pipe. Grease also can over-power a septic system (see the "Septic Systems" section). Septic tanks rely on anaerobic bacteria to break down household waste; excess grease can destroy this bacterial action and gum up the works.

HOW YOUR PLUMBING SYSTEM WORKS

Your home's water-supply system delivers water under pressure to fixtures and appliances. The drain/waste-vent (DWV) system relies on gravity to carry liquid and solid wastes to the main house drain, which slopes down to a sewer line or a septic tank. U-shaped traps (actually called P-traps) in the drainpipe of most fixtures hold water that acts as a seal to keep sewer gases from entering the house. Clean-out plugs in the main and branch drains provide access for removal of blockages. Vent pipes connected to the drainage system allow sewer gases to escape and keep P-trap seals in place.

Insulate your pipes. Insulation won't prevent exposed water-supply pipes from freezing (and possibly bursting) during a long cold spell, but it will help during a short-term cold snap. It also reduces heat loss from hot-water pipes and keeps warm, humid air from condensing on cold-water pipes in the summer, which causes them to "sweat." For more on protecting your pipes from the cold, thawing them out if they freeze, and patching them if they burst, see the "Snow and Cold" section.

Drain your spigots. Before winter, disconnect all hoses from outside spigots. Inside the house, find the spigots' shutoff valves and turn them off. If the spigot has a small cap on it in addition to the handle, remove it to let water drain out of the valve and pipes. Go outside, open each spigot, and let the remaining water dribble out. Leave the spigots open. This way, there will be no water inside to freeze, expand, and break the pipes.

Winterize your system. If you leave a house or cottage unheated during the winter, frozen water in the pipes will cause them to burst. Protect your pipes and your home by having the plumbing and hot-water or steam-heating systems drained and winterized before you leave. The procedure, in brief, involves turning off the water supply at the main shut-off valve, opening all the faucets, flushing all the toilets, removing all the water in fixture traps, shutting off and draining the water heater and the boiler and heating pipes (if any), and filling toilet bowls and traps with automotive windshield-washing fluid or RV-type antifreeze. It's a complicated job best left to a professional plumber, but it will save you a lot of headaches.

Easy Fixes

Unsticking shutoff valves. When a water-supply shutoff valve isn't used for a while, it can get stuck or start leaking after you turn it. To fix a drippy valve, try gently tightening its packing nut with a wrench, or opening and shutting the valve several times until the drip stops. To loosen a stuck valve, put a few drops of oil around the stem near the packing nut. Loosen the nut about one turn, and retighten it by hand. Wait a few minutes for the oil to soak in, and you should be able to turn the valve easily.

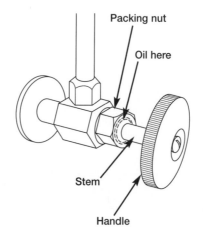

Packing nut

Oil here

Stem

Handle

Clearing clogs in branch and main drains involves removing clean-out plugs and often the use of heavy-duty, power-driven augers. This is definitely a job for a professional plumber.

Draining the plumbing system. This is a possible, if temporary, fix for thumping or banging pipes, also known as water hammer—it's quick and won't cost you a dime. Begin by turning off the main water-supply shutoff valve. Find the lowest faucet or spigot in your home and open it. Open a few of the highest faucets as well. When the lowest faucet stops dripping, close all the faucets and turn the main shutoff back on. Expect some banging and sputtering when you turn on the faucets again for the first time.

Getting air out of pipes. Once it gets into pipes, air will make a banging noise as it travels through them. If you suspect an air problem, turn on all the faucets, hot and cold, and flush the toilets once or twice. After a couple of minutes, any trapped air will have been flushed out. Turn off the faucets. If the noise persists, something else is causing the problem.

QUIETING NOISY PIPES

Plumbing systems emit all sorts of noises: some are annoying but benign, and others indicate trouble. How can you tell which pipes are causing the trouble? Use your ears to follow the noise to its source, if you can. If you're led to exposed pipes, you can usually see if they're vibrating, knocking against studs, or have loosened supports. Quieting these pipes can be as simple as adding or cushioning pipe supports (of course, exposed pipes are far easier to silence than those covered by drywall). Here's a rundown of the most common plumbing noises and what you can do to silence them:

- Rattling or banging when the water is turned on may be caused by a pipe that's loose within its strap, U-clamp, pipe hanger, or support block.

Resecure or tighten the supports or add more straps or hangers, as needed. If a rattling pipe runs through exposed joists, try installing pipe inserts—split plastic sleeves that fit around the pipe and slide into the hole in the joist.

- Clicking, ticking, or squeaking when the hot water is turned on may indicate that a now heat-expanded pipe is too tightly anchored. Loosen the clamp or strap or add a piece of rubber or felt between the pipe and its support.

- Thumping or banging when a faucet or an appliance is turned off is known as water hammer. It's caused by the spike in pressure that occurs when water moving under pressure is suddenly stopped

by the closing of a valve. (The problem is more common with certain appliance valves, which shut off almost instantly, than with hand-controlled faucets.) In addition to being annoying, water hammer causes pipes to shake, which can eventually damage pipes and valves and weaken connections. What you need is a device called a water hammer arrester.

- Whistling may be caused by a shutoff valve that's not fully open or by high water pressure, which can worsen a water-hammer problem. Make sure all water-supply shutoff valves are completely open. In some cases, a pressure-reducing valve may have to be installed in the supply line near the water meter.

WATER HAMMER ARRESTER

equipment spotlight

A water hammer arrester is an air-filled cylinder or ball that's installed in the supply line near valves that are causing water hammer. The air chamber acts as a shock absorber against the water-pressure spike and silences the pipes. Many older homes have arresters that are simply capped lengths of vertical pipe. These become waterlogged over time as the air gets absorbed into the water supply. You can recharge them by draining the plumbing system. But recharging is only a temporary solution, as the air will be absorbed again. If water hammer persists, have a plumber install engineered arresters sold at hardware stores and home centers. These come equipped with a piston with rubber gaskets that isolates an air pocket from the water in the pipes. Screw-in water arrestors that mount between the hot and cold faucets and the washing machine are also available, and are easy for homeowners to install.

Finding a clog. The first step to clearing a clog is finding it. If only one fixture is clogged, the problem is either in the fixture itself, in its trap, or in the drain leading away from it. If several fixtures are clogged, the problem is in a branch line that all of them drain into. Since water flows downhill, the clog will be below the lowest stopped-up fixture and above the highest working one. If many or all fixtures are running sluggishly, the clog is probably in one of the main drain lines. (Tree roots working their way through sewer lines in the main drain are a possible culprit.) If fixtures drain sluggishly and smell bad, the roof vent on the system's main vent pipe may be clogged, which prevents sewer gases from escaping. A clogged vent may also cause sink or tub drains to gurgle when you flush the toilet. For more on clogs and how to deal with them, see the chapters titled "Sinks and Their Fixtures," "Tubs, Showers, and Their Fixtures," and "Toilets."

Septic Systems

If your home is not hooked up to a municipal sewer system, you probably have a septic system to break down and dispose of household wastewater. A well-designed (and just as important, a well-maintained) septic system will perform its job efficiently for decades. Mistreat a septic system and it can turn into huge money pit—as a matter of fact, there are few home repairs that are more costly than a new septic system. Just how expensive are they, you ask? About $15,000. That's plenty of impetus for you to treat yours right!

Care and Maintenance

Conserve water. This is one of the surest ways to maintain the health of your septic system. Large volumes of water, especially when delivered over a short time (as happens when too many showers are taken back to back or too many loads of laundry are washed in one day), can flush suspended, untreated waste particles into the drainage field, eventually clogging it. If you rely on a septic system, here are some water-saving techniques to consider:

- Take shorter showers and replace old showerheads with water-saving models.
- Repair dripping faucets and turn off the tap when you're shaving or brushing your teeth.
- Replace old toilets, washing machines, and dishwashers with new water-saving models.
- Wash full loads of clothes, or set the washing machine water level for smaller loads.

take care

If there's foul-smelling water rising from the drainage field or if water backs up out of drains, the septic system is failing. Call your septic service company without delay.

Have your septic system inspected every two or three years. Also have the tank pumped as necessary to remove built-up sludge and scum. How often the tank will need to be cleaned out depends on its size and on the number of people in your home.

Try to stagger baths and wash loads. This will help you avoid overloading the system.

HOW A SEPTIC SYSTEM WORKS

In a traditional private septic system, household waste is piped into a waterproof holding tank (the septic tank), where anaerobic bacteria (microorganisms that grow in the absence of air) break the waste down into solids (sludge), liquid (effluent), and scum. The solids settle to the bottom, where bacteria further decompose them. The scum, composed of waste that's lighter than water, floats to the top. The middle layer of effluent flows out via a distribution box and travels through underground perforated pipes into the drainage, or leach, field. There, gravel and soil act as biological filters to purify the wastewater as it is absorbed into the ground (see illustration). Excess grease and other contaminants can destroy the bacterial action essential to the proper functioning of a septic system and interfere with effluent absorption in the leach field. In some systems, a grease trap in the waste line removes excess grease from wastewater before it flows into the main septic tank. Being careful about what you pour down your drains is the key to avoiding septic system problems: You just want to avoid clogging the system, and you want to keep the bacteria in it alive, healthy, and on the job.

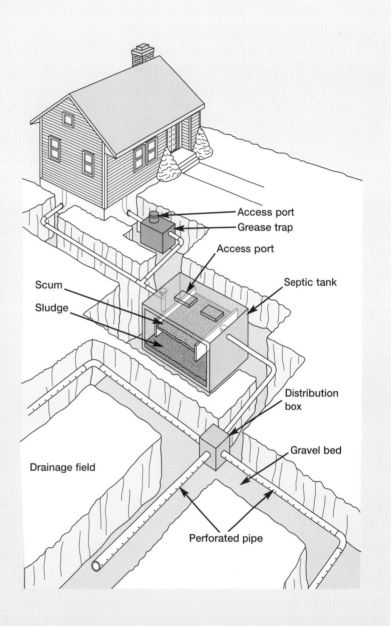

Access port
Grease trap
Access port
Scum
Sludge
Septic tank
Distribution box
Gravel bed
Drainage field
Perforated pipe

Don't dispose of anything in sinks or toilets that the bacteria in the septic system can't break down. Such items include grease, fat, oils, coffee grounds, any paper product other than toilet tissue, cat litter, disposable diapers, feminine hygiene products, condoms, bandages, aluminum foil, and cigarette butts.

Don't pour bacteria-killing toxins down the drain. These include drain cleaners, bleaches, antibacterial soaps, disinfectants, acids, discarded prescription medicines, oil-based paints and solvents, pesticides, and fertilizers.

If you have a garbage disposal, use it sparingly. The ground-up solids the disposer sends down the drain can overload a septic tank's filtration system, allowing food particles into the leach field, where they can cause or accelerate clogging. If you don't have a disposal, try to continue making do without one.

Direct runoff from gutters or drainage spouts away from the drainage field. Water constantly seeps from the septic tank into the drain field. If the drain field is saturated with rainwater, the water from your septic tank has nowhere to go.

Don't park or drive over the drainage field. A septic drainage field needs oxygen to work properly. Driving over it compresses the soil, squeezing out the air in it.

Watch what you plant. Only grass should be planted over and near your septic tank and drain field. Tree and shrub roots could damage the system.

Water Wells

If you don't live in a community with its own municipal water system, your home's water probably comes from a private well. In a typical private system, a pump draws water from the well and sends it to a pressure tank inside the house. Although water from a properly located and installed well is naturally filtered, it can be subject to contamination from a variety of sources, including septic systems, leaking underground fuel tanks, animal wastes, and pesticides. Testing your well water regularly is essential to ensure the safety and purity of your supply.

YOUR COST SAVINGS

$5,000

Cost to replace a contaminated water well with a new one (including the cost to drill the new well).

Care and Maintenance

Test your water every year. It's your responsibility to maintain the safety of your drinking-water supply. Have your well water tested once a year for bacteria, nitrates, and other impurities. Call your local health department to arrange a test or to request a list of state-certified water testing laboratories in your area.

Consider a bigger tank. If your well can't keep up with demand, you may have a much cheaper option than drilling a new one. A well installer may be able to install a larger size holding tank or pressure tank that the pump can then fill at night and during times of low use. Occupants can use this reserve while the pump "catches up."

SMART IDEA

Hang on to the well log filed by the contractor when the well was built. It contains important information about the well, its construction, and the ground surrounding it.

5 EASY WAYS TO KEEP YOUR WELL IN GREAT SHAPE

1. Inspect the exposed parts of the well—the casing and well cap—several times a year to make sure the cap is tightly secured and there are no cracks or openings that could let in pollutants.

2. Make sure the ground around the well slopes away from it, and when mowing near the well, be careful not to damage its casing.

3. Hire a qualified well contractor to annually inspect the entire system. Have him check the well, pump, pressure tank, pipes, valves, and water flow.

4. Do not use hazardous chemicals, such as gasoline, paints, solvents, pesticides, and fertilizers, near the well.

5. Install an anti-siphon valve on all faucets with hose connections. This will keep unsanitary water from being pulled back (back-siphoned) through a garden hose and contaminating your well water system.

Plumbing Emergencies

A pipe bursts, a toilet overflows, the washing machine floods your basement. The first step in dealing with most plumbing emergencies is to shut off the water supply to the whole house or to an individual fixture or appliance. The next steps are to stay calm and remember all that you've learned here about emergency troubleshooting. The longer you wait to fix the problem, the worse it is likely to get—and the more you'll have to spend on repair costs and the replacement of water-damaged items.

SMART IDEA

If a washing machine or dishwasher floods, use beach towels and other large absorbent materials to build a dam around the spillage. Confining the water this way makes it easier to mop up.

Easy Fixes

My house is flooding—what's the best damage control? If your home falls victim to a broken pipe or an overflowing washing machine or dishwasher, taking these steps immediately will minimize the damage:

- Turn off the main water-shutoff valve.

- To prevent electrical shock, shut off electricity to the flooded area, but only if you can get to the service panel without having to step through the floodwater. Wading through water that's in contact with electrical outlets or appliances can give you a severe, possibly deadly, shock.

- Wear rubber boots and gloves if the leak was in a drain line or has been mixed with sewage. Disinfect the area thoroughly after it has been cleaned and allowed to dry.

- Try to mop up the water as quickly as possible to prevent floor damage.

- Repairing or replacing a broken pipe is a job for a plumber, but in an emergency, patch a pipe however you can.

- While your burst pipe is fresh on your mind, inspect the rest of your home's pipes and hosing. Broken washing machine hoses are a common cause of household flooding. Standard rubber hoses weaken and crack with age and can eventually burst. To avoid what could be a costly problem, replace washer hoses every two years or so.

I've dropped a piece of jewelry down the drain—what do I do? The ring you drop down the drain is not lost forever. It will wash down the drainpipe and stop in the bottom of the U-shaped trap. Some traps have a plug on the bottom that you can unscrew to retrieve valuables. Put a bucket underneath the plug before removing it—the trap is filled with water. If there's no plug, use the bucket anyway, then loosen the large nuts above and below the trap with a pipe wrench to remove the entire trap. Empty the water into the bucket, fish out the item, and then replace the trap.

Help! My toilet is overflowing! When it looks like the water is about to spill over, stand back and trust the toilet's design. If the toilet overflows, remove the tank lid and push the flush-valve flapper or tank ball into the valve seat at the bottom of the tank to stop the flow of water into the bowl. Turn off the toilet's shutoff valve or the main shutoff valve. Bail out excess water, if possible, or just wait. Water will slowly leak through even the worst clog, and the water level in the bowl will drop slowly to the point where you can begin plunging.

HOW DO I TURN OFF THE WATER?

When a pipe breaks or an appliance floods, your first job is to stop the water flow. This means quickly turning off the nearest valve feeding water to the problem area—or even the main water valve supplying the house, if need be. Identify and mark all such valves in your house now so you won't have to search for the right one in an emergency. To shut valves off, turn them clockwise. Or, if they're lever valves, turn the handle perpendicular to the pipe. Periodically check shutoff valves to make sure they open and close freely.

TO SHUT OFF WATER TO THIS LOCATION	LOOK FOR A SHUTOFF VALVE HERE
The entire house	On either side of your water meter—on an exterior wall, in your basement, or in a concrete enclosure near the street. If you have a well, you'll find a valve by the pressure tank (cut the power to the tank, too).
All the hot water in the house	On the pipe leading into your water heater.
Sink	Underneath the sink—there are usually two shutoff valves in the cabinet underneath, one for hot water and one for cold.
Bathtub	Either in the basement or behind an access panel in the faucet wall.
Toilet	Under the toilet tank.
Dishwasher	First look under the kitchen sink, where you'll probably find a valve on the line leading to the dishwasher. If not, go to the basement and inspect the pipes underneath the appliance.
Clothes washer	Follow the short hoses that feed hot and cold water to the appliance. Where they connect to the plumbing, you should find two valves.

Forced-Air Systems

YOUR
COST SAVINGS
$1,250
What you'd pay a heating
and cooling professional to
install a new high-efficiency,
gas-fired, 80,000 BTU
forced-air furnace.

Forced-air systems are among the most common whole-house heating systems in contemporary homes. Relatively inexpensive to purchase, they're easy to maintain and provide effective climate control. All it takes to get years of comfort is attention to the occasional needs of your system's main components—the furnace, blower, ductwork, registers, and thermostat—and you'll be sitting pretty, in every room and in every season.

SMART IDEA

For better performance and air quality, purchase the most sophisticated filter style your system can handle. Woven fiberglass filters are the cheapest, but they are designed to filter out only larger dust particles, enough just to protect the blower and other furnace parts. Pleated and electrostatic styles filter out a wider range of contaminants. (Check your manual before installing more restrictive, higher-efficiency filters.)

Care and Maintenance

Get a pro to do your annual once-over. Whether the furnace in your forced-air system has a burner fueled by gas or oil, it needs an annual inspection before heating season, and that's a job you may not be knowledgeable enough to tackle yourself. Before cold weather sets in, give your gas or oil supplier a ring—they'll either dispatch a staff technician or recommend another trustworthy pro for the job. A proper furnace inspection will include a careful check for cracks in the heat exchanger (the part of the furnace that heats the air before it's blown through the house) and detection of dangerous carbon monoxide leaks. If you have an automatic fuel delivery plan with your supplier, this inspection may come free with your plan.

Take a free tour of your heat-and-air system. Learning the ins and outs of duct systems can be overwhelming for a novice. Don't be shy about asking the technician doing your inspection what this or that lever or button does and any other questions you may have about how your system functions. (These guys really know their stuff.) If you have more detailed inquiries, ask a heating and cooling contractor to come out and show you how things work.

Use your garden hose to improve your indoor air quality. Dirty filters slow airflow, making your forced-air system work harder than it has to—and guess what that means for you, the homeowner? Higher energy bills. Dusty buildup can also find its way back into the machinery that powers the climate control, leading to expensive repairs or even mechanical failure. Once a month, check the furnace filter for dust and grime, and replace it as needed. (If you have a reusable filter, wash it with a garden hose, and let it dry completely before sliding it back into place.) Furnace filters generally need to be replaced or washed every three months, monthly at the height of the heating and cooling seasons.

Get your ductwork cleaned. Cleaning ductwork is an expensive and sensitive endeavor, and if it's done poorly, it can have an adverse affect on your indoor air quality. It's certainly not a yearly chore—every five years is more like it—and only if there are visible signs of trouble, such as mold growth within ducts, rodent or insect infestations, or if excessive dust or debris is coming through the heating registers. When your ductwork does require cleaning, contact the National Air Duct Cleaners

How to Balance Your Forced-Air System

If your forced-air system includes air-conditioning, you may need to do some between-seasons tweaking. Heated air and cooled air mix and move differently but are carried through ductwork that treats them pretty much the same. Tweaking your system's duct dampers gets air moving in the right direction and balances the indoor climate. This exercise takes a little time on the first go-round (usually a day or so), but once you've selected and marked the optimum damper settings for the season, you'll be good to go at the start of winter and summer every year afterward. Here's what to do:

1. Set up a TEMPERATURE-MONI-TORING scheme by assembling a set of identical tabletop thermometers. Place one in each room of your house.

----

2. Open all the DUCT DAMPERS and registers in your forced-air system, then set the thermostat to 68 degrees and fire up the furnace.

----

3. After half an hour, CHECK YOUR THERMOMETER READINGS and partially close the dampers in the warmest rooms in the house. Readjust those dampers and the dampers in all other rooms until you've achieved the desired temperature throughout the house.

----

4. Use a PERMANENT MARKER to mark the final handle position you've set on each damper, noting "W" or "winter" next

to the mark you've made. When you do a pre-summer balancing run, note an "S" or "summer" next to that season's marks. You're set now, no matter what the season.

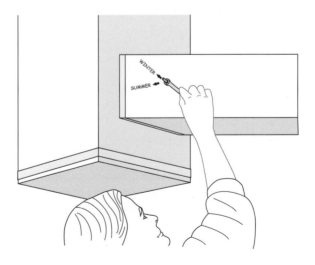

Association in Canada (www.nadca.com) and carefully screen candidates by getting multiple estimates, comparing service claims, and checking licenses and references.

How to Tune Up Your **Furnace**

Though you'll want to bring in a pro for your annual inspection, this simple tune-up is something that any homeowner can handle. Taking care of this "fall cleaning" a month or so before heating season kicks off will ensure a warm winter indoors.

1. TURN OFF THE GAS to the furnace and cut power to it by turning off both the switch at the side of the furnace and the appropriate circuit breaker or fuse at your service panel (see the "Electrical Smarts" chapter).

2. VACUUM THE BASE AND BURNERS of the furnace, extending the vacuum hose with a drain tube to reach the farthest nooks and crannies.

3. CLEAN DUSTY BLOWER BLADES by removing the bolts that hold the blower in place and lifting away blade debris with the vacuum or a small brush. Be careful not to touch fan blade counterweights or the delicate wiring.

4. CHECK THE FILTER, and replace or clean it if it's dirty.

5. INSPECT THE DRIVE BELT on the motor and blower, and replace it if it's cracked or frayed. Adjust the belt tension so that it deflects by about the thickness of your index finger. To adjust the tension, loosen the motor mounting bolts and move the motor away from or toward the blower. (Check your service manual for instructions on setting the tension or replacing the belt on your particular model.)

6. If you have an OLDER FURNACE, its two motor and two blower shaft bearings require an annual oiling. To do this, first clean the area around the oil caps, then take them off and apply no more than three drops of 20-weight machine oil to each bearing.

7. While your heating system is on your mind, take the opportunity to ADJUST DAMPER SETTINGS for the new season; those settings should be marked on the duct surface from the prior year's balancing (see "How to Balance Your Forced-Air System," on the preceding page).

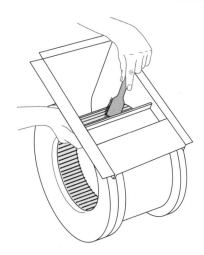

Put your thermostat on autopilot. Today's smart thermostats can help you save valuable energy dollars—and even pay for themselves within a season—with programming to match your at-home schedule. During winter months, for example, take advantage of a digital model's seven-day settings by programming it to reduce the indoor temperature by 10°F (-6°C) overnight or when you're away for more than six hours, and then heat things up again about an hour before you wake or return. You can also arrange your home's climate around your weekend schedule, and manually override the settings if your plans change.

Easy Fixes

Sealing the ducts. Up to 20 percent of precious cooled or heated air can escape through leaky ductwork. You want to seal the system tightly, but you've got to use the right materials. Fabric-backed duct tape doesn't have as much staying power as you need, so go with special metal-backed tape made for the purpose or, for minor leaks, an application of duct sealant. Seal all seams and connections tightly, and follow with an insulation wrap where possible.

Quieting a noisy blower. An out-of-whack drive belt can make a racket, so if you're hearing squeaks and squeals from your furnace, check the belt's alignment with a straightedge. For silent, smooth operation, the belt should be perpendicular to the motor shaft, and the blower and motor pulleys should line up. If you need to make any adjustments, loosen the setscrew to move the motor pulley.

Boosting your ducts. If one room stays much cooler than the rest of the house when the heat's on full blast—and adjusting the dampers doesn't help—consider having a duct booster fan installed in the spot in your ductwork system that's closest to the chilly room. The fan can be either wired to a manual switch or connected to the furnace's blower fan, which will power it up simultaneously.

Gas Burners

Gas burners efficiently burn a combination of gas (either natural or propane) and air to heat either air or water in your furnace or boiler. They are relatively straightforward devices. When trouble arises, it's generally just ignition problems and clogged burners. In addition to scheduling an annual professional inspection, you can enhance your burner's efficiency by staying on top of a few simple maintenance tasks.

SMART IDEA

Know the location of your gas shutoff valves. The main valve is usually located near the gas meter—you'll need a wrench to turn it off. You should know where the manual shutoff valve is for each gas fixture in your house. To shut off a manual valve, turn its handle until it's perpendicular to the pipe.

Care and Maintenance

Unclog your pilot light with a toothpick. If the burner's pilot doesn't light, the pilot orifice may be clogged. To clean it, turn off the electrical switch and main gas shutoff valve. Remove the access panel and unscrew the bracket holding the pilot and the thermocouple (the gizmo next to the pilot that turns off the gas flow when the pilot light goes out). Then clean the orifice with a toothpick. Dust around its edges with a cotton swab or a very thin paintbrush.

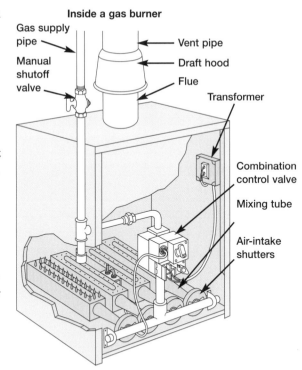

Inside a gas burner

Gas supply pipe

Manual shutoff valve

Vent pipe

Draft hood

Flue

Transformer

Combination control valve

Mixing tube

Air-intake shutters

Keep burner tubes clean. Dirty burner tubes cut down on system efficiency, so clean them up by shutting off the system's gas and electricity and carefully lifting tubes away from their supporting brackets (if the tubes are attached to the brackets, unscrew the connections and gently twist the tubes to remove them). Taking extra care around burner ports, clean the tubes with a vacuum or brush, and unclog ports with a length of stiff wire.

Easy Fixes

Saving your life with a stick of incense. A gas-powered furnace or water heater needs air to properly exhaust, and a house that's too airtight prevents it from getting the amount it requires. This leads to back drafting, a dangerous condition in which flue gases are sucked down the furnace or chimney, allowing carbon monoxide to linger indoors. Carbon monoxide poisoning, of course, can be fatal. Here's an easy test you can do to make sure your home is getting enough fresh air:

- Close all windows and doors and your fireplace damper, and turn on all household exhaust fans (such as those in your kitchen over the stove, in the bathrooms, etc.).

- Power up the furnace, water heater, and any other vented gas appliances.

- Stand by for 10 minutes to allow drafts to stabilize, then head to the furnace and hold an incense stick (a lit match also works) below the air intake on the burner draft hood. If the resulting smoke is pulled up into the hood, you've got enough fresh air for safe operation; if the smoke blows away from the hood or the match is extinguished, back drafting is in effect. Call your utility company immediately.

take care

If you smell a gas leak, shut off the main gas valve, extinguish any open flames, and get out of the house right away. Do not try to relight the pilot, make any other adjustments to the furnace, operate electrical switches, or even use the phone. Leave the door open behind you as you exit and call your gas company or the fire department from a neighbor's house. Remain outside until the dispatched professional has assessed and corrected the problem and given you permission to reenter your home.

How to Relight the Pilot

1. IF YOUR BURNER IS A NEWER ONE with a combination control, turn off the gas knob and main electric switch, and lower the thermostat.

2. AIR THE BURNER for five minutes, then turn the gas knob to "Pilot." (In older burners, close both the main and pilot gas-supply valves. Wait five minutes, then open the pilot gas valve only.)

3. While depressing the RESET BUTTON OR GAS KNOB (it will be one or the other, depending on your model), light the pilot and wait one minute before releasing the button or knob.

4. If the PILOT GOES OUT, wait five minutes and repeat Step 3, this time depressing the reset button for a little longer than a minute. If the pilot still won't light, the thermocouple may be defective. Call your gas company for service.

5. Once the PILOT IGNITES and stays lit, restore the main gas supply and electricity to the unit, and raise the thermostat.

Checking the color of your burner flame. To operate efficiently, a gas burner requires the correct gas-to-air balance. You can tell if the balance is correct by looking at the color of the burner's flame:

- If your burner isn't getting enough air: yellow flame tip; lazy inner flame.
- If your burner is getting too much air: blue flame with a sharp outline and a hard-edged inner flame.
- If your burner has just the right gas-air balance: mostly blue, soft-edged flame with a blue-green inner flame.

If your flame's color looks off, call a service technician and ask him to adjust the air-intake shutters on the burner tubes.

Adjusting the pilot flame. The pilot flame should wrap around the thermocouple by about half an inch. If it's too low, the thermocouple will cut off the gas supply. To adjust the pilot on newer burners, look for a pilot adjustment screw on the unit's combination control. Remove the screw cap, if any, and turn the screw counterclockwise to raise the flame or clockwise to lower it. Models and procedures vary; check your service manual.

Oil Burners and Oil Tanks

Oil burners come in several varieties, but the gun-type, high-pressure burner is the most common these days. Although oil-fired furnaces require more maintenance than their gas counterparts, there's less of it that homeowners can—or should—do for themselves. Oil tanks, on the other hand, are easily maintained but can mean big losses for you if they break down: Leaks that seep into the earth (or worse, into a water supply) can cost you thousands of dollars to repair, not to mention countless hours sparring with environmental officials.

YOUR COST SAVINGS
$1,600
Cost to install a new, 275-gallon (1,100 litres) above-ground fuel oil tank.

Care and Maintenance

Get a gander at the flame. Just as with gas burners, the look of an oil burner's flame will let you know if it's doing its job efficiently. If your furnace (or boiler) has an observation window, take a peek inside every so often. You should see a bright yellow flame with no trace of smoke. If the flame is dark orange or sooty (or if you

How to Do an Emergency Restart on Your Oil Furnace

So, your oil burner just won't start. You've tried raising the thermostat, and that doesn't get it going. Your next course of action is to check your home's service panel for tripped circuit breakers or blown fuses. If the problem persists, there's something else you can do before you call a service technician. Now, pay attention: When you follow the directions below, make sure you press the reset button only once. Pressing it more than once could cause an overload of fuel oil in the system, which could cause it to explode.

1. Confirm that the system's EMERGENCY SWITCH is on (there may be a few switches, with one on the furnace and one on a wall at a nearby entry).

2. Using the fuel storage tank's GAUGE or a clean, 8-foot-long (2.5 metres) dipstick, check the fuel oil level.

3. Look on the BURNER MOTOR for a reset button. Press it *only once*.

4. Head to the PRIMARY CONTROL and press its reset button *once*. If the furnace doesn't start after this step, shut down the power and call a service professional for assistance.

spot smoke spewing from the chimney outside), it's time to call a service professional for a burner adjustment.

Keep the furnace area tidy. Between annual professional service calls, it's your job to keep the area around the furnace free of dust and grime. Don't sweep dirt under the burner unit, and use your vacuum's crevice tool to clear out the opening that admits air to the burner's blower. Otherwise, dust can impede the blower; dirt can cause the burner to fail. It might be possible, in extreme cases, for either to cause an ignition problem in your furnace.

SMART IDEA

Think twice before doing any maintenance work on the burner itself. You'll likely void your service contract.

THE 7 GOLDEN RULES OF FUEL OIL TANK MAINTENANCE

Just like an oil-fired furnace, the oil tank that supplies it requires regular inspections and maintenance. If it's above ground, it's at risk because it's exposed to the elements; underground tanks that fail can cause serious environmental damage that's very expensive and time-consuming to remedy.

1. Have your tank professionally inspected every year before the start of the heating season and keep an eye out for signs of trouble (e.g., rust, dents, leaks) between inspections.

2. Make sure that the legs and foundations of an above-ground tank are stable and its surface is free of rust, oily stains that look like they're dripping down the sides of the tank (called "weepage" by heating and cooling pros), and excessive denting. Rust and oily stains along the bottom of the tank are clear signs that it needs to be replaced.

3. Look for evidence of spillage near the tank's fill and vent pipes. Call your serviceperson if you find any.

4. Whether the tank is indoors or out, keep the area around it free of debris so you can check underneath it for leaks. Make sure the tank and its fuel lines are protected against possible damage by bicycles, heavy objects, and snow or ice falling off the roof.

5. Keep the tank vent clear of snow, ice, birds' nests, and other debris.

6. Underground tanks can corrode and leak without leaving telltale signs on the surface. If you have an underground oil tank, be alert to any unexplained increases in fuel usage, which can signal that the tank is leaking.

7. If you suspect a leak anywhere in the system, contact your oil burner technician or local environmental authority without delay.

Steam and Hot-Water Systems

Steam and hot-water heating systems have been around for ages, but even with such innovations as convectors and wall-mounted radiators, the basics of how they work remain the same: Water is heated in a gas, oil, or electric boiler, and is circulated as liquid or steam through pipes, which lead to radiators or finned convectors that give off heat. As with oil and gas systems, it's important for you to get a professional maintenance check once a year, before cold weather sets in. There are also a few easy things that you can do yourself to keep your steam or hot-water system percolating efficiently and noiselessly.

YOUR COST SAVINGS

$4,000

How much it would cost to have a new high-efficiency boiler installed.

Care and Maintenance

Clean your radiator. Dusty radiators are less efficient than clean ones. While you're doing your weekly housekeeping, take a few moments to dust the radiator's surfaces, and do more intensive cleaning twice a year. Vacuum away surface dust with a brush attachment, and use a crevice tool to clean between the radiator's tubes.

Vacuum your convectors. Most modern hot-water heating systems use baseboard convectors instead of old-fashioned radiators. Hot water from the boiler flows through a finned pipe in the convector; the fins in turn transfer heat to the surrounding air. What you don't want is dust building up between the fins—the convectors won't operate as efficiently. Periodically vacuum baseboard convectors with a brush attachment. Take off the covers to get at the fins inside, but be careful not to bend them. If you do see bent fins, use needle-nose pliers to straighten them.

Easy Fixes

Bleeding your hot-water system Air that's trapped in the radiators or convectors of a hot-water system will keep hot water from flowing into them freely. But there's an easy way to prevent this from happening: Once a year (before the heating season kicks in), "bleed" or empty the radiators or convectors. With the boiler on, grab a cup or thick towel and head to the unit farthest from the boiler (start on the second floor if your house has one). Using a screwdriver (some units require a special key), slowly and carefully open the bleed valve on that unit. (Look for the valve under the cover of a convector or on the top corner of a radiator at the end opposite the inlet valve.) Catch the hot water that spurts out in the cup or towel. Leave the valve open until

CARING FOR A STEAM SYSTEM

Steam-heating systems require a special level of care: The combination of high temperatures and contents under pressure can be a dangerous one (that's yet another reason why that professional annual maintenance check is important). But once the mercury drops, there are a few tasks you should perform to make sure that you stay warm all winter:

- With the boiler cycle off, check the system's glass water-level gauge every 10 to 14 days. If the water is below the halfway point on the gauge, turn off the boiler system and give it an hour or so to cool down. Then open its water-supply valve until the water level reaches the ideal zone, between about halfway to two-thirds up the gauge. Why is this important? Your system's water levels need to be within a certain range for the boiler to work. If it falls below the recommended range, the boiler can overheat and sustain damage or even explode.

- If the water does fall below the recommended range, your steam system's low-

water cutoff will shut off the burner. Sometimes the burner will shut off not because the water's low, but because sediment buildup clogs the cutoff. It's important that this cutoff mechanism works. Here's how to flush your low-water cutoff: First, turn down the thermostat and put a bucket under the pipe. Open the cutoff's drain valve and let water run out until it's

clear (be careful, it will be very hot!). Then close the valve, and refill the boiler to its proper level.

- Once a year, test the boiler's pressure safety valve. With the boiler running, pull up the valve's lever and let a little steam escape. If the valve reseals without leaking, it's okay. If it clogs or sticks, shut off the power to the boiler and have the valve replaced.

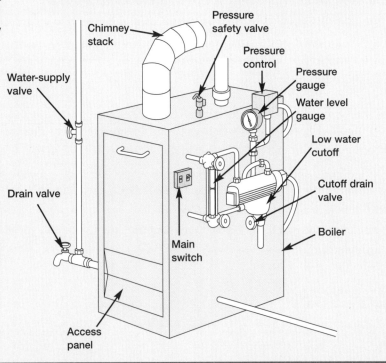

water flows out without sputtering. Taking care not to burn yourself—you may want to wear gloves or use a potholder—close the valve and repeat the process on the next radiator and then the next, working your way back toward the boiler.

Stopping the knocking. Radiator knocks are the bane of one-pipe steam-heating systems, in which steam flows to radiators and condensate (that is, water) flows back to the boiler via the same pipe. If the radiator doesn't slope down toward the inlet valve and the pipe doesn't slope down toward the boiler, water collects in the system and impedes the flow of steam, creating a lot of noise in the process. Adjusting the pipe is a job for a plumber, but quieting a radiator is simple. Some units have height-adjustment bolts in the legs on the end opposite the inlet valve. Turn the bolts with a wrench to increase the radiator's slope. If your model doesn't have adjustment bolts, slip shims under its legs.

Quieting your inlet valves. Another way to prevent knocking in a one-pipe steam system is to keep radiator inlet valves either fully open or fully closed. A partially open valve allows water and steam to mix, which causes the knocking.

Replacing problematic vents. The air vent on a steam radiator (it's on the end of the radiator opposite the inlet pipe) lets out air, but not steam, as the radiator fills with steam. If the vent spits, drips, or hisses (or if the radiator fails to heat evenly), the vent may be clogged and should be replaced with another one of the same size. To remove the air vent, shut off the radiator's inlet valve, let the unit cool, then unscrew the vent (you may need a wrench).

SMART IDEA

Before replacing a clogged air vent, try shaking out any debris and then soaking the vent in distilled vinegar for 30 minutes. If you can blow air through the vent when it's upright, you may not have to replace it after all.

Electric Heat

Electric heaters provide targeted warmth quickly and efficiently. Since they don't burn fuel on the premises and therefore don't require chimneys, vents, fuel tanks, or complicated ductwork to do their job, electric heaters are much more versatile in terms of placement and much less of a hassle when it comes to maintenance. Keep them free of dust and debris and observe safety guidelines, and they'll deliver secure comfort to any living space.

Care and Maintenance

Clean up before it gets cold. Accumulated dust and debris can hinder an electrical unit's heating speed and output, which is why it's best to clear away off-season buildup before the weather gets chilly. With the heater off and cool, carefully vacuum the heating element, reflector surface, and housing using a brush attachment. When they're not being used, store portable space heaters in their original packaging or in plastic garbage bags that you've tied shut.

TYPES OF ELECTRIC HEATERS

Cove heaters Installed just below the ceiling, these heaters direct radiant heat straight down to the floor. Insulated tile or other hard-surface flooring is best suited to holding and releasing a cove heater's warmth.

Wall heaters This type of heater is mounted between two wall studs, its front grille usually flush with the wall's surface. Most are intended for heating a single room, require a dedicated electrical circuit, and include a built-in thermostat. In radiant versions, a reflective back panel directs heat from electric heater coils out into the room. Convective units have a fan that circulates heated air.

Baseboard and kick-space heaters Inconspicuous and low to the ground, these heaters keep your feet toasty as they spread warmth in a room. Baseboard styles use passive convection heat (cool air is drawn through the unit's lower slot, rises as it flows past the heating element, and exits through a top vent). Under-cabinet toe-kick models use fan-forced convection controlled by a thermostat.

Portable space heaters These convenient heaters come in radiant, convection, ceramic convection, and liquid-filled models. In general, radiant heaters are best for heating a small space quickly. Choose a convection heater to distribute warm air quickly in a large space. Ceramic heaters are usually small and therefore good for countertop and under-the-desk use. Liquid-filled units are very efficient and quiet.

Open the drapes and move the dresser. A common cause of electric heater malfunction is air flow that's blocked by furniture, draperies, or debris. Set up a space heater away from any obstructions that can impede the flow of air around it.

Easy Fix

Fixing fan problems. If the fan in a fan-equipped convection heater stops spinning, shut off the heater, unplug it, allow it to cool, and then do a little investigating. If the blades seem to be jammed, remove the heater cover for access and clear away any debris. Give the fan a spin by hand to see if bent components are the problem; try straightening them out, if possible, with pliers. If the fan seems to be loose, tighten the setscrew at the fan's hub. If none of this does the trick, the fan motor may be defective.

BUYING THE RIGHT SIZE HEATER

Single-room electric heaters are rated by the amount of energy they consume; typical ratings range from 750 to 5,000 watts (portable units max out at 1,500 watts). To figure out how much heater wattage you'll need to heat a room with a normal ceiling height, calculate the room's area (length in metres multiplied by width in metres) and multiply the figure by 100 (that is, 100 watts per square metre). Adjust your result up or down depending on such factors as the room's location, ceiling height, number of windows and exterior walls, amount of insulation, and the presence of other heat sources.

Thermostats

Your thermostat is Mission Control for your home's climatic comfort. This temperature-sensitive, typically low-voltage device switches the furnace and/or the air conditioner on and off according to settings you specify. Mechanical thermostats may need an occasional recalibration and tune-up; newer, smarter electronic models have fewer problem-causing parts. The latest generation of thermostats offers extra customization and energy savings with seven-day programming. Using an Energy Star-rated programmable thermostat can save you about $150 in heating costs per year.

Care and Maintenance

Test your thermometer every fall. The only way you're going to get the temperature in your home just to your liking is to make sure that the thermostat's thermometer is accurate. Every fall, before the heating season begins, do this simple test: Tape a household thermometer (one that you know is accurate) to the wall next to the thermostat. Give the thermometer about 15 minutes to settle on its temperature reading, and then compare that reading to the thermostat's. If the difference between the two is more than 5 degrees, recalibrate your thermostat (see below).

Easy Fixes

Adjusting the anticipator. A thermostat's heat anticipator tells it to shut off the furnace or boiler a little early, allowing residual heat to keep room temperature at the desired level. If your heating system cycles on and off too often (or not often enough), a few pokes at the anticipator ought to solve the problem. Access the inside of the thermostat and nudge the anticipator pointer toward a higher setting on its scale if the system is cycling too often; adjust the other way if it isn't cycling often enough.

Recalibrating the thermostat. You've got to get at the guts of the thermostat to tune it. Start by removing its cover. Then, if you need to, unscrew the base plate containing the unit's working parts. Your thermostat's thermometer is usually a bimetallic coil whose components expand or contract at different rates when they're heated or cooled. The flexing of the coil trips a switch (sometimes a mercury-filled glass bulb) that turns the system on or off. Recalibrating the thermometer usually involves turning the coil's adjustment screw or nut with a small screwdriver or needle-nose pliers. Double-check the manufacturer's instructions if you have them.

How to Replace an Old Thermostat with a Programmable Version

Today's high-tech, programmable thermostats allow you to create a heating and cooling plan that suits your schedule *and* cuts your energy consumption. It doesn't take much time to replace an old mechanical thermostat with an electronic one; just make sure the new unit you select works on the same voltage as and is compatible with your HVAC system. (For some upgrades, you may have to have an electrician run new wiring.)

1. TURN OFF POWER to your boiler, furnace, and/or air conditioner.

----

2. Remove the OLD THERMOSTAT'S COVER, unscrew the front assembly, and disconnect its wires. Remove the front assembly; unscrew and remove the wall plate, if there is one. (Check with a local recycler about how best to dispose of the old thermostat, especially if it has a mercury switch.)

----

3. If the wires aren't already COLOR-CODED, tag them with the letters of the terminals to which they were attached. To keep the wires from slipping back into the access hole, secure them with a clothespin or tie them around a pencil.

----

4. SLIP THE WIRES through the new thermostat's wall plate. Level the plate on the wall and mark the fastener hole locations. Use anchors and screws to secure the plate firmly to the wall.

----

5. Follow the MANUFACTURER'S INSTRUCTIONS to connect the wires to the new unit's terminal screws. Install backup batteries if necessary, and snap the thermostat onto the wall plate. Restore system power and program your new thermostat.

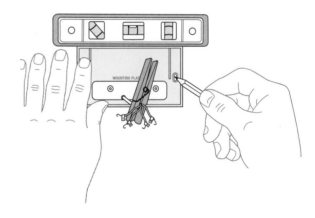

Central Air-Conditioning

A central air conditioner circulates cool air through ducts and registers, typically those of an existing forced-air heating system. Few home maintenance chores yield a greater pay-off, in terms of comfort and dollars saved, than keeping your A/C system clean. Benign neglect, on the other hand, can lead to major malfunctions—and very high replacement fees. The cost of replacing an old system averages about $3,000; expect to pay double or triple that if you're installing a new system and new ductwork.

SMART IDEA

Fire ants, mice, and other critters love to set up housekeeping around the warmth of the condenser unit. Before screwing the top grille back on, make sure you evict any unwanted residents.

Care and Maintenance

Cut the power first. Before you go poking around your central A/C's system, turn the power off at its shutoff box (this is usually on an exterior wall near the system's outdoor unit). Some shutoffs are pulled out; others have a handle that you flip down or, less commonly, a fuse to remove. If there is no outdoor shutoff, cut power to the air conditioner at the main circuit breaker panel or fuse box.

Clean the filter. Making sure your air conditioner's filter is clean is probably the most important thing you can do to keep the system working at its peak. Check the filter at least once a month during the cooling season and replace it as needed. Remember, too, that it's equally important to balance the airflow through your duct-work in summer and winter. Don't forget to change damper handles to summer settings at the start of the cooling season (see "How to Balance Your Forced-Air System," on page 219).

Keep plants away from the unit. The outdoor unit of your air-conditioning system needs to be free and clear to do its job. For maximum airflow, you'll need to maintain the area around it well:

- Keep at least a 2-foot (60 cm) radius clear of landscape plantings.
- When mowing the lawn, make sure grass clippings are directed away from the unit.
- To limit the amount of dust the fan draws into the unit, cover the ground around it with gravel, and add a layer of mulch to nearby flower beds.

Use bleach for your A/C cleanup. For part two of your central air conditioner spring cleanup, head indoors and turn your attention to the furnace's blower compartment. With the power turned off, open the blower compartment and vacuum it and the blower, and service the blower motor and belt. Also, check the condensation drain tube for sludge and algae buildup. To get rid of algae, carefully pour a solution of 1 part bleach to 16 parts water down a rigid drain tube (remove a flexible drain tube to flush it out). If possible, poke a wire into the drain port to clear it.

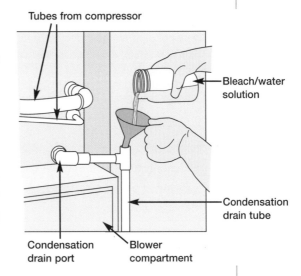

Tubes from compressor

Bleach/water solution

Condensation drain tube

Condensation drain port

Blower compartment

Get your system serviced. We've said it before with regard to furnaces and boilers, but the advice applies to central air conditioners, too: It's important that you have your system professionally inspected and serviced every year in early spring. In addition, give it a thorough cleaning and tune-up at the beginning of each cooling season.

HOW A CENTRAL AIR CONDITIONER WORKS

Central air-conditioning systems consist of an outdoor unit containing a compressor and its motor, a condenser coil, and a fan, and an indoor unit consisting of an evaporator coil usually located in the main supply duct (or plenum) above the furnace blower. Copper tubes—one insulated, the other bare—transfer refrigerant between the two units. In other words, the compressor pumps refrigerant back and forth between the evaporator coil, where the refrigerant absorbs heat from the air, thereby cooling it, and the condenser coil, where heat is released.

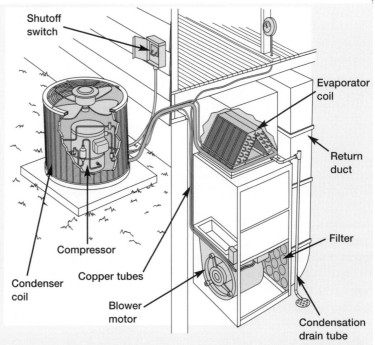

Shutoff switch

Evaporator coil

Return duct

Filter

Compressor

Copper tubes

Condenser coil

Blower motor

Condensation drain tube

Rouse your sleeping A/C the right way. When it's time for your central A/C system to come out of hibernation (or after a prolonged in-season shutdown for maintenance or repairs), you need to power it up properly. First, make sure the thermostat is switched to "off." Next, restore power and let the system run for 24 hours so that the compressor's lubricant has a chance to warm up before use. Then you can switch your thermostat to "cool" and set the desired temperature to activate your air conditioner.

If there's a brief power interruption while the air conditioner is on (or if the system is accidentally turned off), switch the thermostat to "off" and keep it that way for at least five or six minutes before restarting the system. Restoring power right away can damage the compressor.

How to Clean an Outdoor A/C Unit

Don't worry, this task is much easier than it looks, although it does take more than a few minutes. You might want to ask someone to help you move and hold the unit's top grille. Here's what to do:

1. TURN OFF POWER to the air conditioner, as described above. To access the condenser coil and its fins, you may have to first remove a protective metal case covering the unit (if there is one, it's usually screwed or bolted in place at the base). Vacuum the condenser coil's fins with a soft-bristle brush, being careful not to bend or distort any of the delicate fins as you go. Use a fin straightener comb, sold at HVAC parts suppliers, to straighten any bent fins you encounter.

2. RAKE UP AND REMOVE leaves and other debris surrounding the coil that could potentially block airflow.

3. Here's where the assistant comes in handy: UNSCREW THE TOP GRILLE and hold it open. The unit's fan and motor are usually attached to the grille, which needs to be supported carefully to avoid straining electrical wires and connections.

4. Using a GARDEN HOSE equipped with a trigger-controlled nozzle, spray the fins from the inside out, moving around the perimeter of the condenser to clean the entire coil. Remove any debris that has collected on the inside bottom of the condenser unit.

5. OIL THE MOTOR at its ports (if any) with either a manufacturer-recommended lubricant or 20-weight machine oil. Replace the top grille.

6. RESTORE POWER and set the indoor thermostat to "cool" so that the compressor comes on. Listen for any noises that might indicate trouble. After 10 minutes, feel the tubes that carry refrigerant to the unit: the uninsulated one should be warm to the touch and the insulated one should be cool.

Easy Fixes

Reducing indoor humidity levels. To keep your indoor air from feeling too sticky, reduce your air conditioner's blower speed. Air moving in slower motion over the evaporator coil removes more moisture from living areas. Be sure to consult with the unit's manufacturer before taking this step, and avoid dropping the speed too drastically, which can result in the coils icing up.

Stopping a rattling compressor. It has probably happened to you before, and boy, did it get on your last nerve: What's more annoying than a loud, rattling outdoor A/C compressor when you're trying to spend leisure time outside? Here are a few things to do to your compressor to make sure that doesn't happen again:

- Make sure nothing is obstructing the fan. Turn off power to the system and remove the unit's top grille. Clear out any debris around the fan.
- Tighten the bolts or setscrews holding the blades in place.
- Inspect the unit for loose housing screws and tighten them.
- If the fan motor has oil ports, make sure that they're lubricated.

If your motor starts making noise and these four tricks don't solve the problem, the fan motor may need to be serviced or replaced. Call a technician.

take care

Don't run the air conditioning if it's cool outside. You risk damaging the compressor if you operate the system when the outside temperature is below 60°F. (15°C).

5 SIMPLE WAYS TO SLASH YOUR A/C BILLS

1. **Close your blinds.** Windows can let in about 25 percent of summer heat. Block the heat with shades or blinds during the sunniest daylight hours.

2. **Insulate attics and walls.** The attic and exterior walls of your home will keep out the heat with proper insulation. Most kinds of insulation are inexpensive, though you may want to hire someone to install it.

3. **Strip in the cool.** Weather stripping can keep cool air from escaping through doors and windows. It's very inexpensive; you can strip the area around a door in less than half an hour. (See the "Weather Stripping" section for further details.)

4. **Spin some coolness.** Ceiling fans and stand-alone units can augment the output of a central air conditioner. A whole-house fan draws cool outside air indoors through slightly opened windows around the house, and pushes warm air up and out through the attic for a fast, efficient change in temperature. You'll save money by decreasing the time you need to run your A/C.

5. **Do your baking and washing at night.** Large appliances give off significant heat. Save the operation of ovens, ranges, dishwashers, and clothes washers and dryers for evening hours when cooler temperatures will offset their output.

Window and Room Air Conditioners

YOUR COST SAVINGS

$400

Price you'd pay for a new 8,000-BTU air conditioner to replace a poorly maintained unit.

Window and room air conditioners operate on the same principles and with the same basic components—compressor and condenser coil on the outside, evaporator coil on the inside—as a central air conditioner. The difference is that in the more portable versions, all the elements are bundled into one compact unit that can be mounted into a window opening or through a wall to deliver cool to a targeted living area. Replacing these units typically costs a few hundred dollars; the trouble and expense of reinstalling these heavy units is even more of a headache than the upfront costs are!

Care and Maintenance

Keep your home cool with dishwashing liquid. Cleaning the air-conditioning filter at least once a month during the cooling season is essential. Wash a foam or metal mesh filter in warm water with a squirt of dishwashing liquid. Rinse and let dry thoroughly before reinstalling it. Replace disposable filters with a new version of the same model.

Check the gaskets. Each spring, check the seals and gaskets around it to make sure they're not leaking air. Repair or replace any that are deteriorated.

Fend off algae with ammonia. As the air-conditioning season wears on, there's a good chance that your unit's drain tube could become clogged by algae. Check your A/C's drain tube by inserting a piece of wire into the drain tube, which is accessible from the underside of the unit, and moving the wire around the tube's interior. This

SHOULD YOU STOW THE AIR CONDITIONER DURING THE WINTER?

Off-season care and storage of your air conditioner can vary, depending on the location of a unit and your personal preference. Both window- and wall-mounted units can stay in place, with winter drafts sealed out using specially made insulation kits that cover either the exterior of the air conditioner or its indoor panel. However, if you'll be putting up storm windows, a window-mounted unit will have to be taken out and stored. Either way, do a little post-season cleanup: Straighten out any bent fins, vacuum the unit thoroughly, and remove any rust from the drain pan and cabinet.

should clean out the algae, if there is any. Next, either pour in or use an old medicine dropper to drip a teaspoon of household ammonia into the tube to prevent new growth.

Keep the A/C in the shade. Window air conditioners work less efficiently in direct sunlight. If you can, install yours in a shady wall, or put an awning over it.

How to Clean a Room Air Conditioner

Cleaning a room air conditioner is fairly easy, but if you've never done it, you might want to give yourself a few hours to learn how to take the machine apart and put it back together. To clean it thoroughly, you'll first need to remove the unit from its window or wall opening. Get someone to help you with this—air conditioners are very heavy. The routine described below applies to most air conditioners, but check your owner's manual for more specific instructions.

1. UNPLUG THE UNIT and lift it out of the window or wall opening. Place it on a work surface, and remove its front cover and case according to the manufacturer's instructions.

2. REMOVE THE FILTER from the front grille and either wash or replace it.

3. Using a BRUSH ATTACHMENT, thoroughly and carefully vacuum the evaporator fins. Straighten any bent fins with a fin straightener comb, sold at HVAC parts suppliers.

4. To wash the CONDENSER COIL (this is best done outdoors), first make sure the unit's drain holes are open, and cover the fan motor and its wiring compartment with a plastic bag. Use a garden hose to spray down the condenser coil from the outside. Rinse away any grime that collects in the unit's drain pan, and wipe off any water left after the pan has drained.

5. When the air conditioner is completely dry, LUBRICATE THE MOTOR with electric motor oil (five drops at each accessible port should do the trick, but consult your owner's manual for specifics).

6. REPLACE the unit's casing and cover, and return it to its mounted position.

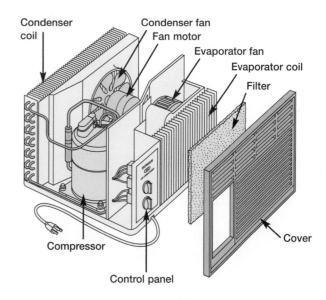

Condenser coil · Condenser fan · Fan motor · Evaporator fan · Evaporator coil · Filter · Cover · Compressor · Control panel

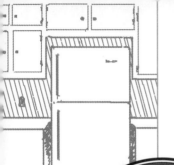

Refrigerators

It's the small things that cause the most damage to this major appliance: Dust on your refrigerator's coils can lessen its efficiency and shorten its life, minerals in water can clog ice makers and water dispensers, and algae and food particles can clog the drain. The good news is that these little troublemakers are a cinch to defeat yourself, which saves you the expense of professional servicing—or a new unit!

SMART IDEA

A stocked freezer isn't just good news for your belly—it also keeps your freezer running at maximum efficiency. (More volume means less circulating air that has to be cooled.) If your unit isn't stuffed, fill your empty spaces with jugs of water. They'll not only help your freezer's performance, they'll keep your food cold in the event of a power outage.

Care and Maintenance

Give your fridge room to breathe. Your fridge functions most efficiently when you give it a little space: Allow at least half an inch (1 cm) on the left and right and 1 inch (2.5 cm) behind it, and don't stack anything on top of the unit. If it is in direct sunlight, move it or install a window shade. Avoid keeping a refrigerator in an uninsulated garage or basement, because extreme temperatures can harm it.

Clean your icebox from the top down. Start high, and go one shelf at a time, from top to bottom—that way if you dribble crumbs, sauce, or even your detergent, you're not dirtying shelves you've already cleaned. If the shelves are removable, clean them in the sink with warm water and mild detergent, and dry them thoroughly before you put your food back on top of them. Soak refrigerator drawers in warm, soapy water in the sink. Use the same water-and-detergent when you're wiping up spills and other messes.

Keep your cool longer by vacuuming the coils. Your refrigerator's coils are notorious dust catchers, but they're simple to clean: You'll find them by removing the toe plate below the refrigerator door. On a cycle-defrost model, the coils are at the back of the unit. They look kind of like a grid of wire-like pipes. Make sure your fridge is unplugged, then vacuum the coils using the vacuum's crevice-cleaning attachment. If you don't have a vacuum, use a coil brush, or even a yardstick with a rag attached. Clean the coils quarterly or more often if you have pets. Dirt and dust on the coils can inhibit the dissipation of heat, causing the unit to run poorly, cycle on and off too often, or not run at all.

Put your fridge on the level. Your fridge may not be level because your floors may not be perfectly flat. That's okay—this is an easy fix, and one worth doing because your refrigerator is most efficient when it's level. Look for the unit's feet or casters, and raise or lower them with an adjustable wrench; adjust casters by turning their leveling screws with a screwdriver. On some refrigerators, you may have to remove the toe plate. Use your carpenter's level to make sure it's balanced.

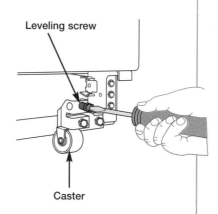

Leveling screw

Caster

Watch for water line leaks. Check the water line monthly for leaks. The line often traverses cabinets or walls, where small drips can create big problems.

Prevent defroster problems. In frost-free freezers, a hose carries moisture out of the freezer into a drain pan at the bottom of the unit. If the hose gets clogged with algae or food, the defrost cycle will cause the melted ice to overflow and drip into the area where food is kept. Here's a once-a-year trick to keep your defrost drain in good working order: Unplug the refrigerator and empty the freezer. Pop the freezer floor out (your manual will explain how to do this), find the drain hole, and remove excess ice from the floor of the freezer and tray. Mix 1/2 gallon (2 litres) of hot water with 1/2 cup (125 ml) of chlorine bleach and pour the solution into the hose *a little bit at a time*—you may not need to use all of the solution. When the ice is melted and flowing down the drain hole, blow down the drain hole with a small rubber tube to force the leftover particles out. When the hose allows a free flow, rinse it with clear water. Finally, empty, clean, and dry the drip pan.

WHEN IT'S TIME FOR A NEW MODEL

Refrigerators that are sold today use 40 percent less energy than those that were sold in 2001. The Association of Home Appliance Manufacturers claims that a new, 20.6-cubic-foot refrigerator with a top freezer uses no more electricity than a 75-watt lightbulb. Twentieth-century models may well account for as much as 15 percent of your electric bill; to encourage customers to replace their old units with more energy-efficient ones, some utility companies offer incentive rebates. That new model could pay for itself faster than you'd think!

Give your door gaskets the dollar-bill test. If the gaskets on your refrigerator door aren't sealing tightly, your food will spoil more quickly, and your energy bill will skyrocket. Here's how a five-dollar bill can save you big bucks: Twice a year, put a five-dollar bill between the door and the refrigerator unit and close the door. Try to pull the bill out. (Try this trick in several places around the door.) If there's no resistance, the gasket's not working. If the gasket appears stiff or cracked, replace it. If your old gasket looks good, lightly coat the flat surface on the more vulnerable hinge side with petroleum jelly to keep it from sticking.

Easy Fixes

Changing your filter. If the ice from your ice maker or water from your refrigerator's spigot tastes funny, changing the filter may help. You can purchase them online or in appliance parts stores. Installing a new filter will take you about two minutes— you snap out the old one and snap in the new one. Swap in a new filter annually (if your water quality is bad, change it every six months).

Fixing a saggy door. If your gasket's in good shape but flunks the five-dollar-bill test, the door may be warped or sagging. To fix it, take everything off the door shelves, loosen the screws behind the gasket or on the plate on top of the door, then grasp the door and flex it until it closes flush with the refrigerator. This is easier to do with a helper. Tighten the screws to hold the door in place.

Stoves, Ovens, and Range Hoods

Your stove is the warming heart of your kitchen; it helps you nourish your family. With that in mind, you want to do everything you can to keep it in good working order. Regular cleaning and maintenance can keep you cooking up a storm for years to come—and can spare you the expense of having to buy a new model.

YOUR COST SAVINGS
$510
How much it would cost to replace a standard, mid-priced freestanding gas range.

Care and Maintenance

Anchor your oven. A freestanding or slide-in oven needs an anti-tip bracket to keep it from toppling if weight is put on the door. (Tipping ovens can start fires and cause burns.) The anti-tip bracket is usually a U-shaped piece of metal screwed to the floor beneath the oven and hooked to one of the oven's rear feet; slide your appliance out a few inches to check for it. If your oven doesn't have one, the manufacturer might supply it for free.

Make it shine. Cleaning the stove isn't anyone's idea of a good time, but it has its benefits beyond just looking tidy. Clean stoves transfer heat better and are more energy efficient. Here's how to keep yours in tip-top shape:

- Wipe up spilled food promptly. Messes are easiest to clean when they're fresh.
- Avoid using abrasive cleansers and cleaning pads. Instead, spray a 50-50 mix of dish soap and water and let it soak into burned-on food for a few minutes. Wipe with a clean cloth.
- If your stove doesn't have a sealed cooktop, you can do more extensive cleaning on its inside, too. (These non-sealed cooktops can be popped open like you would a car hood.) If you can get under the hood, so to speak, use the same 50-50 mix for cleaning.
- If food cakes on one of your burners, clean off as much as you can, then turn the heat to high. The mess should burn right off.

Protect smooth cooktops. Smooth glass and ceramic cooktops are sleek and attractive, but they're also fairly easily damaged. To get the longest possible life out of them, avoid abrasive cleaners, and never use the cooktop as you would a cutting board. Avoid scratching the surface by using only smooth-bottomed cookware, and

SMART IDEA

While an element is removed, clean or replace the drip pan underneath it. Shiny clean pans reflect heat, making the stove more energy efficient.

Using commercial oven cleaners in a self-cleaning oven is a very bad idea. Applying chemical cleaners to self-cleaning ovens can damage the appliance's interior. If you have a self-cleaning oven, for crying out loud, let the oven clean itself. While the oven is cleaning, give the oven racks a mild ammonia bath. Always let the self-cleaning cycle complete before opening the oven door.

stow cookware away after cooking to avoid heat buildup. Finally, don't store heavy items like cookware and canned food in the cabinets above the stove. If they fall, they'll damage the cooktop.

Look under the hood. Most of us take notice (and action) when greasy goo starts building on the top side of the range hood, but how many of us remember to get the gunk out from the underside? Once a month, remove the hood's exhaust filter, toss it in the dishwasher, and wash that gross grease away. If your hood's exhaust fan is making more noise than usual, chances are the filter's clogged. And while you have the filter off the hood, wipe the hood and fan blades with all-purpose cleaner, if you can access them.

Easy Fixes

Keeping the flame burning properly. If your gas stove's flame tips are orange rather than blue, there's probably a problem with the burner. Wait until the stove is cool, then lift the cooktop, remove the burner, soak it in soapy water, and give it a good scrub. Then clean the individual gas jets—this is a cinch to do with a toothpick or a heavy-gauge needle. Clean flash tube ports, the tiny holes where the pipe from the pilot

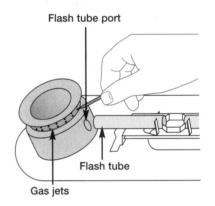

Flash tube port

Flash tube

Gas jets

light connects to the burner, with a fine wire. If the flame still burns orange, it may be a sign that your stove is using the wrong type of gas (say, the stove is set to be used with natural gas and you're using propane instead). No worries—a technician can usually fix it. A final tip: Orange flames aren't always bad news—they aren't uncommon in coastal communities. The color of the flame can be affected by salty air.

Recalibrating your oven. Use an oven thermometer to test a 450°F (232°C) oven; if the temperature's off by more than 35°F (20°C), you need to recalibrate. This can be an easy fix. On manual-control ovens—those with knobs—recalibrating may be a simple matter of turning screws on the back of the oven-temperature knob. Ovens with digital (touch-pad) controls can sometimes be calibrated using a special keypad sequence. Either way, consult your owner's manual. An impossible-to-calibrate oven may have a bad thermostat, which a technician can replace.

De-gunking the sides of your range. Have you ever pulled your stove away from the wall and seen the nasty spills, stains, and crumbs that have stuck to its sides?

This mess is easily avoided by picking up inexpensive T-shaped plastic gaskets from a home-improvement store and slipping them between freestanding stoves and adjacent countertops. When gaskets get soiled (and boy, will they get soiled), simply remove them, wash them, and reinstall them.

Replacing bad elements. If you have an electric stove, you heat your food on "elements," those bull's-eye-looking coils of wire that are covered with nonconductive material. Sometimes they get past the point at which they'll ever be clean again, and sometimes they just up and quit on you. Neither is cause for worry because elements are easy and inexpensive to replace. Here's what to do: Unplug your stove (and if you want to be extra cautious, cut the power at the breaker box, too). Then check the element's connection to the stove's wiring—it'll flip up, plug in, or be soldered in. (The first two options are easy to do for yourself. If it's soldered on, you really should have it replaced by a professional.) Plug in elements can just be tugged out. With flip-up models, you'll just have to remove a screw or two from an insulating block before you detach it. Once you've detached the element, bring it (and the stove's model number) to an appliance store for an exact match.

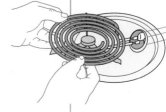

Adjusting warped doors. Discoloration or soot around the oven door indicates a warped door. To adjust, simply open the door and loosen the screws on the inside panel near the corners; these hold the inner and outer panels together. Push down on the door while twisting it from side to side (be extra careful on doors with large windows); then carefully retighten the screws. Close the door and look for gaps; it may take a couple of tries to get it right. Another possible cause of warped doors is bent hinges; these would have to be replaced by a professional.

Replacing electric oven elements. If your electric oven's not cooking properly, its element may be burning out. (Oven elements are bigger versions of stove elements.) Cut power to your oven, let it cool, then remove the screws that hold the element in place. (You may need to remove the door to gain access; check the manual for specifics.) Pull out the element and test it with an electrical continuity tester; most have one probe and one alligator clip. Touch the tester's probe and clip to the two element terminals. If the element is good, the tester's bulb will light.

Replacing oven seals. Open your oven door and inspect the slender gasket clipped to the front of the oven. (Not all models have them.) If it's damaged, burned, or soiled, you can probably replace it with an identical gasket (also called an oven seal) from an appliance-parts store. Don't attempt to replace seals on self-cleaning ovens; leave that to a pro.

Garbage Disposals

Garbage disposals are powerful, but they're not invincible. You'll keep yours running smoothly for years to come if you follow simple guidelines such as keeping out grease and keeping those blades clean and free of obstruction.

SMART IDEA

To deodorize a garbage disposal, pour 1/4 cup (60 ml) of borax down the drain, let it sit for 30 minutes, then flush with water for a few seconds while the disposal is on. (You can use the same treatment to freshen up smelly floor drains!)

Care and Maintenance

When life hands you lemons, clean the garbage disposal. Once a month, turn on your disposal and toss a tray of ice cubes in. It'll make a racket, all right, but the ice does a good job of cleaning the blades. Next, run some cold water down the disposal, followed by a few lemon peels. Suddenly what used to be the murkiest, scariest part of your kitchen will smell fresh and clean. (Other deodorizing options are to use either a cup (250 ml) of white vinegar or a half-cup (125 ml) of baking soda—*not* the two together—followed by more cold water.) Never use liquid drain cleaner in a garbage disposal!

Run cold, not hot, water into your disposal. Hot water softens grease—that's a bad thing. You want fatty foods to harden so that they'll grind up.

Never pour grease or oil in your disposal. Strain it into a glass jar instead. Once the jar is full, put it in the refrigerator overnight so the grease congeals, then toss the glass jar out in the trash.

Don't grind up celery or corn husks. Their fibers can get tangled in the disposal unit's blades, which just spells "big mess" for you. Clam and oyster shells are also too hard—toss those out into the trash. Small bones (like those in fish fillets) are usually okay. Never throw coffee grounds down the disposal, either!

Easy Fix

Stopping leaks with two screws. Where's your disposal unit most likely to leak? At the drainpipe and at the sink. Making sure that these screws are always tightened will keep discarded food in your pipes, not inside your kitchen cabinets:

- At the drainpipe: See that pipe coming out and down from the disposal's side? Tighten the screw that holds it in place.

- At the sink: Use an offset screwdriver or a hex key to tighten the screws on the unit's sink mounting ring.

How to Clear a Jammed Garbage Disposal

1. UNPLUG THE DISPOSAL. If you have a hardwired model, turn power off at the service panel.

----

2. Insert the ALLEN WRENCH that came with the disposer into the bottom-center hole on the machine, and rotate until it moves freely. (The wrench moves the disposal's central drive shaft.) If your disposal didn't come with a wrench, insert a wooden broomstick or plunger handle in the mouth of the disposal to move the blades. Never use your hands.

----

3. PULL FOOD, fibers, or whatever else is jamming the works out of the disposal's maw with needle-nose pliers or tongs.

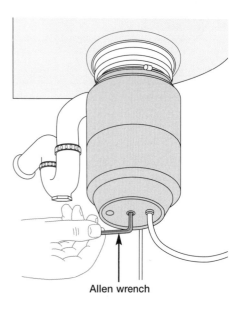

Allen wrench

4. RECONNECT POWER to the unit. If it doesn't power up, push the reset button (if there is one) on the underside of the disposal. Make sure the unit is cool to the touch before pressing reset; the motor can heat up if it is stuck or jammed.

----

5. If the DISPOSAL STILL DOESN'T START, repeat steps 1 through 4 at least twice before calling a service technician.

Dishwashers

For an appliance whose job it is to get things squeaky clean, how is it that your dishwasher is probably the grimiest, most stained and rusty item in your kitchen? Left unchecked, dirt and dings can mean big problems (and big repair bills) for your dishwasher. Giving it a once-over every now and again to check these and the moving parts that can weaken with age—like the doors, spray arms, and hoses—can keep your dishwasher problem free for years to come.

Care and Maintenance

Give the dishwasher a scrub with powdered lemonade mix. A dishwasher needs to be washed to function optimally. When the machine starts to look and smell grimy, there're a few things you can do: The most ingenious dishwasher cleaning secret we know of is to use a scoop of powdered lemonade mix. If you don't have that on hand, give it a rinse with a cup (250 ml) of white vinegar. Whichever cleaner you choose, be sure to run it through an empty dishwasher.

Get rid of mineral deposits with a toothpick and vinegar. Food and mineral deposits may clog the holes in your dishwasher's rotating spray arm. To clear the holes, remove the dish racks, then unscrew the screws that hold the spray tower or

THE RIGHT SUDS

Dishwashers do their best cleaning when the triumvirate of water quality, water temperature, and detergent are in perfect balance. If your appliance just isn't performing up to par:

Adjust your detergent based on water hardness. Your utility company should be able to tell you how hard your water is (measured in grains per gallon, or simply "grains"). Use 1 teaspoon (5 ml) of detergent per grain.

Check your water temperature with a kitchen thermometer. Some dishwashers require water that's hotter than 140°F (60°C). If your dishwasher doesn't have a built-in water heater (check the manual), adjust your home's water heater. Always run hot water from the faucet nearest your dishwasher before starting a cycle to flush cold water from pipes.

Experiment with different types of detergents. Some households swear by gel-style detergents, while others find that they gum things up.

hubcap arm in place. Lift off the arm and clear clogs with a toothpick or nail. Remove mineral deposits with vinegar and a scrub brush.

Replace your dishwasher's hoses before they break. If your washer has a standard reinforced rubber hose, replace it every two years (and consider upgrading to a braided stainless steel hose, which lasts longer). And while we're replacing hoses, be sure to change out the dishwasher drain hose every few years; use a worm-screw clamp instead of a spring clamp to attach it. (The worm-screw clamp connection is more secure than the spring clamp.) Always use new hoses when replacing a dishwasher.

Easy Fixes

Repairing rusty racks. Scour rust spots on dish racks with steel wool, then touch them up with ReRack, Rackcote, or another rack repair product. Epoxy-style paint that's used to fix chips in porcelain sinks will also work. If your rack "fingers" are damaged, cap them with rubber dishwasher "tine caps."

Using petroleum jelly to stave off a flood. Imagine for a minute what would happen if the seals on your dishwasher door went kaput: Your kitchen island would look like Noah's ark! To prevent leaks and keep that seal as tight as can be, regularly clean the gasket (it may be on the tub, or it may be on the door—some dishwashers also have an extra gasket along the bottom of the tub, so look for that, too) with warm, soapy water, give it a light coat of petroleum jelly, and check it visually. In most cases, a bad gasket is easy to replace; again, just order it online or from your local appliance-parts store.

Replacing door springs. If you find that your door doesn't spring back as easily as it once did, there's no need to bust out the duct tape. When you open your dishwasher door forcefully, its springs can stretch and break. Here's what to do: Pick up a set of inexpensive replacement springs at your appliance-parts store (just tell the salesperson the dishwasher's make and model). Once you have them, pull the dishwasher out a few inches from under the cabinet, open the door, and look for the springs near the hinges. Install them on both sides. Usually this is an easy pull-off, hook-on operation.

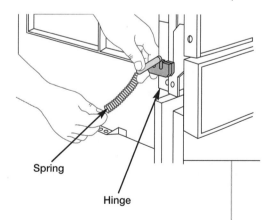

Spring

Hinge

Clothes Washers

If you've ever had an issue with your washing machine, you know that the problem is rarely with the machine itself—it's with the water that the washer uses, coming into and out of the appliance. A flooded basement as a result of a broken washer hose, for example, can be a costly disaster, but fortunately, these water-related occurrences are easy to prevent with routine care.

SMART IDEA

Leave the washer door open for a few hours after a load and allow the water to evaporate. This helps prevent rust on the washer tub and will keep your washer from smelling musty.

Care and Maintenance

Balance loads—it's critical. In all washers, but in top-loading washers in particular, off-kilter loads of laundry can put a great strain on the bearings and mechanism that rotate the tub. Save yourself the cost of these new parts by keeping your ears open for the beginning of the spin cycle and redistributing the wet clothes, if need be, after you stop the spinning, usually by opening the lid. After any unbalanced load is finished and out of the washer, tip the machine forward a few inches (onto its front legs) to get the self-adjusting rear legs to drop back into place.

Don't overload the machine. Stuffing your washer like a Thanksgiving turkey is only going to tax the machine's inner workings. Follow the capacity parameters that are listed in the instruction manual (they also may be printed inside the lid of top-loading washers).

Understand that more detergent doesn't mean cleaner clothes. Use only as much detergent as the package says—using too much can cause a sudsy overflow to pour from your washer (and damage the machine in the process). If you see the high efficiency (HE) logo on your washer, use only HE-designated detergent. It sudses less, causing the machine to be more water and energy efficient.

Replace your washer's hoses. The standard rubber hot and cold water hoses connected to your washing machine can harden, crack, and burst, which is why it's smart to replace them every two years. Consider a stainless steel–reinforced hose, which lasts much longer and can withstand higher water pressure. When you change hoses, mark the date of replacement on the hose.

Keep your washer from frying. Protect your washer's high-tech controls and digital displays by plugging the appliance into a surge protector made for appliances. This is an especially smart move if your community is prone to frequent brownouts, blackouts, or power spikes. And don't set the surge suppressor on the ground, where it might get wet.

Level your machine. A washing machine that's not level will be out of balance, causing it to break down and wear out sooner than necessary. On most models, leveling is very easy: Use a carpenter's level to check that the back of the machine is level from side to side. (It probably is because most machines have self-adjusting back legs.) Next, check whether the machine is level from front to back on one side, and adjust the front foot on that side with a wrench as necessary. (You may need to temporarily prop up the front of the washer on a block of wood to access the legs.) Then adjust the front-to-back level for the other side. When both sides are level, check the front of the machine for side-to-side levelness. Finally, tighten the lock nuts on the front legs to prevent the machine from jiggling out of place.

Going on vacation? Send your washer on one, too. To relieve pressure on a washer's hoses and inlet valves (and eliminate the possibility of a hose bursting and causing a flood), it's a good idea to shut off both hot and cold water to your washer when it's not in use. (The valves should be visible and accessible behind the machine.) At the very least, you should do this when you'll be away from home for several days. Warning: These valves will probably be sticky if you haven't turned them in a while. If they're not budging, don't force them—you'll only bring on the flood that you're trying to prevent. Instead, have a plumber repair or replace them.

Catch small leaks before they become big problems. A heavy-duty waterproof polyethylene pan, available at home centers, can be installed under the washer as added insurance against minor washer leaks. Sometimes these pans are required by building codes, particularly if your washer is not in the basement.

Clean the inlet screens. Between the hoses and the washer you'll find small filters that clog easily, particularly if your water is hard. You have reason to suspect clogged filters if the machine fills slowly with water or doesn't fill at all—in any case, they're easy to unclog. Turn off the washer's water valves, then unscrew the hoses from the washer. You'll find the filters inside the ends of the hoses. Remove them by prying them off the hose with a screwdriver, then scrub them clean with a toothbrush. If the screens are hopelessly clogged, replace them. It's okay to replace plastic screens with metal ones, but don't replace metal screens with plastic ones.

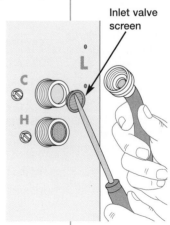

Inlet valve screen

Clothes Dryers

There are really only two things that will muck up your clothes dryer's function: lint and airflow problems. Keeping that air flowing freely—both into the dryer and, even more importantly, out of the exhaust duct—is key to keeping your dryer in tip-top shape. Lint is a clothes dryer's worst enemy: Lint buildup doesn't just slow the speed of drying; it's also a big fire hazard.

Care and Maintenance

Before *every* use, clean lint from the dryer's lint screen. This is the single easiest way to take care of your dryer. At least twice a year, augment your de-linting using a skinny, long-handled dryer vent brush, available at home centers and online. Insert the brush into the lint-screen vent, and twist it to grab and remove lint from the vent.

SMART IDEA

If your dryer is in a small, enclosed laundry room, leave the door open while the dryer is running. This will improve airflow to your dryer, which increases its efficiency. You may also consider installing a louvered door on your laundry room.

Take the lint screen test. Remove your dryer's lint screen and stick it under a running faucet. If the water beads up and rolls off, your screen is probably clogged with microscopic fibers and chemicals (you can thank your fabric-softening dryer sheets for those). Scrub the lint screen with mild soap and an old toothbrush, and let it air dry before replacing it. If you regularly use dryer sheets, scrub your screen at least twice a year.

Vacuum underneath it. Every six months or so, remove the dryer's toe panel (just jimmy it loose with a putty knife, starting at the top center) and vacuum as much dust and lint as you can—this is easy if you have a skinny crevice-cleaning attachment. For fire safety reasons, cleaning out the lint here is particularly important on gas dryers. Caution: Do not try to clean inside the burner on gas units—you can break the ignitor.

Clean the dryer duct. At least once a year, use a long-handled dryer duct brush and a vacuum cleaner hose to clean out the dryer duct. (You'll need to unplug your dryer and disconnect the duct first.) The trick to using a dryer duct brush is to rotate it constantly as you insert it, and to pull it out frequently so you don't create a plug of lint in a hard-to-reach place. Brush out the duct from the dryer end first, and then do the same from the outside vent hood, working inward toward the dryer. And while the dryer is pulled out and disconnected from the duct, vacuum the duct connection, too.

Do without fabric-softening dryer sheets. Those sneaky little things can clog the dryer's exhaust vent. If you throw one in the dryer, be sure to remove it along with your laundry. You might be able to do without dryer sheets altogether and still avoid static cling by setting the dryer's auto-dry level a little lower, or by using liquid fabric softener in the clothes washer.

Use a tissue to test the seal on your dryer door. With your dryer going, run a piece of thin paper (facial tissue will work) around the edge of the door. If it's sucked in, the dryer door gasket isn't sealing. Note your dryer's make and model and order a replacement from an appliance-parts store or online. Remove the old seal (it should come off with just a little prying), clean away the adhesive with mineral spirits, and install the new seal using the adhesive that comes with it.

Easy Fixes

Putting an end to oily marks on clothes. Built-up detergent and fabric softener from your washer are probably the culprits. Bleach is the cheap secret to getting this gunk out of your washer and off your clothes. Get the washer tub clean by setting the water temperature to hot and the water-level control at the highest setting, and run the machine while empty. When the tub is full, add 2 cups (500 ml) of bleach and let the machine agitate for a few minutes. Stop the cycle before it drains (lifting the lid usually does the trick) and let the full tub sit for a half hour. Close the lid, finish the wash cycle, and then run the machine again with a load of clean rags or old clothes.

Watching for wildlife. Make sure that your dryer's outside vent hood has a louvered door and a basket-style cover to keep out rodents, birds, and other critters that seek a warm, dry place to nest. Choose a cover that snaps off so that you can clean the ducts easily.

Cleaning the moisture sensor. If your dryer can sense whether clothes are wet, damp, or dry, it has a moisture sensor (most newer models have one). Check the manual to find out where the sensor is (or stick your head in the drum and look around—the moisture sensor is usually two shiny metal strips near the lint screen).

take care

Make sure your dryer ducting is metal, not white vinyl—the latter is a huge fire hazard. (Call a pro if you need this replaced.) Also, dryer ducting should carry the dryer's hot air all the way to the outside of your home, not to the attic or to any interior space. Venting a dryer indoors increases the humidity inside your house, and humidity can cause condensation, mold, and other moisture-related problems.

The moisture sensor checks the clothes for dampness as they tumble past by using electrical resistance—the dryer the clothes, the greater the resistance. When the sensor is coated with that waxy, dryer-sheet residue, it's less effective. Give the sensor a squirt of gentle all-purpose cleaner and a quick wipe. While you're in there, wipe down the entire drum to remove residue. You're back in business!

Checking the length of your dryer duct. A general rule of thumb to follow is that a straight path from the dryer to the outdoors should be no more than 22 feet (7 metres) long, with 5 feet (1.5 metres) subtracted for every right-angle bend. In other words, if the path your duct takes requires two 90-degree bends, the total length should be no more than 12 feet (4 metres).

Check all your buttons and switches. You'd be surprised how often a homeowner shells out $75 to $100 for a service call—only to have the repairman flip a switch, say "Thank you," and walk out the door. If your dryer isn't working, don't overlook the obvious.

- If your dryer won't start, check to make sure it's plugged in and that the circuit breaker hasn't tripped or fuse hasn't blown. Make sure the door is completely closed, so the door switch can signal the dryer it's okay to start.
- If your gas dryer won't heat, first make sure your control switch isn't set to the "fluff/air dry" mode. On gas dryers check to make sure the valve is on; the handle should run parallel to the pipe.
- If your dryer takes a long time to finish a load, make sure your washing machine is on the right setting and operating correctly; sopping wet clothes will take hours to dry. Also, clean the lint screen and check the outside vent to make sure nothing is blocking the exhaust; lint, nests, ice and stuck flaps are all possible suspects. If the vent is okay, check the duct for debris or blockages as previously described.

Water Heaters

You turn on a faucet, and hot water pours forth as if by magic. Of course, it's not magic—it's your water heater at work. We tend to take this relatively simple device for granted, that is, until it conks out on us and costs us several hundred dollars to replace. Want it to work better and last longer? A little routine maintenance is all it takes.

YOUR COST SAVINGS

$800

How much it would cost to replace a standard 50-gallon (200 litres) electric water heater.

Care and Maintenance

Keep your tank from toppling. A 50-gallon (200 litres) water heater weighs more than 500 pounds (227 kilograms) when it's full. It can easily topple in an earthquake, causing fire and water damage. Secure yours by wrapping it with two lengths of steel plumber's tape and securing the tape to nearby wall studs (wrap one length of tape near the top of the heater and the other near the bottom). You can also buy a water heater strapping kit at the hardware store.

Tuck your tank in. Wrapping your tank in an insulating blanket can save energy. But this isn't a job for grandma's handmade quilt—go buy a tank blanket at a home center (make sure it has an insulating value of at least R-8) and follow the easy installation instructions. You'll want to wear gloves to protect your hands against glass fibers. Be sure to cut ample holes in the blanket around your heater's connections and access panels, and don't cover the instruction and caution labels on the tank.

Test your TPR valve. Your water heater tank is equipped with a safety feature called the temperature and pressure relief (TPR) valve. The valve sticks out of the top or side of your water heater tank; there's a pipe attached that runs down the side of the unit. If the temperature or pressure in the tank gets too high, the valve opens to prevent the tank from exploding. If the valve is rusty or malfunctioning, your tank could explode. Twice a year, test the valve by flipping its lever open. Be careful: If it's working, hot water will come out of the pipe! If no water comes out or if there's rust or mineral build-up around the TPR valve, have a plumber replace it.

take care

Got junk stored around your water heater? Get rid of it. For safety's sake, you want an empty, 3-foot (1 metre) radius around the water heater. It's always a good idea to keep debris away from a heat source; you should also guard the tank from items that can absorb moisture. They could cause the tank to corrode.

Keep your tank from rusting. Submerged in every water heater tank is an aluminum or magnesium rod whose purpose is to corrode over time and, by doing so, keep the tank itself from rusting. Every four years or so (or every two years if your water is hard) drain the water heater. Then unscrew the anode rod from the top of the tank (have a friend brace the water heater so it doesn't fall) and remove it. Replace it with whatever kind of rod was there before unless your water has a sulfurous "rotten egg" smell, in which case you should go with an aluminum rod. If you can't pull out the old anode because the ceiling is too low, pull it up as far as you can and then grab it at the top of the heater with vice grips. Break it off above the vice grips, pull it up some more, and repeat the process. Replace it with a flexible link-style anode.

Easy Fixes

Catching slow leaks. Install a water heater pan that's 2 inches (5 cm) in diameter larger than your tank. The pans cost less than $15, are available in rustproof aluminum or plastic, and have optional fittings that channel water flow to a floor drain.

Draining your water heater. Cleaning out the sediment that settles in the bottom of your water heater will help it last longer and run more efficiently. Turn off the electricity or gas to your water heater, and turn off the cold water supply pipe leading to the tank. Attach a hose to the drain valve at the base of the tank and direct the opposite end into a floor drain. Open the hot water side of any faucet, then open the drain valve and let the water and sediment drain out. Shut the drain valve and refill the tank.

NO HOT WATER: WHAT DO I DO?

IF YOU HAVE A ...	THE PROBLEM MAY BE ...	HERE'S HOW TO FIX IT ...
Gas water heater	A burned out pilot light	Check the light—it probably needs to be relit.
Electric water heater	The high-temperature cutoff may have tripped	Press the reset button
Electric water heater	A faulty thermostat	Call for help—this is a job for a professional.
Electric water heater, with only cold water from your showerhead	The tank's top heating element may be burned out	Replace top element
Electric water heater, with a little hot water that runs out quickly	The tank's bottom heating element may be burned out	Replace bottom element

Your Property

Yard work gives you a chance to enjoy the outdoors, exercise your muscles, and save some money while you do the work. It doesn't matter how young or old you are, either. There are yard chores almost anyone can do.

You may have memories of planting bulbs with your grandmother, building a shed with your dad, or mowing the lawn for the first time. Working in the yard and taking care of your home's outdoor structures don't require highly specialized skills or a lot of money.

In fact, the primary talent that's needed is good planning, especially when it comes to tending to your lawn and garden. The rest is easy. By the time you're done reading this section, you'll have learned the secrets to fixing sagging fence gates, getting rid of the ants on your patio, sealing your driveway, winterizing your in-ground sprinkler system, and lots more.

More important, we'll tell you which crucial small repairs you can make today (like patching a cracked concrete walk or adjusting the backfill in a retaining wall) that can spare you major headaches down the road. Before long, the only thing you'll dread about yard work is having to turn down your neighbors' requests to help them with theirs.

Grass and Ground Cover

A lush, green lawn can boost your home's "curb appeal," but did you know that it can also be an energy-saving asset? The moisture that a lush lawn gives off can do more to cool a house than an air conditioner. As most homeowners know, lawn maintenance is a perpetual balancing act of feeding, watering, mowing, and weeding. Here's how to get that elusive green lawn—and save a lot of green, too.

Care and Maintenance

Test your soil. Before you can grow a healthy lawn or garden, you need to determine whether your soil is healthy. The easiest way to do this is to contact your local soil-testing laboratory for information about testing and conducting a soil test. They will tell you how to collect the soil sample and what the analysis costs. You can find one online or ask a nearby garden center or university to recommend a private soil-testing lab. In addition to determining the pH (acidity/alkalinity) of your soil, the test will let you know what nutrients can be added to your soil to improve grass or plant growth. Do-it-yourself soil-test kits and electronic soil-testers are also widely available, although their results are not as comprehensive as a professional test. Landscaping professionals recommend having the soil around your property tested every one to three years to adequately monitor growing conditions. Test soil in late fall or early spring to maximize the benefits of any needed adjustments.

Gauge when, and how much, to water. Grass should be watered deeply and on an infrequent (but regular) schedule. Most types of grasses need about an inch (25 mm) of water every week—including rainfall—preferably in one fell swoop rather than frequent, shallow waterings. (Two exceptions are newly seeded lawns, which need to be kept moist until germination, and grass grown in sandy soil, which tends to do best with two or three waterings of 1/2 inch/1 cm per week.) Early morning watering is the way to go, because watering at night can invite fungus and disease and watering during the heat of the day loses more water to evaporation.

Get your lawn greener by eating canned tuna. To gauge how long you need to run your sprinkler, scatter several empty tuna cans around the area. Each can

How to Collect a Soil Sample

Most testing facilities provide instructions for collecting a soil sample. For lawns, the procedure is essentially the same everywhere.

1. Use a clean TROWEL AND BUCKET (chemical residue will affect the results of the test). Collect the sample when the ground is slightly moist, *not* wet.

----

2. For small lawns, randomly select at least FIVE LOCATIONS to sample; for larger plots, select 10 to 15 locations.

----

3. SCRAPE AWAY any debris, and insert the trowel 2 to 3 inches (5 to 8 cm) for an established lawn or 6 inches (15 cm) for a new lawn. Push on the handle to make a wide opening.

----

4. Use the trowel to take a 3/4-inch-thick (2 cm) SLICE of soil from the side of the opening, extending from top to bottom. Place the soil in the bucket.

----

5. Repeat steps 3 and 4 at all locations. Thoroughly MIX THE SOIL in the bucket, then fill the soil-sample bag to the indicated amount.

----

6. Include all requested information on the SAMPLE BAG before taking it in to be tested.

----

holds about an inch (2.5 cm) of water; when they're full, you'll know that your lawn is adequately saturated.

Cut no more than one-third off of your lawn's height. You're not the first person to think that cutting your lawn extra short is a genius idea: You're right, you may not have to mow the lawn as often, but you'll weaken the blades and roll out the welcome mat for weeds and invasive grasses. Although ideal mowing heights vary depending on the kind of grass, there is a golden rule to lawn mowing: Never remove more than one-third of the blade. Giving your lawn a trim rather than a close crop encourages deeper root growth and healthier grass overall.

Know exceptions to the "one-third" rule. Increase height of mower by 1/2 inch (1 cm) after a drought, when you're mowing shaded areas, or when the grass has been stressed by high traffic. In cool climates, your last mow of the season should be about 30 percent lower than normal—that'll help you prevent matted grass and snow mold fungus.

Use coffee grounds and other organic matter instead of chemical fertilizers. For those who don't want to dump a bunch of chemicals on their lawn, there are good organic fertilizer options. Our favorite? Used coffee grounds! Ground corn, soy, cottonseed, alfalfa meal, and organic fertilizer are also effective. Unlike their chemical counterparts, organic fertilizers can be used any time of year; they need about three weeks to break down in the soil, so be sure to apply them well in advance of seeding.

Determine what kind of grass seed you need. Before you do anything else, find out which types of grass grow best in your area. You can find this out by consulting the soil-testing laboratory or a local garden center or nursery (or you can ask a neighbor with a nice lawn what kind of seed he uses). Once you're out shopping, pay close attention to the packaging: The makeup of even "identical" blends from the same manufacturer can vary because seeds come from different sources. Two of the phrases you want to look out for are "weed content" and "other crop seed" (this "other" category can contain anything not specifically classified as a noxious weed). The only way to guarantee that you're not sowing a fair number of weeds along with your grass is to select a box that says "0 percent" in those categories. You should also avoid grass seed packages marked "VNS," which stands for "variety not stated," and those that contain more than 0.5 percent annual grasses; this is important because you want to limit the amount of annual grass that's going into your yard—it will die off after that first growing season. Finally, look for a high germination rate—at least 85 percent for Kentucky bluegrass, fine fescue, and turf-type tall fescue (TTTF).

SMART IDEA

Apply fertilizer during the spring growing season or in late fall—never during the hot summer months, when it can cause turf burn or promote weed growth.

THE 4-1-1 ON FERTILIZER NUMBERS

All commercial fertilizers use three-number designations, which correspond to their ratios by weight of nitrogen, phosphorus, and potassium (N-P-K); slow-release 3-1-2 or 4-1-2 formulations are generally considered safe for most lawns. Although newly seeded lawns need all three nutrients, established grasses usually require supplemental nitrogen and little, if any, phosphorus and potassium.

Get rid of weeds once and for all. Removing them by hand is the safest course, especially if you have only a few. The way to do it is to grab them at their base when the soil is moist. Use a trowel or a weeding knife to dig up dandelions and other weeds with taproots. If you have a pervasive weed problem, you may need to bring in the big guns: herbicides. These are potent chemicals—always

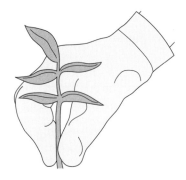

follow manufacturers' safety and usage guidelines. If you want to minimize potential damage to your lawn, consider a spot spray herbicide, such as Ortho's Weed-B-Gon. Some folks use paintbrushes to apply the herbicide directly to the weeds, though this could get tedious. Keep an eye on the mercury: The risk of damaging your lawn increases as the temperature rises.

How to Start a **Lawn** from Scratch

If more than half of your lawn consists of bare patches, invasive grasses, or weeds, it's easier to start anew than it is to repair the damage. A complete lawn renovation takes 15 to 20 days and should be done in the early fall for cold-season grasses, or in the late spring for warm-season grasses.

1. KILL the old grass and weeds. On a windless day, apply Roundup (or generic glyphosphate) or an organic weed-and-grass killer such as Burnout II over the surface (add some food coloring to the weed killer to see where you've sprayed). After a week, inspect the lawn; if you see living plants, apply another round.

- -

2. MOW your lawn using the mower's lowest possible setting. (Yes, in this case, you break the one-third rule we told you about a few pages ago.)

- -

3. TILL the earth to a depth of 4 to 6 inches (10 to 15 cm).

- -

4. RAKE vigorously to remove rocks and debris, and create a level planting surface.

- -

5. MIX a slow-release 3-1-2 fertilizer into the soil.

- -

6. Use a DROP SPREADER to overseed your new lawn with one and a half times the recommended rate of seed.

- -

7. Use a water-filled ROLLER to tamp down the seed. This helps keep the seed moist between waterings by putting it in contact with the soil.

- -

8. WATER the lawn 10 to 15 minutes twice a day for two weeks until the seeds germinate.

- -

9. MOW the grass when it is tall enough to be cut at your mower's highest setting.

- -

10. Gradually CUT BACK on watering once the grass has reached the desired density.

- -

Aerate your lawn. Make this a top priority every spring. When you aerate, you essentially punch numerous holes in a moist lawn by using a special tool to remove plug-like cores of soil, thatch, and grass. There are plenty of good reasons to do this: Aeration boosts lawn growth by bringing water and fertilizer closer to the roots, which eases soil compaction, removes thatch, and improves drainage. After you aerate, fertilize, water, and, if needed, seed your lawn. Leave the soil cores where they fall; they'll provide a beneficial top dressing as they break down. Several types of core aerators are available. Mechanical walk-behind models are expensive to buy but don't cost much to rent. There are also aerator attachments for garden tillers and inexpensive manual aerators suitable for small lawns.

Don't want to deal with grass? Go with a ground cover. This broad category of low-growing, spreading plants comes in a variety of colors, textures, flowers, and foliage; most need from one to three years to fill in. Although most ground covers prefer rich soil, you can find varieties suited to just about any growing condition. Looking for a low-maintenance, shade-loving evergreen? It doesn't get any easier than pachysandra. How about a ground cover you can walk on that thrives in sandy soil and full sun? Wooly thyme should fit the bill. Be wary of invasive species, especially English ivy, ground ivy, periwinkle (*vinca minor*), and goutweed (bishop's weed). There's nothing wrong with the way they look, but you may wind up with more coverage than you planned on.

Be kind to your rotary mower. A rotary mulching mower is a worthwhile investment for most home gardeners. Here's how to treat it well and get years of reliable service out of it:

- When accessing the underside of a mower, turn it so that the air-filter side of the mower is up.
- Check the air filter. Replace the filter if it's dirty and grimy—on average, about every two years. If it's just dirty, try shaking out some of the dust before reattaching it.
- Keep the undercarriage clean. If the mower's undercarriage is mucked up with caked-on grass and mud, it's a rust problem waiting to happen. The blade may also have trouble moving properly. Grass and mud buildups are easy to remove—a screwdriver wrapped in a piece of cloth or a stiff brush will do the trick.
- Keep blades clean. Before each mowing, give your blades a blast of Pam cooking spray. It will prevent grass from sticking to the blades and overtaxing the engine.
- Change the oil. The oil in your mower should be replaced annually, or after 40 hours of use. It's a simple endeavor: While the engine is still warm, drain old oil into a container through the drain plug or, if necessary, through the filter hole. Refill with new oil.

SMART IDEA

Why spend $1,000 or more for a power rake, aerator, or other piece of heavy equipment you'll use only a few times? Instead, call local garden centers and equipment rental suppliers to find the best rental deals. Calculate exactly how long you'll need the machinery; there can be a big difference in price between renting for a whole day versus a few hours. Be sure to ask for tips on equipment setup and safety.

- Stow it away for the winter. Empty the gas tank before winter storage, or use a gas stabilizer. Run the tank dry after the last mowing of the season.

Easy Fixes

Inspecting for thatch. Thatch is a layer of partially decomposed grass stems and roots at the soil line. Annual raking or aeration often keeps it in check, but if thatch gets too thick, it can prevent water and fertilizer from reaching the roots, providing a breeding ground for insects or diseases. Because this can cause the turf to become spongy, it's more difficult to mow your lawn. To inspect for thatch, use a knife or trowel to cut a 3-inch-wide by 3-inch-deep (8 by 8 cm) circle from your lawn. If the layer just above the soil is dark, spongy, and more than 1/2 inch (1 cm) thick, it's time to dethatch.

Dethatching your lawn. First, mow your lawn to about half its normal mowing height, then make several passes with a power rake, moving both horizontally and vertically. Be sure to remove remaining thatch with a lawn rake. Dethatching will stress your lawn, so it's best done just before the active growing season. While you're at it, reseed and fertilize after you dethatch.

Using ground covers to prevent weeds. If you don't want to be bothered pulling out weeds and replenishing mulch around your shrubs, cover the soil beneath them with a shallow-rooted, shade-loving ground cover. It will keep weeds at bay while cooling the soil. Good choices include bugleweed, foamflower, pachysandra, and star jasmine.

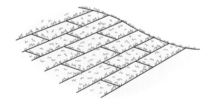

Sodding your lawn. Sod costs about 20 times more than seed does, but it provides faster results. First, level and prepare your yard as for seed (skip the initial fertilizing, though). Make sure the soil is moist to encourage rooting. After the sod is delivered, keep it wet. Store it in a shaded area or cover it, if possible. Install it within 24 hours of delivery. Laying the strips in a staggered brick pattern will help those telltale sod lines disappear quickly; this pattern will also prevent the sod from slipping downhill. Moving both horizontally and vertically, roll over newly laid sod with a water-filled roller. Keep your yard moist for the first two weeks with two to six light sprinklings per day. Gradually reduce watering frequency while increasing the duration of each watering. Fertilize after one month.

Trees and Shrubs

Most people view trees and shrubs as long-term investments that add to the beauty of their homes and surroundings. Like all investments, trees and shrubs should be selected and maintained carefully; they should be planted with enough room to grow. Keep older trees healthy with occasional pruning and some tender loving care, and they'll look handsome (and improve your property's value) for many years to come. Not maintaining them means bad news not just for your landscaping: Ailing or dead trees can also damage your home.

YOUR COST SAVINGS
$300
The amount you could save per year on your air conditioning cooling costs by maintaining healthy shade trees around your house.

Care and Maintenance

Take care around your tree's roots. Most tree roots grow just below ground level. When surface roots appear aboveground, cover them with 2 inches (5 cm) or less of topsoil or plant a ground cover to conceal them; never pile up soil over roots or around trunks. Don't garden aggressively directly beneath a tree as the constant digging can damage roots, and avoid driving or parking your car over a tree's root zone.

Make a drip irrigator with a plastic jug. Young trees and shrubs need about 3 inches (8 cm) of water per week during their first growing season. Keep them hydrated by giving each its own watering system: Use a thin nail to pierce holes in a 1-gallon (4 litres) plastic jug. Bury the jug a few feet from the plant so that the spout sticks out just above soil level. Fill the jug with water, which will slowly seep out to the roots.

Want your roses to grow? Prune them. Keep rose bushes full and healthy by pruning them in early spring before new growth appears. Use a sharp pair of bypass or scissors-type shears, which make cleaner cuts than anvil shears. For hybrid and floribunda roses, cut the strongest canes to about half their height; less vigorous canes should be cut back by a third. Make cuts on a 45-degree angle, about 1/4 inch (0.5 cm) above and slanting away from outward-facing buds. Remove dead or damaged canes and suckers (shoots from the roots or the lower part of the plant's stem). Tear or pull out suckers at the base; cutting them will only result in more suckers. Be sure to wear protective gloves.

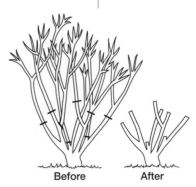

Before   After

Don't top trees. "Tree topping"—drastically cutting back large branches on mature trees—is among the most damaging things you can do to a tree. Not only does it leave trees looking deformed and more prone to disease and decay, but the tree will ultimately grow back taller and bushier. Always prune a tree with care, and never remove more than one-third of the crown in a single pruning.

Avoid girdling injuries. Bumps from lawnmowers and lashings from dog chains can cause damage around a tree's circumference. Such "girdling" injuries can destroy a tree's transport system, and ultimately kill the tree. Prevent mishaps by laying mulch around the tree (leave some bare ground around the trunk) or by installing shallow edging a few feet (60–90 cm) from the trunk.

Easy Fixes

Trimming trees. Exercise caution when removing tree limbs and large branches. Never use a chain saw above waist height; use a bow saw or pruning saw. For accessible limbs, make the first cut from underneath, halfway through the limb, about 1 foot (30 cm) from the trunk. Make a second cut from the top, about 1 to 2 inches (2.5 to 5 cm) out from the first cut, and remove the first section of the limb. Remove the remaining stub with a single cut from top to bottom just beyond the base of the limb (essentially flush with the trunk). Use a pole saw or long-handled lopper for large or high limbs, and remove them in two or more sections. Before cutting, fasten a rope around the sections and loop it around a lower limb to control the speed and direction of their fall. Such jobs require two or more people.

DETERMINING YOUR HARDINESS ZONE

Before you invest in plants and landscaping costs, make sure the trees and shrubs you choose are right for your yard. The first step is knowing your hardiness zone, a climatic zone determined by average annual minimum temperature. Several Web sites, including the Agriculture Canada site (http://sis.agr.gc.ca), make it easy to pinpoint your zone. When selecting a tree, calculate its ultimate height, spread, and root mass. Also, weigh its susceptibility to splitting from storm damage (poor choices include Bradford pear, mulberry, and weeping willow), as well as potential annoyances, such as messy or unpleasant-smelling fruit and flowers (for example, female ginkgo, black cherry, and umbrella magnolia). Avoid planting the tree too close to your house, or where it may interfere with power lines, pipes, driveways, or walkways.

Flower Beds

There's an unmistakably regal quality to well-tended flower beds, but you don't have to pay a princely sum to have your own. If you start plants from seed, use compost, and keep an eye out for bargains, you can get by on quite a modest budget. Plan your beds well, mulch, and water regularly, then sit back and admire the crown jewels in your garden.

YOUR COST SAVINGS

$275

The amount you could save by starting flowers from seed versus buying plants from a garden center.

Care and Maintenance

Test your soil's drainage. Before you dig a flower bed, have the soil tested (see the "Grass and Ground Cover" chapter). Then check the site's drainage: Dig a hole, 1 foot (30 cm) deep by 2 feet (60 cm) wide, and fill it with water. If it takes more than four hours to drain, you'll need to improve the drainage, either by digging furrows around the edges to accommodate runoff, adding organic matter to the soil, or building a raised bed.

Prep new flower beds properly. Early fall is the best time to prepare a flower bed. Select the site, then lay out the desired shape with a garden hose; for straight lines, tie string between stakes. Use a spade to remove the sod or soil within the outline, then remove the hose or stakes. Place a tarp alongside the bed. Dig up the topsoil and place it on the tarp. Add a generous amount (up to 25 percent) of compost, peat moss, or mulched leaves, and mix it thoroughly. Use a spading fork to loosen the soil in the bed to a depth of 6 to 10 inches (15 to 25 cm); remove any large stones, weeds, or roots. Spread several inches of compost over the soil, turn it over completely, and then shovel in the improved topsoil. Level the surface with a flathead rake.

Start a flower bed from scratch using newspaper or cardboard. An easy way to turn an overgrown patch of your yard into a flower bed is to cover the ground with a layer of 8 to 12 sheets of newspaper (use only black-and-white pages) or a few pieces of cardboard. Lay several inches of compost or topsoil over the paper and you're set. The paper layer will kill off everything growing beneath it and eventually break down into the soil.

Germinate seeds using coffee filters. You can plant a flower bed for less than $20 if you start from seed. For the best results, germinate them indoors, using coffee filters (not paper towels). Soak the filter in water, and then squeeze until damp. Place seeds on a quarter section of the filter. Fold the filter in half, and tuck the side opposite the seeds underneath. Put the filter inside a plastic sandwich bag, let in some air, and seal it. Label each bag with the plant name, flower color, and date. Store the bags in a warm 65–75°F (18 to 24°C) location, away from direct sunlight.

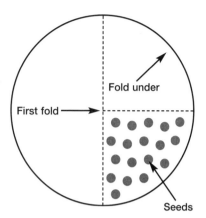

Check the seeds' moisture level every two days. Lightly mist as needed with 95 parts water and 5 parts hydrogen peroxide, to prevent mold. Upon sprouting, gently place seedlings in a sterile, soil-less mix. Position plants 2 to 4 inches (5 to 10 cm) under two 40-watt fluorescent bulbs; provide 12 to 16 hours of light per day for at least two weeks. Keep the planting medium moist at all times; begin half-strength feeding with a water-soluble fertilizer after five days.

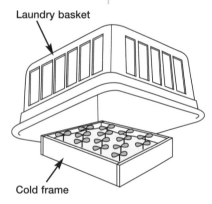

Toughen up tender shoots. Seedlings with at least two sets of mature leaves can be moved outdoors, but they must be "hardened off" before planting. Move the plants outside in a cold frame (a box designed for growing plants outdoors, like a mini-greenhouse), placed where there is no direct sunlight: in a well-shaded area or under an inverted, weighted-down laundry basket. Bring them indoors if nighttime temperatures drop below 45°F (7°C). After one week, remove the cover, and gradually increase the amount of sunlight the plants receive during the morning and afternoon hours, but avoid exposure to midday sun. The hardening-off process takes 10 to 14 days after the risk of frost has passed. Don't forget to water the plants while they're being acclimated.

Harvest more beautiful blooms by deadheading and pinching back. Most plants will grow fuller and have more flowers if they're pinched back occasionally. Just press your thumbnail against your index finger between two sets of leaves, and snip off the top. Another way to get more blooms from established plants is to prevent them from setting seed by deadheading them. If new buds are forming, simply cut off the spent blooms just above the bud. Otherwise, cut old blooms back to the base of the stem. Deadheading isn't effective for flowering bulbs and most perennials, but it works like a charm for annu-

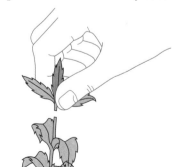

als. You can also promote fewer but larger blooms in plants such as chrysanthemums and peonies by disbudding, or snipping off the small side growth; this lets plants conserve their energy, which goes toward producing a few large blooms.

Decide whether or not fertilizing is for you. Most established flowers don't require supplemental fertilizing if there's enough organic matter in the soil. Fertilizer is most beneficial when growing seedlings and at planting time. Some perennials, such as astilbes and clematis, do enjoy a feeding in early spring. But don't go heavy on the nitrogen; that could result in spindly growth and too many leaves. A water-soluble 15-30-15 fertilizer is preferable in most cases. Use manure with caution; most annuals can't tolerate it. Any manure should be very well composted before it's put in your flower bed.

Control pests the nontoxic way. One of the most common alternatives to pesticides is companion planting, grouping certain plants to repel animals, insects, and diseases. For instance, planting a garlic barrier around flowers can protect them from gophers, rabbits, squirrels, and voles. You can also make effective bug sprays from

SMART IDEA

Pesky slugs and snails can be eradicated by burying a container half filled with beer so that its opening is flush with the ground. Leave it overnight; in the morning you'll find dozens of dead-drunk snails in the brew.

COMPOSTING 101

In addition to the many ways compost helps plants—providing essential nutrients, maintaining a healthy soil pH, combating disease, retaining moisture, and boosting the activity of beneficial soil organisms—composting also benefits the environment by reducing household waste.

While you can keep a compost pile in your yard, most people prefer the convenience of bins, which can be bought or constructed from salvaged building materials, wooden pallets, or recycled plastic. Include slats or air holes to permit good ventilation, which is necessary for decomposition.

The key to making compost is heat, which results from layering a good mix of "browns" (fall leaves, sawdust, shredded news-paper) and "greens" (grass clippings, coffee grounds, kitchen scraps). You can also add corn husks, eggshells, farm manure, paper towels, shredded cardboard, paper bags, and lots of other things.

Don't add: human and pet wastes, animal products, plastics and other petroleum products, barbecue ash, diseased plant parts, perennial weeds, seeds, and herbicides and pesticides. Turn piles a few times each month to ensure good airflow.

New additions—especially malodorous ones like farm manure and fish parts—should be placed deep inside the pile. Also, don't forget to add moisture (leftover tea, coffee, cooking water), but keep a cover handy to prevent the compost from getting too wet.

When it's ready, your compost should have a sweet, earthy smell (foul-smelling compost means it's not getting enough air). Spread it liberally around your garden and lawn, and let nature take its course.

A three-compartment pallet composter

diluted solutions of alcohol, ammonia, liquid soap, vinegar, or vegetable oil. (For some handy recipes go to http://faq.gardenweb.com/faq/organic and click on "What Are Some Great Natural Pesticidal and Fungicidal Recipes?") Don't use this solution containing ammonia in hot weather (or at least test it on a single plant before using it widely): Ammonia might injure some plants' leaves when the weather is very warm.

Easy Fixes

Mulching new flower beds. Mulch is good for your garden, and saves you time and trouble. A protective layer of organic matter that sits atop the soil, mulch keeps weeds at bay, retains moisture, and improves soil fertility. Mulching materials include chipped wood or bark, pine needles, tree leaves, coffee grounds, grass clippings, seed or nut hulls, and even shredded newspaper. Mulch new flower beds to a depth of 2 to 3 inches (5 to 8 cm) after planting. Mulch breaks down over time, so replenish it at least once a year—preferably in early spring, when most perennials are dormant. Overdoing it, though, may result in rot, soil imbalances, and insect or rodent infestations.

Protecting bulbs with chicken wire. Squirrels, chipmunks, and other animals look at your flower bulbs and see lunch, not would-be blooms. Lock these pests out of the lunchroom by placing a layer of chicken wire on the ground (under the mulch) after planting or while the bulbs are dormant in early spring. Anchor it by pushing the edges deep into the soil. You can also mix broken clamshells or pruned rose canes into the soil around your bulbs; animals hate digging around sharp objects.

4 TIPS FOR SMART PLANT SHOPPING

1. Look for plants that are compatible with your planting site, and purchase only those with healthy foliage, abundant new growth, and unopened buds.

2. Shake plants to make sure no insects fall out.

3. If possible, slip the plant from its pot and examine the roots, which should be light-colored and firm and surrounded by a good amount of soil.

4. Avoid plants with yellowed or wilting leaves, weeds or moss on the soil surface (such plants will be difficult to establish), stunted or dead growth, or roots that are crowded and tangled or protrude outside the container.

Sprinklers and Hoses

A garden's survival depends on good irrigation. Fortunately, today's gardeners can choose from a wide variety of sprinklers and hoses—everything from automated, in-ground systems to economical, environmentally friendly soaker hoses. With simple, periodic maintenance to repair leaks and remove blockages, even inexpensive revolving and oscillator sprinklers should last for years. Keeping this equipment in good condition will keep your landscaping healthy, potentially saving you hundreds of dollars on yard maintenance and even tree care.

YOUR COST SAVINGS

$4,000

What you'd pay to have an in-ground sprinkler system in a 50-by-90-foot (15 by 27 metres) yard replaced.

Care and Maintenance

Invest in a water timer. Forgetting about that sprinkler running in your yard is a surefire way of inviting a host of unpleasant surprises—to say nothing of inflated water bills. Those headaches can be avoided by using automatic water timers on your hoses. Most automatic timers cost less than $60 and attach between an outdoor faucet and the hose; some higher-end models can accommodate multiple watering zones.

Make your water go both ways. Tired of lugging the garden hose from one side of your yard to the other? A splitter can make life easier for you. These inexpensive accessories let you connect two or more hoses to a single faucet, with independent on/off controls for each one, so you won't have to constantly move sprinklers back and forth. Inexpensive plastic splitters can be found for less than $3, but the best ones (costing up to $20) are zinc-plated or brass and won't rust or bond with the faucet.

Hose-proof your flower beds. Trailing garden hoses have been responsible for flattening many a prized plant. Protect your flower and vegetable beds by placing permanent bumpers at the outer corners of your beds. Simply drive a couple of branches or wooden stakes into the ground, and cover each with a short piece of PVC pipe.

Winterize your in-ground sprinklers. If winter temperatures drop below freezing where you live, you'll need to winterize your in-ground sprinkler system.

take care

Don't drink water from your garden hose. Most garden hoses leach lead and other hazardous chemicals into water that's left standing inside them. Some newer hoses carry warning labels about the lead content, although many don't. It's best to err on the side of caution: Sip only from hoses labeled as safe for drinking—or don't drink at all.

Removing all standing water is essential to prevent damage to pipes and other components. Although you can empty the water using manual or automatic drain valves, it's preferable to have a professional "blow out" the system with a compressor. Make sure that the water is turned off at the main shut-off valve (typically located in the basement of your home, but if it's outdoors, make sure it's below the frost line or wrapped with insulation). Finally, if you have an automatic sprinkler system, don't forget to shut down the controller/timer or put it into "rain mode," which lets it retain all programmed information.

Impact sprinkler head

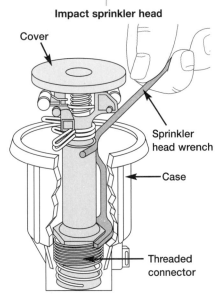

Cover

Sprinkler head wrench

Case

Threaded connector

Easy Fixes

Unclogging sprinkler heads. Before you call a service company to fix a malfunctioning sprinkler head, check to see if it's clogged. For fixed sprinklers, use the corner of a plastic card or utensil—*not* a screwdriver or other metal object—to push out dirt lodged in the sprayer. Examine the screen by removing the sprinkler head assembly (turn the water off first!), unscrewing the nozzle, and sliding it out. If it has holes or tears, replace it with a new one made for that brand or model. Dislodge clogs in impact sprinklers by inserting a screwdriver between the cover and the case; clean out the case by unscrewing the head from its base with a sprinkler head wrench.

Unclogging oscillator sprinklers. If your oscillating sprinkler shoots out uneven streams of water, use a hat pin or upholstery needle to dig out dirt or debris that may be clogging the nozzles. To remove lime and mineral deposits, use pliers to detach the nozzles and let them soak in a cup of vinegar for about one hour. Then clear both ends of each nozzle with a pin and reattach them.

Stopping leaks with new washers. Before buying a replacement for your leaky sprinkler, try replacing the filter washer where the sprinkler connects to the hose. It should cost about $1. To fix a leak under the arm of a revolving sprinkler, unscrew the bearing assembly column from the base and replace any worn-out washers or O-rings. Bring the worn parts to a hardware store and ask for duplicates.

Revolving sprinkler

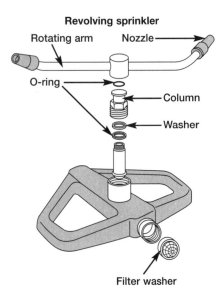

Rotating arm   Nozzle

O-ring

Column

Washer

Filter washer

Driveways and Walkways

Concrete and asphalt may be among the most durable of building materials, but they still require some maintenance. Asphalt requires periodic sealing and patching, while concrete can chip or flake and weaken around the joints between sections. Both are subject to damage from water, road salt, and petroleum products. No matter the task—whether it's removing an oil stain from your driveway or repairing a crack in the sidewalk in front of your house—don't put off fixing it. Small concrete and asphalt jobs invariably become big ones if they're put off long enough.

YOUR COST SAVINGS

$275

What you would pay to have an existing 10-by-50-foot (3 by 15 metres) asphalt driveway resealed.

Care and Maintenance

Clean your concrete walkways once a year. Doing this not only leaves them looking fresh, it also clears them of debris or stains that might cause you to slip. Here's how to give them a good cleaning: First, wet the concrete, then scrub it with a stiff brush or broom and a mild degreaser or commercial concrete cleaner. If the concrete is uncolored, you can substitute laundry detergent or—if no plants are nearby—bleach. Let the cleanser sit on the surface for 15 to 20 minutes, then rinse well with a hose sprayer or pressure washer set at 3,000 psi (20 MPa).

Seal your driveway every three years. A couple of coats of sealant every few years gives asphalt driveways needed protection against weather and wear. Two types of sealants are available: coal-tar emulsion, which is better at repelling motor oil and other petroleum products that eat away at asphalt, and asphalt emulsion, which is less caustic to use. Regardless of which you choose, buying one with the highest grade possible (with a five- or six-year warranty) will pay off with better and longer protection.

Prep surfaces well before applying sealant. Prepare your driveway for sealing by washing it with soapy water and a stiff bristle brush, followed by a thorough rinsing. Dig out any weeds or grass, and patch small cracks with crack-filler compound (see page 275). Mix the sealer for the time specified; poor mixing is the leading cause of subsequent problems. Work on 100 square feet (9 square metres) at a time, using

Kill weeds or grass growing in the crevices of walkways or between patio pavers by pouring a pot of boiling water over them. You can also make an effective, all-natural weed killer by mixing 1 cup (250 ml) of salt and 1 teaspoon (5 ml) of dishwashing liquid in 1 gallon (4 litres) of white vinegar. Pour a small amount directly on weeds to stop them in their tracks. Save noxious herbicides for serious weed invasions.

a sealing brush, a push broom, or a roller. Apply two thin coats rather than a single thick one; it will dry faster and bond better. To improve traction, spread a thin coat of sand over the wet sealer. Let the driveway dry for two days.

Seal concrete joints with epoxy. Expansion joints let sections of concrete expand and contract in response to temperature changes. Over time, these joints can also become the primary points at which water seeps in under the cement and causes cracks and erosion. Seal any leaky joints in driveways and walkways with an epoxy joint sealant. Before applying the sealant with a caulk gun, sweep out the joint and scrub it clean.

Familiarize yourself with less corrosive alternatives to rock salt. Be cautious when using deicers containing rock salt (sodium chloride) or magnesium chloride. They're highly effective, but also highly corrosive to asphalt, brick, and concrete surfaces—not to mention auto bodies, lawns, and wood floors. New deicing products using calcium magnesium acetate (CMA), a noncorrosive, water-soluble acid, offer a safer, equally effective alternative, though they can cost up to five times as much as salt-based products. If you stick with salt, look for a deicer with added corrosion inhibitors.

Easy Fixes

Fixing spalled concrete. If a concrete surface isn't cured properly, the mix contained too much water, or if it is subjected to a heavy impact, the concrete will eventually chip or flake in a process called spalling. But you don't have to repave the entire area. Instead, break up all the damaged concrete with a small sledgehammer (you should hear a hollow sound when you hit weakened concrete). Using a wire brush, scrub the surface until all the loose material has been removed, then rinse well. Once it has dried, cover the surface with latex patching compound or a mixture of portland cement, fine sand, and water. Smooth it with a steel trowel or a wood float.

Filling large gaps. If there are large gaps—pencil-width or wider—where your sidewalk or stairs meet your foundation, water can seep into your basement, or freeze and expand causing greater damage. Fill the gap with foam backer rod, apply

FIXING CRACKS IN CONCRETE AND ASPHALT

TO FIX THIS ...	DO THIS ...
A small crack (less than 1/4 inch or 0.5 cm wide) in asphalt	Start by digging out any weeds or grass, then clean off remaining dirt with a broom or shop vac. Next, use a stiff brush and a premixed driveway cleaner (or a solution of laundry detergent in water) to scrub away residual oils or dust. Rinse well and let it dry. Patch the crack with asphalt crack-filler, a caulk-like compound. Smooth it with a putty knife to keep moisture from getting under the crack.
Blacktop potholes and cracks wider than 1/4 inch (0.5 cm)	Follow the preparatory steps above, leaving the area wet (but with no standing water). Use a trowel to fill the hole with cold-patch compound. Half-fill holes deeper than 4 inches (10 cm) with coarse gravel, tamped down with a 4x4, before adding compound. If more than one layer of compound is needed, tamp down after each application, and let it dry before applying the next layer. Asphalt patches require 24 to 48 hours to set completely.
A hairline crack in concrete	Dip a rubber-gloved finger in some auto-body filler, press it into the fissure, and smooth it. You can also use any urethane-based caulk to fill cracks up to 1/8 inch (3 mm) deep.
Larger concrete cracks	Use a narrow cold chisel to chip out loose edges, then clean out any remaining pieces of cement and dust with a wire brush. Use a trowel to fill in the crack with latex patching concrete, and smooth it with a wood float.

a thick bead of urethane caulk, then use the back of a spoon dipped in mineral spirits to smooth the joint.

Removing oil stains from the driveway A car leaking oil can wreak havoc on your driveway, leaving behind unsightly stains that are even harsher on the pavement than they are on your eyes. There are plenty of commercial stain removers available, but you might want to try this cheaper home-brew solution: Spread a thick layer of ordinary cat litter over the stain, grind it in with your heel, cover it with newspaper, and let it stand overnight. Sweep up the used litter, cover the stain with a paste of laundry detergent and water, and let it sit overnight. The next day, remove most of the soap paste and scrub the stain with a stiff bristle brush, adding more water and paste if needed as you work.

take care

Always wear safety goggles when breaking up concrete. Protect the hand in which you're holding your chisel by wrapping an ordinary sponge ball around the chisel. Further protect your eyes and face from wayward fragments by pushing the chisel through a piece of window screening before you begin chipping away.

Patios and Paths

Patios and paths are made for walking—as such, the last thing you need is for these surfaces to become hazards for your family and guests. Loose or damaged patio pavers, bricks, or stones should be reset or replaced as soon as possible; slippery moss needs to be eliminated; and path materials, such as gravel or wood chips, should be evenly dispersed underfoot and replenished as needed. Appearances are also important, of course. Fortunately, all it takes is vigilance and a little timely maintenance to keep patios and paths looking and performing their best.

SMART IDEA

Keep extra pavers or bricks on hand in case you need to replace any in your patio. To ensure that your surplus stock will weather at the same rate and be the same color as those you may want to replace, store them outdoors.

Care and Maintenance

Give patios a clean sweep. Don't allow dead leaves, spent tree blossoms, seedpods, and other organic matter to pile up on your patio. In addition to being unsightly, such debris can harbor insects and leave behind dark spots on concrete and flagstones. Keep patios neat by regularly sweeping them with an outdoor-quality straw broom or a leaf-blower.

Scrub away stains. Grease from barbecue grills, rusty patio furniture, and leaf tannins can all leave their marks on your patio. Most stains can be rubbed out with a bit of scouring. Spot-treat grease, leaf marks, and other stains with a solution of 1 gallon (4 litres) of warm water and 1 cup (250 ml) of trisodium phosphate (TSP) or TSP substitute, a heavy-duty cleanser available at most hardware stores. Scrub well with a long-handled, stiff-bristle brush, then hose the spot off (the runoff won't harm surrounding plants). You can also use this solution to give your patio an annual spring scrub-down.

Remove orange rust with lemonade. Few things can mar a patio's appearance worse than orange rust stains, but the good news is you don't have to learn to live with them. Remove rust from concrete by sprinkling some dry cement powder over it and rubbing with a small piece of flagstone. This pumice-like combination effectively scrubs off the stain. Rust on patio stones can often be removed by the citric acid found in powdered lemonade mixes. First, wet the stone, then cover the stain with the mix. Cover the powder with a sheet of plastic (to prevent the moisture from evaporating), and put a weight on top to hold it in place for 10 to 20 minutes. Then scrub with a stiff-bristled brush, and rinse off.

Power wash your patio. A few blasts from a pressure or power washer can work wonders on a tired-looking brick, stone, or concrete patio. To avoid damaging the patio material or injuring yourself, don't use a power washer rated higher than 3,000 psi (20 MPa) or one with a pinpoint nozzle. Instead, use a 15- or 25-degree fan nozzle. Also, take care to avoid positioning the jet too close to the patio surface, which can cause etching. Pressure washers can be rented for a small daily fee; if you've never used one, request a demonstration and detailed safety guidelines from the rental service.

Restore aging patio blocks. Although they're not as popular today as they once were, patio blocks are still found outside plenty of homes. Typically made of sandstone, concrete, or other porous material, the blocks can hold a lot of dirt and debris. First, try scrubbing them with a stiff brush dipped in some mild laundry detergent and water, then hose them off. If your blocks are extremely dirty, rent a pressure washer to give them a deep cleaning, which will also remove a small amount of the surface. If they're chipped or pitted from age, flip them over, rinse off any ground-in dirt, and presto—you have a brand-new block.

Use plastic edging to hold mortarless brick or paver patios and paths in place. This edging is sold at most building and masonry supply stores. The edging is secured with steel spikes and can be flexed around curves and cut to size with a hacksaw. If you're making a path with parallel sides, be sure to keep the sides evenly spaced, then simply drive stakes through the guide holes and you're done. The edging won't rot, and it will practically disappear after the grass grows back.

Border pavers

Flexible plastic edging

10" (25 cm) steel spike

1" (2.5 cm) sand bed

Crushed rock base

Paver patio

Rid your stone patio of moss. If you live in a warm, humid climate, you probably struggle with moss. It grows practically everywhere and can make patios and steps perilously slippery. The easiest way to get rid of moss is to scrub it away with a stiff-bristled brush, using a solution of 1 part household bleach in 2 parts water. If you have colored stone or concrete in your patio, test the solution on an inconspicuous corner to make sure it won't cause discoloration. To keep moss from returning, seal the surface with a brick sealer.

Evict ants from your patio's crevices. Have ants started colonizing the paver joints or crevices in your patio? Before you call the exterminator or reach for the bug spray, try flooding them out by pouring boiling water over the mounds. Another approach is to spray the mounds and surrounding area with a 50/50 solution of water and white vinegar or commercial glass cleaner (such as Windex) mixed with some dishwashing soap. Sprinkling some ground black pepper or cayenne powder on top of the mounds is yet another way to send the ants packing.

Rake and replenish your path. Loose path material—gravel, pebbles, or wood or bark chips—typically gets displaced to the edges, where there is less traffic. To restore its even distribution, use a lawn rake to pull the material back into place. This actually serves two purposes, as it also helps dislodge weeds, leaves, twigs, and other debris. Don't forget to replenish your path material as needed.

Seal your stones. Coating pavers, flagstones, or bricks with a water sealer will enhance their color and provide protection against stains. Clean the stone before applying the sealer; use a power washer, if needed. Reapply the sealer every two to five years.

Easy Fixes

Stopping sand loss. If the sand in your stone path is slowly washing away, it might be that the joints between the flagstones are too wide to hold the fill. If you need to reset the stones, set them in sand as before. Instead of filling the joints with plain sand, however, mix a little dry portland cement in with the sand and pack it firmly between the stones. Then, sprinkle a bit of water over the joints to set the filler. You won't have to worry about lost sand again.

How to Replace or Reset Cracked or Settled Patio Pavers

Constant exposure to the elements can cause bricks or pavers in your sand-based patio to crack, or for larger areas to settle. Don't put off these repairs. Here's how to replace broken pavers and get your patio looking good as new:

1. CUT a wire coat hanger and fashion it into two pieces with a slight hook at one end (see illustration).

2. SLIDE the wire hooks under opposite sides of the paver and lift up. If you have large patio bricks you may need another set of pullers (as well as someone to help you lift them).

3. Once the first PAVER is removed, carefully use a screwdriver or chisel to pry up and remove surrounding pavers that are damaged or have settled.

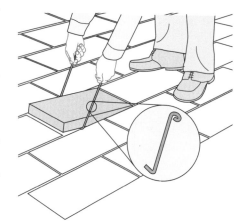

4. CLEAN sand and debris away from the area.

5. Put down a layer of fresh SAND. Use a wood float to spread sand to the corners and tamp it down. Repeat until the sand base is level with that of the surrounding pavers.

6. RESET the pavers (or set new ones, if the old ones were broken).

7. POUR sand over the paver, and evenly fill the gaps.

8. Gently TAP IN THE PAVER with a mallet, and sweep away the remaining sand.

Cutting flagstones down to size. Is your piece of flagstone too big to fit in the allotted space? You don't need a masonry saw to get it to fit. Score the desired cut a few times on one side using a stonemason's or straight chisel and a 2-pound (1 kilogram) hammer. Flip it over and score the other side. You may have to repeat this a few times before the pieces break off. The secret is to take your time; rushing the job is likely to result in a cracked stone. Make sure to wear goggles when doing this.

Retaining Walls

The truth is that retaining walls don't require much care as long as they're built on a solid, level, and well-compacted base. Simple maintenance—like replacing loose stones, keeping plant life at bay, and checking for low spots behind the wall—is usually all that's needed. Replacing retaining walls isn't just an ordeal that involves ripping up your yard; it's also a big expense.

Care and Maintenance

See if your wall is settling. Watch for excessive settling or low spots behind your wall that allow water to pool or build up. Over time, such areas will get larger and collect more water that can eventually seep behind the wall, resulting in a weight buildup that could cause a collapse. Prevent problems by lifting the mulch or sod on top of the wall each spring and adding enough new backfill to raise the cap back to its correct level.

RETAINING WALL PROS AND CONS

There are three basic types of retaining walls: natural stone, wood timber, and modular concrete. Each has its own strengths and weaknesses.

MATERIAL	PROS	CONS
Natural stone	Attractive and long lasting; wide variety of materials to choose from; can be installed to accommodate curves and contours	Require more time and skill to install; more expensive (unless you have access to free stone); soil can wash through gaps
Wood timber	Inexpensive, quick installation, requires only carpentry tools for installation	Short lifespan (10-25 years); limited color and design options
Modular concrete block	Go up quickly once first course is in place; wide variety of colors and shapes; easy to integrate steps or multiple tiers	Moderately expensive; heavy (some blocks can weigh up to 75 pounds (34 kg); special tools required for cutting

HOW ARE RETAINING WALLS BUILT?

A 4-foot-high (1 metre), concrete-block retaining wall starts with a trench that's dug deep enough to hold 4 to 6 inches (10 to 15 cm) of compacted base material, 1 inch (2.5 cm) of leveling sand, and half the height of the bottom layer of blocks. The trench also needs to be wide enough to leave a gap of at least 12 inches (30 cm) between the undisturbed soil and the rear edge of the blocks. Succeeding layers of blocks are each stepped back 3/4 inch (2 cm), with vertical joints overlapping by at least 4 inches (10 cm), and rows secured to each other with "lips" molded into the bottom edge of each block or with plastic or steel reinforcement pins. Crushed rock is used to backfill, except for a 6-inch (15 cm) "cap" of compacted native soil on top to keep surface water from seeping into the trench.

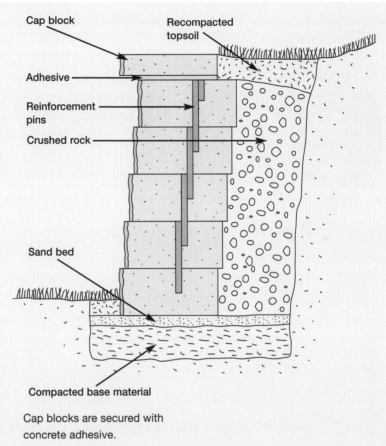

Cap blocks are secured with concrete adhesive.

Yank out interloping weeds and plants. Weeds, vines, and seedlings have an uncanny ability to take hold in gaps in a wall. Although they may look harmless, the weight of a vine or a sapling's roots can shorten your wall's longevity. Hand-pull anything you see growing on top of or on the face of your wall (or give the wall an annual spraying with an herbicide).

Replace loose stones. One loose stone in a wall always seems to beget another. If one or two stones become loose due to freezing and thawing or the impact of a car bumper, odds are they'll be joined by their neighbors. To avoid a major repair job, reset stones as soon as they become loose. Use mortar to keep them in place if necessary.

Fences

YOUR COST SAVINGS

$6,500

What you would pay to install a new 200-foot-long (61 metres), 6-foot-high (2 metres) cedar fence.

Not only does a fence provide privacy and security, it can add a decorative touch to your yard. Maintaining a fence requires diligence, however: Always be on the lookout for structural problems and take care of them right away. Making simple spot repairs can add years to the life of your fence, and save you the huge expense of replacing it.

Care and Maintenance

Inspect the perimeter. Check fences every few months for trouble spots. Caulk any gaps between the fence posts and concrete footings to prevent water from seeping in and causing rot. Wooden fences—except for unpainted cedar fences—should be painted or stained every two to three years; in the meantime, scrape off flaking or peeling paint or worn stain and reapply a fresh coat to prevent the wood from being exposed. Replace any rusted screws, brackets, or wire ties, and make sure all gate hinges are tightly secured and well oiled.

Keep vegetation at a safe distance. Vines and weeds growing near a wooden fence increase moisture in the area and severely cut back on needed air circulation. Keep plants at bay by putting down a weed barrier of roofing felt or landscape fabric a few inches below the grade on both sides of your fence and cover the barrier with gravel.

Trim or cap fence posts. Flat surfaces on wooden fence posts allow water to sit and soak in, which encourages wet rot, mold, and algae growth, and a host of other problems. Don't look for trouble. Trim or cut posts to a point or arched shape so rain will run off them. Use preformed metal or wood caps ($5–10 each) to protect the 4x4 support posts in a board fence.

Power wash your unfinished cedar fence. Improve your unpainted cedar fence's appearance by cleaning it with a power washer (rent one for about $40 for four hours). Select a model that operates at 1,500 or 2,000 psi (10.34 or 13.79 MPa), and get both 15- and 25-degree spray tips. (Although power washers are easy to operate, ask for a demonstration if you've never used one.) Start with the 25-degree spray tip; use the 15-degree tip, which is faster and more powerful, after you've gained experience with the washer. Keep it about 18 inches (45 cm) from the wood when you begin spraying, then move in a few inches closer, swinging the tip slowly along the length of the board. Keep the width of the spray aligned across the boards. The wood's color will brighten as the surface is stripped away. Stop stripping when the wood stops changing color.

Use mineral spirits to clean vinyl fences. Although they're largely maintenance-free, most vinyl fences need occasional cleaning. Avoid stiff brushes and abrasive cleansers, which can scratch or discolor the surface. Mineral spirits or naphtha tar remover will dispatch most stains, including crayon, asphalt, and grease. Apply the cleaner with a soft cloth; afterward, rinse the area with water.

Easy Fixes

Treating cedar for rot. Cedar posts, which are often buried directly in the ground, are at risk for developing rot, but early detection can keep the problem from spreading. Use an ice pick or an awl to test the wood; if the tool penetrates more than 1/8 inch (3 mm), the post may need to be replaced. If the damage is shallower, scrape or chip away any affected material until you see healthy wood—make sure you remove all signs of rot to prevent it from recurring—then saturate it with a wood preservative or apply a clear epoxy sealer (or a new coat of paint or stain).

Repairing wooden rails. Rot will also cause wood rails to separate from their posts. If the rot is widespread, replace the affected rails. Reattach salvageable rails with galvanized steel T-brackets and screws. First, chip off the rotted wood, and liberally apply a wood preservative to the rail and post. Level the rail before positioning the bracket and drilling the pilot holes. Then insert and tighten the screws and caulk the joint.

Fixing a sagging gate. A wobbly gatepost can be set straight by pushing it back into place and securing it to the top and bottom rails with a pair of L-brackets. Pick up a sagging gate by tightening the hinge screws. If the screws are stripped, replace them with longer ones or fill the holes with wood putty, and refasten the hinges. To keep the gate from sagging, raise it on support blocks, fully extend a turnbuckle, and install it diagonally across the gate with lag bolts. Tighten the turnbuckle with a pry bar or wrench.

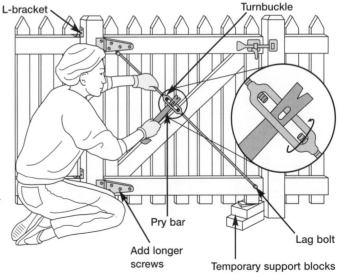

L-bracket
Turnbuckle
Pry bar
Add longer screws
Lag bolt
Temporary support blocks

Storage Sheds
and Other Outdoor Structures

The structures in your yard should only add to the happiness your home brings you; they shouldn't be heartaches and eyesores. A little routine maintenance can go a long way in keeping outdoor buildings in great shape for years to come: Small steps like inspecting your shed's wood for worn spots and tightening loose fasteners on play sets, arbors, and gazebos will allow you many years of safe enjoyment outdoors.

Care and Maintenance

Tighten fasteners in the spring. Temperature changes from one season to the next cause wooden structures to expand and contract. This, in turn, causes the metal fasteners holding them together to loosen, which results in slackened joints that let organic matter and water seep in—now you've got an ideal environment for rot! Calamities relating to your shed and other outdoor structures can be easily prevented; all it takes is a quick stroll around your yard each spring. Bring a screwdriver along to tighten loose screws and a hammer to reset wobbly nails. If you come across nails that have become too loose to reset, replace them with larger, rust-resistant nails or screws. Have a notepad and pencil handy so that you can jot down any other problems.

take care

Pergolas and arbors may look lovely covered in grapevines, but birds and wasps will also be attracted to the fruit. Not only can such intruders spoil your quality time outdoors, they can leave quite a mess. To get the best use from these structures, don't use them to grow crops. Stick with ivy or a flowering vine.

Protect unfinished wood. Although it isn't necessary to paint or stain redwood and cedar structures, such as arbors, play sets, sheds, and pergolas, adding a coat of water-repellant wood preservative every few years will keep moss and algae at bay and slow aging due to exposure to the sun's UV rays. Use a water-based, nontoxic preservative.

Keep greenhouses well ventilated. Good air circulation is essential to grow healthy plants and prevent mold growth and other problems. You can keep fresh air circulating by installing one or more vents on each side of the roof and on each side wall. While temperatures are rising in the morning, keep the vents open, but close them in the afternoon to conserve heat. To avoid having to manually adjust the vents, consider installing automatic vent openers, which can be set to open and close at predetermined temperatures.

PAINTING AN OUTDOOR SHED

A couple of coats of acrylic latex paint could be all you need to spruce up a faded outdoor wooden shed. If you're painting a new wooden structure, prime it first with one coat of an alkyd, oil-based primer before applying one or more coats as needed of acrylic latex paint. Don't apply more than one coat of the primer. Oil-based paint is more likely than latex-based paint to trap moisture that can give rise to blistering and rot. It can also become brittle and crack or peel as wood contracts and expands.

Instead of paint, you may be better off applying a solid-color latex stain. Although it doesn't last quite as long as paint, stain doesn't peel or blister. Whichever you choose, don't wait too long to paint or stain your new outdoor wood. Wood that is allowed to weather won't hold the finish as long as wood that's painted right away.

Give your greenhouse a summer cleaning. Take advantage of the warm summer months, when plants are moved outdoors, to clean and make repairs to your greenhouse. Give windows and shelves a thorough washing with detergent and disinfectant (both are necessary for battling insects and diseases, but avoid any contact with plants). Use an algaecide to eliminate slime from flooring and benches. Also, be sure to inspect the windows for damage. Temporarily repair cracks with glazing tape, but replace broken panes as soon as possible. Don't forget to check all hoses for leaks, and repair or replace any rusted shelving, frame parts, or faucets.

Easy Fixes

Repairing a leaky tin roof. A garden shed with a tin roof may have charm aplenty, but there's nothing charming about one that leaks. It's easy to determine the source of a leak—just inspect the roof from the inside on the next rainy day. Once you've located the source of the leak, paint a circle around the area. On a clear day, measure the distance from the mark you've painted to two points on the roof's edge, and measure the same distances on the outside. Clean the area (on the roof's exterior) with a wire brush and patch it with siliconized acrylic caulk or polyurethane roof and flashing sealant. (Make sure the roof is dry before you start; otherwise the caulk won't adhere.) An even better, though more expensive, solution is to reseal the roof using an acrylic elastomeric coating that you brush on in layers.

Pools

Owning a pool is major commitment. Pools require regular monitoring and upkeep, including testing the safety of the water several times a week and handling strong chemicals. It's no surprise there are so many thriving pool service companies. Although you'll have to buy your own chemicals, performing your own pool maintenance will not only save you a considerable sum of money, it will bring the peace of mind that comes from knowing you don't have to rely on others for your family's safety and enjoyment.

Care and Maintenance

Test your chemicals frequently. You're not the only one enjoying your pool: It's also an excellent breeding ground for harmful bacteria and other microorganisms. Applying a sanitizer (usually chlorine) can keep them in check. Monitoring and adjusting the chemical levels regularly is essential—you have to make sure that the creepy-crawlies aren't thriving in your water! Two to three times a week, use a pool water test kit to test pH (the ideal range is 7.2–7.6) and chlorine levels (1.0–3.0 parts per million). Thoroughly rinse

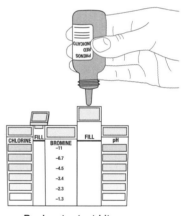

Pool water test kit

vials and cells before filling them, and collect water samples from about 18 inches (45 cm) below the pool's surface. Additional testing for total alkalinity (80–120 ppm), calcium hardness (200–300 ppm), total dissolved solids (500–1,500 ppm), and, in the case of outdoor pools, stabilizer/cyanuric acid (20–50 ppm), should be done once a month. Always use caution when handling all pool chemicals, particularly acids.

Make your own floaters. Protect your concrete pool against ice damage by filling three or four plastic gallon (4 litre) jugs with a bit of water and placing them around your pool before closing it. In the event your pool ices over, the jugs will absorb the stress instead of your pool walls. In vinyl pools, use large pieces of foam rubber instead of jugs.

Make sure your pool is childproof. No pool task is more important than keeping young children away from the water during off hours with either a pool fence, a pool cover, or a pool safety net. (This applies even if you don't have children in the home—kids from the neighborhood still pose a risk.) There's no shortage of products or suppliers of childproof pool gear, so shop around for a good price and warranty. Some of the leading companies include All-Safe (www.allsafepool.com), Katchakid (www.katchakid.com), and Life Saver Pool Fence (www.poolfence.com).

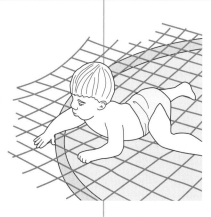

CLOSING YOUR POOL FOR THE WINTER

The coming of fall signals the end of pool season in most areas. Close your pool when daytime temperatures hover between 60 and 70 degrees (15 and 21°C). Follow this pool-closing checklist:

- Three to five days before closing, balance the water, adjusting the pH to between 7.2 and 7.6.
- Apply winter shock (a chlorine formulation for winterizing pools).

- Clean and store all ladders, diving boards, skimmer baskets, ropes, and wall fittings.
- Drain water to 3 to 6 inches (8 to 15 cm) below the tile level for solid covers, 12 to 18 inches (30 to 45 cm) for mesh covers.
- Disconnect and drain all pumps and filters according to manufacturers' instructions.
- Clean, brush, and vacuum pool walls and floor, skimming off all debris.

- Blow out pool plumbing with an air compressor, and plug return lines with expandable stoppers.
- Add winterizing algicide and pool-grade antifreeze.
- Shut off all electricity to the pool.
- Coat any exposed metal with petroleum jelly to prevent rust.
- Cover the pool.

Easy Fixes

Shocking your pool. An overpowering chlorine odor is a sure sign that your pool is in need of shock treatment. What you smell is actually chloramine, or combined chlorine, a compound that forms when chlorine combines with perspiration, rainwater, cosmetics, urine, and other substances. Despite its strong smell, combined chlorine is a weak sanitizer and can cause eye and skin irritations. To restore the efficiency of the sanitizer, you'll need to add a large amount of granular chlorine (a process known as super-chlorination), or use a nonchlorine shock containing either potassium monopersulfate or lithium hypochlorite. Pools should be shocked when they're first opened and once a week thereafter (more frequently if they're used by many bathers).

Is it time to repaint or replaster? Over time, pool chemicals and extreme fluctuations in water temperature will take their toll on a concrete pool. On average, pools in temperate zones need to be replastered every 10 to 15 years or repainted every three to five years. Your timing may vary, though. If you notice an excessive amount of flaking, it's probably a good time to call the contractor.

Do you suspect a leak? Think your pool may have a leak? Try this: Place a 5-gallon (19 litres) bucket on the second step and fill it to the water level of the pool (place a brick inside to keep it in place). Mark the water level inside the bucket. Shut off any pumps, mark the pool's water level on the outside of the bucket, then restart the equipment. After one to two days, check the bucket; if the pool level is lower than the bucket's, there's a leak. You may be able to pinpoint its location with a dye test. Use an empty reagent bottle or a small squeeze bottle filled with food coloring. Squeeze out a bit of dye in suspected areas, especially behind ladders, near steps and lights, and around corners and tile fittings. If the dye gets sucked in, you've found your leak.

GARDEN POND MAINTENANCE

Water gardens are another popular outdoor water feature. They're a soothing, restful landscape element—as long as they don't leak. Here's how to track down and fix three common types of leaks.

Punctured liners The toughest part about fixing a hole in a liner is finding its location. Let the water level drop; the water will stop draining at the level of the leak. Transition areas where ponds flow over waterfalls or into other ponds are common problem spots. Carefully move plants and rocks, and examine the liner. Once you find the hole or slash, scrub the area with a scouring pad to remove dirt and debris, then dry the area thoroughly. Using a repair kit (around $10 at garden centers) apply the adhesive and patching material, then let it dry and cure based on directions.

Drooping liners and wicking water Flexible liners can settle and water will creep over the edge. Look for wet spots around the perimeter of the pond, then prop up the sagging liner by raising the edge up with soil. Water can also use plants or exposed areas of soil to climb up and out of a pond. The solution is to move the plants away from the edge of the pond or create a break in the "bridge" to stop the wicking.

Plumbing leaks Check the soil around pumps, valves and hoses for wet areas. If the leak is in a pipe or hose, carefully unearth the pipe then, with the pump running, track down the exact location of the leak. Sometimes the solution is as simple as retightening a hose clamp. If a hose or pipe is leaking the simplest solution is often to splice in a new section.

Threats to You and Your Home

This part of the book could scare you, but it shouldn't. In fact, it's designed to put your mind at ease. It's no surprise that Mother Nature can turn nasty, bringing devastation

through fires, storms, and earthquakes. And when she isn't throwing big things at you, she can send little things to wreak havoc, such as rot and mold, poisonous gases, and invasive insects. Even when nature is behaving, there's no lack of burglars out there looking to abscond with your prized possessions. Fortunately, there are many precautions you can take to guard against these threats and keep yourself, your family, and your home safe. That's what this part is all about.

On these next few pages, we'll teach you how to guard against fire, poisonous gases, and burglars. You'll also learn how to keep insects, rot, and mold out of your home. The final section is a primer on preparing for and dealing with natural disasters. We've also included in this section two special features that apply across the board to all natural disasters: What to stash in your emergency kit, and how to cope after a natural disaster. Read through those features—and this entire section—carefully, then do what you need to do. Finally, relax. You're ready to adopt a new motto: "Don't be scared. Be prepared."

Fire Safety

A fire in your home is one of the most devastating things that can happen to you, both emotionally and economically. Fires can destroy your property and threaten the lives of your family; they can also inspire feelings of hopelessness and helplessness. The good news is that there are easy steps you can take to protect your family and your home from a fire. Here's your guide to learning what to do if a fire occurs and how to plan ahead so that you and your family know what to do if you experience one.

OUNCE OF PREVENTION

$65

The cost of three smoke alarms and one ABC fire extinguisher—fire-prevention essentials you need to protect your home and family.

Preventing Fires

Maintain your smoke detectors. Smoke detectors won't do you any good if they're not operating properly. To make sure that yours will sound when they're needed, adopt the following routine:

- Once a month, check each detector by pressing the test button until the alarm sounds. If the unit has no test button, light a candle, blow it out, and hold the smoking wick near the detector. If the alarm doesn't sound in 30 seconds, replace the battery.
- Twice a year open the case and gently vacuum the interior using the soft-brush attachment. If the case doesn't open, vacuum through the holes.
- Change the battery once a year. Doing it on your birthday is a sure way to remember!
- After 10 years, install a new detector.

Keep the appropriate fire extinguishers handy. Fire extinguishers are rated A, B, or C—each kind is designed to put out a particular type of fire. Class A fires involve wood, paper, and cloth. Class B fires involve grease, gasoline, chemical solvents, and other oils. Class C fires involve electrical equipment. Although extinguishers rated ABC are a bit more expensive, it makes sense to keep these multipurpose extinguishers in your home. Keep one in every room of the house, preferably near an exit. In addition, keep BC extinguishers in your kitchen and garage; this type of extinguisher is best suited for these locations. Because fire extinguishers eventually lose their charge, choose models that have pressure gauges and can be recharged. When the gauge shows low pressure, have the unit recharged immediately to keep it functioning.

Rehearse a family escape plan. Don't wait for a fire to break out to start thinking about an escape strategy—make your plans now. Draw a rough map of your house, showing all its doors, windows, hallways, porches, and porch roofs. Determine two escape routes for each room and mark the routes on the map, using different colors for each route. Acquaint your entire family with the map, and hold occasional fire drills at night so that it becomes routine and everyone can follow the shortest routes to the outside automatically. Also assign one person to help anyone who has difficulty moving about, and establish an outdoor meeting place where you can count heads and know that everyone is safe.

THE DOS AND DON'TS OF FIRE PREVENTION

DO …

- Install and maintain smoke detectors and have charged fire extinguishers on hand.

- Keep passageways, doors, and stairways clear and easy to navigate.

- Keep drapes, bedding, and upholstered furniture away from heating vents, space heaters, fireplaces, and woodstoves.

- Unplug TVs, computers, and appliances when you won't be using them for a while.

- Sleep with your door closed. If there's a fire in another room, it will be hampered from getting to you before you can wake up.

- Check extension cords for defects, and replace any that are damaged.

- Keep curtains and other flammables away from stoves and cooktops.

- Replace frame and panel doors to the basement and garage with steel doors—or at least solid wood ones.

- Regularly clean your clothes dryer's lint trap.

- Keep a flashlight near your bed in case a fire causes a power failure.

- Position your outdoor grill at least 2 feet (60 cm) from anything that could conceivably burn. If it is a gas grill, make sure it is totally rust-free; a rusted area could develop into a gas leak and create a fire.

- If you install a woodstove, position it at least 3 feet (1 metre) from the wall. Install the stovepipe with clearances recommended by the manufacturer. Over time the wood framing in walls and ceilings can dry out from the heat of a stove and may ignite at a temperature as low as 200°F (93°C).

DON'T …

- Smoke in bed or in an easy chair in front of the TV when you're tired or drinking.

- Overload electrical circuits. Multiple devices plugged into a socket can cause a fire.

- Leave unattended candles burning.

- Allow children to play with matches, lighters, or candles.

- Keep anything combustible within 3 feet (1 metre) of your water heater.

- Try to restart a dwindling fire by squirting it with lighter fluid. Add kindling instead.

- Don't keep piles of newspapers, oily cloths, or flammable chemicals indoors. If they become too warm, they may catch fire through spontaneous combustion.

In Case of Fire

Contain small fires quickly. If a small fire breaks out, get everyone out of the house and call the fire department. Then, if the fire is still small, try to put it out with a fire extinguisher. When using an extinguisher, position yourself between the fire and an escape route. Work with a sweeping motion, aiming the nozzle at the bottom of the flames. If the fire gets out of control, leave the house quickly, closing all doors behind you to help contain the fire.

Keep your family safe. At the first signs of smoke or fire, get everyone out of the house as quickly as possible. Don't stop to collect valuables or keepsakes. Don't even stop to call the fire department; call from outside on a cell phone or from a neighbor's house. In escaping from a burning house, keep yourself and your family safe by doing the following:

- Don't panic. Keep a cool head and concentrate on getting to safety.
- If you're trapped in a room, stay near the floor. If you can't get out through the window, open it both from the bottom (to let you breathe) and from the top (to let out the smoke).
- If you can get out and you know where the fire is, use a route that moves away from it.
- Remember the details of the escape map you drew and take the safest exit route, as you practiced in your fire drills.
- Close all doors behind you as you pass through the house to the outside.
- Feel any door in your path with your hand. If it's hot, don't open it. If it's cool, open it slowly and stay behind it. If you feel heat or pressure coming through the door, slam it shut.
- If a hall or stairway is filled with smoke, try to find another way out.

SMART IDEA

Chimney flue fires are one of the most common types of fireplace-related fires. Relining a damaged flue can cost $3,000 or more, and damage to other parts of the house can soar into the tens of thousands of dollars. There's evidence that creosote-cleaning fire logs can help reduce the incidence of chimney flue fires. They won't take the place of regular chimney cleanings, but burning them is cheap insurance.

SMOKE DETECTORS

equipment spotlight

The best defense against fire is early detection. It's critical that you install smoke detectors on all levels of your house including the basement and outside each sleeping area (inside the room if anyone sleeps with the door closed, as is recommended). To avoid false alarms, install them at a safe distance from steamy showers and cooking ranges. There are two basic types of alarms: An ionization unit emits a small amount of radiation that is detected by a sensor and sounds an alarm when smoke blocks the radiation from reaching the sensor; it is best for detecting fast-burning fires from paper, wood, and fat. A photoelectric unit is triggered when smoke breaks a beam of light; it is better at sensing smoky fires, such as smoldering mattresses. Either type will give you sufficient warning, but if you want to cover all your bases you can always purchase a combined photoelectric/ionization model.

- If you must pass through a smoke-filled area, crawl along the floor, where the air is clearer.
- In a smoke-filled area, take only short breaths through your nose. Cover your nose with a damp handkerchief, if possible.
- Once outside, don't go back into the house until the firefighters tell you it's okay.

Stop, drop, and roll. If clothing catches fire, act quickly. If it's your own clothing, cross your arms over your chest, drop to the ground, and roll over and over slowly. If a wool blanket, coat, rug, or heavy drape is within reach, wrap yourself in it and roll on the floor. If someone else's clothing catches fire, get him on the floor quickly, tripping him if necessary. Smother the fire with a wool blanket, coat, rug, or drape. Spray the person with a fire extinguisher if one is handy, but be careful to keep the spray away from the person's face. Once the fire is out, do not pull burned clothing away from the skin as you might cause serious injury. Call for emergency medical services right away.

How to Install a Smoke Detector

Some smoke detectors have to be connected to the house's hard wiring—that kind should be installed by a licensed electrician. Battery-operated units are either stuck in place with adhesive backing or screwed in. Install smoke detectors at least 12 inches (30 cm) away from corners and 3 feet (1 metre) away from windows (breezes can delay the alarm). Here's how to install the screw-in type:

1. Holding the unit's mounting bracket in place, make pencil marks on the wall through the screw openings. Remove the bracket. At the marks, drill holes to accept anchors for the screws.

2. Tap the anchors into place and reposition the bracket. Attach it by driving the mounting screws into the anchors. Put in the battery, then snap on the unit's cover.

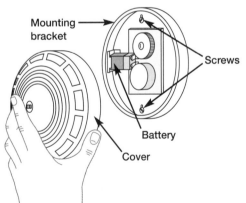

After a Fire

Exercise caution when reentering a damaged home. If you have a major fire in your house, stay away until the firefighters tell you it is safe to go back inside. After a severe fire, a house can be a dangerous place. Charred beams may break away and fall. Water used to put the fire out can collect above the ceiling and suddenly break through, bringing ceiling fixtures and drywall down on your head. You may step on a weak spot in the floor and sink, breaking your leg—or worse. There is also the danger of electrical shocks from exposed wires in wet surroundings. Once the house is declared safe enough to enter, however, work fast to prevent further damage. If you don't do all you can, the insurance company may not cover the damage you could have prevented.

take care

When drilling into damp drywall, never use an electric drill—its contact with the moist wall may give you a severe electrical shock.

Drain a sagging ceiling. If firefighters pumped water into the attic or an upper floor, you may see a sag in the ceiling below. If the sag is severe, stay out of the room and call in a professional contractor. If the sag is slight, however, put on a face mask and use a hand drill to make a small hole at the center of the sag. As the water flows out, catch it in a bucket, keeping your face out of the way. Drill other holes, one at a time, until all the water has drained.

Wash away the soot. Wearing rubber gloves and safety glasses, scrub your walls, ceilings, and floors to get rid of soot left by the fire. Put warm water in a bucket, and for every gallon of water stir in 1 cup (250 ml) of chlorine bleach and 5 tablespoons (75 ml) of trisodium phosphate (TSP), which is available in paint and hardware stores. After scrubbing hard, rinse the surfaces with clear, warm water.

Salvage your furniture. Scrub any mud and grime from wood furniture with a brush dipped in a cleaning solution with a pine-oil base. Let it dry thoroughly in a well-ventilated room or in a shady outdoor spot. Don't dry it in the sun, which might cause it to warp. Clean and dry the drawers separately to prevent later sticking. If mildew appears, brush it away, using a solution of 1 cup of chlorine bleach to 1 quart of water, then rinse it.

Dry it all out. To prevent mold, mildew, and rot problems further down the road, it's necessary to thoroughly dry out all building materials that have gotten wet. If floors have sustained water damage, pull up and remove the carpet and the carpet pad. If walls have become wet, remove the sheetrock (and any insulation behind it) and let the wall cavities dry out. If electrical components have become wet, have a qualified electrician check them over and replace them as necessary.

A POST-FIRE TO-DO LIST

As soon after a fire as it's safe to do so, you need to get on your way rebuilding your home (and your life). Doing these few things will prevent theft and further damage to your home.

- Board up damaged windows and doors to keep burglars at bay.
- Have debris carted away.
- Have the roof repaired before it rains.
- Remove damaged items to a safe place until an insurance inspector sees them.
- Have a licensed electrician check the house and make sure that it is safe.
- In cold weather, heat the house with a portable stove, or have the water system drained and pour antifreeze into all the drains and toilets.
- If water has collected in the basement or in any other area, pump it out.
- Roll up wet rugs (and the padding underneath them) and take them outdoors. Unroll them there and let them dry in the sun.
- If your electricity is on, dry the floors with fans or blowers and leave the house open as much as you can for ventilation without inviting looters.
- Take up water-soaked resilient flooring, such as linoleum or soft vinyl tiles, to let the wood underneath dry without warping or causing odors. If the flooring is brittle, use a heat lamp to make it pliable enough to handle and save for reinstalling.
- Send clothing to a dry cleaner that has an ozone chamber, which prevents smoke odors from setting in the fabric.
- Wipe leather goods with a damp cloth, then a dry one. Dry them away from sunlight or heat, and then clean them with saddle soap.
- Stuff wet shoes and handbags with newspaper to keep them from drying stiff and out of shape.
- Put wet papers, books, and paintings into a freezer to stop the moisture from soaking in farther and causing more damage. Later you can have a specialist restore them.

Radon and Carbon Monoxide

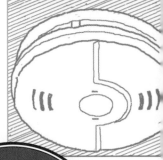

Poisonous gases in your home can cause severe health problems. Radon, a radioactive gas that collects in the soil and seeps into your house, can increase your chances of developing lung cancer. Poisoning by carbon monoxide (CO), which emanates from heaters and nonelectric stoves, can lead to illness and even death. Although both gases are invisible and odorless, you must take steps to rid your house of them. It's a matter of life and death.

OUNCE OF PREVENTION

$20

The cost of a carbon monoxide detector. 300: Number of people in North America who die annually after being overcome by carbon monoxide.

Minimizing Radon Exposure

Test your home for radon. The potential for radon poisoning varies by region. While there is generally less risk in some areas, local variations can be dramatic. Check with your provincial radon department or look online at http://www.radiationsafety.ca. Even if you live in a low-risk area, you'd be wise to check your home's radon levels. You can buy kits that include free lab analysis. Radon is measured in picocuries per liter of air (pCi/L). More than 4 pCi/L is considered hazardous. Because false readings sometimes occur, repeat the test in a few weeks. Never rely on your neighbor's tests, as radon levels can vary dramatically in structures that are only a few feet apart.

Breathe easy. Minimizing your exposure to radon is as simple as ventilating the spaces where you're most likely to find the gas and not spending much time while you're in them:

- Never linger in places where radon buildup is likely to be greatest.
- Increase the ventilation throughout your home, particularly in the basement.
- Don't smoke indoors. Smoke combined with radon makes you even more susceptible to cancer.
- Install a vapor barrier in your crawl space; always keep the space's vents open.

If necessary, call the pros. If your radon levels are consistently above 4 pCi/L, have a professional assess your home's problems and install a radon mitigation system. This expert may also install pipes or a collector mat under the basement floor, seal floor drains, cover the sump pump, or install a fan that vents air away from your house.

SMART IDEA

Have your home tested for radon *before* you put it on the market. In one case, a home inspection conducted by the buyers just before purchasing the house revealed high levels of radon. The result? The deal fell through and the homeowners eventually wound up settling on an amount $25,000 less than the original offer.

Preventing Carbon Monoxide Poisoning

Know the signs of carbon monoxide poisoning. Inhaling carbon monoxide causes headaches, dizziness, nausea, and drowsiness. Get anyone suffering these symptoms into the open air quickly. Have someone call EMS, and administer CPR if you're qualified. Once the person is safe, quickly open all doors and windows of the contaminated room, turn off any combustion appliances, and leave the house. Call your fire department and report what's happened. Before turning your fuel-burning appliances back on, make sure a qualified serviceperson checks them.

Install a carbon monoxide detector. The best models have test buttons and digital displays that show the room's level of carbon monoxide. All sound an alarm when levels are unacceptable. The concentration of carbon monoxide is measured in parts per million (ppm). Health effects from exposure to levels of 1 to 70 ppm don't affect most people, but heart patients might experience an increase in chest pain. Levels above 70 ppm may cause headache, fatigue, or nausea. Levels above 150 ppm can cause disorientation, unconsciousness, and even death.

Test your detector once a month. Hold the test button for 10 to 15 seconds; if the alarm doesn't sound, replace the battery. If that doesn't work, the unit is malfunctioning. Replace it. If your unit has no test button, hold burning incense near it; the alarm should sound within five minutes.

Check your furnace's flame. If it's yellow, the fuel is not burning thoroughly and may be releasing carbon monoxide into the air. Have the furnace's combustion regulated so the flame burns blue with a yellow halo (for more information, see the "Gas Burners" section).

6 WAYS TO MINIMIZE YOUR CARBON MONOXIDE EXPOSURE

1. Have a technician check and service your heating system, chimneys, and vents annually.

2. Never use gas appliances to heat your home.

3. If a pilot light on your stove or water heater goes out, relight it immediately. Before doing so, be sure the air is free of gas that may have escaped while the pilot light was out.

4. Never operate fuel-burning appliances inside your home, garage, or any enclosed space unless they are safely vented to the outside.

5. Never leave a car running in an attached garage, even with the garage door open. Carbon monoxide may seep into the house.

6. On every floor of your home and near sleeping areas, install a carbon monoxide detector that meets the requirements of the current ULC standard. Make sure it is not blocked by furniture or draperies.

Home Security

Keeping your house safe from burglars is mostly a matter of making it look like it's more trouble than it's worth for thieves to break in. The easiest way to keep your home from looking like an easy target is to keep all of your doors and windows securely locked. Here are a few other "aha!" tips to keep your family, and your belongings, secure.

OUNCE OF PREVENTION

$55

The price of a Grade 1 deadbolt lock. The rate of home invasions in Canada: around 23 per 100,000 population.

Preventive Measures

Secure all doors and windows. It won't do much good to lock your doors and windows unless they're solid and perfectly secured. Try the following:

- Replace hollow-core outside doors with steel doors.
- Don't rely on door chains. They can be broken easily. Opt instead for dead bolts.
- Install a wide-angle (180-degree) peephole in your front door. Simply drill a hole to put it in. If the bell rings and you don't see anyone through the peephole, don't open the door.
- To keep intruders from lifting a sliding door out of its frame from the outside, drive a couple of screws partway into the top track on the inside. No one will be able to lift out the doors without removing the screws first.
- Install decorative grillwork over low windows (unless that violates local building or fire codes).
- Add keyed pin locks to all windows, even on the second floor. Burglars know how to use ladders.
- Trim shrubbery bordering your home. Doing so both allows you a clear view through your windows, and prevents burglars from lying in wait behind them.
- Install dead bolts on outside doors.
- If you have cellar or basement doors that lead to the outside, secure them from the inside with sliding crossbars.

Put your lamps on a schedule. Programming your lamps to turn on and off while you're away will make people (namely, burglars) believe that you're home. There are several ways to do this: One way is to screw light-sensing sockets into standard lamp sockets that will turn the lights on automatically at dusk. You can also use a plug-in timer to turn lamps on and off at certain hours. Finally, you can replace a standard light switch with a switch timer that you set by turning a dial. Some models memorize and repeat your daily lighting pattern; others can be set to go on and off at random times to give the appearance of normal activity.

Light up your home's exterior. Install lights at each side of your entrance door and leave them on all night; if one burns out, you'll still have a lighted entrance. To make outdoor walkways safer at night, line them with low-voltage ground lighting or solar lights. Finally, have an electrician install floodlights with motion-sensing switches; if anyone approaches your home, the lights will detect his or her movements and turn on, alerting you to the interloper's presence. You can adjust the direction of the sensors, the size of the field, and the sensitivity of the system to avoid spotlighting the neighborhood stray cat. Most models have an override switch.

Secure the extra key. Most people want to leave a spare key outside to accommodate repairmen or unexpected relatives, or to use when they forget their own keys. Hiding a key outdoors is tantamount to an engraved invitation for burglars, because they know *all* the common hiding places. One solution to this problem is to keep the spare key in a special key box that is mounted on the wall and closed with a combination lock. Real estate agents often use these devices, which are available at locksmith shops. Only give the combination to people you want to have access to your house.

Reset your garage door opener. You can make your garage-door opener more burglarproof by resetting its frequency. This will keep thieves who carry collections of standard transmitters from finding one that will open your garage. Remove the cover of your remote transmitter and randomly reset the tiny switches inside. Then take the cover off the receiver mounted in your garage and reset its switches to match. Reprogram any extra transmitters, as well. If your transmitter doesn't have a set of switches, it was individualized at the factory and doesn't need resetting, as it's already burglarproof.

Take precautions before you go on vacation. When you're out of town, you don't want potential burglars to know your house is empty. If practicable, arrange for a full-time house sitter. If you can't do that, take the following precautions before leaving:

- Stop mail and newspaper delivery. Piled-up newspapers and mail signal your absence. (Better yet, have a neighbor pick up your mail and newspapers. What if your paper delivery person spreads the word that you're not home?)
- Hire a neighborhood teenager to mow your lawn and water your plants.
- Stash empty garbage cans in the garage.
- Leave a car parked in your driveway, and ask a neighbor to move it from time to time. Or ask the neighbor to park his own car in your driveway periodically.
- Turn off your electric garage door opener, padlock the garage door, and lock the door that connects the garage and the house.
- Install timers on interior lamps so that they turn on and off automatically, giving the impression that you are home (even when you're not).
- Leave curtains and blinds open, as you would if you were at home during the day.
- Tune a radio to a talk station at a volume loud enough to be barely heard outside, but not understood. Put the radio on a timer programmed to turn it on and off. Burglars don't want to break into homes if they hear voices inside (they probably won't be able to tell that it's the radio!).
- Turn off your phone ringer. An unanswered phone signals that no one is home.
- Leave a key with a friend, along with an itinerary and instructions on how you can be reached. Leave the phone numbers of your plumber and electrician with the neighbor in case of an emergency.
- Phone the local police and let them known you'll be away.
- Turn on all security alarms and timers.

WHICH ALARM SYSTEM IS RIGHT FOR YOU?

Don't rely on your barking dog to alert you to burglars. If you want maximum security, have a burglar alarm system installed. There are two basic types of burglar alarms: perimeter systems and motion detectors.

PERIMETER SYSTEMS

A perimeter system sounds an alarm if someone opens a door or window. Magnetic sensors are installed on closed windows and doors, and adjacent switches are recessed into the frame. When the door or window is closed, the magnet and switch are close enough together to form an electric circuit. If the window or door is opened when the system is armed, the circuit is broken and the alarm sounds. For additional protection, fit your windows with security screens, which are window screens interwoven with wires that form a protective circuit that sounds an alarm if cut. Glass-break alarms that adhere to any glass window or door and sound when the glass receives any abrupt shock are another option.

MOTION DETECTORS

Motion detectors sound an alarm when something moves inside a room, cutting across the invisible beam cast by the detector. These kinds of detectors should be installed across doorways and other passageways a few feet above the floor (if they're too low, they may ring when your pet saunters by). It's also a good idea to position sensors in the corners of each room near the ceiling to survey crucial traffic areas.

All alarm systems consist of sensors that are connected to a control box, a remote-control key switch to turn the system on and off, and an alarm that rings a bell or siren or dials the police (or security company) or your cell phone. The control panel should be near the door you use most often, but out of reach from the outside if a window is broken.

The most efficient burglar alarms are hard-wired systems that combine both perimeter alarms and motion detectors. However, there are also wireless systems that use radio frequency signals to monitor the components, many of which simply plug into wall outlets or are battery-powered. Unless you're an expert do-it-yourselfer, you'd probably be wise to have a full burglar alarm system installed professionally. However, if you don't want to spring for a full system, use individual motion detectors that scan single rooms and sound an alarm if anyone enters.

Termites and Other Pests

Nature is great when you're walking through your yard or hiking through the woods, but you don't want it invading your home. The best way to keep insects and other pests at bay is to understand the ways in which they try to get in. Avert a raft of pest-related headaches with vigilance, preventive maintenance, and a rapid response to problems that arise. If you are not vigilant, it could cost you thousands of dollars to get the critters out once and for all and repair your home's structure.

Preventive Measures

Inspect your home yearly. Take an annual walk-around of your house, inside and out, looking for such telltale signs of insect infestation as rotting wood, termite swarms, and mud tubes leading from the soil to sill plates and other wooden areas.

Keep insects outside. It's far easier to keep pests out than to get rid of them once they've invaded your indoor turf. But it's not as though they march single-file through the front door: Check every likely entry, including foundation cracks, gaps around outdoor faucets, openings created by loose siding or flashing, and those small, round insertion points for your cable and electrical wires. Seal any gaps or holes you find with caulk, siding or sheet metal, or metal screening. Cut back branches touching the roof or siding that serve as insect "bridges."

Stay dry inside and out. Insect pests love moisture, which is why you must rid your house and its environs of areas where water can collect or infiltrate. Seal cracks and holes in your foundation with caulk or cement. Repair plumbing leaks. Eliminate anything—including old tires, empty flowerpots, and wading pools—that can hold stagnant water.

Use high-quality latex caulk to seal small gaps around telephone and cable lines. For larger gaps, use moldable putty, available in the electrical supplies section of your local home center.

WHAT'S BUGGING YOU?

PROBLEM INSECTS	HOW TO KEEP THEM OUT OF YOUR HOUSE
Ants	Seal up all sweets and greasy foods, which attract ants. Washing countertops, cabinets, and floors with a vinegar-and-water solution kills the scents that guide ants to food.
Bees	There are over 10,000 kinds of bees. If the bee that's bugging you is fuzzy with brown and yellow stripes, you may be dealing with honey bees. If so, there's a chance a local beekeeper will take them off your hands for free. Large infestations of other types of bees may require a call to the exterminator.
Carpenter ants	Find and fix the moisture problems (usually roof or plumbing leaks) that attract them. Lay a line of chili powder or powdered charcoal to bar their points of entry. Or sprinkle boric acid* on a spoonful of apple-mint jelly, mix it in, and spread the jelly on an index card. Place the card near the ant colony. For a severe infestation, call in professional help.
Fleas	If your pet has fleas, you need to treat your home, too. Vacuum all areas where your pet sleeps or sits. Vacuum his bedding and then wash it in hot water. (Seal up and discard the vacuum bags.) Be sure to keep your pet's flea treatments up to date.
Moths	To prevent infestation by pantry moths, store food in tight-lidded glass or sturdy plastic containers. Clean your pantry with a disinfecting cleanser or a vinegar-and-water solution. If you find holes in woolen or other clothing, check the corners of closets and behind furniture for webbing or small cocoons, which are signs that clothes moths are present. Pheromone traps, which use a natural insect bait, can be used for both types of moth.
Roaches	Paper and glue attract roaches, so don't stockpile empty grocery bags. Sprinkle boric acid* under cabinets and in corners where these pests are known to travel. Keep your kitchen sparkling clean, fix leaky faucets immediately, and if necessary schedule regular exterminator visits.
Termites	Follow this chapter's tips carefully. If you think you have an infestation, call a reputable exterminator, find and fix the moisture problems that attracted the termites, and then repair damaged or compromised wood.
Wasps	If you notice a small wasp nest under a roof eave, wait until after dark on a cool evening when the insects are inactive. Use a long pole to knock the nest from its mooring, and the wasps won't return. Treat larger hanging nests or ground nests with wasp and hornet spray killer (follow package directions).

It is not advisable to use boric acid in homes in which small children or pets live.

Is it a termite or a carpenter ant? Winged, antlike bugs spell trouble whether they're carpenter ants or termites. Carpenter ants have segmented bodies, pronounced "waists," back wings that are shorter than their front wings, and elbowed antennae. Termites lack a defined waist and have straight antennae.

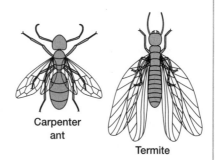

Carpenter ant

Termite

Find a qualified professional. Look for a certified exterminator who guarantees his work.
Asking friends or neighbors for references, checking your phone book, or seeking out reviews online (at sites such as www.pestcontrolcanada.com) should yield you a few good pest-control contractors in your area. Get several estimates before you hire someone; try to secure a maximum price from whomever you hire.

HOW TO SPOT TERMITE DAMAGE

It's estimated that termites cause approximately $5 billion worth of property damage in Canada alone every year—imagine what the figure is worldwide! While termite swarms and mud tubes are easy to spot, other signs of infestation are more subtle. Tap at your baseboards to see whether they've been hollowed out from within. Check for small, brownish-black spots or small piles of "dry powdery muck" that looks like pepper (it's actually termite waste) along baseboards or in kitchen cupboards. If you think you may have termites, don't dawdle. Have a state-certified, pest-management professional inspect your home right away.

Easy Fixes

Keeping raccoons out of your trash. If the neighborhood raccoons are making nightly visits to your trash can, try sprinkling Epsom salts around the area. Other home remedies include spraying the cans with vinegar or a solution of half-strength ammonia.

Preventing deer from grazing in your garden. Try placing scented soap or hair clippings in old pantyhose and hanging them on stakes around the garden. Some folks claim that soaking rags in vinegar and placing them on the fence or on stakes surrounding garden beds also works.

Mold and Dry Rot

No one likes to think about it, but molds and fungi are all around us. Since we just can't eliminate them all, a more realistic goal is to control their growth. The best way to do that is to keep moisture at bay. Even dry rot—a somewhat misleading term—is moisture-related. Whether it's mold or dry rot that threatens, vigilance, ventilation, and controlling moisture are the keys to prevention. Mold remediation on your home is a very expensive endeavor: You'll have to pay for any structural damage that mold has caused, *and* you'll have to pony up for removing any materials and possessions contaminated by the mold, not to mention the cost of making sure that it never returns.

Preventive Measures

Patrol your property for moisture. Inspect your property regularly for signs of mold and rot and the moisture problems that cause them:

SMART IDEA

If you keep potted plants on a deck or wood patio, avoid moisture problems by setting the planters on pot feet (available at home and garden centers), which allow air to circulate underneath.

- At least twice a year, check your roof for leaks. Look for loose roof shingles and popped roofing nails.
- Inspect your basement, crawl spaces, attic, porch, deck, house perimeter, and other areas where water can collect or seep in.
- Check roof eaves and door and window frames for the signs of dry rot: soft, crumbly wood and a powdery surface.
- Keep gutters clean and free of leaf accumulations, which trap moisture. Consider upgrading to self-cleaning gutters.
- Examine the caulking around windows, doors, and utility openings, and recaulk as needed. Make sure weather stripping around doors and windows is doing its job of keeping moisture out.
- On your deck, inspect the ground-to-post contact points.
- Inside the house, check bathroom and kitchen plumbing for leaks. Look for signs of mold growth around showers and tubs and on tiles.
- Make certain dryer, bathroom, and stove exhaust vents lead outside. You don't want them dumping moisture-laden air into your attic.

Keep bathroom air circulating. Proper ventilation is essential to discouraging the growth of mold and mildew in bathrooms. After showers and baths, be sure to run the exhaust fan for about 20 minutes, or long enough to dry out the room. If your bathroom lacks a fan, have one installed. To increase air flow to bathroom closets, consider replacing solid doors with louvered ones.

Bleach it. To remove surface mold from tile corners in showers and bathtubs, use a solution of 1 part bleach to 10 parts water in a plastic spray bottle. Make sure the room is well-ventilated—open windows and keep the bathroom door open—before spraying directly on the mold spots. Wait a bit, then wipe with a sponge.

Blast it. To remove deep-seated mold and keep it from coming back, use a more powerful solution of trisodium phosphate (TSP), bleach, and water. Mix 1 quart (1 litre) of bleach, 3 quarts (3 litres) of water, and 2/3 cup (160 ml) of TSP, available at hardware stores, and apply the solution to the affected surfaces with a sponge. Don't forget to wear safety gear.

Freshen up. To get rid of musty odors, you need to—you guessed it—eliminate moisture problems and ventilate, ventilate, ventilate. In addition, scrub affected walls with a bleach-and-water solution (see above) and a nylon-bristled brush. If necessary, paint affected walls and ceilings with a paint that contains mildewcide.

Exhaust warm air. To move out warm, moist air collecting in the upper reaches of your attic, consider installing a roof ridge vent system. Or use an electric attic fan.

Vent the dryer. Your clothes dryer is another source of hot air that needs to be expelled. Make sure the dryer is properly vented to the outside. Once a year, inspect the dryer's exhaust duct and clean it out.

Direct water away from your house. Make sure the ground slopes away from the perimeter of your house. Channel water from downspouts away from the foundation. Trim tree branches that overhang your roof, and clear excess plant growth from around the foundation. Encroaching foliage provides opportunities for moisture to collect, while roots near the foundation can interfere with perimeter drainage systems.

Hurricanes and Other Windstorms

Luckily, we don't experience many hurricanes in Canada, however, we do see the remnants of many southern storms. Each ocean has its own hurricane season, with most falling between May and November. And when you add typhoons to the mix of international tropical cyclones, as these windstorms are called, well, it's always windy season somewhere in the world. You should have plans in place for what you will do in case a storm comes your way. Even if you don't live on a coast, you could still be hit by a tornado or other devastating windstorm. Although winds do a lot of harm, most damage from storms comes from water, not to mention fires that break out due to fallen power lines and ruptured gas lines. If hurricanes or tornados are common in your area, take steps now to prepare your house. Not doing so can mean spending thousands of dollars replacing damaged items and repairing (or rebuilding) your home.

SMART IDEA

Garage doors are just as vulnerable as windows in a windstorm. If the garage door is compromised, a domino effect where garage—and even house—walls and roofs can collapse rapidly. Invest in a hurricane-rated door or a code-approved metal bracing system to minimize possible damage.

In Advance

Invest in hurricane windows. If you live in a hurricane zone, you may want to install so-called "hurricane windows," which will survive longer than ordinary ones and may save you a bundle. (Just know that, no matter what a window salesman says, there's no guarantee that these special windows will stand up to the worst hurricane winds.) Get the best windows you can afford, because they are the most vulnerable parts of the house in a windstorm. Not only can the wind shatter the glass and let in rain, but very strong winds can stream through a broken window and exert enough upward pressure on the roof to blow it off. If this happens, the walls of the house could also collapse.

Prepare window coverings well in advance. You can buy removable and roll-down metal storm shutters to protect glass doors and windows. If you don't want to invest in commercial shutters, the best option is to board up your windows when a storm approaches. This preparation needs to be done in advance, because you won't have time to measure, cut to fit, and install boards after a storm warning is given. Use 1/2 (1 cm)- or preferably 3/4 (2 cm)-inch outdoor (CDX) plywood and cut it 5 inches (13 cm) larger than the window on all sides. So that you can install them quickly when the time comes, predrill screw holes along the edges of the plywood 8 to 12 inches (20 to 30 cm) apart; install anchors in corresponding parts of the studs around the windows (not in the flimsy window frames). When the hurricane comes, you'll only need to position the boards and drive in the screws.

Make a video tour of your home's contents. If your home suffers damage, you may need proof of how things were to justify insurance claims or tax deductions for losses. This is why it makes sense not just to make a list of all your furniture, appliances, and other contents of your home, but to take photos (or video) of *everything*. Write down serial numbers, where applicable, and save receipts for big-ticket purchases. Store these photos and records in a safety deposit box or another safe, off-site location.

Climb up and check your roof. Roofs are vulnerable to high winds, which will lift any loose edges and tear away shingles. Before the storm season starts, look for any loose or cracked shingles and repair them right away (or hire someone to do this for you, if you can't work in high places). Driving rains will find and enlarge the tiniest openings, resulting in bad leaks that can damage the rooms below.

Keep your trees trimmed. During a windstorm, trees and limbs can fall onto your house and cause severe damage. Prune away some inside branches of the trees near your house—the less dense branches are, the more wind can pass through them. You should also check your trees for signs of weakness: Remove any trees that are drying out, leaning more than 15 degrees, or have heavily damaged roots.

Invest in an emergency generator. Hurricanes and other windstorms frequently blow down power lines, causing power outages. An emergency generator will allow you to keep running essential appliances and lights. This is particularly important for people who rely on electrical medical equipment.

Establish an evacuation plan. One of the most common reasons that people die in hurricanes is because they refuse to evacuate—don't be part of these grim statistics. When you know a storm is approaching, get out of its path quickly. Planning your evacuation in advance is the surest, quickest way to get you to safety in the event of an emergency. Here's what to do:

- Identify ahead of time where you'll go—the home of a friend or relative in another town, a distant motel, or an emergency shelter. Have both a first choice and a back-up plan.
- In your car, keep a list of the phone numbers for these alternative shelters. You'll also need a road map—if roads are blocked or washed out, you may have to take unfamiliar routes.
- Gather extra clothing and bedding to take along, as well as an emergency care kit (see next page).

SMART IDEA

Be sure you're up to date on all the insurance coverage that you need in your part of the country. You want to be covered for wind, water, and fire damage—not just storm damage and homeowner's insurance.

- Give an out-of-town friend or relative a list of family names and phone numbers to call in case of emergency. When disaster strikes, it is sometimes easier to call long distance than locally. Have family members call the liaison for information if they can't reach you.

SMART IDEA

If a hurricane is coming and you live in a mobile home (or another insubstantial structure) you should seek sturdier emergency shelter, whether or not you're instructed to evacuate. Better to be safe than sorry!

As a Storm Approaches

Tune in for up-to-date news. If a storm is heading your way, tune to a local television or radio station for advice, and follow it. Keep a battery-operated radio and extra batteries handy in case of a power outage.

Take other important pre-storm precautions. Each of these things takes just a few minutes but could save you unnecessary worry (or damage) once the storm hits:

- Set your freezer to its highest temperature in case the power fails. Super-cold food will have a better chance of staying unspoiled until the power is restored.
- Bring outdoor furniture and equipment inside. Tie down objects too large to move.
- Fill the bathtub with water in case the water supply is affected; you may need extra water for cleaning or for flushing toilets.
- If there's a chance you'll need to make a fast getaway, fill your car's tank with gas; gas pumps won't work during a power failure.
- If you won't be using your car, put it in the garage.
- Moor your boat and leave it.
- Evacuate if you're told to, or stay indoors and away from windows.

EMERGENCY CARE KIT

When a natural disaster strikes, whether in the form of a fierce storm, flood, or earthquake, or when the power simply goes out, it's almost always too late to try to start throwing together the survival items you'll need. That's why you should assemble this kit in advance and have it at the ready. Be sure to routinely replace any perishable items in your bag (such as water and batteries). Include the following items, plus anything else your family might need to survive:

- Flashlight with extra batteries or a crank-up model
- Portable radio with extra batteries or a crank-up model
- First-aid kit
- Prescription drugs and other necessary medical supplies
- At least 1 gallon (4 litres) of drinking water per person per day for at least three days; replace the supply every six months
- Small supply (ideally a three-day supply) of ready-to-eat food (energy bars and the like are a good place to start)
- Manual can opener
- A waterproof, fireproof container with valuable papers, including passports and insurance policies—or copies of these important papers if you keep the originals in a safe-deposit box

During a Storm

Lock down. If you're at home during a hurricane, lock doors and windows to reduce vibration, and close drapes and blinds to help contain broken glass. Stay away from windows. If the rain is beating under the doors, place folded towels along the insides of sills to absorb the water.

Hurricane winds suddenly dying off? Wait. The eye may be passing overhead. The most damaging part of the storm will follow: Once the eye has passed, the winds will blow from the opposite direction, and trees, shrubs, houses, sheds, garages, signs, and other objects that were damaged by the first winds will be hit from the other side.

Stabilize broken windows. If a window cracks during a not-too-fierce storm, put duct tape over the crack to prevent it from spreading and producing an even larger break. If the break is too large to stabilize with tape, put on heavy work gloves and carefully pull out the broken glass, working from the top of the pane down. Then staple or tape polyethylene sheeting or a heavy-duty plastic garbage bag over the open area and nail a piece of plywood over it to keep out the wind.

Beware of follow-up tornados. Even after a hurricane is over, don't get too smug—it's common for tornadoes to follow soon afterward. Stay indoors until you are sure it's safe to go outside. Whether or not they come in the aftermath of a hurricane, tornadoes can be devastating, and they can develop quickly. If a tornado approaches, find a low, windowless, structurally strong place to take shelter. Good places include: under a staircase; in the basement; under a solid table, desk, bed, or an upholstered chair that's tipped over against an inside wall at the center of the house; or an inside hall or closet on the lowest floor.

A tornado is due to hit any minute—what should I do? If you're outside when a tornado's on the way, take refuge in a steel-framed or reinforced concrete building. If you're in open country, move away from the tornado's path at a right angle. If you can't escape, lie down in a ditch. Shield your head and cover your face with clothing to avoid choking on dust. Don't stay in a car, mobile home, or trailer.

Stabilizing broken windows

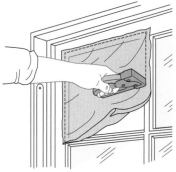

Step 1

Step 2

After a Storm

Be very careful. Hurricanes and tornadoes cause major damage—everything from blown-out roofs and shattered windows to flooding, falling trees, and downed power lines. Danger may lurk inside your home, too: Waterlogged ceilings may come crashing down, and floors may give way under foot. If you've evacuated, don't return home until the authorities assure you it's safe. When you do return, take the precautions listed in "Picking Up the Pieces After a Natural Disaster" on the next spread.

Trim troublesome trees. Storms wreak havoc on trees, and damaged trees can be a threat to you and your property. If a storm partially uproots a tree, splinters a large branch, or causes a major split at a fork (where two major branches meet), the tree or heavy branches may weaken in time and fall onto your roof or pose a threat to passersby. It's probably best to hire a professional tree service to remove or trim large branches or trees. For small trees or small, low branches, you may be able to do the job.

Take inventory. Save swatches of damaged flooring materials, window coverings, and furnishings, and take pictures of all interior and exterior damage to show your insurance claims adjuster or agent.

Check it out. Before using any storm-damaged appliances, furnaces, or air conditioners, have them inspected and repaired by qualified personnel.

Air it out. Speed the drying process by opening windows, doors, drawers, and cabinets. If you have electricity, turn on dehumidifiers, fans, and air conditioners to remove moisture from the air.

Floods

Devastating floods could happen anytime, in most parts of the country. Because they're so unpredictable (and so distressing), it's important to know now what you'd do in the event of a flood in your area. There are basically two types of floods: River flooding, which occurs when a river overflows its banks (usually in the spring); and flash floods, caused when heavy rains fall over a brief period, leaving more water than the ground or drains can take in. Flash floods often occur during heavy rain or windstorms and can come with little or no warning. Here's what you need to know so that you can protect your family, your home, and your belongings should the unlucky day ever come.

OUNCE OF PREVENTION

$8,000

A simple flood cleanup and disinfection of a Canadian home can cost up to $8,000.

In Advance

Get flood insurance. If you want to avoid catastrophic costs due to floods, the number one rule is to have proper insurance. Most homeowners' basic insurance policies don't cover losses due to floods, unless you have purchased extra coverage. If your house is in an area prone to flooding, you should consider buying additional flood insurance (even if you're not in a likely area, you might want to consider purchasing it anyway). Financial assistance could be available from your municipality should catastrophic flooding occur in your area. If you require more information about flooding, you could go to the Canada Mortgage and Housing Corporation's website "About Your House—General Series, After the Flood—A Homemaker's Checklist" at http://www.cmhc-schl.gc.ca.

Give your house a lift. This is an extreme solution, but it's one that might make sense if you live in a flood-prone area: Consider elevating your home. Yes, it's a costly procedure, but it may save you a bundle in reconstruction or repairs if floodwaters enter your house. Just an inch or two of water in your home can do thousands of dollars worth of damage.

take care

If there's danger of a flood, tune in to a local radio or television station to keep track of what's happening. If you're advised to evacuate, do so—but first turn off the gas, electricity, and water. Lock up the house and leave quickly.

Take inventory. Make a detailed list of your home's contents, and take photos of everything. If a flood causes damage and you want to make an insurance claim or claim a tax deduction, you'll need to prove what exactly was inside.

Don't get shocked. In case of a flood, you'll need to be able to reach your electrical control panel safely, without stepping in water—that's why it's important to situate this panel very carefully. Basements are not the ideal places for your control panel, because they are the usually first places to flood. If your control panel isn't well positioned, have an electrician move it to a safer place.

Keep an emergency kit at the ready. Store emergency essentials in a duffel bag or another portable pack on a high shelf on an upper floor. (See the "Hurricanes and Other Windstorms" chapter for a list of what should go into your emergency kit.) If you're forced out of your house by floodwaters, you'll have everything you need to survive for a few days.

Give your appliances a boost. If you know in advance that your area will flood, prop up any appliances that are in the basement or on the first floor. (Get those power tools and dehumidifiers off the floor!) Place bricks, concrete blocks, or layers of boards under the corners of the appliances, or, if possible, move them to a higher floor. Unplug everything that isn't essential, at least until the storm passes.

During a Flood

Don't go anywhere. If you're at home when a flood begins, stay there. Don't try to wade through the water to drier land, and, above all, don't drive through flooded streets. Six inches (15 cm) of moving water can sweep people off their feet; 12 inches (30 cm) can wash away a vehicle. About half of flood-related deaths occur when people are trapped in automobiles that stall while being driven through flooded areas. If your car stalls, abandon it immediately. Instead of leaving home, do the following:

- Open the basement windows so that pressure from water outside doesn't cause your walls to cave in.
- If necessary, seal the outside doors of the house with plywood and plastic sheeting.
- If the waters start creeping in and you can't leave the house, move to a higher floor or the attic. Take warm clothing and your emergency care kit with you wherever you go.
- Fill sinks and bathtubs with water. You may need it later if the water supply becomes contaminated.
- If the floor is flooded or any wiring gets wet, turn off the electric power at the main control panel.

After a Flood

Get rid of that swimming pool in your basement. If you get water in your basement, you can pump it out with a gasoline-driven pump. Keep the pump outside and lower the intake hose through a window. Gas-powered pumps release toxic fumes, which you can inhale if you're in an enclosed space. Lower the water level no more than 2 feet (60 cm) per day. If you pump out too much water within a short period of time, pressure from the water-saturated soil outside could cause the basement walls to collapse. Use a shop vacuum to suck out the remaining puddles.

Proceed with the utmost caution. Just because the flood water recedes doesn't mean that danger is behind you; there's still a risk of injury or infection. The house foundation may have been weakened, the electrical system may have shorted, and

PICKING UP THE PIECES AFTER A NATURAL DISASTER

After any major natural disaster that affects your home (be it a flood, storm, or earthquake), take great care to keep yourself and your family safe. First of all, stay out of disaster areas; not only are they dangerous, but your presence might hamper rescue efforts. Use your phone for emergencies only; you don't want to tie up lines that might be needed for rescue efforts. Don't drive if it's not absolutely necessary. If you do drive, be alert to downed power lines, damaged roads, and mudslides. Above all, stay out of damaged homes and buildings until professionals have deemed them safe.

When you finally reenter your damaged home, take great care (even if it's been deemed safe). Wear sturdy shoes to avoid cutting your feet. Carefully watch every step you take, and use a flashlight or a battery-powered lantern to light your way. *Never use candles.* Even lighting a match can be dangerous if there is a gas leak. As you move through the house, take photos of all damage and check for the following:

- If you smell gas, turn off the gas line and get outside at once.

- Keep a lookout for unstable floors, walls, staircases, and windows. If you find any, get out of the house until they're fixed.

- Check for electrical system damage, such as ruptured wires. If the power is still on and you find electrical damage, turn off the power immediately and call for help.

- Check for sagging ceilings or loose plaster or drywall. Have a contractor repair the damage before you return to the house.

- Check the house foundation for cracks.

- If there's a water leak in your house, turn off the water supply. Also check for damaged water lines. If you find any, call a plumber and avoid using water from the tap.

- Check for damaged sewage lines. If you suspect damage, don't use the toilets. Call a plumber.

- Clear away spilled medical supplies, toxic cleaning materials, and all flammable materials.

- Watch for animals and snakes that may be hiding in the house. Use a stick to poke through debris.

the floodwaters may have been contaminated with sewage or other things that might make you sick. Don't eat food that has been touched by floodwater. Boil drinking water. In addition, follow the precautions listed below and in the "Picking Up the Pieces After a Natural Disaster" box on the previous page:

- Do not enter any building that is surrounded by water. Floodwaters often undermine foundations, causing sinking and cracks and breaks in floors. These structures can collapse, leaving you trapped inside.
- Open your windows. You want to get the inside of your house dry before mildew or toxic molds set in. If a window sticks, use a pry bar to open it.
- Unplug appliances, clean and dry them, and spray electrical components and other working parts with contact cleaner (available at hardware and electronics stores).
- Check drains and have them cleared if they're stopped up. Check the valves in the sewer traps.
- Shovel and hose out mud and silt, then scrub and disinfect the floors and woodwork.
- Let walls, floors, and insulation dry thoroughly before covering or repainting them. If a wall is waterlogged, replace the wallboard and insulation to above the waterline.
- Service damaged septic tanks, cesspools, pits, and leaching systems as soon as possible to prevent health hazards.

Snow and Cold

Winter is a time to stay inside and keep warm, but you can only accomplish this if your home's heating system is up to par. Before the start of the cold season, have your heating system checked to make sure it is in good working order. But even if your system is working at maximum efficiency, you may still have problems with frozen water pipes or storms that leave you snowbound. Planning ahead and taking a few precautions will keep you and your home safe and warm during cold winter weather.

OUNCE OF PREVENTION

$40

Cost of a pipe-heating cable—a great tool that can prevent pipes from freezing.

In Advance

Do all you can to keep your water pipes from freezing and bursting. Frozen pipes (which sometimes burst) are probably the most common cold-weather problem that homeowners face. Water expands as it freezes and eventually pipes, whether they're PVC plastic or metal, give way. The most susceptible pipes are the ones that take water to outside faucets, sprinkling systems, and swimming pools. In less severe climates, water pipes often pass through underinsulated attics or crawl spaces, and they burst when an occasional freeze descends. Burst pipes result in major plumbing bills; the water that gushes forth can ruin floors, rugs, furniture, and other belongings. To prevent these headaches, try the following:

- Consider having a plumber relocate exposed pipes.
- Insulate and seal your basement or crawl space.
- Before the first cold spell, drain water-sprinkler supply lines. Don't use antifreeze in these pipes unless instructed to do so by the manufacturer. Antifreeze is harmful to humans, pets, wildlife, and landscaping.
- Disconnect hoses from outdoor faucets, drain them, and store them indoors. Turn off the valves that control the water supply to these faucets, and open the faucets a bit to let any stored water drain.
- If water pipes run through the garage, keep the garage doors closed in cold weather.
- Insulate pipes that run through unheated spaces, including those that carry hot water. These pipes can still freeze when the water heater is not operating.

- If you plan to be away from home for an extended period during cold weather, leave the heat on, setting the thermostat to 55°F (12°C).
- When the weather is very cold, let water drip from faucets served by exposed pipes. Moving water is less likely to freeze. Open doors to cabinets and closets that house pipes and sinks to allow heat in.

WHAT SHOULD I USE TO INSULATE MY PIPES?

A variety of insulating materials is available at hardware and home supply stores. You can buy lengths of pre-shaped pipe insulation, cut them to length with a knife, and secure them around pipes with clamps or tape. You can also wrap pipes with aluminum insulating tape; with each wrap, overlap the tape by half an inch and secure the entire job at the pipe ends with duct tape. If an electrical outlet is nearby, you can use electrified heat tape or heat cable to warm pipes; some brands even have thermostats that turn the device on and off as needed. When wrapping heat tape around a pipe, leave a half-inch (1 cm) gap between the turns. In a pinch, you could wrap the pipes with thick layers of newspaper.

Winterize to keep your home warm and cozy. Follow these simple suggestions throughout the winter to keep out the cold:

- Clean gutters and downspouts in late autumn—after the last leaves have fallen—to prevent ice blockage and help runoff.
- Check areas that let cold air in, such as basements, crawl spaces, attics, garages, and spaces under kitchen and bathroom cabinets. Caulk any openings or add insulation.
- Make sure storm windows shut tightly. Plug window drafts with rope caulk, wide tape, or (as a stopgap) folded newspapers.
- Add insulation to the attic and take other measures to prevent ice dams.
- If you have a forced-air heating system, vacuum the duct openings and get a supply of air filters.
- Remove room air conditioners. Another alternative is to insulate each unit by removing the front panel and placing plastic sheeting inside, then replacing the panel and covering the unit.
- Trim any tree branches that may damage the house or the outside wiring in a storm.
- Keep a good supply of fuel on hand.
- If you go away, leave the heat on. If you'll be gone for a long time, consider having a plumber drain and winterize your water system.

During a Winter Storm

Stay tuned. Listen to local television and radio stations, and evacuate if you are advised to do so. Be sure to turn off the electric power and the gas and water coming into the house before you go.

Get the car in gear. Prepare your car by filling it with gas, putting on snow tires (snow tires are now mandatory in winter in Québec), and parking it in the garage or where the engine is protected from blowing snow. Keep a small emergency kit in your car during the winter, including a bag of sand, blankets or sleeping bags, non-perishable snacks, drinking water, a flashlight, jumper cables, extra batteries, a shovel, a window scraper, a warm hat, waterproof gloves, and a first-aid kit. Drive through a snowstorm only in genuine emergencies—but never alone—and stick to the main roads. Tell someone where you're going and when you're expected to arrive.

What if I'm snowbound? If you plan on staying put for the duration of the storm, there are a few things you should do to ensure that you're comfortable and safe:

- Have extra clothing and blankets ready for use in case the power goes out.°
- Line up an alternative form of heating, such as kerosene or propane space heaters, plus enough fuel to last a week. If you have a fireplace or wood-burning stove, stock up on wood.
- Keep your community's emergency phone numbers on hand, including emergency medical numbers.
- If you normally cook with electricity, have an alternative cooking method (such as a camp stove or a gas grill) at the ready. Caution: It is unsafe to use many of these alternative appliances indoors—be sure to keep them outside, or use them only in the other well-ventilated places indicated in the manufacturer's instructions.
- Stock up on enough food and water to last a week.
- Prepare an emergency care kit (see the "Hurricanes and Other Windstorms" chapter for details on what should be inside).
- Store the snow-clearing tools or materials you might need—rock salt, shovels, scrapers, snowblowers—in a place that you can easily access, even after a heavy snowfall. Also keep a supply of silicone spray to lubricate snow-blowing machinery.

What if I get stuck outdoors? If you're caught outside in a snowstorm while you're on foot, head for the nearest shelter. If the snow keeps you from seeing ahead, follow a fence or ruts in the road. Tie a scarf over your nose and mouth to protect your lungs, ears, and face and to prevent suffocation from the wind and snow. If you're stranded in a car, don't get out. Run the engine occasionally for warmth, but keep a window open. Be sure the exhaust pipe isn't blocked by snow, or carbon monoxide may back up into the car. If the car runs out of gas, keep all the windows shut, but be on the lookout for help constantly. Exercise or at least move your arms and legs for warmth and to keep yourself awake. Don't go to sleep under any circumstances.

Remain cautious even after the storm passes. Continue to listen for news flashes and updated weather information, even after the snow stops. Major winter storms are often followed by even colder conditions. If you go outdoors, dress warmly and watch out for falling icicles; knock them down with a rake or pole. Avoid overexertion. Many people have heart attacks while shoveling snow. It is also a strain on the heart to walk through heavy snow or to push a car through it. Avoid driving until the roads are clear.

Easy Fixes

Thawing frozen pipes. If you turn on a faucet and only a trickle of water comes out, a section of one of your water pipes is probably frozen. You can find the frozen spot by swabbing along the pipe with a moist rag; frost will form when you reach the frozen area. Thaw the pipe along its length before it bursts, starting at the end nearest a faucet. Leaving the faucet open, apply heat with a hair dryer, portable space heater, or electric heating pad, or wrap the pipe in rags or towels and pour boiling water over it, catching the water in a pan beneath the pipe. Don't use a propane torch, as it may heat the water in the pipe to the boiling point and make the pipe explode.

Patching leaking pipes. If you don't thaw a frozen pipe in time and it develops a leak, you can fix it temporarily while awaiting a plumber. First, shut off the water supply and dry the pipe. Fix a small leak by wrapping plastic or duct tape tightly around the damaged section. For a larger repair, slit a section of rubber hose and slip it over the pipe, then hold it in place with tightly twisted wires or two or more hose clamps.

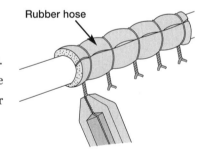

Rubber hose

Earthquakes

If you live in an area that is subject to earthquakes, don't wait for a quake to strike to decide what to do or where to go. Earthquakes begin without notice and, though they last only seconds or minutes, can be devastating. Prudent planning can help keep your family and your house from being badly harmed.

OUNCE OF PREVENTION

$20

Cost of water-heater restraint straps, which prevent damage from broken gas and water lines.

Before and After a Quake

Make your home a fortress. If you live in an earthquake zone, have a structural engineer examine your house—especially if it is old—to determine whether or not it is sound enough to survive a quake. You may need to add extra bracing and foundation bolts or have the chimney reinforced. Also, it's a good idea to have flexible gas connectors installed where gas lines meet appliances; they'll be far less likely to pull apart in an earthquake. Finally, take the following do-it-yourself precautions:

- Put secure latches on your cabinet doors to keep them from opening during a quake (you don't want your fine china and treasures to fly across the room, do you?).
- Stabilize your water heater by wrapping it with steel plumber's strap and attaching the strap to wall studs.
- Anchor top-heavy furniture like bookcases by attaching it to a wall with L-shaped brackets.
- Lock the rollers on your refrigerator or on any other appliance or piece of furniture that has casters.
- Learn how to turn off the gas, water, and electric power where these utilities enter the house.
- Keep an emergency care kit on hand (for details, see the box in the "Hurricanes and Other Windstorms" chapter).
- Keep an inventory list. Take photos of your house and everything inside, or, better yet, videotape it. If an earthquake causes damage, you may need proof of your home's condition and contents to justify insurance claims or tax deductions.

take care

Animals often get wild after an earthquake. If your pet seems agitated, don't approach him too suddenly and don't touch him, or he may lash out and bite or scratch. Stay at a safe distance and to one side, and speak calmly and reassuringly. If he calms down, approach him slowly and pet him gently. If your pet keeps acting erratically, try to isolate him until he recovers from the fright caused by the quake.

Evaluate the damage carefully. Don't enter the house until the authorities tell you it's safe to go inside. And when you do go in, move through slowly, and keep your eyes open. Check floors, walls, foundations, and chimneys for cracks. Look for damage to electric wires, water pipes, and gas lines. Open closets carefully to check for leaks or damage. For other post-quake tips, see "Picking Up the Pieces After a Natural Disaster" in the "Floods" section.

DOS AND DON'TS OF EARTHQUAKE SAFETY

DO ...

- Stand in a sturdy interior doorway or against an inside wall, if you're in a building. Alternatively, get under a bed, desk, or sturdy table.

- If you're outdoors, move away from buildings, power lines, utility wires, and anything that may topple. Stay in the open until the shaking stops.

- Turn on a local TV or radio station to get up-to-the-minute reports on safety after the quake.

- Be wary of aftershocks, which can occur minutes, days, or weeks after the main quake. If you feel one starting, seek cover.

- Extinguish any small fires. Call the fire department to put out larger ones.

- Check yourself for injuries, and then check others, providing any needed first aid or calling for a rescue squad. Don't move an injured person unless she is in immediate danger of further injury.

DON'T ...

- Use elevators.

- Go outdoors.

- Stand near or hide under windows, ceiling fixtures, mirrors, china closets, masonry walls, or chimneys.

- Remain in low-lying areas (especially if you live near water). Get to higher ground quickly—quakes can cause flooding.

- Get out of the vehicle, if you're driving. Stop in open areas. If you're on a bridge or overpass, drive off of it into an open space.

Power Outages

Electrical power can go out as the result of a severe storm or earthquake, or simply because the power company experiences mechanical failure. Blackouts that last for more than a few hours can be frustrating and expensive—you'll probably have to toss out the contents of your refrigerator and freezer and restock them. However, if you keep emergency supplies on hand and plan in advance, you and your family (and your food supply) can come through a blackout unscathed.

OUNCE OF PREVENTION
$15
Cost of a 10-pound (4.5 kg) block of dry ice, which can keep perishable foods cold during a power outage.

In Advance

Generate your own power. If your neighborhood experiences frequent power outages or if someone in your household relies on electric power to run a life-support system, you may want to invest in an emergency generator. A generator connects to the electrical service panel of the house and can supply enough power to run the furnace, well pump, refrigerator, and lights. Have the generator installed by a qualified electrician.

Make up an emergency kit. You won't want to be rummaging in the dark, so prepare your kit in advance and keep it handy.

Install a surge suppressor. It can protect your computers, phones, TVs, and other electric-powered devices.

Keep plastic jugs of water in the freezer. Leave an inch (2.5 cm) of free space at the top of the jug, as water expands when it freezes. The ice will extend the time the freezer stays cold and provide extra water when it melts.

Have a landline phone with a handset connected by a cord. Cordless phones won't work when the power is out because they rely on electricity. Also, make sure that your cell phone is fully charged, and buy a car charger for your cell phone.

Set your freezer as low as it can go. If you have reason to expect a blackout (such as an approaching hurricane), set your freezer at its coldest setting (most go to about -20°F or -29°C).

Fill your car's gas tank before a storm. Gas station pumps are electrically powered and may not be in service.

Know where the manual release is on your garage door opener. The remote won't work without electricity.

Put a plan of action in place for the physically handicapped. Keep a back-up manual wheelchair on hand (or an extra battery on hand for a motorized wheel chair or scooter). Ask the power company about emergency measures for power-dependent people.

Coping During a Power Outage

Survey the situation, and conserve the residual power that you have. First, check if there's power in your neighborhood. If only your house is affected, try resetting your circuit breakers or replacing the fuses. (But don't touch a service panel in a flooded area; wait until the water is gone.) If the rest of your neighborhood is dark, call the power company. Tune in to a local radio station (on your battery-powered radio) and follow the advice you're given.

Turn off the electrical equipment you were using when the power went out. Leave one radio or lamp turned on to let you know when the power is back.

Pack those perishables. If you have advance warning that a storm is coming, pack eggs, dairy products, meat, and fish in a cooler and surround them with ice.

Keep the refrigerator and freezer doors closed. An unopened refrigerator will stay cold for a few hours. A half-full freezer will keep food frozen for up to 24 hours, a full freezer for 48 hours.

If your freezer is without power for more than a day, stash some dry ice inside. Use 25 pounds per 10 cubic feet (11 kilograms per 0.3 cubic metre) of freezer space. Place heavy cardboard on top of the food and dry ice on top of the cardboard. In a full freezer, dry ice will keep food frozen for three or four days.

If perishable food is kept at above 40°F (4°C) for more than two hours, discard it. If frozen food is coated with ice crystals and has not reached a temperature of 40°F (4°C) or more, refreeze it. Never refreeze foods that are completely thawed.

If you have medication that requires refrigeration, keep it in a closed refrigerator. It should remain safe for several hours without a problem, but ask your pharmacist in advance how long it will keep if the temperature rises.

If the weather is cold, use your fireplace or a kerosene heater approved for indoor use. Don't use stoves or heaters designed for outdoor use.

Index

A

accidents, *see* safety

acrylic, 73

acrylic latex, 160, 167, 199, 285

acrylic latex with silicone, 160

adapter, 172

adhesive, 66, 67, 68

adjustable hacksaw, 20

adjustable wrench, 20

aerator, 194–96

AFCI, *see* arc-fault circuit interrupter

air circulation, 164, 307

air-conditioning:
  care and maintenance, 234–36
  central, 234–37
  cleaning, 235, 236, 238, 239
  easy fixes, 237
  in forced-air system, 219
  slashing bills, 237
  window and room, 238–39, 318
  workings of, 235

air flow, 252

air leak, 154

alcohol, 187

algae, 238

alkyd paint, 43, 44, 285

aluminum:
  doors, 114
  ladders, 172
  roof, 133
  screens, 117, 163
  siding, 89–91
  window frames, 103
  wiring, 178–79

aluminum-clad windows, 106

aluminum foil, 67, 146

ammonia:
  for algae in air conditioner, 238
  in bug spray, 270
  as household cleaner, 24
  on wood floor, 61

amps, 175, 176

anaerobic bacteria, 208, 213

anchors, 21

animals:
  urine stains, 76
  see also pests; pets

anticipator, 232

anti-scald valve, 201

anti-siphon valve, 215

antiskid tape, 200

ants, 278, 304, 305

appliances:
  during flood, 314
  electrical cords attached to, 171
  overloading on circuits, 175
  power to start up, 174
  unplugging, 172, 177, 316
  use during evening hours, 237
  see also specific appliances

arbor, 284

arc-fault circuit interrupter (AFCI), 178

area rug, 59

asbestos, 152

asphalt, 95, 273, 274, 275

asphalt aluminum paint, 132

asphalt roll roofing, 132, 133

asphalt roof cement, 25

asphalt shingles, 122–24

attached ceiling tiles, 58

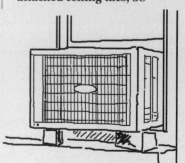

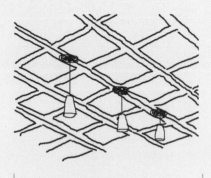

D

F

grout saw, 54, 71

guarantees, 30

gutters, 306

   care and maintenance,
     134–35

   cleaning, 134, 318

   easy fixes, 135

   leaky, 135

   patching, 135

   sagging, 135

   salt on, 136

   screen guards, 135

   seepage from, 144, 214

gypsum, 36

H

hacksaw, 20, 85, 128

hair, 27

hair dryer, 68, 146

hairspray, 59, 65

hall, 47

hammer, 18, 85, 123

hand drill, 19

handheld shower attachment,
   201

handicapped, 324

handrail, *see* banister

handsaw, 28

hardboard, 50

hardiness zone, 266

hazardous chemicals, 215,
   271

headlamp, 140

heaters:

   baseboard, 230

   ceramic, 230

   cove, 230

   kerosene, 324

   kick-space, 230

   liquid-filled, 230

   space, 230, 231

   wall, 230

   water, 255–56, 321

heating systems, 218–31, 317

   electric, 230–31

   forced air, 218–21

   gas, 222–24

   oil, 225–26

   steam and hot water,
     227–29

   thermostat, 221, 232–33

heavy-duty stapler, 22

heel scuffs/marks, 62, 68

herbicides, 262

hinged doors, 108–13

   anatomy of, 109

   binding, 110

   care and maintenance,
     108–10

   cleaning, 108

   doorknob, 108

   easy fixes, 110–12

   entry, 109

   hard-to-close, 111

   hardware, 108

   hollow-core, 112

   kick plate, 112

   latches, 111

   locks, 108–9, 112

   security of, 113

   self-closing, 111

   silencing, 110–11

   strike plate, 112

   weather stripping, 109–10

hinges, 109, 111

hinge screws, 110

holes:

   in basement wall, 144, 146

   in flashing, 130

   in floor, 61

   patching small, 37, 61

   in plaster wall, 41

hollow-core door, 109, 112

hollow-wall anchor, 21

home:

   exterior, 16, 17, 81–82

   indoor systems, 16, 17,
     33–34

   painting, 87–88

   preservation, 13–15

   security, 299–302

   value, 13

   see also home maintenance;
     specific areas of home

home maintenance:

   caulking, 159

   checklist, 17

   making time for, 16–17

   must-have items for, 14

   positive attitude about, 15

   seasonal, 16–17

homeowners insurance, 13,
   309, 313

hooking, 179

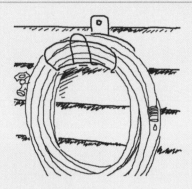

hook scraper, 88

hoses, 249, 250, 251, 271, 288

hot water, 210

hot-water systems, 227–29

hourly rate, 30

household cleaners, 24

household items, 14

household supplies, 23–25

house wrap, 93

hurricanes, 308–12

hybrid roses, 265

hydraulic cement, 146

hydrogen peroxide, 57

I

icebox, *see* freezer

ice dam, 88, 136–37, 150

ice maker, 242

icicles, 150

indoor systems, 16, 17, 33–34

see also specific systems

ink stains, 76

inlet screens, 251

inlet valves, 229, 251

insecticides, 303

insects, 192, 269, 278, 303–5

instant-start lighting tubes, 185

insulation:

of attic, 136, 149, 152, 237, 318

electricity and, 172

fiberglass, 150, 151, 152

of floors, 153

of pipes, 144, 209, 318

types of, 151

of walls, 149, 237

of windows, 156

see also weather stripping

insurance, 13, 30, 309, 313

interlocking metal weather stripping, 155

inventory, 309, 314, 321

ionization smoke detector, 293

J

joint compound, 36

joints:

brick, 93, 94

caulking, 159

chimney, 139

concrete, 273, 274

foundation, 140, 142

leaky, 144

roof, 130, 131

joint tape, 23

joists, 63, 64, 152, 210

juice stains, 76

K

kerosene heater, 324

keys, 112, 300

key turnbuckles, 101

kick plate, 112

kick-space heater, 230

kitchens:

dishwasher, 248–49

garbage disposal, 214, 246–47

ovens and stoves, 243–45

refrigerator, 240–42, 321, 324

sink, 193–98

wall coverings, 47

walls, 42, 54–56

wattage needed in, 183

kneeling, 27

kneepads, 27

L

ladders, 21, 125–26, 172, 300

lag screws, 79

lamps, 171, 172, 299–300, 324

lap siding, *see* clapboard

latches, 111

latex caulk, 303

latex gloves, 158

latex paint, 43, 44

latex primer, 45

latex stain, 285

lath, 40

lattice, 162, 165

lawn, 259–64

M

under crawl space, 152

on deck, 164, 165

in foundation, 140–41

garage doors and, 120

mold and rot and, 306, 307

paint and, 88

on roof, 127, 133

in service panel, 173

standing water, 83, 164, 272

behind stucco, 98

vapor barriers, 150

in walls, 35

from weep holes, 92, 117

on windows, 52, 154

wooden doors and, 111

moisture sensor, 253

mold:

in bathroom, 307

on brick, 95

crawl space, 141

after fire, 295

on floors, 62

preventive measures, 306–7

molding, 52–53, 159

molly bolt, 21

mortar, 93, 94, 142

mortgage insurance, 13

moss, 128

moths, 304

motion sensors, 192, 300

mounting strap, 184

mowing, 260–61, 262

mulching, 270

multipurpose tool, 21

muriatic acid, 55, 70, 92, 145, 277

N

nail apron, 27

nail head, 87

nail polish, 61, 71, 117

nails:

in molding, 52

in nail apron, 27

in newel post, 79

as part of toolbox, 18–19

popped, 36, 51, 166

removing, 21

in shed, 284

in trim, 53

nail set, 21

natural disasters, 315

earthquakes, 321–22

floods, 313–16

hurricanes, 308–12

winter storms, 319–20

natural fiber wall covering, 47

needle-nose pliers, 21

neighborhood watch programs, 300

newel post, 78, 79, 163

noise, 27, 63, 110–11, 120, 210

noncontact voltage tester, 182

nosing, 78

notched trowel, 71

nuts, 20

nylon carpeting, 73

O

"octopus" plugs, 171

odors, 307

oil:

in garbage disposal, 246

on hinges, 109

as lubricant, 24, 119

in mower, 263

stains, 62, 76, 168, 226, 275

on tools, 26

oil burner, 225–26

oil tank, 225–26

Olefin carpeting, 73

open-end wrench, 20

organic fertilizer, 261

oscillator sprinkler, 272

outdoor electrical fixtures, 189–92

see also specific fixtures

outdoor grill, 292

outdoor structures, 284–85

outlet, *see* **electrical outlet**

oven, 243–45

oven cleaner, 244

overcurrent protection device, 173

oxygen bleach, 165

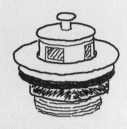

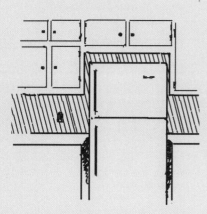

T

pressure-balancing, 201

shutoff, 209, 210, 222, 272

TPR, 255

valve seat, 207

vapor barrier, 140–41, 150

vapors, 27

varnish, 61, 62

ventilating lock, 101

ventilation, 149

of attic, 136, 150

of basement, 144

of clothes dryer, 307

of greenhouse, 284

see also vents

vent pipe, 131

vents:

attic, 150, 153

caulking, 159

roof ridge, 307

soffit, 153

steam radiator, 229

vermiculite, 152

vinegar:

for ants on patio, 278

for concrete floor, 145

for dishwasher, 248

for grout, 70

as household cleaner, 24

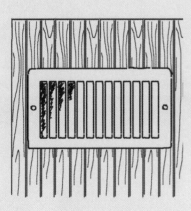

on lime, 194

for shower door, 200

vinyl-clad window, 106

vinyl-coated paper, 47

vinyl fence, 283

vinyl flooring, 65–69

black spots on, 69

blisters, 67

care and maintenance, 65–67

cleaning, 65–66

doormats, 65

easy fixes, 67–69

patching sheet vinyl, 68, 69

protecting exposed edges, 67

replacing tile, 67, 68

vinyl siding, 89–91

care and maintenance, 89

cleaning, 89

cracks in, 90

dents in, 90

easy fixes, 90–91

loose panels, 89

matching new to old, 91

painting, 90

replacing damaged, 91

vinyl tubing, 156

vinyl weather stripping, 155

voltage tester, 172, 177

volts, 175

V-strips, 155, 156

W

walkway, 273–75

wallboard walls, 35–38

care and maintenance, 35

chair dents, 35

easy fixes, 36

filling cracks, 36–38

fixing blisters, 38

fixing scratches and dents, 36

leaks and moisture in, 35

patching material, 36

patching small hole with kit, 37

repairing banged-up corners, 38

replacing popped nails, 36

sanding, 38

wall coverings, 46–49

care and maintenance, 46–48

cleaning, 46–47

easy fixes, 48–49

fixing curled seams, 49

painting or repapering over, 49

over paneling, 51

patching, 49

popping bubbles, 48

regluing peeling borders, 49

seam adhesive and rollers, 46

selection guide, 47

stains, 48

vacuuming, 46

wall heater, 230

wallpaper, *see* **wall coverings**

wallpaper dough, 48

wall rack, 168

walls:

basement, 143, 144, 145, 146

brick veneer, 93

ceramic tile, 54–56

exterior, 84

Lumber

Builder's Slang	Actual Size (US-inches)	Actual Size (Metric-mm)
2 x 2	1-1/2 x 1-1/2	38 x 88
2 x 4	1-1/2 x 3-1/2	38 x 89
2 x 6	1-1/2 x 5-1/2	38 x 140
2 x 8	1-1/2 x 7-1/4	38 x 184
2 x 10	1-1/2 x 9-1/4	38 x 235
4 x 4	3-1/2 x 3-1/2	89 x 89
4 x 6	3-1/2 x 5-1/2	89 x 140

Nails

Common Name	Length (US-inches)	Length (Metric-mm)
4d	1-1/2 inches	35 mm
5d	1-3/4 inches	45 mm
6d	2 inches	50 mm
8d	2-1/2 inches	60 mm
10d	3 inches	75 mm
16d	3-1/2 inches	85 mm
20d	4 inches	100 mm

Weights

US (Pounds)	Metric (Grams)
1/4	125
1/2	250
2/3	300
3/4	375
1	500
2	1 kg (kilogram)
3	1.5 kg
5	2 kg
10	5 kg
15	7 kg
20	9 kg
25	11 kg
50	22 kg
100	45 kg

Measurements given have been rounded up for convenience.

Other Helpful Building and DIY Conversions

	From US Units	To Metric Units	Multiply by
Power	BTU/second	watts	1054
	horsepower	watts	745.7
Pressure	pounds/sq. inch	kilograms/sq. meter	4.882
Force	pound (lb)	newton (N)	4.4482
Volume	acre foot	cubic meters	1.233
	cubic yard	cubic meters	0.7646
Velocity	miles per hour	meters per second	0.447
	miles per hour	kilometers per hour	1.609

Liquid Volume

US	Metric (mL)
1 teaspoon	5 mL
1 tablespoon **or** 1/2 fluid ounce	15 mL
1 fluid ounce **or** 1/8 cup	30 mL
1/4 cup **or** 2 fluid ounces	60 mL
1/3 cup	75 mL
1/2 cup **or** 4 fluid ounces	125 mL
2/3 cup	150 mL
3/4 cup **or** 6 fluid ounces	175 mL
1 cup **or** 8 fluid ounces **or** 1/2 pint	250 mL
1-1/2 cups **or** 12 fluid ounces	375 mL
2 cups **or** 1 pint **or** 16 fluid ounces	500 mL
3 cups **or** 1-1/2 pints	750 mL
4 cups **or** 2 pints **or** 1 quart	1 L
4 quarts **or** 1 gallon	4 L

Measurements given have been rounded up for convenience.

Length

US	Metric
1/8 inch	3 mm
1/4 inch	5 mm
1/2 inch	1 cm
3/4 inch	19 mm
1 inch	2.5 cm
2 inches	5 cm
3 inches	7.5 cm
4 inches	10 cm
5 inches	13 cm
6 inches	15 cm
7 inches	18 cm
8 inches	20 cm
9 inches	23 cm
10 inches	25 cm
11 inches	28 cm
12 inches or 1 foot	30 cm

Conversion Symbols

Multiplication Factor	Prefix	Symbol
$1,000,000,000 = 10^9$	giga	G
$1,000,000 = 10^6$	mega	M
$1,000 = 10^3$	kilo	k
$100 = 10^2$	hecto	h
$0.01 = 10^{-2}$	centi	c
$0.001 = 10^{-3}$	milli	m
$0.000001 = 10^{-6}$	micro	u
$0.000000001 = 10^{-9}$	nano	n

Common Units of Measure

US	Metric
acre	hectare (ha)
cubic foot	cubic meter (m^3)
cubic yard	cubic meter (m^3)
gallon	liter (L)
hundred weight	kilogram (kg)
linear foot	meter (m)
mile	kilometer (km)
pound	kilogram (kg) for mass newton (N) for force
ton	tonne (t)

Notes

Notes

Plans

Plans